Primer of
Educational Research

W. Newton Suter
University of Arkansas at Little Rock

Allyn and Bacon
Boston • London • Toronto • Sydney • Tokyo • Singapore

Senior Vice President and Publisher, Education: Nancy Forsyth
Series Editorial Assistant: Cheryl Ouellette
Marketing Manager: Kris Farnsworth
Composition and Prepress Buyer: Linda Cox
Manufacturing Buyer: Suzanne Lareau
Cover Administrator: Suzanne Harbison
Production Coordinator: Christopher H. Rawlings
Editorial-Production Service: Omegatype Typography, Inc.

Copyright © 1998 by Allyn and Bacon
A Viacom Company
160 Gould Street
Needham Heights, MA 02194

Internet: www.abacon.com
America Online: Keyword: College Online

Library of Congress Cataloging-in-Publication Data
Suter, W. Newton,
    Primer of educational research / W. Newton Suter.
       p.   cm.
    Includes bibliographical references (p.) and index.
    ISBN 0-205-27014-X (alk. paper)
    1. Education—Research—Methodology.   I. Title.
LB1028.S945   1998
370'.7'2—dc21   97-6810
                                          CIP

Printed in the United States of America
0 9 8 7 6 5 4 3 2   02 01 00 99 98

To Walter and Thalia
Paula and Meredith

Contents

Preface

I confess, and my colleagues have confessed too: Research Methods in Education is our favorite course, the one we enjoy teaching over and over. Many factors help explain this favoritism, and this text embodies most of them. I recall the thrill I experienced as a student in learning how the research process—the very heart of science—can supplant other far less trustworthy ways of knowing. I see the same interest and excitement with my students today as they begin to understand the process of research and develop skills in evaluating published research reports. Students have had some prior exposure to the content of most education courses, such as history, philosophy, or psychology; because of this, many students feel insecure—almost threatened—about taking a course with which they have few personal linkages to relate new information. They often recall reading research articles in other classes; the idea of learning more about the "fine-print" sections of those articles often leads to, quite simply, dread. What students don't always realize is that learning about research methods and statistical analysis is far more conceptual than technical, and that courses in which these methods are explored often turn out to be most enjoyable and interesting. This text captures much of that interest in the study of research methods.

The purpose of this book is *not* to guide students through their own research project from start to finish, as you might expect in a course for students writing their dissertation. Rather, its purpose is to make research *accessible* to education (and social science) students by equipping them with the skills needed to understand and critically evaluate published educational research. Oriented toward the *consumers* of research, this text is appropriate for a first course in research methods at the undergraduate or graduate level. All of the major components of the research process and the principles of sound methodology are also introduced for the eventual *producer* of research. Students can acquire research skills by completing the application exercises and by inspecting carefully the fourteen published research reports which were chosen especially for their value in illustrating principles of sound research methods. Above all else, students using this book will understand how and why researchers think like they do.

The text is organized into twelve chapters in a manner which heightens interest and systematically eases students into reading and critiquing solid educational research, both quantitative and qualitative. Chapter 1 piques interest through the use of a motivational pretest. Chapters 2 and 3 introduce basic terms and describe research as a process. Chapters 4 and 5 focus on research hypotheses and the variety of approaches used by researchers to test them. Chapters 2 through 5 are loaded with concrete examples to maximize students' understanding. Chapter 6 focuses on sampling, Chapter 7 on measurement soundness, and Chapter 8 on research bias and control, all of which draw heavily on examples. Chapters 9 and 10 describe common experimental and non-experimental research designs, and Chapter 11 covers the analysis of data. The concluding Chapter 12 focuses on the task of critiquing educational research. Chapters 2–11 each contain at least one short published research report which is presented as a "Guided Tour" with a running narrative explanation. This approach guarantees little chance of the students missing the major points of the chapter as illustrated in the report.

I know this method of teaching research methods *works*, because it has evolved through a process of fine-tuning of the many semesters of teaching this subject to students at the University of Arkansas at Little Rock. I thank them for their patience and feedback during many field trials. I also thank the following reviewers whose suggestions resulted in many improvements: George Petersen, Bowling Green State University; Doris Prater, University of Houston, Clear Lake; and Paul H. Westmeyer, University of Texas at San Antonio. Finally, I thank Nancy Forsyth and the staff at Allyn & Bacon and Mary Ann Monk at Omegatype Typography, Inc. for their admirable work during the acquisition, editing, and production of the book.

Primer of Educational Research

Chapter 1

RESEARCH AWARENESS

INTRODUCTION

Educational researchers are committed to improving the quality of education by increasing their knowledge of the art and science of teaching and the process of learning. Educational practitioners, such as teachers, counselors, administrators, and curriculum specialists, become most effective when their skills and classroom wisdom are combined with their knowledge of educational research. The goal of this book is to *make educational research accessible* to practicing educational professionals, those ultimately responsible for improving learning in the classrooms. Making research accessible requires the ability to read and critique published educational research. Each chapter of this book is concerned with an important facet of educational research, one that enables you to read research reports with greater comprehension and critical appraisal. Each of the remaining chapters will include one or two short reprints of published research. You will be guided through each research report to see how concepts described in each chapter have been applied in an actual research setting. By the end of this book, you will understand the most important principles and concepts of educational research *and* be able to read and evaluate research reports. This will put you in a good position to make decisions about applying educational research in your practice.

One final note: Reading journal articles that report research results is not easy. (It does get easier with practice.) The scholarly literature in any field is often dense and filled with jargon; it is always slow reading. But I believe it holds the key to improving the art and science of teaching and learning. You could probably go to easier sources for information about "what works," like popular magazines, brief workshops, biased television, so-called experts who follow the pendulum swings, or tidbits off the Internet. (I am reminded of the drunk who lost his wallet in the dark alley but searched under the street lamp because the light was better.) However, the simplicity of these sources greatly distorts the complex reality. The *scientific* basis of the art of teaching is revealed only by the research literature. Understanding the published scientific literature involves bringing new light to previously dim areas (to continue the lost wallet metaphor). This book will illuminate the process of educational research so you are in a better position to read, understand, and apply it in your own practice.

Before we examine the important concepts of educational research, let's take a brief pretest. Its purpose is to stimulate your thinking about research, not to assess your knowledge. It will make you aware of your own ideas about research, even though you probably don't think about them in a formal way.

The pretest on the next page introduces many important ideas, ones that apply to all types of scientific research in diverse fields of study. Some of the most dramatic examples of important research principles can be found in medicine. (Medical research, it seems, attracts more news media than many other fields of study, so some of what you already know about the research process may be the result of widely disseminated medical research findings.) For this reason, some of the concepts described in the chapter pretest have been couched in the context of medicine. It is important to remember that these research principles are widely applicable since they are embedded in the scientific research process in general, and are shared by the fields of education, psychology, nursing, business, communications, sociology, neuroscience, political science, biology, and hundreds of others. The remaining chapters will elaborate on the ideas introduced in the pretest (and many others), all within the context of educational research.

RESEARCH AWARENESS PRETEST: TRUE OR FALSE?

1. When two research studies which have been designed to answer the same question yield opposite conclusions, the most likely explanation is an error in statistical analysis or coding.

   T _____   F _____

2. Biases in research studies are usually obvious and can nearly always be detected by researchers without special training.

   T _____   F _____

3. Standardized achievement tests—used so often in educational research— are distinctly American and have roots dating back to the early 1900s.

   T _____   F _____

4. Sampling blunders in research are rare and easy to avoid.

   T _____   F _____

5. The best surveys are large ones, involving around 25,000 respondents, and using sophisticated sampling techniques.

   T _____   F _____

6. What may be considered sloppy reasoning or misused data are rare occurrences in the practice of research.

   T _____   F _____

7. Research studies are only commissioned by so-called disinterested, independent, and impartial researchers with no vested interests in the outcome.

   T _____   F _____

8. In research the term, "statistically significant" means roughly the same as "important" or "substantial."

   T _____   F _____

9. Educational researchers can prove theories by collecting data in order to prove hypotheses.

   T _____   F _____

10. Control groups in educational research are considered a luxury and are not needed to evaluate the effectiveness of new interventions.

    T _____   F _____

ANSWERS WITH EXPLANATIONS

1. When two research studies which have been designed to answer the same question yield opposite conclusions, the most likely explanation is an error in statistical analysis or coding.   Answer: False.

The most likely explanation can be found in the *design* and *procedural* differences between the two studies. Let's consider a clear example from the field of medicine. In 1985, the *New England Journal of Medicine* published back-to-back studies designed to answer the question, "Does estrogen use in postmenopausal women affect the risk of heart disease?" One study involving more than 1200 women reported that estrogen use *increases* the risk of heart disease (Wilson, Garrison, & Castelli, 1985), while the second study involving more than 32,000 women reported that estrogen use *decreases* the risk of heart disease (Stampfer et al., 1985). How can these contradictory findings be explained? By a catastrophic error in analysis? No, not usually. By fundamental differences in the methods used to answer the question? Yes, very likely. And what differences are the most likely explanations? The answer to this question is explored in the following paragraphs.

Very often, one finds differences in *instrumentation,* or the process of collecting data in a research study. In the estrogen research, one study used mailed questionnaires to collect data, while the other study used physical examinations. Faced with a questionnaire, you might check *No* to the question, "Have you had any cardiac disorders in the past five years?" A physician checking an EKG recording, however, may have a very different answer to that question. And what about chest pain? It may be interpreted as indigestion on a questionnaire, but as angina by a doctor who asks other questions. Other differences in instrumentation are present in the estrogen studies, including the period of followup (four versus eight years). It may be the case that estrogen use decreases the risk of heart disease for a period of time, and then increases it after a longer period of time (or has no effect).

Another explanation for opposing conclusions may be found in *sampling,* or the process used to select research participants. This is a likely explanation because it may be the case that estrogen use lowers the risk of heart disease in one group of people but increases it in another. One study collected data from women aged thirty to fifty-five, while the other used women aged fifty to eighty-three. It may also be possible that estrogen use has a protective effect for nonsmokers, but a harmful effect for smokers. Does estrogen affect diabetics differently? Might it affect differently those with a family history of heart disease? The list of intervening sample characteristics is almost endless.

Yet another explanation for opposing conclusions may be found in the *intervention,* or the process of manipulating the treatment conditions. In the estrogen example, it is possible that its influence may depend on type (natural versus synthetic) or dosage, with small amounts showing a protective effect and larger amounts showing a harmful effect.

These differences in instrumentation, sampling, and intervention, of course, have counterparts in educational research. For example, it is possible that cooperative learning efforts as implemented by one particular teacher may have positive effects on a very specific outcome with only one type of student. A change in any one of these factors may offset or possibly reverse the positive effect.

This discussion reminds me of the humor in research. One especially good cartoon was drawn by Walt Handelsman at the *The Times-Picayune* in New Orleans. It shows a newspaper with the following headlines: "Oat bran good, study says. Oat bran not effective study says. Coffee may be harmful study cited. Study: Coffee good for sex life. Milk bad for kids, says study. Milk good for kids, study says. Aspirin bad for stomach, study finds. Aspirin good for heart, study reveals. Margarine harmful, study claims." Another newspaper shows: "STUDIES MAY BE HARMFUL, study claims. More study needed."

2. Biases in research studies are usually obvious and can nearly always be detected by researchers without special training.   Answer: False.

Let's once again borrow a dramatic example from medicine. In 1988, the journal *Nature* published a celebrated research study (Davenas et al., 1988) with remarkable claims made in support of a discredited branch of medicine known as homeopathy (the use of very dilute substances to cure a disease which, at full strength, would cause the disease in healthy people). *Nature* agreed to publish these findings if a team assembled by the journal could observe a *replication* (or repeat) of the experiments. One member of the observation team was particularly interesting: Mr. James Randi, also known as The Amazing Randi, a professional psychic debunker. A magician by training, the Amazing Randi successfully uncovers the tricks used by frauds who claim to have psychic powers. The homeopathic researchers never claimed to have such powers, but it was believed by the *Nature* team that they may have been less than careful and, without the researchers' knowledge or awareness, may have allowed a source of bias to creep in and somehow influence their findings in an unintentional way. The real issue was not fraud, but contaminating bias so subtle that it was beyond the researchers' level of awareness.

The homeopathic experiments were replicated under the watchful eyes of The Amazing Randi with the appropriate controls for experimenter bias such as *blinding* (or being "in the dark"), whereby the researchers were kept unaware of which conditions were supposed to (according to homeopathic theory) result in higher measurements. With these controls (and others) in place, the *Nature* team found that the homeopathic effects disappeared and concluded that they were originally the result of research bias. The scientific community, including educational researchers, benefitted from the reminder that some contaminating biases are so subtle that their discovery requires keen perception, like that of the caliber of James Randi. All consumers of research, it seems, must be aware of the perils of "wishful science."

The introduction of subtle influences beneath the awareness of those responsible is not a new discovery. About one hundred years ago in Germany, a horse named Hans bewildered spectators with displays of unusual intelligence, especially in math (Pfungst, 1911). The owner, Mr. von Osten, tested Hans in front of an audience by holding flash cards. Hans would, for example, see "4 + 5" and commence to tap his hoof nine times for a correct answer. Hans would even answer a flash card showing, say, "¼ + ½" by tapping three times, then four times. Amazing! said the crowds and reporters. Worldwide fame was bestowed on the animal now known as "Clever Hans." This remarkable display lasted several years before the truth was uncovered by Oskar Pfungst, a psychologist with training in—you guessed it—the scientific method. It was revealed by Pfungst that Clever Hans responded to very subtle cues from von Osten—cues that von Osten *himself* was oblivious to. Body posture and facial cues (like raised eyebrows, widened eyes, flared nostrils) were the inevitable result of the owner's excitement as the hoof tapping approached the correct number. When the right number was tapped, the height of excitement was displayed all over von Osten's face. This, then, became the signal to stop tapping. Once the research-oriented psychologist put in place the appropriate controls, like showing the flash cards to the horse only (not to von Osten, who was therefore "blind"), then the hoof tapping began to look more like random responses and Clever Hans didn't seem so "clever" after all. Von Osten himself was never accused of being a fraud, for the communication was below his awareness (and imperceptible to spectators). Although the Clever Hans phenomenon was not discovered in a research setting, it is a valuable reminder that one cannot be too careful when investigating all types of effects, from magic in medicine to genius in horses.

3. Standardized achievement tests—used so often in educational research—are distinctly American and have roots dating back to the early 1900s.   Answer: False.

Although there is much current national debate about the value of standardized tests such as the SAT or the Scholastic Assessment Test (formerly the Scholastic Aptitude Test), the debate is nothing new. Standardized achievement testing, in fact, is believed to be about 3,000 years old! (For an interesting account of this history see DuBois, 1966.) The ancient Chinese in about 1,000 B.C. tested its citizenry in seven basic areas in order to select those most talented for positions of ruling authority (called *Mandarins*). Scholars believe that they used clay tablets and private cubicles with serious penalties for cheating (they were beheaded!). These ancient civil service exams tested the following core "arts": music, archery, horsemanship, writing, arithmetic, and the rites and ceremonies of public and private life.

Incidentally, history has a way of reinventing itself. Perhaps the most currently accepted theory of intelligence is described by Howard Gardner (1983) in *Frames of Mind: The Theory of Multiple Intelligences.* This theory of "multiple intelligences" is currently the basis of many attempts at curricular reform and posits seven (you guessed it) intelligences: music, spatial, bodily/kinesthetic, linguistic, logical/mathematical, interpersonal, and intrapersonal. Can you match these with the ancient Chinese counterparts? (They are listed in corresponding order.)

4. Sampling blunders in research are rare and easy to avoid.   Answer: False.

There are literally thousands of ways to introduce a sampling bias. Perhaps the most dramatic blunder occurred in politics just prior to the 1936 presidential election ("Landon," 1936). This is especially interesting since the survey was one of the largest on record. Nearly 2.5 million potential voters returned cards through the mail resulting in a prediction that the Republican candidate, Alf Landon, would defeat Democrat Franklin D. Roosevelt by a wide margin. (The poll was conducted reasonably close in time to the election, and no major influencing event like a scandal occurred between the poll and the election.) Of course, Landon was not elected President, and FDR won by one of the largest landslides in election history. How can you explain such an error? Like most sampling errors, the problem was a general one: the sample was simply not representative of the population. This lack of representativeness resulted from the pollster's selection of potential voters from, at least in part, automobile registration lists! Who was most likely to own automobiles in the midst of the Depression Era? The wealthy. And were they more likely to be Republicans or Democrats? Republican. As a result of this blunder, the survey was predominantly a survey of Republican voters.

5. The best surveys are large ones, involving around 25,000 respondents, and using sophisticated sampling techniques.   Answer: False.

Most national surveys use about 1,000 or so respondents in their sample. This number produces a "margin of error" of around 2%, in other words, a boundary within which the entire population would most likely fall. For example, if a sample size of 1,000 reveals that 66% of parents—plus or minus 2%—favor year-round schooling, then we know that the true percentage in the population of millions of parents will most likely be 64% to 68%. Notice that sample size is determined by the desired precision (2% or 3% is customary) and *not* by a certain percentage, say 10%, of the population. If this were so, then polling organizations such as Gallup would have to survey millions of people for their attitudes toward public education. The Gallup sample size (at least in their survey of attitudes toward education) is about 1,320, and the population they generalize to includes all adults eighteen years or older, except those in institutions such as prisons, hospitals, etc. and those in the military. This is over one hundred million people! Also, recent Gallup survey methodology (Elam, Rose, & Gallup, 1996) is hardly sophisticated. It involves a computer that randomly dials a valid telephone number. When the phone is answered, the interviewer asks to speak to the *youngest male* living in the household, and if no male lives there, the interviewer asks to speak to the *oldest female* in the household. Really! Remarkably, this simple technique, which sounds terribly biased, produces a sample that matches the age and sex distribution in the general population, and their findings generalize to the population of all households in this country with a very small margin of error.

6. What may be considered sloppy reasoning or misused data are rare occurrences in the practice of research.   Answer: False.

Misinterpretations of data are actually quite common and instances of flawed reasoning abound. Let's consider a few examples. In an attempt to show that it is not advisable to simply throw money at education to increase educational productivity, a nationally known columnist recently cited the "Iowa first phenomenon" in support of his argument. Iowa, the argument goes, scores highest in the nation on the SAT, but doesn't rank high in terms of state per-pupil expenditure. Is this a meaningful comparison? No, according to Powell (1993), especially when you consider that *only about 5% of the high school seniors in Iowa take the SAT*. Most take the ACT (the American College Testing program is headquartered in Iowa). A select few take the SAT in pursuit of universities beyond their borders—such as Stanford, Yale, and Harvard. This academically talented group inflates the SAT average and is meaningless when compared with, for example, New Jersey's SAT average (home of the Educational Testing Service, which administers the SAT). New Jersey ranks high in per-pupil expenditure, but relatively low in SAT scores. To no surprise, the majority (76%) of New Jersey high school seniors, including the less academically able, take the SAT.

Some of the most widely known and influential studies conducted also illustrate the problem of data misinterpretation. In education, perhaps the most dramatic example is Robert Rosenthal and Lenore Jacobson's experiment with teacher's self-fulfilling prophecy. This study, described in their book *Pygmalion in the Classroom: Teacher Expectation and Pupils' Intellectual Development* (1968) received a tremendous amount of media coverage and remains as one of the most frequently cited studies ever conducted in the social sciences. The study suggested that children's intelligence can move up merely in response to teachers' *expectation* that it will do so. Unfortunately, the media frenzy over this experiment overshadowed the scientific criticism occurring in less accessible outlets (Elashoff & Snow, 1971; Wineburg, 1987). Richard Snow (1969), for example, observed that in Rosenthal's original data, one student whose IQ was expected to increase moved from 17 to 148! Another jumped from 18 to 122! Because IQs hover around 100 and rarely exceed the boundaries of 70 to 130, one can only conclude that the original data was flawed and meaningless. The idea of teachers' self-fulfilling prophecies took hold despite the data errors, however, and continues to this day. (There is ample evidence that teachers do have expectations of student performance based on seemingly irrelevant characteristics and that they may behave in accordance with those expectations. There is no evidence, however, that students' measured intelligence can spurt in the manner originally suggested by Rosenthal's interpretation of the data.)

One of psychology's best known research biases—the Hawthorne effect—is also a case study in the misinterpretation of data. The Hawthorne effect was "discovered" during a series of experiments at the Hawthorne Western Electric plant during 1924–32. This effect refers to a change in behavior as a result of simply being studied. It is also referred to as the *novelty* effect or the *guinea pig* effect and is generally believed to stem from the increased attention that research subjects receive during the course of a study. The Hawthorne effect suggested that an increase in workers' production level attributed to, for example the installation of a conveyer belt, could actually stem from the attention they received from being studied in response to a change (any change). Whatever the cause, the Hawthorne experiments are believed to be a major impetus in the launching of industrial psychology as a discipline. The major findings of this study (Roethlisberger & Dickson, 1939) were interpreted *impressionistically* by the researchers, and because the Hawthorne effect became so entrenched in the minds of researchers, it wasn't until fifty years later that the original data were analyzed objectively and statistically (Franke & Kaul, 1978). Remarkably, Chadwick, Bahr, & Albrecht (1984) reported that "the findings of this first statistical interpretation of the Hawthorne studies are in direct and dramatic opposition to the findings for which the study is famous" (p. 273). In other words, an objective analysis revealed (at least in these data) that the Hawthorne effect was a myth. In truth, there may be a Hawthorne effect in other contexts, but we know that its existence is not supported by the original Hawthorne data.

I am reminded of an old story about the psychologist who trained a flea to jump on command. This sadistic psychologist then investigated what effect removing a leg, one at a time, would have on its ability to jump. He found that even with one leg, the flea could jump at the command "Jump!" Upon removing the flea's last leg, he found that the flea made no attempt to jump. After thinking about this outcome for a while, he wrote up his findings and concluded, "When a flea has all legs removed, it becomes deaf." His finding was consistent with that interpretation, but it is simply not the most reasonable one.

7. Research studies are only commissioned by so-called disinterested, independent, and impartial researchers with no vested interests in the outcome.   Answer: False.

Let's consider a 1993 report published in *JAMA* (*Journal of the American Medical Association*) and described in the March 8, 1993 issue of *Newsweek* titled "A Really Bad Hair Day." The report suggested that men who have a balding pattern on the crown of their head are up to three times more likely to have a heart attack than men without such a balding pattern. Who commissioned this study? According to *Newsweek* it was Upjohn Co., the pharmaceutical giant which produces Rogaine, a preparation advertised to restore hair. (I am reminded of talk about the study linking a crease in earlobes to heart disease. If you had such a crease, would you run off to a cosmetic surgeon to have the crease removed in an attempt to stave off heart disease? I hope not…).

Be advised that publishers of instructional materials also commission product evaluations, and may fine-tune research studies with desired outcomes in mind. I am not suggesting fraud, only that some of the hundreds of decisions that must be made in the course of a research study may be guided somewhat by "wishful science."

8. In research the term, "statistically significant" means roughly the same as "important" or "substantial."   Answer: False.

Perhaps the single best phrase to capture the meaning of *statistically significant* is "probably not due to chance." It carries no connotation like "important" or "valuable" or "strong." Very small effects, for example training in test taking skills that "boost" SAT scores in a group from 500 to 510 might be statistically significant, but of little practical importance.

The term statistically significant does not in any way suggest an *explanation* of findings either—only that an observed relationship is probably not due to chance. For example, let's pretend that your friend claims to have psychic powers, that is, can affect the outcome of a coin toss. As the coin is tossed, your friend can "will" more heads as an outcome than would be expected by chance. After one hundred tosses, the results are in: the coin turned up heads sixty times. Is this statistically significant? Yes, because a coin tossed one hundred times would be expected to land heads with a frequency of about forty-three to fifty-seven most of the time. ("Most of the time" means ninety-five percent, hence if you were to toss a coin one hundred times and repeat this for one hundred trials, ninety-five of the trials would produce between forty-three to fifty-seven heads.) Notice that sixty heads was a statistically significant outcome since it was beyond the limits imposed by chance ninety-five percent of the time. But also notice that no explanation is offered by the term "statistically significant." There are many explanations other than "psychic ability." Perhaps the coin was not a fair one, or mistakes were made in the tally of heads, or the "psychic" was a cunning trickster. Also, there always exists the possibility that the outcome of the coin toss was indeed a chance occurrence, although this explanation is correct less than five percent of the time. Note: The concept of statistical significance is undoubtedly the single most difficult one in the introductory study of educational research. Don't worry how those numbers were determined in the coin toss example. This will be fully explained in a later chapter (more conceptually than mathematically).

9. Educational researchers can prove theories by collecting data in order to prove hypotheses.   Answer: False.

"Prove" is a word that is best dropped from your vocabulary, at least during your study of educational research. Unlike students who prove theorems in geometry, students who conduct educational research will most likely *test* theories by finding *support* for a specific hypothesis derived from a theory. For example, constructivist theory predicts that students who *construct* meaning by, for example, creating a metaphor to help their understanding, will learn new material better than students who passively receive new material prepackaged in a lecture. If in fact a researcher found that the "constructed" group learned the new material faster than the "lectured" group, he would conclude that the research hypothesis was *supported* (not proven) and the theory which spawned the hypothesis, in turn, becomes more credible.

There are at least two reasons why educational researchers cannot prove hypotheses or theories. First, research findings are usually evaluated with regard to their statistical significance, which involves the computation of a p value, referring to the *probability* (not proof) that a certain finding was due to chance factors. Although the p values can be extraordinarily low (e.g., .000001, or one chance out of a million that the findings were due to chance), they cannot drop to zero. So there is always the possibility—however small—that the findings could be attributable to chance.

Second, no matter how well controlled a study is, there always exists the possibility that the findings could be the result of some influence other than the one systematically studied by the researcher. For example, a researcher might compare the relative effectiveness of learning to spell on a computer versus the "old-fashioned" way of writing words by hand. If the computer group learned to spell better and faster than the handwriting group, might there be reasons other than the computers for the better performance? Yes, there might be several. For example, maybe the teachers of the computer group were different, possibly more enthusiastic or more motivating. It might be the enthusiasm or motivation by itself that resulted in better spelling performance. If the more enthusiastic and motivating teachers had taught the handwriting method, then the handwriting group may have outperformed the computer group. Consider another example. The computing group was taught in the morning, and the handwriting group in the afternoon. If the computing group outperformed the handwriting group, how would you know whether the better performance was a teaching-method effect or a time-of-day effect? You would not.

10. Control groups in educational research are considered a luxury and are not needed to evaluate the effectiveness of new interventions.   Answer: False.

Control groups serve a vital function by enabling researchers who test new methods to answer the question Compared to what? Let's consider a dramatic example in medicine once again to illustrate this point. Assume that a researcher wanted to test the effectiveness of acupuncture on lower back pain. She recruited one hundred patients with such pain and asked them to rate their pain on a one to ten scale before undergoing acupuncture three times a week for ten weeks. At the end of the ten weeks, the patients rated their back pain once again, and, as expected by the researcher, the pain was greatly reduced. She concluded that acupuncture was effective for reducing low back pain.

Are there other explanations for this finding? You bet, and the researcher should have controlled for these alternative, rival explanations with appropriate control groups before any conclusions were drawn. For starters, what about the mere passage of time—is not time one of the best healers? Maybe the patients' back pain would have greatly reduced ten weeks later if they had done nothing. (Have you ever had a backache? Did it go away without any treatment?) A good control for this explanation would be a ten-week "waiting list" control group which simply waited for the acupuncture in the absence of any treatment. What about the effect resulting from simply resting three times a week for 10 weeks? Or an effect due to the awareness of undergoing an alternative treatment? Or an effect simply due to lying down on a special acupuncture table? Or an effect simply due to piercing the skin? An appropriate control in this instance would be a group treated *exactly* the same as the acupuncture group, including having their skin pierced superficially while lying down three times a week on a special acupuncture platform. In fact, members should not be aware that they are in the control group. In the jargon of research, this is referred to as *blinding* the control group to the influence stemming from the awareness of special treatment. This control group, then, controls for the influence of time, resting prone during the day, receiving special attention, and many other factors as well, including the simple expectation that pain will go away (often referred to as the *placebo* effect). Note: In this book the labels "control" group and "comparison" group are used interchangeably since no attempt is made to differentiate them. The labels "experimental" group and "treatment" group are used interchangeably for the same reason.

We hope that this little pretest has stimulated your interest in the process of scientific research in general and in educational research in particular. In the next chapter, we will examine some important basic terms used in educational research. We will also review our first published research report.

APPLICATION EXERCISES

1. Visit your library and locate a journal that publishes the findings of research studies, such as the *American Educational Research Journal, Journal of Educational Psychology,* or the *Journal of Educational Research.* Find a study that uses a control group and explain its function. In other words, what does the control group control?

2. Using the same resources in your library, find two studies that present contradictory findings. Then try to explain how it is possible that the two studies could yield opposite results. Hint: This is not as difficult as you might think. Two studies could be located by reading a third study in an area of interest. Authors of the third study in their review of previous research in the beginning of their article will often cite several studies revealing one outcome and several others that reveal a different outcome. Find one in each opposing group and examine the study differences carefully.

MULTIPLE CHOICE QUESTIONS

1. When two studies designed to answer the same question yield opposite conclusions, the most likely explanation is related to:
   a. coding errors
   b. fraudulent procedures
   c. differences in methodology
   d. quality of reporting journals
   e. timing of data collection

2. From a research perspective, what do Clever Hans and The Amazing Randi have in common?
   a. They highlight the importance of informed consent
   b. They illustrate why researchers use statistical tests
   c. They emphasize the value of multiple measures
   d. They remind us that laboratory mice are not like people
   e. They reveal why researchers control bias by blinding

3. Gardner's theory of multiple intelligences reminds us that contemporary theories are not always:
   a. new
   b. simple
   c. correct
   d. supported
   e. believable

4. The Alf Landon and Franklin D. Roosevelt poll revealed which of the following?
   a. Polls themselves can change voters' minds
   b. Polls are usually greatly "off target"
   c. Polls can be more accurate than actual voting
   d. Polls can be very large but also very biased
   e. Polls lead to "voter burnout"

5. The Gallup national poll of attitudes toward education reveals that representative samples are possible if the sampling plan targets respondents':
   a. age and sex
   b. ethnicity and socioeconomic status
   c. occupation and year of birth
   d. zip codes and income
   e. education and family size

6. The "Iowa first phenomenon," Hawthorne effect, and *Pygmalion in the Classroom* all remind us that:
   a. samples must be large (10,000+) to be representative
   b. data can be easily misinterpreted
   c. subjects can be abused in research studies
   d. good theories can be proven
   e. statistical "blips" can occur

7. Researchers who (maybe unknowingly) fine-tune studies with desired outcomes in mind call attention to the problems associated with:
   a. "soft data"
   b. "sham groups"
   c. "wishful science"
   d. "sabotaging subjects"
   e. "untestable theories"

8. Which of the following is the best description of "statistically significant"?
   a. "important and powerful"
   b. "probably not due to chance"
   c. "worthy of recognition"
   d. "substantial or large"
   e. "theoretically interesting"

9. Which of the following makes little or no sense from a research perspective?
    a. "We tested the hypothesis"
    b. "We predicted no difference"
    c. "We analyzed the results"
    d. "We proved the theory"
    e. "We replicated the findings"

10. The fact that back pain often disappears by itself over time reminds us why researchers must use:
    a. control groups
    b. objective measurements
    c. statistical analysis
    d. consenting participants
    e. multiple observations

Answers: 1) c   2) e   3) a   4) d   5) a   6) b   7) c   8) b   9) d   10) a

CONSTRUCTS, VARIABLES, AND HYPOTHESES

OVERVIEW

The conduct of educational research is best understood as a *process*, or series of integrated steps. These steps will be elaborated in Chapter 3, but understanding this process requires familiarity with several terms, such as constructs, variables, and hypotheses. These basic concepts will be introduced with many concrete examples. They are part of the "language" of research. Understanding the research language is sometimes demanding, but the language is fundamental. Your ability to critically evaluate published research requires knowledge that the research process forms an integrated whole. This chapter will lay some groundwork for this knowledge and ability.

CONSTRUCTS AND OPERATIONAL DEFINITIONS

Educational research is challenging in part because educators are interested in complex abstractions, such as *motivation, self-esteem,* or *creativity.* Other researchers might study soil samples under the microscope, distances with a telescope, or tumors with a magnetic resonance imaging machine. The abstract dimensions that interest educational researchers are called *constructs* because they are constructed or invented labels, a short-hand way of describing many interrelated behaviors, all of which are postulated to represent the same trait or ability. For example, all of the behaviors and skills believed to reflect intelligence may be bundled conceptually and referred to collectively as "intelligence." The underlying dimension inferred by the construct such as intelligence (or self-esteem, motivation, etc.) is only postulated to exist. We cannot see it directly; it is "in the head," so to speak.

Although we cannot see these constructs, we can test the *theory* (explanation) behind the construct by directly studying the presumed indicators of the construct. These indicators are referred to as the *operational definition* of the construct. Intelligence (the construct) may be inferred from "intelligent" behavior (the indicators), such as correctly solving a logic problem, answering questions about word meanings, repeating backwards a string of eight numbers, solving a math problem, using "street smarts" to achieve a goal, starting a new business, paraphrasing the theme of a written paragraph, solving an equation, or executing a triple lutz. The major point is this: abstract constructs must be defined in a way that makes them observable. They may be defined in many different ways, some of which are more appropriate than others.

Some operational definitions clearly do not reflect the rich complexity of the construct. Consider love, for example. Just as people who have intelligence are expected to acted in predictable ways, people who have love (or are "in love," as they say) are expected to act in predictable ways, or at least have predictable characteristics. Love with all its complex emotions could be operationally defined as the level of an endorphin-like chemical found in the blood. (Increases in this chemical, also found in chocolate, are believed to be responsible for the euphoric high that falling in love brings. Its decrease is believed to be responsible for the "honeymoon is over" feeling.) Or it could be operationally defined by the frequency of romantic kissing, a self-report rating scale (on a one to ten metric, ranging from "I'm Indifferent" to "I'm Going Crazy With Love"), or even the credit limit that one imposes on a partner's charge card at J. C. Penny's. In any case, these abstract constructs must be measurable in some form or another.

Perhaps the best way to think about operational definitions is this: it is the *rule for putting numbers or codes next to names* in a research study. Consider the construct test anxiety, for example. Most people know what this means, and the label itself has allowed us to communicate fairly well about test anxiety. But how would you know if an intervention designed to lower test anxiety was effective? General impressions are not acceptable, because they are especially prone to bias. Researchers usually find a more empirical indicator of test anxiety. *Empirical,* in this sense, means objective, first-hand, and verifiable. It would not be acceptable to say that the subjects "just kinda looked less uptight." More empirical measures might include heart rate, average number of eye blinks per minute, level of perspiration, number of fidgets, or blood pressure. But does heart rate, for example, really capture the essence of test anxiety, in the same way that an endorphin-like chemical captures the essence of love? Hardly. Here is the troubling tradeoff: Constructs often loose their meaning when they are operationalized, that is, when the numbers are put next to names.

Consider a few more examples, such as creativity, for instance. It is generally understood what is meant by this term, and because of this, we can talk about classroom ideas that foster creativity, home environments that are most conducive for enabling creative behavior to flourish, and many other factors that might be linked to creativity in students. Let us pretend that a biochemical theory of creativity posits that babies who were breast fed tend to be more creative in high school than babies who were bottle fed. One hundred students were located and classified into the breast versus bottle group. However difficult that may be, consider the harder part: how to measure creativity. Maybe teachers' ratings on a one to ten scale? Number of recognized science projects? The number of unusual uses for a brick named within one minute? Ratings of a short story written by students as judged by a creativity "expert"? Score on a researcher-developed test of creativity? Do any of these measures really capture the essence of creativity? Needless to say, the method chosen for putting numbers next to names has great implications for the value and meaning of the research.

Some systems for putting numbers next to names could render the research meaningless, as it is possible that a researcher might be testing a hypothesis very different from what was intended. For example, a researcher might test the hypothesis, *"The quality of the home environment before school age is linked to intelligence ten years later."* The researcher decides to use high school GPA and SAT scores as measures of intelligence, but these measures may be, more appropriately, indicators of motivation rather than intelligence. And then there's the problem of operationally defining the "quality of the home environment." The number of educational toys accessible? The frequency of verbal interaction between parents and children? The type of verbal interaction? The frequency of parents' reading to their children? The sheer variety of daily stimulation? The frequency of parents' punitive and restrictive behaviors? The simple presence of two parents? When operational definitions do not accurately reflect the construct being investigated, the research results are, at best, open to competing interpretations. I hope you can see that the decisions made regarding the operational definitions of constructs are among the most far-reaching. Other examples of constructs and operational definitions appear in Table 2.1.

TABLE 2.1   Examples of Constructs and (not necessarily good) Operational Definitions

Construct	Operational definition
Intelligence	Score on Graduate Record Exam (GRE); score on Stanford-Binet scale
Anxiety	Heart rate; blood pressure; self-report rating
Motivation	Grade point average (GPA)
Self-esteem	Score on Coopersmith test
Creativity	Number of novel uses for a paper clip described in three minutes
Love	Credit limit allowed on spouse's Mastercard; level of endorphin-like chemical in the blood
Hyperactivity	Number of fidgets in fifteen minutes
Stress	Eye blinks per minute
Charisma	Rating on a 7-point scale
Aggression	Observers' tally of hits and kicks
Teaching effectiveness	End-of-course student ratings; principal's rating; student achievement scores; student reflective ratings after graduation

TYPES OF VARIABLES

All educational research involves the description or explanation of *variables*, those changing qualities or characteristics of learners, teachers, environments, teaching methods, instructional materials, assessment instruments, and virtually all other factors related to education in the broadest sense. A *variable*, then, refers to any dimension that has two or more changing values. Examples of learner variables include sex (male or female), achievement (one of ninety-nine percentiles), self-esteem (low, average, high), socioeconomic status (upper, middle, lower), prior knowledge (none, some, extensive), learning style (visual, auditory, tactile/kinesthetic), or the amount of musical experience prior to age eight. Examples of teacher variables include experience (one year, two years, three years, four or more years), educational background (BA versus MA/MS degree), or grade level (K–12). Examples of environments include class size (ranging from one to forty) or setting (inner city, rural, suburban). Examples of teaching methods include level of technological support (none versus computer at every desk) or size of cooperative learning groups (three, five, seven). Prominent instructional materials include use of color on musical scores (yes or no) or the number of analogies found in a physics lesson (zero, one, two). And finally, examples of assessment variables include type of test (multiple choice versus essay), type of grading (pass/fail versus A–F letters), or type of graduation requirement (portfolio versus standardized achievement test). As you can see, the number of variables of interest to educational researchers is almost limitless.

The practice of research requires that variables be clearly identified and categorized. The following categories are common and generally accepted:

- Independent (two types)
  - true
  - quasi
- Dependent
- Attribute
- Extraneous

Independent Variables: True and Quasi

Variables categorized here are under the command of the researcher and usually reflect a treatment or intervention of some type. They are "free" to vary (hence *independent*) in the sense that the researcher can determine the conditions or categories that define the variable. For example, size of learning group might be an independent variable with levels determined by the researcher to be three, five, or seven. Independent variables are believed to be the cause of some resultant effect. The researcher might suspect that small learning groups result in better learning. Here's another example. A researcher might believe that preschoolers' training in music leads to better math reasoning in adolescence. The independent variable would be type of musical training, with categories being no training, piano lessons once a week, and piano lessons twice a week.

Two types of independent variables exist: *true* and *quasi*. True independent variables are (1) manipulated by the researcher, that is, the variable and its categories are created by the researcher, and (2) research participants can be randomly assigned to any one of the categories. For example, I might believe that students learn to spell words faster with handwriting practice than with computer keyboard practice. Notice that I created this variation in spelling practice and could also create whatever differences between the groups that I want. I might settle on three groups: handwriting only, keyboarding only, and combination handwriting/keyboarding. I could also assign learners randomly to conditions if I wanted since each student could practice in any one of the three groups. This is a true independent variable because I believe it will cause differences in the rate of spelling acquisition, I created it by determining which conditions would exist, and I am free to assign students randomly to the three different conditions. These interrelated notions of *presumed cause* and *created conditions* are referred to as a *manipulation* of an independent variable by researchers. The fact that the manipulation was coupled with *random assignment* defines the independent variable as true.

A different type of independent variable is referred to as a *quasi independent variable*. (*Quasi* means "having a likeness or resemblance to something," as in quasi formal.) These quasi independent variables are still believed to be the cause of some effect and their created conditions qualify as a manipulation, but restrictions are in place which prohibit the random assignment of subjects to groups. For example, let's presume that a school purchased one hundred computers for use in their classrooms. Teachers believe that the use of these computers results in faster spelling achievement, hence they encourage students to practice spelling by using the computer as often as they can. In order to assess the effectiveness of the computers, a school is found that is not using computers but is as similar as possible in other respects to the school that is. Notice that these two conditions were not created in a truly experimental way; the school which received computers could not be determined randomly. (Quasi independent variables are more akin to "natural" interventions where the researcher has less control over conditions and their assignments.) Recall that true independent variables have researcher-determined conditions with random assignment. *This distinction is critical.* The simple technique of random assignment will determine in large part how confident you can be that, for example, the computer was the cause of observed differences in spelling. As we will see in a later chapter, the use of quasi independent variables will define *quasi-experimental* research designs, which are less persuasive in establishing cause-and-effect relationships than their true experimental design counterparts, those with random assignment.

Dependent Variables

Variables categorized as dependent are also called *outcome* variables or measures. (Sometimes they are called *criterion* measures.) The values of this variable are presumably *dependent* on the particular condition of the independent variable. Using the computer versus handwriting study described previously, one reasonable dependent variable might be the number of practice sessions needed to spell words correctly or the number spelled correctly on a final spelling test. The dependent variables are the effects of the causal variation induced by the independent variables. A research study may indeed have several dependent variables. In the example on spelling practice through the use of a computer, other possible dependent variables include the spelling score on a standardized achievement test (spelling subtest), the number of recognized spelling errors in a short story, or the students' level of enjoyment during spelling lessons.

Dependent variables often take the form of operationally-defined constructs, as discussed earlier in this chapter. They are the "blank" in the expression "...as measured by _____." For example, if a research study investigated the influence of school size on overall achievement, the dependent variable might be "...as measured by the *Stanford Achievement Tests*." Or if a research study investigated the influence of greater autonomy on teacher morale, the dependent variable might be "...as measured by the *rate of absenteeism*." Or if a research study investigated the influence of cooperative learning groups on self-esteem, the dependent variable might be "...as measured by the *Coopersmith Self-Esteem Inventory*." Or if a study investigated the influence of sugar on hyperactivity, the dependent measure might be "...as measured by the *duration of fidgeting*." Of course, observers would have to be trained to recognize what constitutes a fidget.

Do you remember the old adage "An apple a day keeps the doctor away"? If this were tested empirically, can you determine the independent and dependent variables? The independent variable would be whether or not an apple was eaten each day, and the dependent variable would be how many doctor visits were needed by the apple eaters and non-apple eaters. Or more generally, the independent variable might be type of diet (good versus poor) and the dependent variable would be the frequency of colds, flu, or whatever index of health was chosen.

Attribute Variables

A great many variables of interest to researchers include the characteristics (*attributes*) of students, such as sex, anxiety, socioeconomic status, intelligence, learning style, creativity, prior knowledge, exposure to lead paint, musical training prior to kindergarten, and hunger to name a few. Such variables are rarely manipulated in order to function as true independent variables (because it is either impossible, impractical, or unethical). These attribute variables contribute to the astonishing array of learner differences, more commonly called "diversity." Because of the increasingly recognized importance of diversity, these variables are rarely ignored in educational research studies. And for good reason: they are important. Their importance is revealed by studies examining how they relate to independent and dependent variables. For example, one approach to teaching a lesson may work extraordinarily well for low anxiety students but fail miserably for high anxiety students. Some students may have to hear a lesson, others may have to see it, still others may have to feel it. Some learn best in groups, others learn best alone. Ambiguity may frustrate some students, others may thrive on it. The answer to many research questions investigating the effect of a particular teaching method is, *"It depends."* What it depends on are attribute variables.

Failure to consider attribute variables in the design of educational research may render the research meaningless. For example, let us suppose that two different teaching methods (the independent variable) were compared: lecture versus discussion. Achievement test scores functioned as the dependent variable. The results: no difference overall between the two groups; both scored seventy percent. If students had been assessed and classified in accordance with their anxiety level (high versus low), a dramatic difference could result. High anxiety students could have scored ninety percent versus fifty percent in the lecture and discussion groups, respectively (averaging seventy percent). Low anxiety students could have scored fifty and ninety percent, respectively, essentially reversing the findings of the high anxiety group, but still averaging seventy percent. The finding of "no difference" of course would not have been accurate since the anxiety groups functioned to essentially cancel the strong teaching method effect. The best answer, then, to the question, *"What is the effect of lecture versus discussion methods on achievement?"* is *It depends on anxiety.* (This is simply a hypothetical example.) Admittedly, it is probably rare that the influence of an independent variable such as teaching method would be wiped out so completely by failing to consider attribute variables. The point is that the influence of an independent variable could be masked by unattended learner characteristics. Attribute variables are not limited to student characteristics. Teachers, classrooms, schools, families and many other variables all have characteristics that may function in this "it depends" manner. (More will be said about this idea in Chapter 9, where the concept of interaction is described.)

One final note about attribute variables: they may also be referred to as *subject* variables or possibly *moderator* variables. To make matters even more confusing, they may also be referred to as a type of independent variable, namely a *measured* or *selected* independent variable. Differences, hence confusion, in terminology is unfortunate but is a reality. Because it is doubtful that all researchers will ever use agreed-upon common labels, critical readers of published research must be alert to this variation in terms. It is not as frustrating as it sounds, for the type of variable should be obvious in context despite its masquerading under different names. Don't think that all research terminology is clouded by differences in labels. It appears that "types of variables" offers the worst offense in this regard.

Extraneous Variables

This class of variables, unlike the other three, usually number in the hundreds or thousands in any given research study. These variables are sometimes referred to as *nuisance* or *control* variables, and for good reason: they are a nuisance and must be controlled. They all have in common the potential to influence the dependent variable, but are extraneous (not relevant or important) to the research hypothesis or question. Because of this, these extraneous variables must be controlled so that their influence is not contaminating the results. For example, in the computer versus handwriting study of spelling achievement described earlier, the following variables might be considered extraneous:

- Time of day students practiced spelling
- Amount of students' physical exercise
- Noise level in the room
- Motivation level of the student
- Alertness of the student
- Charisma of the teacher
- Learning style of the student
- Prior knowledge of the student
- Lead poisoning levels
- Prior experience with computers

All of these variables—unless they are independent or attribute variables—must be controlled so that their influence does not jeopardize the meaningfulness of the study. Fortunately, most of the variables can be controlled by a single action—random assignment of students to conditions. This simple but powerful technique can neutralize the influence of countless extraneous variables that are related to the student, such as motivation, prior knowledge, lead levels, etc. The extraneous variables related to the teacher and environment often require special procedures in order to neutralize or control their influence. These control techniques are described in Chapter 8. For now, it is important to recognize this category of variables as *virtually all sources of influence on the dependent variable other than the independent and attribute variables.* The differences between the four major types of variables are summarized in Table 2.2.

Confounding. When extraneous variables are not controlled, they sometimes exert their influence in a troublesome way. Failure to recognize and control for extraneous variables may result in a form of contamination known as a *confounding.* This special term is described below.

The term *confounding* is used often in educational research, but its meaning is not widely understood. It is used in everyday contexts to mean "confused," "bewildered," or "mixed up." In research, you can think about confounding as "mixed up" results. Specifically, a confounding occurs whenever a researcher has allowed two or more variables to change together. The independent variable (IV), of course, should vary because this is the treatment or intervention that the researcher has deliberately created in order to change systematically (the manipulation). When any other extraneous variable (EV) changes along with the deliberate change in the IV, it is said the independent variable is confounded with the extraneous variable. For example, if two methods of teaching were studied by comparing one method in the fall with the other method in the spring, it would be said the teaching method (IV) is confounded with time of year (EV). If more able teachers taught one method, and less able teachers taught another method, it is said that teaching method (IV) is confounded with teachers' ability (EV). If less able students were taught using one method and more able students were taught using another method, it is said that teaching method (IV) is confounded with student ability (EV). And if one method was used in a red room, and another method used in a blue room, then teaching method (IV) is confounded with room color (EV). Figure 2.1 illustrates how a careless researcher might introduce a confounding variable into a research setting. Examples of other confoundings are presented in Table 2.3.

Notice that the appropriate use of this term is the confounding of *independent* and *extraneous* variables; it is *not* the dependent variable that is confounded. Confoundings are sometimes eliminated by sound research designs which exert control over the extraneous variables (described in Chapters 9 and 10). They are also eliminated with a variety of statistical techniques (e.g., partial correlation, as described in Chapter 10). Confoundings in educational research are best prevented with a host of control strategies. These techniques are described in Chapter 8. Extraneous variables that are successfully controlled through these maneuvers are sometimes referred to, quite appropriately, as *controlled variables.*

TABLE 2.2 Four Major Types of Variables Used by Researchers in the Test of "An Apple a Day Keeps the Doctor Away"

Variable	Key Characteristic	Example
Independent	Presumed cause	Eating apples (none or one per day)
Dependent	Measured outcome (effect)	Number of doctor visits for colds or flu
Attribute	Subject characteristic	Male versus female
Extraneous	Controlled influence	Prior health, other foods

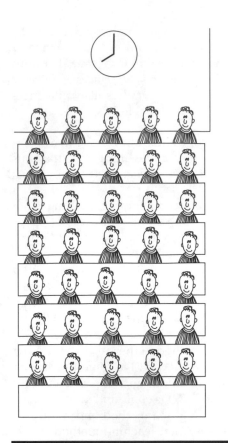 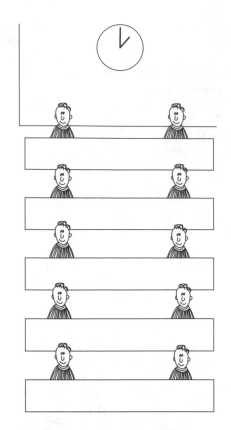

FIGURE 2.1 Is class size related to achievement? A careless researcher might allow class size to be confounded with the extraneous variable of time of day. If so, achievement differences could be due to variation in the independent variable (size) or the extraneous variable (time). The results would be uninterpretable.

TABLE 2.3 Hypothetical Examples of Independent (IV) and Extraneous (EV) Variables Which Are Confounded.

Independent Variable	Extraneous Variable	Confounding
Amount of sugar in breakfast	Day of week	High sugar on Monday; low sugar on Friday
Length of class	Type of teacher	One-hour class by Mr. Smith; two-hour class by Mrs. Woo
Type of teaching	Location	Lecture in Room 012; discussion in Room 812
Use of a drug hypothesized to reduce hyperactivity	Color of room	Hyperactivity medicine group in off-white room; placebo in red room
Use of questions in text	Interest level	Interesting text with questions; boring one without
School uniforms	Type of school	Uniforms in single-sex school; no uniforms in coed school
School schedule	Type of school	9-month public schools; 11-month private schools
Type of kindergarten	Parent socio-economic status	Montessori for wealthier parent; public for less wealthy parents

As the IV changes so does the EV, rendering the results uninterpretable. When this happens, the differences in the dependent variable (not stated in this table, but they can be imagined) could be due to the IV *or* the EV (or some combination of both).

HYPOTHESES

In addition to the four different types of variables described above, educational researchers are concerned with the following three different classes of hypotheses:

- Research hypothesis
- Alternative hypothesis
- Null hypothesis

Let's examine each one in turn and then see how they interrelate.

Research Hypothesis

The *research hypothesis* is what you probably think of as the main hypothesis. It is the researcher's best guess about the outcome of the research study. These expectations about the outcome usually come from the theory that generated the hypothesis in the first place. Research hypotheses are more than vague hunches about the outcome; they are precise statements regarding clear outcomes. They sometimes appear in an *If A, then B* format where *A* refers to the independent variable, and *B* refers to the dependent variable. Some examples are shown below:

- If children are taught to read via whole language, then their reading comprehension will be higher.
- If children watch three or more hours of television per day, then their behavior on the playground will be more aggressive.
- If children learn in small cooperative groups, then their social interactions will be more positive.
- If teachers earn master's degrees, then their job satisfaction will increase.
- If young children take piano lessons, then they will have higher math aptitude ten years later.
- If exercise immediately precedes a geometry lesson, students will learn faster.

Research hypotheses may not appear in the *If A, then B* form. Sometimes they appear as statements or claims such as, "Young children who take piano lessons will have higher math aptitude ten years later," or, "Exercising immediately before a geometry lesson will result in faster learning." Research hypotheses may even appear as a question, for example, "Will young children who take piano lessons have higher math aptitude ten years later?" Or, "Does exercise immediately before a geometry lesson result in faster learning?"

The particular form of the research hypothesis is not as important as its content. It must specify in some way which variables are being studied, and, if known, what potential outcome is expected. It is important to understand that educational researchers do not simply gather data on a hodgepodge of many variables in a helter-skelter manner only to fish around aimlessly in the hopes of finding something "significant." The problem with this "shotgun" approach is that "significant" relationships **will** surface, but their significance is illusory because of the workings of mere chance. We will have more to say about the research hypothesis in Chapter 4 and the meaning of significance in Chapter 11.

Alternative Hypothesis

The *alternative hypotheses* are developed or conceptualized by researchers only to be eliminated. They are referred to as alternative in the sense that they rival the research hypothesis as an explanation for the outcome. (In fact, they are sometimes called *rival hypotheses*.) For example, let's suppose that a new method of teaching reading—Total Immersion—was compared to an existing or traditional method. The research hypothesis might be, "If students are taught to read using Total Immersion, then they will learn to read with greater comprehension." A critic might say, "There is an alternative hypothesis—better teachers used the Total Immersion method, and that is why Total Immersion students read better. Those teachers are so good that their students would read better no matter what method they used!" Another critic might say, "There is another alternative hypothesis—more able students were taught using Total Immersion, and those students would read better no matter what method was used." But the careful researcher would have already anticipated these alternative hypotheses and taken steps to rule them out. For example, the same teachers were used to teach reading via the Total Immersion and traditional methods. Further, the researcher arranged for students to be randomly assigned to each method to assure that the groups were comparable at the start of the research.

Alternative hypotheses (or simply, blunders) are avoided by careful researchers for obvious reasons—the findings could be "explained away" by rival interpretations, rendering the research results difficult to interpret. When critical reviewers of research ask the question What else could have possibly explained these results? they are asking for plausible, rival, alternative hypotheses. Cautious researchers anticipate these problems related to potential alternative hypotheses. Then they make certain that they are eliminated, or at least made implausible.

Example: Perceptual Defense.   Research in psychology provides excellent examples of alternative hypotheses. Consider the example of the *perceptual defense phenomenon*. McGinnies (1949) attempted to test the credibility of Freudian psychodynamic theory, which suggests that many of our motives stem from unconscious influences and long forgotten early experiences. The problem with psychodynamic theory, from a scientific point of view, is that the theory (however interesting) does not generate easily testable research hypotheses. Good scientific theories must "stick their neck out" and be vulnerable in the sense that hypotheses spun from the theory can be tested directly. However difficult, McGinnies' experiment tested the notion that the perceptual defense mechanism is capable of recognizing disturbing, anxiety provoking stimuli at the *unconscious* level. This monitoring device, according to the theory, was constantly on the alert and blocked out environmental threats before they entered our awareness. It was, generally, a protective gateway to our conscious awareness.

This idea of a perceptual defense mechanism was tested in an ingenious (but flawed) way by flashing words on a screen by a machine at speeds much faster than could be recognized. These words were flashed slower and slower by the experimenter until the research subjects could recognize the words, at which point they simply announced the word out loud. The speed at which subjects could recognize and announce the word was called their *threshold*. McGinnies was especially interested in whether thresholds were longer for emotionally threatening (nasty, or taboo) words as compared to neutral words. If the perceptual defense mechanism were doing its job, it should have prevented or at least delayed the threatening words from entering conscious awareness until the force was too strong, hence lengthening the threshold. The gate would simply burst open, allowing the inevitable recognition of the emotionally charged words. The research hypothesis, then, was, "If subjects view taboo words compared to neutral words, then their recognition thresholds would be longer." In fact this is just what McGinnies found—subjects took longer to recognize taboo words than neutral words. This outcome, therefore, provided support for the perceptual defense mechanism and added credibility to the psychodynamic theory which predicted this outcome.

But wait a minute. Recall that alternative hypotheses are rival explanations of the research findings. How else could this result be explained? In several ways. Perhaps subjects recognized the taboo words just as quickly as the neutral words, but hesitated before announcing something embarrassing to the experimenter, especially if they were wrong! Subjects may have "jumped the gun" in their announcement of neutral words (to appear fast, hence intelligent) but delayed somewhat for taboo words until they were absolutely certain that what they actually saw was indeed what they thought they saw. The alternative hypothesis, then, was, "If subjects are shown taboo words compared to neutral words, then they will take longer to announce them, in an attempt to be certain about what they saw."

Researchers have another name for problems such as this: *artifact*. "Artifact" is a general term referring to unwanted and unintended sources of bias in the collection or analysis of data; as such they function as alternative hypotheses. A critic might say that McGinnies's (1949) findings were an artifact of his data collection procedure since his subjects may have hesitated before announcing the nasty words, consequently lengthening their perceptual thresholds. Artifacts are common in behavioral research because people's behavior is often influenced by the very process of observation. Subjects may react in unintended ways to the mere presence of a camcorder or clipboard (e.g., show nervousness, be better behaved, etc.). In this case the artifact is also referred to as a *reactive measure* since subjects are reacting to the research procedures required for observation. (A counterpart in medicine might be "white coat fever" whereby blood pressure may skyrocket in response to physicians and all their paraphernalia.) Artifacts are clearly undesirable since they can "explain away" the findings. To say that specific research findings are an artifact of the data collection procedure is to say that the findings are distorted and not to be trusted.

Another alternative hypothesis in the McGinnies (1949) study might be related to the frequency that neutral and taboo words appear in printed materials (newspapers, magazines, books, advertising signs, etc.). Words that appear more commonly in our language might be recognized faster simply because we are more familiar with them. And if neutral words (compared to taboo words) do indeed appear more frequently in print (hence we are more familiar with them), then another alternative hypothesis would be, "If subjects are shown more familiar versus less familiar words, then they will recognize more familiar words faster." You might have recognized this rival explanation as a confounding: the type of word changes as it should since it is the IV (neutral versus taboo) but familiarity changes with it as well (more familiar versus less familiar). If recognition differences are found between neutral and taboo words, one would not know whether the difference was due to the type of word or the familiarity of the word.

Example: Learning Spelling. Cunningham and Stanovich (1990) provided another illustration of an alternative hypothesis. They tested whether young students learn to spell best by practicing on a computer, using scrabble-like tiles, or by handwriting. After practicing new words in one of the three groups, students were given a final test, much like a spelling bee, except that the students wrote down each word after it was pronounced by the teacher. The researchers found that the handwriting condition was far better than the computer and scrabble-tile conditions in terms of the number of correctly spelled words. Can you think of an alternative hypothesis? (The clue lies in how the students were tested: all were tested using handwriting.) The alternative hypothesis was, "If students are tested with the *same* method used for studying, then they will score higher." Perhaps the computer group would have scored highest if they were tested using the computer; similarly, the scrabble-tile condition might have been superior if they were tested with scrabble-tiles. This practice–testing match, therefore, becomes a rival explanation for the findings, since the only condition with the same practice and testing format was the handwriting condition. (This problem, however, was recognized by the researchers and was eliminated in their second experiment. The results, however, were still the same, hence the title of their article: "Writing Beats the Computer.")

It should be clear by now that rival (but plausible) alternative hypotheses are clearly undesirable in the research process. Essentially, these hypotheses are statements about research blunders. Cautious researchers must think carefully about these hypotheses and take steps to avoid them so that they are not rival explanations for their research outcomes.

Null Hypothesis

The third type of hypothesis used by researchers comes into play during the statistical analysis of data. For this reason, the null hypothesis will be mentioned only briefly in this section. A more complete explanation appears in Chapter 11 where we discuss research results and their interpretation.

The *null hypothesis* is a statistical assumption about the population from which the sample was drawn. The assumption is that there is *no* relationship between the independent, dependent, or attribute variables. Why in the world, you might ask, does the researcher assume there is no relationship among variables in the population? This is a temporary assumption, and is believed to be true, so to speak, only while the computer is running during the analysis of the data. The researcher really believes its opposite: the research hypothesis. The computer will then tell the researcher how likely it is that the actual findings in the sample would be obtained if the null hypothesis were true. If the likelihood is very small, for instance, only one in a hundred chances that the null hypothesis is true, the researcher would be entitled to reject it, and conclude that there is probably a relationship in the population from which the sample was drawn. The null hypothesis functions in this temporary way, only to be rejected if the probability of it being true is very low. Most researchers indeed want to discard ("reject") the null hypothesis, for its rejection is interpreted as support for the research hypothesis. This is a difficult idea, and some confusion may be unavoidable at this point without greater elaboration. The null hypothesis will be explained further in Chapter 11, in which its vital role will become clearer. Other examples of research, alternative, and null hypotheses are found in Table 2.4.

TABLE 2.4   Examples of Research, Alternative, and Null Hypotheses

Hypothesis	Example
Research	If children watch violent television, then they will act more aggressively at recess.
Alternative	Children prone toward aggression simply watch more violent television.
Null	In a the population of school-age children there is no relationship between television violence and aggressive behavior.
Research	Children who use computers to learn geometry will learn faster than children who use paper and pencil
Alternative	Children learn faster on the computer because a local news story made them more attentive.
Null	In a population of students there is no difference between those who learn geometry with computers versus paper and pencil in the speed of learning.
Research	Children will learn to spell better in a spelling bee format than in solo seatwork.
Alternative	Children learn better in the spelling bee format because the poor spellers drop out.
Null	In a population of children there is no difference in spelling achievement between those who learn in a spelling bee versus solo seatwork.

CHAPTER SUMMARY

The research process often begins with a theory—or explanation—of some phenomenon or construct (an unobservable trait). All abstract constructs must be operationally defined before they are researchable; that is, defined in terms of the operations used to produce or measure them (as in the expression "as measured by..."). The data collection step in the research process is guided by a research design that manages four different types of variables: independent, or presumed causes; dependent, or presumed effects; attribute, or subject characteristics; and extraneous, or controlled influences. Researchers anticipate biasing sources of contamination or confounding in the research process and use many control procedures to hold them in check. The whole process is guided further by three different types of hypotheses: the research hypothesis, or predicted outcome; the alternative hypothesis, or rival interpretation of results (such as a confounding); and the null hypothesis, or the assertion that no relationship exists in a population. The null hypothesis becomes relevant only in the statistical analysis phase of the research. The interpretation of findings may lead to a refinement of the theory and forms the basis for subsequent research.

GUIDED TOUR

Let's turn our attention now to a guided tour of published educational research. This will help solidify important terms and concepts described in this chapter.

Brief Report

NOTE-TAKING FOSTERS GENERATIVE LEARNING STRATEGIES IN NOVICES

Leslie Shrager and Richard E. Mayer

University of California, Santa Barbara

Subjects were instructed to take notes or not take notes while watching a videotaped lecture on cameras. Note-takers performed better than non-note-takers on recall and transfer tests for students with low prior knowledge of cameras but not for students with high prior knowledge. The results replicated previous At-

[Note] *Most published educational research begins with a summary. This is called the abstract.*

This article is based on an Honors Thesis submitted by the first author.

Correspondence concerning this article should be addressed to Richard E. Mayer, Department of Psychology, University of California, Santa Barbara, California 93106.

tribute × Treatment interactions observed for different materials and supported the generative hypothesis (Peper & Mayer, 1978, 1986).

In a review of research on Attribute × Treatment interactions (ATIs), Snow and Lohman (1984) concluded that special methods of instruction that directly force learners to use appropriate learning strategies are more effective for less skilled learners whereas conventional methods are more effective for more skilled learners. Consistent with this observation, previous research by Peper and Mayer (1978, 1986) found that requiring students to take notes on a lecture produced positive effects on problem-solving transfer for students who scored low in prior knowledge or domain aptitude but not for students who scored high; and furthermore, that the same pattern or ATI was not observed for performance on tests of fact retention or verbatim recognition.

Such results are consistent with a generative theory of learning in which the outcome or learning depends both on what is presented and on the learning strategies used by students (Wittrock, 1974). [1] Presumably, highly skilled learners are more likely to possess and to spontaneously use generative learning strategies, whereas less skilled learners are more likely to use generative learning strategies only when directly guided to do so during learning. Furthermore, the use of generative learning strategies is more likely to result in improved performance on semantic tests such as problem-solving transfer or semantic recall than on verbatim tests such as fact retention or verbatim recognition (Weinstein & Mayer, 1985).

In light of the lack of consistently replicated ATIs in the literature (Snow & Lohman, 1984), we conducted the present replication of Peper and Mayer's (1978, 1986) ATI results. However, to broaden the scope of the study we used different

[1] *In the broadest sense, the construct being investigated by these researchers is "learning." Recall that a construct is a complex abstraction, an inference about something presumed to exist "in the mind." As is true for all constructs, these researchers will have to translate this abstraction into operational terms which are clearly measurable (observable).*

materials (i.e., a lecture on cameras rather than a lecture on automobile engines or statistics), a different attribute measure (i.e., prior knowledge with cameras rather than prior knowledge of car repair or mathematical aptitude), and an additional dependent measure (i.e., recall of the idea units in the lecture). [2] According to the generative theory (Peper & Mayer, 1978, 1986), we predicted that note-taking would result in improved problem-solving transfer and semantic recall but not verbatim recognition or verbatim fact retention for low-knowledge learners but would have essentially no effects on test performance for high-knowledge learners. [3]

Method

Subjects and Design

The subjects were 60 college students from the University of California, Santa Barbara, with 17 students in the low-knowledge/note-taking group, 14 in the low-knowledge/non-note-taking group, 14 in the high-knowledge/note-taking group, and 15 in the high-knowledge/non-note-taking group.

Materials and Apparatus

The apparatus consisted of four television monitors and a video recorder. The materials consisted of (a) an 11-min video-taped presentation adapted from Bromage and Mayer (1981) and entitled "How to Use a Camera," (b) a subject questionnaire that asked students to indicate their familiarity with 35-mm cameras on a 5-point scale ranging from never having used a 35-mm camera to being an expert photographer, (c) a recall test sheet that asked the students to write down all they could remember from the lecture, [4] (d) a transfer test sheet containing four essay problems such as how to design a simple camera for children, (e) a verbatim recognition test consisting of 12 pairs of sentences with one sentence taken from the lec-

[2] *Like most educational research, this study is theory driven. Here we see a clear statement about the role of generative theory in producing the research hypotheses tested by these researchers. (Generative theory emphasizes the important role of learners' actively constructing, or generating, their own understanding by building mental frameworks, making connections, creating metaphors, etc.) The value of this approach is that the findings may support the theory, which itself will help us understand in a much broader sense how students learn. A credible theory, then, does a good job explaining a construct, and the practical implications of a credible theory can lead to improved teaching and enhanced learning ("theory into practice").*

[3] *Here is a precise statement of the research hypothesis, or expected relationship. Recall that the hypothesis is not a vague statement about many different relationships which could be found. It is a very specific relationship, one expected by the researchers, if in fact the theory which spawned the hypothesis is correct. From this hypothesis, one can see that "learning" is defined using a four-pronged approach: transfer, recall, recognition, retention. These will have to be operationally defined in some meaningful way (hopefully). This clear statement also suggests how this research will arrange for the operation of its independent (manipulated), dependent (outcome), and attribute (subject characteristic) variables.*

[4] *Here we find that there are four dependent variables: a recall test score, transfer test score, verbatim recognition test score, and a verbatim fact retention score. This is also seen clearly in Table 1, p. 264 of their article under "test type." When asked to describe the dependent variables in a table such as this, remember that they refer to the measured outcome, that is, the numbers within the table itself.*

ture and the other sentence conveying the same meaning, and (f) a verbatim fact retention test consisting of 10 factual questions such as asking what "ASA" stands for.

Procedure

Subjects were tested in groups of one to four with each subject seated in front of a separate monitor. [5] Subjects who indicated a basic understanding of or a lot of experience with 35-mm cameras were categorized as high-knowledge learners whereas those who had never or rarely used a 35-mm camera were categorized as low-knowledge learners. Subjects randomly assigned to the note-taking group were instructed to take notes whereas those randomly assigned to the non-note-taking group were told to watch the presentation closely. [6] Then, the videotaped lecture was presented followed by the recall test (with a 5-min time limit), the verbatim fact retention test (with a 4-min time limit), the transfer test (with an 8-min time limit), and the verbatim recognition test (with a 3-min time limit).

Results and Discussion

Scoring

The recall test was scored by counting the number of idea units in each student's protocol out of a total possible of 135 idea units using a procedure described by Bromage and Mayer (1981). The transfer test was scored by giving 1 point for each creative idea in each answer out of a total possible score of 37 using a procedure described by Bromage and Mayer. [7] The verbatim recognition test was scored by counting the total number of correct answers out of a possible 12. The verbatim fact retention test was scored by counting the total number of verbatim correct answers out of a possible 10, such as saying "ASA" stood for "American Standards Association."

[5] *Here is a description of an attribute variable. Recall subjects are assigned to categories of this variable on the basis of some pre-existing characteristic, in this case, level of prior knowledge. This attribute variable was important for testing the research hypothesis (see #3), because it was predicted that low-knowledge learners would respond to the treatment (note-taking) differently than high-knowledge learners.*

[6] *Here is a description of the manipulation which defined the researchers' independent variable. Of the subtypes listed earlier in the chapter, this is regarded as a* true *independent variable (opposed to* quasi*) since its categories were created by the researchers and learners could be assigned randomly to each condition (a manipulation). True independent variables are far better suited than quasi-independent variables for the purpose of establishing cause and effect.*

Remember that all researchers must also confront the existence of extraneous variables, all of those influences which can affect the dependent variable (or variables, in this case) but are not relevant to the research hypothesis. As such, their influence must be controlled. The procedure section of a published research article describes the tactics and strategies used for the control of extraneous variables. Recall that researchers, whenever possible, use one very powerful method of control: randomization. In this case, they randomly assigned subjects to categories of the note-taking independent variable. This was an attempt to equalize (control for) extraneous influences related to the learners themselves, such as aptitude, interest, motivation, vision, hearing, etc. as these influences would tend to spread out equally across the note-taking and non-note-taking groups.

As we have seen, extraneous variables which are not controlled can sometimes result in disastrous problems such as a confounding. For example, if learners merely chose, by signing up, either the note-taking or non-note-taking condition, it is plausible that more enthusiastic learners would congregate in the note-taking condition (instead of being "stuck" in the control group). If the note-takers performed better than the non-note-takers, one would not know whether the difference was due to note-taking per se, or to a heightened interest level among the note-taking learners. Another obvious confounding would be, for example, using a video presentation of the instruction for non-note-takers but a live presentation for the note-takers. If the note-takers performed better, the effect could caused by differences in the method of presentation as well as differences in note-taking.

Furthermore, the procedure section often reflects the researchers' concern about alternative hypotheses, those nasty worries about "what else could explain away the findings." All researchers have these worries. To the ex-

Attribute × Treatment Interactions

Table 1 lists the proportion correct (and standard deviation) for each group on each test. As predicted, separate analyses of variance (ANOVAS) revealed ATIs in which note-takers recalled more than non-note-takers for low-knowledge students but not for high-knowledge students, $F(1, 56) = 6.89$, $MS_e = 16.10$, $p < .01$, and note-takers solved transfer problems better than non-note-takers for low-knowledge students but not for high-knowledge students, $F(1, 56) = 3.79$, $MS_e = 20.48$, $p = .05$. [8] Supplemental t tests performed on the data for low-knowledge students revealed that note-takers recalled more than non-note-takers, $t(29) = 4.96$, $p < .001$, and note-takers solved transfer problems better than non-note-takers, $t(29) = 3.50$, $p < .001$; in contrast, for the high-knowledge students, note-takers did not differ significantly from non-note-takers in recall, $t(27) = .57$, ns, or transfer, $t(27) = .29$, ns. Also as predicted, there was no ATI involving verbatim recognition, $F(1, 56) = .14$, $MS_e = 2.79$, ns, or involving verbatim fact retention, $F(1, 54) = .38$, $MS_e = 3.90$, ns. Supplemental t tests conducted on the data for low-knowledge students revealed no signifi-

tent that the research procedures can eliminate (or at least render implausible) those alternative explanations, the researcher is more confident that the independent variable, and nothing else, caused the obtained differences in the dependent variables. For example, notice that all learners were tested alone or in small groups (up to four people). One alternative hypothesis for the findings might be that note-takers did better because the non-note-takers simply did not pay attention to the videotape. This argument would seem more plausible if learners were tested in groups of forty, where there undoubtedly exist more distractions or maybe greater anonymity ("lost in the crowd" reactions). Simply put, one is more likely to "phase out" in a larger crowd, and get away with it. This alternative hypothesis cannot be ruled out definitely, but it seems less plausible.

[7] This section presents information related to the operational definitions of learning. Recall that operational definitions describe the rule for "putting numbers next to names." This is an important description in any research article, for it not only allows replication to take place, it also provides information for readers' evaluation of the worth of their definitions. If operational definitions are poor translations of the construct, then the researchers are not really studying what they intended to study.

[8] Recall that researchers must attend to another type of hypothesis—the null hypothesis. As we have said before, this is a difficult concept, one that is described more fully in Chapter 11. But for now, we know that the null

TABLE 1　Proportions of Correct Response for Four Groups on Four Tests

| | Test type | | | | | | | |
| | Semantic recall[a] | | Problem-Solving transfer[b] | | Verbatim recognition[c] | | Verbatim fact retention[d] | |
Treatment group	Proportion	SD	Proportion	SD	Proportion	SD	Proportion	SD
Low knowledge								
Notes ($n = 17$)	.11	.02	.32	.09	.64	.11	.47	.22
No notes ($n = 14$)	.06	.03	.21	.08	.60	.11	.39	.17
High knowledge								
Notes ($n = 14$)	.09	.04	.31	.16	.64	.16	.58	.16
No notes ($n = 15$)	.08	.02	.34	.14	.62	.13	.44	.22

[a]Maximum = 135.　[b]Maximum = 37.　[c]Maximum = 12.　[d]Maximum = 10.

cant difference between the groups on verbatim recognition, $t(29) = 1.17$, *ns*, or on verbatim fact retention, $t(29) = 1.10$, *ns*; similarly, *t* tests on the data for high-knowledge students revealed no significant difference between the groups on verbatim recognition, $t(27) = .33$, *ns*, or on verbatim fact retention, $t(27) = 2.00$, *ns*.

By replicating the pattern of previous ATIs, these results add reliability to Snow and Lohman's (1984) observation that instructional methods that force students to use generative learning strategies are likely to be more effective for less skilled learners than for more skilled learners. [9] In addition, the pattern of interactions observed in this study supports two important predictions of the generative hypothesis: that requiring students to take notes has a different effect on low- versus high-prior-knowledge learners, and that requiring low-prior-knowledge students to take notes will improve performance on semantic tasks such as problem solving and recall but not on verbatim tasks such as recognition or fact retention. The persistence of these findings across this study and two others (Peper & Mayer, 1978, 1986) is noteworthy and encourages the conclusion that note-taking can foster generative learning strategies, particularly in students who won't normally engage in generative learning.

hypothesis is nearly always one that the researcher wants to "reject." This is because the null hypothesis is a statement that there is no relationship among the independent, dependent, and attribute variables being studied. The "p" value in the results section of a published report tells us how likely it is that the null hypothesis is true. In this case, you can see a p value less than .01, which is not very likely. Because this null hypothesis can be rejected as not being very likely, the researcher is entitled to conclude that its opposite—the research hypothesis—is probably true.

[9] *We have seen that the practice of educational research uses its own language in special ways. This practice often involves a theory (generative theory), a research hypothesis describing independent and dependent variables (note-taking results in improved learning...), constructs and operational definitions (e.g.,transfer learning is evidenced by number of points earned on a test...), control of extraneous variables (e.g., random assignment), data collection (learners were tested in small groups...), analysis (note-takers recalled more, p < .01), interpretation (or conclusion, e.g., note-taking fosters generative learning strategies...). Whew! I guarantee that reading published research articles becomes easier with time!*

References

Bromage, B. K., & Mayer, R. E. (1981). Relationship between what is remembered and creative problem-solving performance in science learning. *Journal of Educational Psychology, 73,* 451–461.

Peper, R. J., & Mayer, R. E. (1978). Notetaking as a generative activity. *Journal of Educational Psychology, 70,* 514–522.

Peper, R. J., & Mayer, R. E. (1986). Generative effects of note-taking during science lectures. *Journal of Educational Psychology, 78,* 34–38.

Snow, R. E., & Lohman, D. F. (1984). Toward a theory of aptitude for learning from instruction. *Journal of Educational Psychology, 76,* 347–376.

Weinstein, C. E., & Mayer, R. E. (1985). The teaching of learning strategies. In M. C. Wittrock (Ed.), *Handbook of research on teaching 3rd ed.* (pp. 315–327). New York: Macmillan.

Wittrock, M. C. (1974). Learning as a generative activity. *Educational Psychologist, 11*, 87–95.

Received July 11, 1988

Revision received December 16, 1988

Accepted December 20, 1988

APPLICATION EXERCISES

1. Describe how you might *operationally* define the following:
   a. happiness
   b. optimism
   c. sociability
   d. cheating
   e. ambition
   f. feeling in control
   g. genius
   h. persistence
   i. authoritarian

2. Consider each of the following scenarios below and identify the *independent, dependent,* and *attribute* variables. Also name one extraneous variable that should be controlled by the researcher
   a. A group of experienced and "fresh" teachers (with ten+ years and less than two years experience, respectively) attended ten workshop sessions in stress reduction techniques (the treatment). A randomized group of experienced and fresh teachers functioned as a control group. Both groups were then compared on a measure of stress (blood pressure). It was found that the treatment was linked to lower levels of stress, with fresh teachers showing a greater effect.
   b. In an attempt to increase the high school graduation rate, a researcher implemented a mentoring program in ten high schools. Another group of ten high schools served as a comparison. The researcher found that the mentoring program increased the graduation rate but was more successful with females than males.
   c. A researcher tested whether students' reading comprehension was greater for material read from text or from a computer monitor. (She believed that the monitor demanded greater attention, hence would increase reading comprehension test scores.) She also analyzed the data by comparing those with and without home computers. She found no differences between the groups tested.
   d. Are students' grades a function of how much sleep the student gets? A researcher wondered about this question, and arranged for one hundred tenth graders to sleep no less than nine hours a night for one semester. A control group slept in accordance with their natural habits, which averaged about six hours a night. She also classified the students into two groups based on their

prior GPA (3.0 or higher versus less than 3.0). She found that increasing sleep resulted in higher grades during the semester; for the students with lower GPAs, the effect was more pronounced.

e. Will students write better if they use a word processor versus handwriting? To answer this question seventh and tenth graders wrote a three-page essay on a computer with a word processing program or by hand on a writing tablet. (The handwritten essays were transferred to type via a word processor so that the graders, not knowing one group from the other, could not be biased either way.) All essays were rated by independent graders on a ten–point scale reflecting overall quality. The researcher found higher ratings across both grades for the word processing group.

f. A researcher showed two different videotapes to fifty junior high school classes on the basic principles of electricity. In one condition, the lecture was summarized with a good metaphor. The other condition simply ended without a metaphor. He also tested students' learning styles, and classified each as visual, auditory, or kinesthetic. To measure students' retention of content one month later, he gave a ten-item multiple-choice test. The findings revealed far greater memory in the metaphor groups but the learning styles made no difference.

3. For each of the following scenarios, describe the confounding that the careless researcher forgot to eliminate.

a. A researcher tested whether students learn more with visual aids in the form of handouts versus slides. He used handouts during a lecture on the biochemistry of memory and projected slides during a lecture on the biochemistry of emotion. He tested students' comprehension via a ten-item multiple-choice test at the end of each lecture. Students scored higher in the projected slides condition. He concluded that slides were superior to handouts for aiding students' understanding.

b. A researcher wanted to know whether students write more "from the heart" using handwriting versus a computer. Students signed up for the condition of their choice (computer versus handwriting), and all students wrote a three-page essay on "My Family." Raters independently and blindly judged the emotional content of each essay on a ten–point scale. The students' essays were clearly more emotional in the handwriting condition. The researcher warned teachers that the use of computers in school will produce robot-like students.

c. A teacher wanted to know if the color of classrooms affects behavior in any noticeable way. He wondered this after all classrooms in his building were painted pale yellow; many students seemed hyperactive. He checked conduct reports at his school and compared them to another school across town that had the same off-white walls that his school used to have. The conducts reports at the off-white comparison school revealed far fewer instances of misbehavior. He concluded that yellow rooms affect behavior in negative ways.

4. For each of the scenarios below describe the research hypothesis in an *If A then B* form. Then offer an alternative hypothesis, that is, a plausible rival explanation for the findings.

a. A researcher tested whether a new electronic system for monitoring halls would reduce the number of tardies at a large high school. Also, a new and somewhat confusing computer system was installed in each classroom for teachers to report tardies. The researcher found that the electronic system significantly reduced the number of tardies after its installation.

b. A researcher tested his hunch that teachers older than sixty are far happier in their positions than their counterparts in private business. He interviewed one hundred senior workers from both occupations and found that indeed teachers were happier than business people in their later years. He recommended that senior workers seek careers in teaching in order to be happier.

c. A researcher tested the idea that gymnastic lessons for kindergartners will lead to greater athletic ability in high school. To test this idea, he located two groups of high school students: those who had had gymnastic lessons as kindergartners and those who had not. Then he tested their athletic prowess with a battery of physical performance measures. He found that those who had early gymnastic lessons were far superior as athletes in high school than those without such lessons. He recommended gymnastic lessons to all youngsters in order to improve their adolescent athletic abilities.

MULTIPLE CHOICE QUESTIONS

1. Which of the following is an *operational* definition of "depression"?

   a. sadness combined with hopelessness
   b. melancholy plus gloom
   c. abnormal despair
   d. rate of speech in words per minute
   e. sense of loss

2. If a researcher administered a new drug, called Calmerix, to one group of hyperactive boys and another new drug called Hyperex to a second group and compared their scores on the Hyper Test, then the independent and dependent variables, would be respectively:

   a. boys vs. girls; Hyper Test scores
   b. type of drug; Calmerix versus Hyperex
   c. type of drug; Hyper Test scores
   d. Hyper Test scores; type of drug
   e. level of hyperactivity; boys on Calmerix

3. If a researcher compared left-handed versus right-handed boys on a reading test after giving half of them special training, then the attribute variable and one likely extraneous variable, would be respectively:

   a. special training; reading scores
   b. handedness; age of student
   c. special training; sex of student
   d. reading scores; ability level
   e. noise level; handedness

4. The critical difference between a true versus quasi independent variable is related to whether subjects can be:

   a. measured
   b. controlled
   c. randomized
   d. operationalized
   e. analyzed

5. Assume that during the fall semester a researcher compared a lecture approach to teaching statistics (using his freshmen class) with a problem-oriented approach (using his junior class). Both sections were given the same statistics test as a final outcome measure. He repeated the same experiment in the spring semester. This scenario is best described as a confounding of:

   a. test scores with teaching approaches
   b. class level with test scores

c. time of year with test scores

d. teaching approaches with class level

e. time of year with teaching approaches

6. Clear expectations about a research outcome, often expressed in an *If A then B* form and sometimes derived from theory, is referred to as a:

a. research hypothesis

b. alternative hypothesis

c. null hypothesis

d. confounding

e. operationalization

7. Which of the following captures the meaning of an alternative hypothesis?

a. presumed hunch based on theory

b. rival explanation or blunder

c. statement about populations

d. measurement in concrete terms

e. constructs not easily measured

8. What do researchers usually do with the null hypothesis?

a. assess it and try to debug it

b. "adopt" it and try to modify it

c. inspect it and try to prove it

d. watch it and try to change it

e. assume it is true but try to reject it

9. Which of the following pairings involving types of variables is *not* correct?

a. extraneous : outcome

b. independent : cause

c. attribute : subject differences

d. dependent : effect

10. Consider the proverb: A rolling stone gathers no moss. If you were to test its validity, what type of variable would be the *rolling stone*?

a. extraneous

b. attribute

c. independent

d. dependent

e. null

Answers: 1) d   2) c   3) b   4) c   5) d   6) a   7) b   8) e   9) a   10) c

RESEARCH AS A PROCESS

OVERVIEW

Recall from Chapter 2 that educational research is best understood as a process, a series of integrated steps with its own language. This chapter will examine these steps more completely. It will explain how the steps structure the entire research process and how they combine to form an integrated whole. Steps in the research process are guided by one of two basic orientations: *theoretical* or *problem-based* (applied). We will examine the processes relevant to both orientations in this chapter. Let's start with the integrated steps characteristic of theory-based research.

THEORY-BASED RESEARCH

The research process guided by theory usually involves constructs or phenomena that require explanation. (Recall from Chapter 2 that constructs are unobservable traits.) Constructs do not exist within a vacuum. The inferred constructs require a theory, or explanation, in order to understand them better. Behind every construct, then, is a theory designed to explain the construct. The theory of intelligence, the theory of motivation, the theory of self-esteem, or the theory of learning would all attempt to explain the origins, development, consequences, or whatever may be required for a better understanding of the construct.

Although a good synonym for theory is explanation, scientific theories are very broad and encompass many phenomena, like the theory of relativity in physics, big bang theory in astronomy, or trickle-down theory in economics. Most educational theories, by contrast, are rather narrow and limited by comparison and frequently (not always) come from outside the field, like psychology or sociology. An example of an education-based theory is Benjamin Bloom's theory of mastery learning, (Bloom, 1976) which relates students' characteristics, instruction, and learning outcomes and explains how all children can reach their full potential in school. Another example of an education theory—an exception since it is so broad and widely generalizable—is Robert Gagne's theory of instruction (1985), which explains the process of effective instructional events in terms of learned outcomes and the underlying cognitive structures and processes. An illustration of Gagne's theory with its full explanatory power is shown in Figure 3.1.

Many theories are best understood when their basic premises are displayed visually, sometimes using flow diagrams or geometric models. For example, J. P. Guilford's theory of intelligence can be displayed as a cube; Abraham Maslow's theory of motivation, a pyramid; and Robert Sternberg's theory of intelligence, a triangle. Many

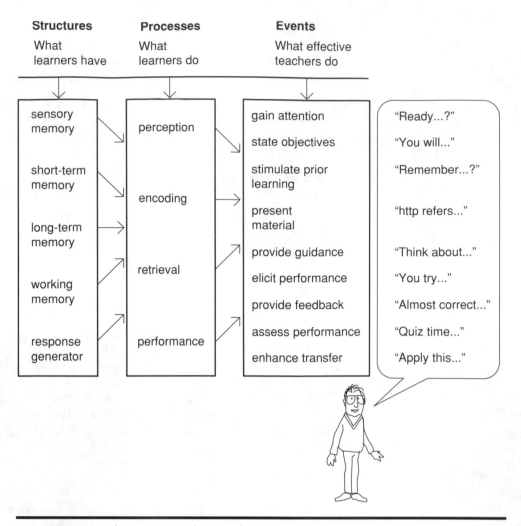

Structures

What
learners have

Processes

What
learners do

Events

What effective
teachers do

sensory memory

short-term memory

long-term memory

working memory

response generator

perception

encoding

retrieval

performance

gain attention

state objectives

stimulate prior learning

present material

provide guidance

elicit performance

provide feedback

assess performance

enhance transfer

"Ready...?"

"You will..."

"Remember...?"

"http refers..."

"Think about..."

"You try..."

"Almost correct..."

"Quiz time..."

"Apply this..."

FIGURE 3.1   Robert Gagne's theory of instruction relates structures, processes, and instructional events in ways that enhance learning and retention. [Adapted from R. M. Gagne, L. J. Briggs, & W. W. Wager, (1992) *Principles of instructional design* (4th ed.). Fort Worth: Harcourt Brace Jovanovich]

theories utilize metaphors to convey their guiding tenets. One particularly interesting theory of how our brain works is provided by Gerald Edelman (1992), a Nobel Prize winner who rejected the computer model of brain functioning and instead likened the working of our brain to that of a *jungle ecosystem,* or a type of neural Darwinism. Good metaphors suggest practical implications of the theory. Sylwester (1993/1994) pointed out that "Edelman's model suggests that a jungle-like brain might thrive best in a jungle-like classroom that includes many sensory, cultural, and problem layers that are closely related to the real-world environment" (p. 50).

Theories explain more than just abstract constructs; they explain important observable phenomena too, such as teenage suicide, gender bias, high school dropout rates, school violence, illegal drug use, boredom with science, or increased absenteeism. Educational phenomena are best understood as trends or observable occurrences. They are different from constructs, in the sense that constructs are akin to abstract traits. Because the purpose of a theory is to *explain* constructs or phenomena, it could be said that the purpose of research is to generate and test theories since the ultimate goal of science is explanation. Examples of theories that interest educational researchers are shown in Table 3.1.

TABLE 3.1 Examples of Theories Tested by Educational Researchers

Theory	Constructs or Ideas
Piaget's theory of cognitive development	schema, equilibration
Bandura's theory of social learning	modeling, efficacy
Atkinson & Shiffrin's theory of memory	stages of information processing; dual-storage
Maslow's theory of humanistic development	needs hierarchy
Vygotsky's theory of sociocultural language learning	zone of proximal development
Bruner's theory of concept learning	scaffolding, discovery
Skinner's theory of operant conditioning	reinforcement
Weiner's theory of motivation	causal attributions
Gagne's theory of learning	information processing, instructional events
Slavin's theory of learning	cooperative groups
Carroll's theory of learning	time
Bloom's theory of learning	mastery
Atkinson's theory of motivation	expectancy
Gardner's theory of intelligence	multiple intelligences
Sternberg's theory of intelligence	triarchy
Kohlberg's theory of moral reasoning	dilemmas
Erikson's theory of personal development	psychosocial crises
Craik's theory of memory	levels of processing
Paivio's theory of memory	visual & verbal codes
Bransford's theory of memory	transfer-appropriate processing
Ausubel's theory of reception learning	expository teaching
Wittrock's theory of constructive learning	generative teaching
Palincsar & Brown's theory of constructive learning	reciprocal teaching

The Research Process

With this background in mind, we can now see how these research components form an integrated, cyclical process as shown in Figure 3.2. We'll see how this applies with three examples, two fairly simple, the other one more complex.

Example: Spelling Acquisition. In an attempt to explain why some children learn to spell new words quickly and with relative ease while others struggle for a longer time, a researcher develops a new theory which she called the Multiple Sensory Modality Theory. An important facet of this theory posits that school learning is enhanced if the learner uses as many sources of sensory feedback as possible to complement the cognitive (thinking) process, including kinesthetic sources (the sensation of body and limb po-

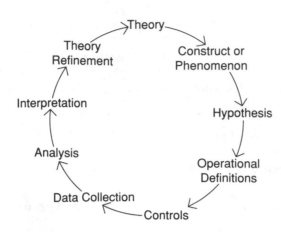

FIGURE 3.2   The cyclical nature of the scientific research process.

sition). This includes fine motor movement, like fingers. The theory suggests that children will learn to spell faster if they practice writing the word with their hand (good old-fashioned handwriting) as opposed to more passively punching the computer keyboard. Hence, high kinesthesia is defined as handwriting practice, and low kinesthesia is defined as computer keyboard punching. This theory also suggests that large handwriting (big, sweeping letters) will result in the fastest learning of correctly spelled words.

In this example, the theory is Multiple Sensory Modality Theory, the *construct* being investigated is learning, and the *operational definition* of learning is the number of spelling practice trials required to learn a list of thirty words with at least ninety percent accuracy. This operational definition functions as the *dependent variable*. The *independent variable* (true) is a type of spelling practice (computer keyboard versus handwriting). A reasonable attribute variable (although not required in a study like this) would be sex. Because girls mature faster than boys, it would be expected according to this theory, that girls would outperform boys since their kinesthetic sense (a major factor in this theory) is more advanced at the same age and presumably capable of enhancing their learning of spelling. Two important extraneous variables in this study—that require stringent control—are students' prior spelling ability and the spelling difficulty of the test words. These extraneous variables would be controlled by using the same words to be learned in both conditions of the independent variable—keyboard versus handwriting—and randomly assigning students to the conditions. This avoids the confounding of type of spelling practice (keyboard versus handwriting) with word difficulty, since both groups would be practicing with the same words. It also avoids confounding type of spelling practice with the prior spelling ability of students. Surely, you would not want the better spellers to practice with handwriting, for then you would not know whether better performance in that group was due to type of practice or type of student.

In this example, the research hypothesis is: "If students practice spelling new words by handwriting opposed to a computer keyboard they will learn to spell faster." One alternative hypothesis is: "If students practice spelling with easier words, they will learn to spell faster." This alternative hypothesis was ruled out because the difficulty of words was controlled by making sure both groups spelled the same words. The null hypothesis for this study is: "In a population of children like these, there will be no difference in the speed of spelling acquisition whether they use handwriting or a computer keyboard." Remember, the null hypothesis comes into play only when the data are being statistically analyzed, a topic described in Chapter 11.

If the results show that the children in the handwriting group learned faster than the computer keyboard group, we would state that the research hypothesis was supported. We would also conclude that the theory which generated the research hypothesis as a result is more credible, and at least for now, does not need further refinement. We would not conclude that anything was proven.

Example: Music and Math. Some older children are quite adept at mathematical reasoning and problem solving; others less so. Let us presume that a researcher suspects that early exposure to music is related to math aptitude. She believes so, let's say, because the math and music "centers" of the brain are in close proximity, and enhancing the circuits of one will help to strengthen the circuits of the other. She also suspects that there exists a "window of opportunity" for the neurological development of music understanding, say between the ages three and six. The earlier the exposure to music, the more profound its effects will be on mathematical reasoning. Lack of exposure to music during these ages, she hypothesizes, takes its toll on the subsequent development of mathematical reasoning. To test this idea, she provides piano lessons and chorus practice to three- to six-year-olds for a period of two years; a control group receives no such systematic training. Ten years later, the SAT math scores are compared between the two groups. As she expected, those children with music experience are more talented in their mathematical reasoning.

Let's examine this research as a process, in accordance with Figure 3.2. The construct being investigated is mathematical reasoning (some might call this "quantitative intelligence" or simply math aptitude). The theory which attempts to explain this construct is the Biology Theory (it details the brain structures and neurochemistry required to explain mathematical thinking). The independent variable is early experience (or lack of it) with music, the dependent variable (operational definition of mathematical intelligence) is the SAT math scores, the attribute variable is age during first exposure, and one of the many extraneous variables might be the number of ear infections during early childhood. The research hypothesis is, "If young children are exposed to systematic training in music, then they will have higher mathematical intelligence as adolescents" (and the younger the exposure, stronger will be the effects). One alternative hypothesis is, "If young children are given music lessons, they have higher socioeconomic status, will attend better schools, and score higher on standardized tests of all types." The null hypothesis is, "In a population of young children, exposure to music will have virtually no effect on their later mathematical intelligence." A major control procedure is the random assignment of children to the music training group (this controls for the extraneous variable of ear infections and greatly reduces the plausibility of the alternative hypothesis concerning socioeconomic status). After the data are collected and analyzed, let us suppose that children with music experience did score substantially higher on the SAT, but the effect was equally strong with all age groups studied. Because the essence of the research hypothesis was supported, the interpretation, then, offered general support (not proof) for the Brain Theory. However, some refinement in the "windows of opportunity" concept would be required since it appears that the earliest exposure did not lead to any enhanced effect. After refinement, the theory will be in a better position to generate a new research hypothesis, which if supported, will add to the theory's credibility.

Example: Gender Bias in the Classroom. Let's consider another example, somewhat more complex. The phenomenon of gender bias, as it is usually studied, refers to the preferential attention that boys receive from their teachers. As such, gender bias would be revealed by teachers simply interacting more with boys, calling on them more than girls, asking more followup questions to boys, or even waiting longer for boys to answer a question, suggesting a positive expectation in the form of "You can do it." This phenomenon can be explained best by one of several theories. Let's offer a Behavioral Theory of gender bias, as contrasted with, say, an expectation theory. According to Behavioral Theory, a teacher begins by calling on boys more than girls simply because of their demanding behavior (wildly waving an outstretched hand, standing up, shouting "Me, me, me, I know, I know." [This might be exaggerated, but you get the idea]). The boys' correct answers are reinforcing to the teacher, in the sense that the correct answers are satisfying for the teacher, and as such, the teachers' behavior (calling on boys) tends to increase in frequency. (The girls would have provided correct answers, too, except they never got a fair chance to contribute because of the boys' more active solicitation of the teacher's attention.) This Behavioral Theory denies that teachers' beliefs or expectations about boys' and girls' school performance are different. (Recall that this is a *behavioral* theory; unobservable constructs such as expectations do not play a role.) This theory, then, assumes there is no difference in teachers' expectations for boys' and girls' achievement. Behavioral Theory also predicts that the differential preference of boys over girls tends to increase over the school year (as you would expect with any reinforced behavior). Because behavior can be shaped without awareness, this theory also predicts that teachers will deny treating boys and girls differently. Eventually, the preferential attention given to boys becomes a teacher's habit and will continue until it is extinguished.

Now let's analyze this problem from the perspective of the research process. First, a theory is advanced as an explanation for a phenomenon, in this case, the theory is Behavioral Theory and the phenomenon is gender bias. This theory then generates research hypotheses about the phenomenon which are consistent with the theory's premises. Several hypotheses could be derived from knowledge of Behavioral Theory as described above. First, if beginning teachers are studied, one would expect to see increasing evidence of gender bias in the classroom over the school year, based on the behavioral principle of reinforcement. Second, one would expect to find no differences in teachers' expectations for boys' versus girls' success in school learning. Third, one would expect to find that teachers are often unaware of their display of gender bias. More formally, a research hypothesis might be, "If novice teachers are observed over the school year, then they will demonstrate increasing evidence of gender bias without their awareness and without differential expectation for school success between boys and girls."

According to Figure 3.2, constructs and phenomena must be operationally defined as described in Chapter 2. "Gender bias" could be defined as the ratio of boys' called on over girls' called on (equated for the number of boys versus girls in the classroom), the frequency of follow-up questions that were asked of boys versus girls, and the average wait time for boys versus girls. (Wait time is the number of seconds teachers wait after asking a question to a student before moving on, probing for more information, or simply answering the question themselves.) These measures could be combined to form a composite, with higher numbers indicating greater interaction and attention to boys, that is, greater gender bias.

Figure 3.2 reveals that control procedures must be implemented so that *alternative hypotheses* are eliminated, or at least minimized. (Recall from Chapter 2 that these are rival explanations of the findings; often they are overlooked sources of contamination or simply research blunders.) For example, class seating charts should assure that boys and girls are spread equally around the room. It would be a problem if boys clustered near the front because some teachers might be inclined to call on students near the front with greater frequency (it might be easier to see their work, hear their responses, etc.). This would be a problem because according to the operational definition of gender bias, a teacher who did have a preference for the front due to hearing or some other extraneous reason would be misidentified as being gender biased. The alternative hypothesis would be, "If teachers are observed over the school year, they will display increasing preferences for calling on students who sit near the front."

The next step in the research process is to gather data, a step elaborated in Chapter 6. For now, it is understood that data should be collected from a sufficient number of subjects in a manner that does not jeopardize its meaningfulness. For example, if classroom observers were recording the number of follow-up questions that were directed at boys versus girls, it would be important that the observers not know that boys were expected to receive more follow-up questions. If they did have this preconceived idea, then it would be too easy to interpret an ambiguous teacher response in a manner that is consistent with what is expected. This technique of keeping data gatherers "in the dark" is called *blinding*.

The end of the cyclical research process involves the analysis of data, the interpretation of the findings in light of the theory which generated the research hypotheses in the first place. It may be that the theory is in need of refinement, revision, or even abandonment. Quite possibly the theory is supported as it stands. If that is the case, then the theory should be even more useful in the future because of its ability to explain complex phenomena in a way that disjointed guesswork could not. The credible theory, of course, would continue to generate testable hypotheses that might ultimately explain other complex phenomena, or possibly help us understand old problems in a new light.

Let's summarize this gender bias illustration by simplifying it. A simple research hypothesis is: "If novice teachers are observed in their first month of teaching (opposed to the ninth month), then they will display less gender bias in the classroom." The independent variable is level of teaching experience (one month versus nine months). The dependent variable is the frequency that boys are called upon. If supported, this research hypothesis adds credence to, not proof of, the Behavioral Theory of gender bias.

PROBLEM-BASED RESEARCH

Problem-based educational research, often called *applied* research, is concerned above all else with solving a practical problem, like improving educational practice or evaluating a specific program for the purpose of making sound decisions. In a sense, all educational research is problem-based (applied) if it is not specifically directed at testing hypotheses sprung from a theoretical framework. The theory/problem distinction actually represents a rather blurry continuum, and there is no point to pigeonholing all research as either/or. It would be hard to imagine researchers who test educational theories completely divorced from any ideas about real-world application. Likewise, it would be hard to imagine applied researchers who never thought about the broader implications of their findings in terms of an explanatory framework (theory). The distinction is important, however, in terms of the *guidance* offered for the integrated steps that comprise the research process. Research based on theory, as we saw earlier in this chapter, is guided by the cyclical nature of the scientific research process as shown in Figure 3.2. Problem-based educational research uses alternative guidance systems, often in the form of what are called *models.*

We will briefly present two guiding models for applied, problem-based research to illustrate how this type of research differs from theory-based research using the cyclical scientific process.

Evaluation Research

Educational evaluations provide data in order to assess the merit or value of educational programs. (The term "program" is used here in a very general sense, referring to a broad range of instructional methods, curriculum materials, and organizations as well as teachers, administrators, and students.) Most educational programs have specific objectives or more general goals, and their success is usually assessed by how well the objectives and goals were met. A distinction is usually made between two types of educational evaluations: formative versus summative (Scriven, 1967). In a *formative* evaluation, data are collected for the purpose of improving specific aspects of a program, like the instructional materials, methods of delivery, and assessment procedures. Recognizing that many educational programs are developed in a trial-and-error manner, formative evaluation research is conducted in the spirit of "forming" a better product or program. Tryouts are followed by revisions (debugging) until the program's outcomes are in line with the program's objectives. In general, formative evaluations are conducted for the purpose of gathering data in order to revise and improve, and thus are an integral part of program development.

In a *summative* evaluation, by contrast, the purpose is to "summarize" the overall success of a program in terms of reaching its goals or achieving its aims. This is usually done after the program has been developed via formative evaluations. Summative evaluations may be used by policy makers or funding agencies to make sound decisions. One classic example of a summative evaluation is provided by the federally funded Head Start preschool program. The general question posed by evaluators of this program was: "Are Head Start children more successful in the later school years than children who do not participate in Head Start?" (The oversimplified answer arising from very complex data is Yes.) Summative evaluations may also compare two competing programs to determine which is more effective.

Program evaluators, as they are often called, must still grapple with the usual challenges faced by scientific researchers who are more theory-driven. They must, for example, restate the aims and objectives of a program in terms of operational definitions so that they can be measured. What, for example, would constitute measures of "success" in a Head Start evaluation? They must also implement controls, often in the form of comparison groups, so that meaningful contrasts can be made between the program and its alternatives. The primary difference is that program evaluators follow models to assess programs (not test theories).

There is a panorama of step-by-step evaluation models used by program evaluators described in some detail by Popham (1993). They range from those emphasizing inputs and outputs to those emphasizing connoisseurship and complex appraisal, as in a work of art. They may be objectives-oriented, management-oriented, consumer-oriented, expertise-oriented, adversary-oriented, or naturalistic and participant-oriented (Worthen & Sanders, 1987). Some emphasize discrepancies between an existing state and a desired state (a "needs assessment") while others emphasize a ratio of cost-to-benefit. One commonly used model is referred to as the "CIPP Model" described by Stufflebeam and his colleagues (1971). The acronym refers to four elements of evaluation: context, input, process, and product, as shown in Figure 3.3. Each facet is associated with specific questions; the answers to these questions will help shape sound decisions. The initial facet of evaluation centers on the context (or environment) where problems are identified, unmet needs are assessed, and decisions are made regarding which objectives should be pursued to meet needs. The input stage of evaluation concerns strategies (plans) and available resources that are required to meet the program's objectives. At this point, important decisions are influenced by information about competing strategies, their effectiveness (and legality) for achieving program goals, and capabilities such as personnel and space. Process evaluation requires the collection of evaluation data, program monitoring, and feedback about program operations while it is underway. Important decisions about data collection methods, record keeping, types of procedural barriers, and the use of materials and facilities will influence how well the program progresses. The last focus in the CIPP Model is product evaluation—the extent to which the goals of the program have been achieved. At this stage, decisions are made with regard to continuing or modifying the program.

Program evaluators operating under this model have specific tasks related to each stage of evaluation. They must determine what kinds of information are needed for each stage ("delineation"), obtain the information, and combine all of the pieces ("synthesis") so that it is useful for making decisions that affect how (or if) the program will continue. Although program evaluation research is conceptualized differently than theory-based scientific research, an important point is worth repeating: the

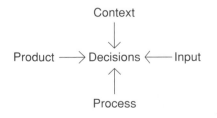

FIGURE 3.3   The CIPP Model emphasizes questions and decisions made in program planning and operation.

major methodological challenges remain the same. These include proper sampling, implementing controls, and using reliable and valid measuring instruments, to name just a few. These topics, among many others, are covered in the chapters to follow.

Action Research

An applied orientation toward research known as *action research* is receiving ever-increasing attention in the professional literature. (Action research is sometimes referred to as *teacher research,* discussed separately in Chapter 5.) This type of research is usually conducted by teachers or other educational practitioners (e.g., administrators, counselors, librarians) for the specific purpose of solving a local problem (meaning in the classroom, school, or district) or gathering information so as to make better decisions. Armed with new knowledge or better information, teachers can "take action" by, for example, improving the way a lesson is presented. One strength of action research is that findings are easily translated into practice. By contrast, some approaches to research leave the practical application a mystery, despite buzzwords such as "theory into practice."

Most action research is carried out by teachers for the purpose of improving their practice and understanding it more deeply. As such, action research contributes to the professional development of teachers by increasing their understanding of the conduct of research and the utilization of findings. Because action research often requires several teachers working collaboratively, a side benefit is the formation of collegial networks, leading to better communication among teachers and reducing feelings of isolation ("separate caves"). Action research encourages teachers to reflect on their practice and enhances the profession of teaching as more teachers assume responsibility for evaluating and improving their practice. Teachers should not be excluded from the research loop, nor be viewed as subservient technicians who merely apply the findings of academic researchers. Newkirk (1992) shows how action research is not simply a scaled-down version of formal, scientific research. Its focus on classroom problems is from the heart, so to speak, and its audience consists of like-minded, reflective, curious, and dedicated practitioners. The "spirit" of action research is captured well by Carol Santa (1993):

> I feel that research studies conducted by teachers are the most powerful way to effect change in the educational system. I know that this is a bold claim, but I believe it intensely. Too often teachers use the same methods year after year, without ever questioning their effectiveness. They don't think enough about what they do or take sufficient time to reflect. Therefore, they don't grow and change. The solution to this problem of entrenchment is teacher research. Teachers must think of their classrooms as research laboratories and involve their students as research collaborators. In this way, learning about teaching never becomes static. We remain alive as teachers, and even more important, our students begin to think of themselves as researchers, too. When we involve students as collaborators, they learn about themselves as learners (p. 401–402).

A model of the action research process (Sagor, 1992) is presented in Figure 3.4. This model describes sequential steps, where each step leads to the next. Problem formulation requires action researchers to identify the issue of greatest concern, what they already know about the issue, and what knowledge is lacking. The problem is then translated into a research question. The credibility of the action research is in large part determined by the data collection step. Sagor (1992) recommends that three sources of data be collected for an adequate answer to each question. Data analysis involves the discovery of trends or patterns in the data and the conclusions (if any) that are possible from the analysis. The reporting of action research results is strongly encouraged via as many appropriate forums as possible. Sagor (1992) states that this step can be especially rewarding as teachers share what they have learned about their practice. The final step involves translating the findings of the systematic inquiry into

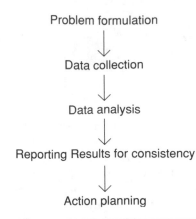

Problem formulation

Data collection

Data analysis

Reporting Results for consistency

Action planning

FIGURE 3.4   Five-step sequential process model of action research. (After Sagor, 1992)

ideas for planning and implementing the school or classroom improvement (the "action"). It is this step that has the potential for revitalizing a learning community.

You will probably find that the results of action research are presented somewhat differently than theory-based, scientific research. The reporting style appears less rigorous than other types of published research. The results are often presented in a quasi-story form, and as such, are more personal and less formal. A story format can be a highly effective way to share findings and ideas, since good stories can be very memorable. Action research can also be presented in the same manner as large-scale, formal research, following standard publication guidelines such as the widely-used "APA Publication Manual" (American Psychological Association, 1994). The increasing influence of action research is also revealed by an international journal launched in 1993 appropriately titled, *Educational Action Research* which welcomes accounts of action research studies and articles which contribute to the debate on the practice of action research and its associated methodologies.

Examples.   Here are three examples of action research provided by Calhoun (1993). A first-grade teacher uses different displays and activities about simple fractions, records students' responses to questions, and determines which presentations are most effective. Four middle school teachers use their science classes to experiment with mnemonic keywords. Their overriding concern is helping students better understand key science concepts. The entire high school faculty try to increase student achievement by adding inductive thinking strategies across the curriculum. Students' responses to the change in instructional emphasis is observed and recorded. Findings are analyzed and plans for implementing changes are discussed. Technical assistance is provided by a regional group sponsored by the state department of education called the Consortium for Action Research.

Another example is provided by three dedicated educators in a Montana school district (Santa, Isaacson, & Manning, 1987). They questioned the value of round robin oral reading, noting that it not only bored students, but seemed to be at odds with research on reading instruction. Students learn most effectively, they argued, when they are taught how to learn. Also, they argued that the best way to change the instructional routines of teachers is to involve them as research collaborators. Two classes were selected; one would receive instruction which encouraged their active involvement in the material. The other was retained as a control, and teaching progressed in the usual way. The classroom reading comprehension test revealed the experimental class had in fact performed significantly better than the control class. They verified their results by choosing a new reading passage and switching the experimental and control classes. The results were the same, superior performance in the actively engaged class. The teacher–researchers explained their findings by reference to the fact that students were not only actively involved in reading, but they had received direct instruction in how to organize information for learning. Santa (1993) also noted that the *process* of experimenting was more important than the results. This is because they discussed the results with their students which stimulated their own thinking about learning, making them aware of metacognition (self-monitoring of learning) and how to gain more control over it. Interestingly, after the results were shared with others via newsletters and meetings, round robin oral reading was no longer the standard routine. Furthermore, other teachers began their own studies to validate alternatives, including the use of journals to improve problem solving in mathematics. These action researchers concluded that as a result of action research, teachers are teaching more, students are learning more, and everybody wins.

CHAPTER SUMMARY

The process of educational research is usually guided by two orientations: theoretical or problem-based (applied). The cyclical nature of the scientific investigation of theories, or explanations, often begins with testing specific research hypotheses generated by the theories, and ends with the support or refinement of theory based on analysis. The process is continual, with each step guided by the scientific method emphasizing control. Problem-based research is concerned with solving practical problems and is often guided by models which prescribe how to evaluate program effectiveness or collect data in order to take action for the purpose of improving classroom learning.

GUIDED TOUR #1

Let's turn our attention now to a guided tour of published educational research. This will help solidify important terms and concepts described in this chapter.

Providing Study Notes: Comparison of Three Types of Notes for Review

Kenneth A. Kiewra

Department of Educational Psychology

University of Nebraska-Lincoln

Nelson F. DuBois

Department of Educational Psychology

State University of New York, Oneonta

David Christian and Anne McShane

Utah State University

Correspondence concerning this article should be addressed to Kenneth A. Kiewra, Department of Educational Psychology, University of Nebraska, Lincoln, Nebraska 68588-0641.

College students viewed a 19-min videotaped lecture and were not allowed to take notes. One week later, these students were provided with one of three different forms of study notes for review: a complete text, a linear outline, or a matrix. Students in a control group were given no notes and reviewed mentally. After review, all students completed three different performance tests. Results from all three tests indicated that reviewing any of the three forms of provided notes significantly raised performance beyond that of the no-notes control group. This finding confirmed the importance or the external storage function of note taking for various forms of provided notes. In addition, the outline and matrix notes generally produced higher recall performance than did the text notes, but only the matrix notes produced higher transfer performance than did the text notes. These differences were explained in relation to the forming of internal connections in memory.

The primary value of note-taking comes not from the recording of ideas, but from the external storage of noted ideas available for review (see Kiewra, 1985a). To benefit most from review, learners must have adequate notes to study. Unfortunately, students are notoriously poor notetakers (e.g., Kiewra, 1985b, 1985c). One way to compensate for deficient note taking is to provide Students with Complete notes to review. Research indicates that students who listen to a lecture without taking notes and who review provided complete notes generally perform better on achievement tests than do those who take and review their own notes (see Kiewra, 1985d). The optimal structure of provided lecture notes, however, has not been researched. This study was designed to investigate three different forms of provided notes. One form was a complete text of the lecture. A second structure was a linear outline of the lecture. All of the lecture ideas were included, but they were organized into a conventional outline form in such a way that the superordinate-subordinate relations among ideas were apparent. The third structure was a two-dimensional matrix that included categories and attributes as respective vertical and horizontal matrix headings. The internal cells of the matrix contained ideas capturing the intersection of those headings. The matrix, therefore, permitted learners to perceive the linear relations within categories, in addition to the relations across categories.

We examined the effectiveness of the three forms of provided notes in relation to one another and to a no-notes control group on three performance tests measuring cued recall, factual recognition, and transfer performance (synthesis/application). Hypotheses were framed by two theoretical principles: external storage (DiVesta & Gray, 1973) and internal connections (Mayer, 1984). [1] On the basis of the external storage principle of note-taking, we hypothesized that those who had notes for review would uniformly outperform those without notes. The internal connections principle suggests that both recall and transfer performance are facilitated when ideas are well organized or connected in memory. The interconnection of ideas aids recall because the recall of one idea often cues the recall of associated notions. Transfer performance is facilitated because such tasks depend on the learner's identifying and understanding relations both within and across categories of information. We therefore expected that the outline and matrix groups would outperform the complete text group because the outline and matrix structures encourage the forming of internal connections. [2] We expected any differences between the outline and matrix group to favor the latter because of their likelihood to form additional internal connections across cate-

[1] *This research tests a theory of memory which includes at least two important principles (external storage and internal connections). Their expression "Hypotheses were framed by two theoretical principles…" illustrates the role of theory in educational research. A good theory not only explains a construct or phenomenon (in this case, deficient note taking results in less learning), but it gives rise to many hypotheses which are directly testable. This is very clear when they state "On the basis of…we hypothesized…" Recall that hypotheses do not exist within a vacuum. Note that when researchers use the term* hypothesis *without any clarification, it is understood that they are referring to the* research *hypothesis (as opposed to the alternative or null hypothesis).*

[2] *Here again these researchers provide the rationale for their second hypothesis. If the presumed cognitive operations are correct as suggested by the underlying theory, then a specific outcome would be anticipated. They state that they "therefore expected," which is another way of saying that they "hypothesized."*

gories. [3] Last, we did not anticipate differences among the three note-review groups on the factual recognition test because it concerned knowledge of isolated facts.

Method

Subjects and Design

Forty-four undergraduate volunteers were randomly assigned to one of four study conditions defined by the notes made available for review: complete text, outline, matrix, or no notes.

Materials and Apparatus

The materials included a videotaped lecture, three types of study notes, and three performance tests. The 19-min videotaped lecture on types of creativity contained 1,881 words and was transmitted on a 19-in. television monitor at a rate of approximately 100 words per minute. The lecture contained a total of 121 idea units that were based on procedures described by Kintsch and van Dijk (1978).

The complete text notes were a typed, seven-page verbatim transcript of the lecture. The outline study notes were typed on five pages and contained all of the 121 lecture ideas expressed in 758 words; they appeared in a linear. outline form paralleling the lecture presentation. The matrix study notes were typed on a single 38 × 20 cm page. Within the 43 cells of the matrix were all 121 ideas expressed in 610 words. One axis named the five types of creativity; the other listed nine associated attributes (e.g., definition, motivation for creativity, distinguishing characteristics, associated myths).

Three types of tests were administered: cued recall, factual recognition, and transfer. On the cued recall test, subjects recalled whatever information they could about specific attributes of the five types of creativity. The specified attributes were identical to those named throughout the lecture and that

[3] *Notice here that researchers can also hypothesize (or "anticipate," as they say) that no differences should be found under some circumstances. Evidently, the theoretical framework predicts that if a task requires mere factual recognition (as opposed to more complex cognitive operations), then the type of note review should be unrelated to learning.*

appeared explicitly in the outline and matrix notes. **[4]** The maximum number or recallable ideas was 121. For the factual recognition test, 20 factual statements were presented (e.g., "Personal satisfaction is the only real motivation") and subjects were to recognize the referent type of creativity. The transfer test consisted or 30 items. Ten of the items were at the synthesis level and required subjects to recognize the types of creativity that shared a common characteristic (e.g., "Which two types take a lifetime to develop?"). The remaining items were at the application level. Each application item provided a novel example that was to be categorized into one of the five types of creativity (e.g., "The thermos was invented by Jose Thermosa who for years contemplated how cold and hot could coexist independently").

Procedure

The 44 volunteers were assembled in a large lecture hall and were randomly given experimental packets with code letters that assigned them to one of the four study conditions as defined by the notes available for review (text, outline, matrix, or no notes). **[5]** Written general instructions informed all participants that they would listen to a lecture without recording notes and would return in 1 week for testing. Subjects were told that notes might be available for review, but the content and format of the notes were not mentioned. Furthermore, the nature of the performance tests was unspecified.

After instructions were read, subjects viewed the videotaped lecture on types or creativity. After the lecture, packets were collected, subjects were instructed not to discuss the experiment, and they were directed to return in 1 week for testing. The following week, packets were returned, and the designated study materials were taken from the packets and were reviewed for 25 min. Subjects in the no-notes group had no notes to review and were instructed to review mentally.

[4] *The scientific process requires that researchers define abstractions such as learning in terms that are directly observable. This section describes the operational definitions of learning, the observable measures which hopefully reflect the underlying abstractions such as "transfer." Recall from Chapter 2 that operational definitions describe the procedures for "putting numbers next to names."*

[5] *The procedure section of a published research report usually describes the controls that were put in place to minimize competing alternative hypotheses (the rival explanations and sources of bias and contamination). Notice that the subjects were randomly assigned to one of the four study conditions. This creates comparable groups at the outset, and rules out an alternative hypotheses which suggest that, for example, the matrix notes subjects performed better because they had better memories, stronger motivation, more prior knowledge, etc. This section also describes how all four groups were treated similarly, except for the intended variation in type of note reviewing. This rules out alternative hypotheses such as, for example, matrix subjects performed best because they heard a better, more dynamic lecture (all lectures were videotaped so they could be exactly the same for each of the four groups). Or matrix subjects performed best because they reviewed longer, or had a shorter interval between the lecture and test administration, etc. This section also describes data collection, a step in the scientific process which may also create alternative hypotheses.*

Participants in all four groups were given lined paper to make additional study notes if they desired.

After the review period, all notes were returned to the packets and subjects had 21 min to complete the cued recall test. After the recall test, subjects had 13 min to complete the transfer test. Last, participants had 6 min to complete the factual recognition test.

Results and Discussion

To assess the statistical effects of the four study materials (text, outline, matrix, and no notes) on performance, we conducted a one-way analysis of variance (ANOVA) on scores from each of the three dependent measures (cued recall, factual recognition, and transfer). [6] Group means for the three tests appear in Table 1.

Each of the three ANOVAS indicated significant differences among the four groups: for cued recall, $F(3, 43) = 20.36$, $p < .001$, $MS_e = 39.62$; for factual recognition, $F(3, 43) = 5.49$, $p < .005$, $MS_e = 9.58$; and for transfer, $F(3, 43) = 17.18$, $p < .001$, $MS_e = 7.53$.[1] [7] Fisher least significant difference (LSD) tests ($p < .05$, in all cases) following up each ANOVA indicated that for each test the three groups given notes to review (text, outline, and matrix) significantly outperformed the no-notes group. These findings confirmed the importance of the external storage effect and uniformly extended it to the review of various types of produced notes.

[6] *Recall that the scientific process requires that the research hypothesis be formulated in such a way that the independent and dependent variables are clearly differentiated. Their research hypotheses reveal that the three performance measures are dependent variables and the four study groups form one independent variable. The subjects' prior knowledge about the topic of creativity would be one of many extraneous variables which must be controlled (see #5 above).*

[7] *This section describes the data analysis step in the research process, an important one that is covered in Chapter 11.*

---

[1] A second, weighted analysis was conducted on transfer scores in which application and synthesis subscores were equally weighted in determining an overall transfer score. The results of this analysis were similar, $F(3, 43) = 15.17$, $p < .001$, $MS_e = 16.24$. Fisher least significant difference tests again revealed that the three groups given notes to review significantly outperformed the no-notes group and that those reviewing the matrix performed significantly higher than those reviewing the text.

TABLE 1 Mean Scores and Standard Deviations for the Four Study Groups on Each of the Three Performance Tests

Study groups	Performance					
	Cued recall		Factual recognition		Transfer	
	M	SD	M	SD	M	SD
Text	13.91	6.16	10.45	2.98	15.82	3.37
Outline	21.09	7.97	11.18	4.09	16.91	3.05
Matrix	20.82	7.01	10.73	2.65	19.00	1.84
No notes	2.82	2.82	6.45	2.38	10.91	2.47

Note. The maximum score was 121 for cued recall, 20 for factual recognition, and 30 for transfer.

In addition, Fisher LSD analyses indicated that both the matrix and outline groups recalled significantly more than the text group on the cued recall test. On the transfer test, those reviewing the matrix again performed significantly higher than those reviewing the text. The advantage of outline and matrix notes over the complete text for recall performance was that the former systems perhaps encouraged students to make more internal connections among ideas (Mayer, 1984). When ideas are interconnected, the recall of one idea may prompt the recall of logically associated ideas as well. Such connections, made at acquisition, may also reduce potential interference among related lecture ideas and thereby support the accurate categorization of ideas at recall. We suspect, however, that the need to both recall and classify related ideas made recall scores relatively low in general.

The superior performance of the matrix note reviewers on the transfer test can perhaps be explained by the nature of the internal connections that they made. [8] Subjects were provided with a two-dimensional matrix that encouraged them not only to make superordinate-subordinate connections down the columns of the matrix, but also to make connections

[8] *This section is concerned with the interpretation of the results. You can see that they are interpreted in light of the theoretical formulation which produced the research hypotheses in the first place. It is likely that other researchers, had they analyzed the results, would present very similar findings yet* have a somewhat different interpretation. It is important to note that interpretations are not findings *(although they are frequently presented as such, especially in the popular news media). Notice that they use the words "perhaps" and "may." Someone with a different theoretical orientation could have a different interpretation and con-clusion. Notice that these researchers did* not *claim that the hypotheses and their generating theory had been* proven. *Research results, at best, can provide supporting evidence of a theory's credibility.*

across columns and categories. Theoretically, matrix reviewers not only made more individual connections, but also gained a more integrated understanding of the material. With this more integrated structure, transfer tasks involving synthesis and application were facilitated.

The fact that all three note-reviewing groups performed similarly on the factual recognition test is consistent with our earlier hypothesis. Items were aimed at the recognition of isolated facts, an outcome not as likely influenced by the forming of internal connections.

In considering the potential effectiveness of matrix notes for recall and transfer tasks, one must keep in mind that students in this experiment were never instructed in how to best use the notes for studying. In fact, we actually observed a few students converting the matrix into a linear outline during the study period! It is our contention that provided matrix notes will under further experimentation prove to be a powerful study device, especially in situations involving training. Perhaps students can ultimately be trained to encode lecture ideas personally in this matrix form. In that sense, this study represents a first step toward determining the type of notes that students should be recording for the purpose of studying.

References

DiVesta, F. J., & Gray, G. S. (1973). Listening and note taking: II. Immediate and delayed recall as functions of variations in thematic continuity, note taking, and length of listening-review intervals *Journal of Educational Psychology, 64*, 278–287.

Kiewra, K. A. (1985a). Investigating notetaking and review. A depth of processing alternative. *Educational Psychologist, 20*, 23–32.

Kiewra, K. A. (1985b). Learning from a lecture: An investigation of notetaking, review, and attendance at a lecture. *Human Learning, 4*, 73–77.

Kiewra, K. A. (1985c). Students' notetaking behaviors and the efficacy of providing the instructor's notes for review. *Contemporary Educational Psychology, 10*, 378–386.

Kiewra, K. A. (1985d). Providing the instructor's notes: An effective addition to student notetaking. *Educational Psychologist, 20*, 033–39.

Kintsch. W., & van Dijk, T. A. (1978). Toward a model of text comprehension and production. *Psychological Review, 85*, 363–394.

Mayer, R. E. (1984). Aids to text comprehension. *Educational Psychologist, 19*, 30–42.

Received February 26, 1988

Revision received June 6, 1988

Accepted June 27, 1988

GUIDED TOUR #2

Let's turn our attention now to a guided tour of published educational research. This will help solidify important terms and concepts described in this chapter.

The Action Research Endeavors of Six Classroom Teachers and Their Perceptions of Action Research

Deborah Sardo-Brown

Counselor and Secondary Education

West Chester University

West Chester, Pennsylvania 19383

Six classroom teachers who taught at the elementary through high school levels conducted a variety of classroom research studies. Two of the teachers studied the effectiveness of school-wide innovations such as a new A.I.D.S. curriculum and a math/science core approach. Three of the teachers studied widely advocated approaches from the research literature such as the use of computer assisted instruction, mastery learning, and metacognitive study methods. Another teacher observed which gender tended to emerge as leader in cooperative learning activities. A myriad of benefits were reported by the teachers as a result of their research including the following: an enhanced sense of professionalism, improved relationships with parents and administrators, and additional information gleaned about student attitudes. Among the areas of frustration for these teachers included difficulty finding time to collect and analyze data and designing research to maximize response rates. On-site support groups for teams of teacher who collect action research data were suggested for the future.

Many authors recently have contended that one important way to promote the reform of schools is to involve teachers in doing research in their own classrooms (Calhoun, 1993; Cochran-Smith & Lytle, 1990; Sardo-Brown, 1990). Since action research is conducted by the practitioner, it provides a way for teachers to investigate issues of interest or concern in their classroom and to incorporate the results into future teaching. This process, which begins with teachers' questions and aims at influencing practice, affords the opportunity for teachers to have greater responsibility for directing their own professional development. Action research is then based around practical problems and is planned and carried out by the person most likely to be interested in and affected by the findings. [1]

Many authors promote teachers' involvement in research as a way in which to empower teachers by increasing their role in school-wide decision-making (Maeroff, 1988). Other authors suggest that action research is a powerful means of promoting

[1] *Here is a brief statement about the purpose and value of action research. This type of research results in teachers' action via changes in practice, not in the advancement of theory. Action research is also distinguished by its effect on the researching practitioner: it often empowers them and leads to greater reflection.*

personal and social reflection (Llorens, 1994). Yet, few investigations have both systematically described action research studies conducted at various grade levels and the way in which teachers reflect upon their completed studies.

Method

The present study will describe the action research undertaken by six classroom teachers, each of whom attended the same master's degree program and were required to complete a written report of action research findings as part of their graduation requirement. Two of the six teachers taught at the elementary level, two at the middle school level, and two at the high school level. Four of the six participating teachers were female and two were male. They possessed a wide range of experience from one to 22 years, with a mean of 8.5 years. Teachers taught in a variety of settings including rural, suburban, and urban. The secondary teachers in the sample taught a variety of subject areas including social studies, English, and science. As a group, these teachers gathered both quantitative and qualitative data to answer their action research questions. All six teachers studied the impact of a specific classroom intervention.

Results

Descriptions of both teachers' action research studies and their reflections on the action research will be presented. [2]

Description of Teachers Action Research

Kim, a veteran fourth grade teacher, wanted to know how effective a new A.I.D.S. curriculum would be in helping fourth grade students acquire knowledge about the HIV virus and methods of its transmission. She also had two additional, related action research questions. Kim always wanted to find out if her students would display an increased sensitivity toward

[2] *You will see that the teachers' action research projects are diverse. Their ideas do not come from an abstract theory; they stem from wanting to know more about their teaching effectiveness and having a desire to change it for the better whenever they can. And notice that their results are not hidden in some obscure journal; they can be applied immediately, whether it be the fine-tuning of a curriculum (Kim), the search for new ways to improve attitudes (Beth) or a change in the way that cooperative learning groups are managed (Lauren).*

HIV positive individuals as a result of material covered in the new A.I.D.S. curriculum. In addition, she wondered if her students would be able to demonstrate first aid skills which would prevent the spread of HIV as a result of instruction they received as part of the new A.I.D.S. curriculum. To answer the first question, Kim compared the pre and post test responses of her 32 students. She found that students' post test scores improved by 88% compared to pre test scores. With regard to the second question, Kim analyzed pre and post journal entries in which she asked students how they would feel toward a classmate who was HIV positive. She found that students were markedly more sensitive toward an HIV infected classmate in the post journal entries than in the journal entries collected before the new A.I.D.S. curriculum was taught. Videotaped data of students performing appropriate first aid procedures showed that approximately 75% of students were able to safely control bleeding on a dummy they practiced on. Kim is now fine-tuning the A.I.D.S. curriculum to include additional hands-on examples designed to appeal to the fact that her students are largely concrete operational thinkers.

Like Kim, Karen's idea for an action research question stemmed from a school-mandated innovation. Karen, in her second year of teaching sixth grade, was curious about the effect of a math-science core approach in which math and science were taught in an interdisciplinary way and within a multi-period block of time. Karen was concerned if using this approach would both improve her 26 students' attitudes toward math and science as well as improve their scores on a district basic skills test compared to her group of 25 students from the previous school year. She administered a 30 item Likert-scale attitude survey to students at the start of the school year and again towards the end of the school year. Karen found that although her male students' attitudes did not vary significantly, her female students were much more likely to indicate they like studying math and science on the post survey. After controlling for pre-existing differences, Karen compared her students' basic skills test performance to the students' test performance from last year. Although she did not find a significant difference, she is hopeful that one will emerge in next year's class as the teachers become more experienced with the math/core block approach.

Another second-year teacher, Beth, became interested in action research after reading a journal article on computer assisted instruction (C.A.I.). Beth hypothesized that an experimental group of 31 eighth grade students who used C.A.I. in conjunction with the traditional textbook would significantly improve their science unit test scores compared to a control group of 29 comparable students who only used the traditional textbook. A t-test analysis of scores did, in fact, indicate that Beth's hypothesis was confirmed. However, although Beth also expected the experimental group of students to display an improved attitude toward science as compared to the control group, her analysis of pre and post Likert scale attitude surveys did not indicate this. Beth is continuing to search for ways to improve her students' attitudes toward studying science.

Mike, a third-year middle school teacher, also was motivated to do action research after reviewing the literature and discovering that little empirical data had been collected on students' opinions about outcomes-based education approaches. He became especially interested in using a form of mastery learning with his four sections of eighth grade social studies in which students were given three opportunities to retake chapter tests if they were unable to score an 85% on the first chapter test. In his form of mastery learning, students did not move on to take tests on new material until they had mastered previous material. In order to assess student attitude about this mastery learning approach, Mike designed a ten item survey with open-ended questions in which students were asked to react to the way in which they were both taught and tested in the mastery learning approach. Mike found that slightly over 90% of his 109 students responded favorably to this approach. Mike would like to continue to assess student attitude toward a new method he plans to incorporate, the use of performance-based examination.

Unlike the previous action research studies, Lauren's interest in her action research question originated from her own experience as a student working in cooperative learning groups. Lauren, a first-year high school English teacher, wondered if the emergence of leader in mixed gender cooperative learning groups would vary depending on the type of activity the groups were assigned. After consulting the literature, Lauren decided to assess how the gender of the emerging leader would vary depending on whether groups were assigned task activities, social activities, or unspecified activities. Task activities are usually male-oriented and are defined as those in which there are direct contributions made to the group. Social activities, which are usually female-oriented, are defined as those contributing to the maintenance of satisfactory morale and interpersonal relations among group members. Unspecified activities are those which do not favor one gender or the other. After videotaping one section of eleventh grade students working in four or five member cooperative learning groups, Lauren had two graduate students from the university code the videotapes using the Bales Interaction analysis. She found that male students typically emerged as leaders in all three forms of activities mentioned above. Because of these findings, Lauren is now routinely assigning specific roles to members of cooperative learning groups on a rotating basis to assure that both genders are able to assume the role of leader in an equitable way.

Don, a veteran high school teacher, was inspired to collect action research data out of concern for the achievement of his vocationally-oriented students. Don hypothesized that teaching his students metacognitive study methods would both improve their performance on social studies chapter tests as well as improve their attitudes toward studying for social studies. Don focused on one of his tenth grade American history sections which was primarily comprised of students who attended the vocational/technical school for half days. As part of the metacognitive study methods Don taught his 22 students how to highlight and underline key words and ideas as they read, how to take good notes in class, and how to use mnemonics such as visualization and rhyming to help them memorize. Don collected several sets of pre and post chapter test scores for this section to determine if students' post test scores significantly improved after instruction in metacognitive study skills. He found a significant improvement in chapter test scores among his lowest achieving students in this section. Don also found that nearly all of these students' attitudes toward studying American history improved as indicated on a ten item Likert-scale questionnaire. Don now wants to continue this with his other sections of students.

Descriptions of Teachers' Reflections on the Action
Research Process

After completing their action research studies, the six teachers responded anonymously in an open-ended questionnaire. The questions contained on the questionnaire included: (1) What are the benefits of doing an action study?; (2) If you could start your action research over, what would you do differently?; (3) How could your school or district facilitate your involvement in action research?; (4) How do you plan to use the findings of your action research study?; and (5) What plans, if any, do you have for doing action in the future?

These six teachers felt they had derived numerous benefits from participating in the action research process. Some of these benefits were directly related to teaching such as a renewed enthusiasm to read about and try out new teaching methods suggested in the research literature, a greater understanding of why they do what they do, and an enhanced sense of professionalism. [3] As one teacher remarked: "I now have validation for what I do and can feel more confident when explaining this to administrators."

Additional benefits included the following: the development of keener observational skills, improved communication with students, and obtaining a personal perspective of the impact of teaching methods learned at the university. For a few of the teachers action research also provided them with a means to obtain information about student attitudes, some of which they had not anticipated. Based on these data, teachers also added they had a better idea about how to revise and improve a particular approach they used. An additional positive outcome noted by three teachers was that they felt that they became better models for student writing since they themselves engaged informally in writing up their action research results. Two teachers remarked that their students were forced to become more reflective since students had to either keep journals or complete surveys which were part of the action research data.

Teachers offered a variety of responses with respect to what they might do differently if they could start their action research studies over. Among the ideas mentioned included: having a contingency plan in place for another action research study in case the initial study is not workable, planning how to control for additional extraneous variables in the classroom,

[3] *Here are some interesting findings related to the impact of action research on the researchers themselves, perhaps the most significant being an enhanced sense of professionalism.*

building in incentives for research subjects to return surveys and journals, carrying out a pilot study, and making earlier requests of school administrators for assistance in either gathering videotaped data or setting up activities which were part of the treatment under study. [4]

Likewise, teachers revealed in the questionnaire that their schools or districts could help facilitate their involvement in action research. Teachers recommended the following ideas here: providing release time to do encouraging a group of building teachers to do an action research study, permitting teachers to have access to school-wide data, and providing money for research supplies.

As a result of doing action research the six teachers also shared some specific plans for using their findings on the questionnaire. [5] These included: sharing findings with other school or district teachers, working with school administration to further explore how the action research results may be used to change school wide policy, sharing action research data with students in order to provide them with a concrete example of how their peers respond to a given treatment, conducting a district in-service based on action research findings, using findings in parent-teacher conferences, and writing up their research for presentation at a professional conference and possible publication.

In addition to the wide variety of ways teachers planned to use their action research data, three of the six teachers expressed a desire to continue to do action research in the future. All of the newly planned action research studies were based on topics in the initial action research. Three of the teachers (Karen, Mike, and Don) seemed to be motivated to continue their research in order to collect data on unanswered questions related to their initial research. Two additional teachers, Kim and Beth, are fine-tuning their curricula as a result of doing

[4] *Action research is research, and as such, it is not immune from bothersome alternative hypotheses. The data collection phase of action research (Figure 3.4) demands attention to potential biases. Action researchers in the classroom have challenges that theory-based researchers might bypass by collecting data in better controlled—but possibly artificial— learning laboratories far removed from real settings.*

[5] *Here is a good illustration of the "action planning" (Figure 3.4) in action research. Note that this includes sharing data with students, a process that can benefit them in a manner illustrated by the Santa et al. (1987) study described earlier in this chapter.*

action research. Kim is in the process of helping to revise the A.I.D.S. curriculum while Beth is involved in creating computer software to augment C.A.I. material she used in her first action research study. Although Lauren does not plan to continue her research, she is currently using her findings to help monitor the interaction patterns between male and female students in cooperative learning groups.

Conclusions

These data suggest that classroom teachers from first through twelfth grade can derive a number of benefits from participating in action research including an enhanced sense of professionalism, improved relationships with administrators and students, and an increased sensitivity to the affective concerns of students. Another benefit derived by classroom teachers was a sense that they were connected to the material found in professional journals. This connection was played out in a number of ways. First, some of the action research studies represented here seem to provide a way for teachers to take research-based findings, such as those on the use of metacognitive study methods, cooperative learning, and computer assisted instruction, and translate them into practice. Second, in some cases the action research studies served as a means for teachers to conduct some ground-breaking investigations on strategies that appear in the literature, but are not thoroughly investigated, such as the impact of an A.I.D.S. curriculum and student attitudes toward mastery learning. [6] Third, in other cases, the action research process forced teachers to question why a strategy they expect to be successful, such as the math/science core block approach, may not affect the kinds of changes desired with their own students.

While doing action research can provide a myriad of beneficial outcomes for classroom teachers, these data also indicate

[6] *The professional literature is loaded with good ideas that remain to be applied in an actual learning situation. Who is in a better position to test these ideas than the teachers who apply them? Her claim that teachers could conduct ground-breaking investigations is especially significant.*

some of the on-going frustrations teachers encounter with the process. Included among these are: difficulty in finding time to collect and analyze data and still maintain a full teaching load, planning the research design and instruments in such a way to maximize response rates, and obtaining administrative support for collection of data. As Sagor (1991) has suggested, perhaps an on-site support group would be helpful in guiding a group of teachers within one school building to pursue an action research study. The work of such a group may be facilitated by interested school administrators and university faculty.

It may also be of great benefit to have teachers within one school district from the elementary and secondary levels share the results of their action research with each other. Judging from the studies described here, such interaction may very well promote a better understanding among faculties as to the struggles faced by teachers at various grade levels.

References

Calhoun, E. F. (1993). Action research: Three approaches. *Educational Leadership, 50*(9), 62–65.

Cochran-Smith, M. & Lytle, S. L. (1990). Research on teaching and teacher research. *Educational Researcher, 19*(2), 2–11.

Llorens, M. B. (1994). Action research: Are teachers finding their voice? *Elementary School Journal, 95*(1), 3–10.

Maeroff, G. (1989). A blueprint for empowering teachers. *Phi Delta Kappan, 69,* 473–477.

Sagor, R. (1991). What project LEARN reveals about collaborative action research. *Educational Leadership, 48*(6), 6–10.

Sardo-Brown, D. (1990). Middle level teachers' perceptions of action research. *Middle school Journal, 22*(3), 30–32.

Sardo-Brown, D. (1995). The action research endeavors of six classroom teachers and their perceptions of action research. *Education, 116*(2), 196–200. Copyright © 1995 by PROJECT INNOVATION. Reprinted with permission.

APPLICATION EXERCISES

1. Educational and psychological researchers develop theories to explain constructs and phenomena. Consider each of the following and offer your own "theory" (explanation). Then visit the library and describe the theories which researchers have advanced as explanations.

    a. achievement decline in American schools
    b. the Flynn effect, or the rise in IQ scores over the past fifty years in most industrialized countries
    c. girls' seventh grade decline in interest, performance, and confidence in math and science (boys and girls are about the same up to the sixth grade)
    d. teenage suicide
    e. aggression
    f. low birth weight
    g. bonding
    h. language development
    i. self-esteem (Note: See what researchers have found to be related to self-esteem; you might be surprised)
    j. juvenile delinquency

2. Propose an action research project related to your current educational practice (teacher, counselor, administrator, etc.). Plan your study in accordance with Figure 3.4, attending to at least the problem formulation and data collection steps. Assume your findings have implications for practice. Then discuss how you would accomplish the action planning step in the process. If you are not currently working in an educational setting, propose an action research project related to the course you are taking which uses this text.

MULTIPLE CHOICE QUESTIONS

1. The educational research process is guided by two general orientations known as:
    a. substantive and derived
    b. theoretical and problem-based (applied)
    c. empirical and holistic
    d. generative and formative
    e. formative and summative

2. Which of the following is best synonym for theory?
    a. construct
    b. abstraction
    c. explanation
    d. idea
    e. hypothesis

3. Educational theories are useful, in part, because they:
    a. guide analyses
    b. prove assumptions
    c. verify observations
    d. simplify data
    e. generate hypotheses

4. Which of the following best describes the nature of the scientific research process?
    a. cyclical
    b. iterative

    c. experiential
    d. authentic
    e. instructive

5. Which of the following best describes the meaning of a construct?
    a. provable proposition
    b. verifiable assumption
    c. unobservable trait
    d. statistical theorem
    e. flexible hypothesis

6. Piaget, Gagne, and Bloom have made significant contributions to education through their explanations more commonly known as:
    a. inputs
    b. outputs
    c. phenomena
    d. theories
    e. hypotheses

7. The CIPP Model is an example of _____, one that emphasizes _____ .
    a. theoretical research; hypotheses
    b. scientific research; control
    c. program evaluation; decisions
    d. applied research; criticism
    e. operations research; data collection

8. What type of research is most appropriate for classroom teachers intent on validating their own classroom practices?
    a. theory-based
    b. action
    c. logical
    d. hypothetical
    e. input-output

9. All types of educational research are best viewed as a(n):
    a. exercise in guesswork
    b. random event
    c. variation of common sense
    d. series of integrated steps
    e. type of "shot in the dark"

10. Theories are often best understood with the aid of models, including examples such as:
    a. pipes and currents
    b. planets and cogwheels
    c. icebergs and tunnels
    d. fusion and magnets
    e. cubes and jungles

Answers: 1) b 2) c 3) e 4) a 5) c 6) d 7) c 8) b 9) d 10) e

Chapter *4*

THE RESEARCH HYPOTHESIS

OVERVIEW

This chapter addresses the major issues surrounding the research hypothesis and the central questions which logically follow. Once the researcher focuses on a research hypothesis (or research question), there are a series of questions that must be answered. The answers to these questions determine whether the researcher should proceed. If the researcher proceeds, then another series of decisions must be made with regard to the *type* of research that is best suited to test the hypothesis. The type of research approach used is crucial since it directly affects the conclusions which are possible after the analysis of data. This chapter is concerned with questions related to the research hypothesis itself. The next chapter is concerned with questions related to the type of research used to test the hypothesis. Research findings are, in part, influenced by how these questions are answered.

THE RESEARCH HYPOTHESIS VERSUS RESEARCH QUESTION

First, let us make a distinction between a research hypothesis and a research question. Generally, researchers reserve the term *research hypothesis* for a study that is closely linked to a theory, usually called theory-based or *basic* research. Recall from Chapter 3 that it is the theory which produces a research hypothesis and, if supported, lends credibility to the theory from which the hypothesis was born. In a published research article, the research hypothesis frequently takes the form *It is predicted that…*or *It is expected that…*or *It is anticipated that…*or some similar statement. Almost all research hypotheses can be recast into the form *If A, then B where A* represents the independent variable, and *B* represents the dependent variable. This form, although helpful for recognizing independent and dependent variables, often produces awkward syntax. Hence, the research hypothesis frequently appears in the *It is expected that…* format.

The *research question,* by contrast, is usually (not always) associated with studies that are more problem-based or applied (less theoretical) as described in Chapter 3. In this case, the research question may arise from a practical (not theoretical) need to know something. For example, a school may evaluate a new in–place system for decreasing absenteeism. The system involves an automatic computer-calling device that informs parents at home when a particular student is not in attendance. Does this system reduce absenteeism? Is it worth the cost? Or consider a case where a superintendent wants to know whether the "magnet" or incentive schools in the district are successful at reducing or eliminating a prior mathematics achievement difference between male and female students. Notice that no theory is being tested in these applied situations; there is simply a real-world concern for more information. In this case, the purpose of the research is usually stated in the form of a research question such as: "Do magnet schools eliminate a math achievement gap between male and female students?" The research question is often referred to by researchers as a *problem statement* or sometimes a research *objective*.

SOURCES OF HYPOTHESES

Whether the purpose of research is stated as a hypothesis or question, then, often tells us how closely the research is linked to a theory or model. The research hypothesis is usually stated in a *directional* form, which means that the researcher can speculate about the direction of differences (higher or lower) or the direction of a relationship (positive or negative). It is the theory which spawned the hypothesis that provides the guidance about which direction the results might take. For example, the constructive theory of learning suggests that learners who take notes themselves during a lecture will remember more than those who follow along with notes that have been provided. The directional hypothesis might be: "If students take notes during a lecture versus follow notes that have been supplied, then they will remember more after the lecture."

Research hypothesis can be formulated in several ways. One common ways is via deductive reasoning, that is, reasoning from general to specific. This was illustrated in Chapter 3, where we saw how general theories produced specific hypotheses. It is also possible to reason in the other direction, or *inductively*, where specific ideas or experiences could lead to general conclusions in the form of a theory. Classroom teachers observe countless phenomena and experience countless specific interactions in their learning environments. These specific but recurring instances may provide good ideas for general teaching practices. A general model, or theory, may summarize the induced hypotheses which arose from specific observations. Teachers may also arrive at induced hypotheses from reading the published research literature in an area. The major point is that some research hypotheses are not theory-based; they may be theory-producing.

Consider an example. A teacher might notice that her young students learn best when they are having fun and are happy. She might wonder whether there a connection between emotion and learning and so tests this idea by measuring learning under varying emotion-laden conditions. Sure enough, she finds that her research hypothesis was supported—children made happy by singing funny songs learned to spell a list of words faster than control children. Support for this specific hunch might lead to tests of its generalization among adults. For example, it might be predicted that adults who are emotionally flat have more trouble learning how to solve several puzzles. Further support might lead to the beginning formulation of a new theory of learning, possibly a biochemical one that links emotion, neurochemical changes associated with emotion, and learned outcomes. In summary, keen classroom observations, specific personal experiences, or careful reading of applied research results may generate educated hunches in the form of research hypotheses, which, if supported, form the basis for a more general understanding or explanation of the teaching and learning process.

In addition to deduction or induction, there is another famous method for arriving at hypotheses. Let's call it *creative visualization*, best illustrated by James Watson and Francis Crick's discovery of the double helix structure of DNA (Watson, 1968). Their training as biochemical scientists was apparently supplemented by dozing before a fireplace in the living room. Here in this hallucinogenic-like state, the structure revealed itself in the flames. It was a hypothesis-to-discovery journey worthy of a Nobel Prize. (If I were you, though, I'd rely on induction or deduction to arrive at hypotheses, and save trance-like states before gamboling fires for other purposes!)

Once the researcher has formulated a question or hypothesis, a series of followup questions usually arise that demand attention. These questions will be described in the following sections.

IS IT RESEARCHABLE?

This question may seem obvious, but it is not. There are many important and fascinating questions that can be asked about education, but in fact many of them are simply not researchable because it is not possible to collect data to answer them. For example, the question: "Should moral or character education be taught in school along with reading, writing, and arithmetic?" is a very reasonable and important question. But what type of data gathered will actually answer it? Questions that are concerned with "should" or "ought" and the like are outside the realm of scientific research; they are more closely aligned with philosophy, ethics, or some other intellectual discipline, maybe even theology. But don't think that research must therefore ignore all questions related to character education. The question, "Do children who receive formal instruction in character education have higher levels of moral reasoning?" is directly answerable, since a researcher could compare the levels of moral reasoning from one group of children given specific instruction in morality with another control group which had received no such instruction. Doing this would require using a specially designed instrument to scale children's thinking along a morality dimension from low to high.

Consider another important question: "What is the best way to teach problem solving skills?" No amount of data collected will answer this question either, since a better teaching method could always be found. What *is* answerable is a question such as, "What method—lecture versus discussion—is most effective for increasing students' problem solving skills?" Answering this would involve measuring students' skills, then placing some in a lecture format and others in a discussion format, followed by a reassessment of skills.

Other questions may just need refining before they are researchable. For example, consider the question, "Why do some students rise to the challenge when facing an obstacle, while others simply give up or withdraw?" This type of general question is best answered by a theory which explains the underlying construct (trait) believed to be responsible for the difference. Maybe the trait is "psychological hardiness" or "educational optimism." The theory behind this trait would have to explain its basic qualities, such as how it manifests itself in the classroom, how it develops, how it is nurtured, why it is stunted, what are its consequences, etc. A more specific, refined question might be, "Do children who delay gratification when they are young tend to pursue more difficult tasks when they are older?" The answer to this question helps us solve the bigger puzzle: Why are some students the way they are. This information can then be incorporated into a more credible theory of hardiness. And, as we have seen, the prevailing theory will then be able to address general questions such as "Why?" Other examples of researchable and nonresearchable questions appear in Table 4.1.

IS IT LEGAL AND ETHICAL?

All researchers in education must adhere to legal codes and conform to ethical guidelines in the conduct of their research. All responsible researchers adhere to these standards with "zero tolerance." From a legal standpoint, research participants are protected under the National Research Act of 1974 from mental, physical, and emotional injury. Also, no responsible researcher can collect personal data without the informed consent of the participants. Furthermore, the 1974 Buckley Amendment assured legal safeguards would be in place to guarantee *confidentiality* (where sensitive information would be held in strict confidence). The law also assured anonymity whenever possible (unless permission was granted to the contrary).

Most schools ensure compliance with the law through the establishment of a review board to make certain that research participants' legal rights are not violated. Researchers may be exempt from formal review by these boards under a variety of situations, including use of existing and publicly available data, the use of routine educational tests that do not identify individual names, and in usual settings (e.g.,

TABLE 4.1   Nonresearchable and Researchable Questions

Nonresearchable	Researchable
Should all children wear uniforms in public school?	Do children in uniformed schools achieve higher than children in non-uniformed schools?
What is the best way to teach reading?	Which group of 3rd graders has higher reading achievement: phonics-based learners or whole language-based learners?
Does research prove watching violence on TV leads to aggression?	Do children who watch more violence on TV behave more aggressively?
Do people unconsciously repress traumatic memories?	Is memory for emotional events more likely to be distorted than memory for non-emotional events?

classrooms) involving usual practices (e.g., teaching strategies) as long as confidentiality is maintained.

Researchers also conduct their business with the full recognition of morality. They know that some practices, although not illegal, would be contrary to ethical guidelines. Ethical treatment of research participants would not, for example, involve deception, denial of opportunity, or the deliberate withholding of educational interventions believed to be beneficial. Unethical behaviors would also include failing to disclose the general nature of research to all participants, treating participants with disrespect, or being less than honest or responsible in the handling and reporting of collected data. There are few charges more serious than one which suggests a researcher may have violated ethical concerns in the conduct of research with human participants. A summary code of ethics governing educational researchers appears in Table 4.2.

IS IT MEANINGFUL?

This is probably the most difficult question researchers must answer, and probably the one which prompts the most disagreement, undoubtedly because of the ambiguity of the term "meaningful." For our purpose, this term means "value," as in the worth of a question in terms of the meaning that could be extracted from its answer. Reviewers of research who are left wondering So what? or Who cares? would seriously question its meaningfulness. Meaningful research questions yield answers that

TABLE 4.2   Summary of Basic Ethical Guidelines for Educational Researchers

Participation in a research study is *voluntary;* no coercion of any kind should be tolerated; participants may freely withdraw.

Informed consent must be obtained from participants; all aspects which might affect the decision to participate must be explained, including all risks.

Avoid deception, cause no harm, and avoid invasion of privacy.

Maintain *confidentiality* and integrity of data; maintain *anonymity* of participants.

Debrief participants and provide information or explanation about the research.

Benefits should outweigh risks after careful consideration.

are often valued in terms of their impact. Some research questions, in fact, do produce answers that are "blockbusters" and are truly ground-breaking. This category would undoubtedly fit Robert Rosenthal's research question posed in "The Oak School Experiment," which is described in detail by Rosenthal and Jacobson (1968). The research question was "...Within a given classroom [will] those children from whom the teacher expected greater intellectual growth show such greater growth"? (p. 61). Rosenthal's answer was a qualified "yes" (but recall the problems with this study as described in Chapter 1). This answer had great meaning for many educators and researchers. For teachers, it meant that they should recognize their expectations of each individual's intellectual growth and harness the energy surrounding those beliefs in ways that foster growth. For researchers, it meant that complex patterns of communication between students and teachers, however subtle, should be studied in order to learn more about how expectations manifest themselves in the classroom. Their job essentially was to develop new theories to help explain the self-fulfilling prophecy in the classroom.

The decade of the 1960s also witnessed another research question and answer that can only be described as a "blockbuster." The question posed by Coleman and his associates was: (paraphrased) "What factors best explain the variation in academic achievement among school children?" (Answer, oversimplified: socioeconomic status.) The answer had great influence, because it shifted attention away from preconceived ideas that were not supported by research data (e.g., achievement was a function of school expenditures).

Other stimulating research questions asked more recently have had great meaning for researchers and practitioners, because they have shifted the direction of research and resulted in widespread changes in classroom practices. A brief sampling of these questions include the following:

- Will classroom practices designed to increase motivation also reduce discipline problems?
- What are the effects of cooperative learning strategies on achievement and attitude?
- Does a model of teaching based on cognitive science result in better comprehension and longer retention than traditional instruction?
- Will portfolio assessment result in better achievement than traditional methods of assessment?
- Will teaching strategies based on students' learning styles result in stronger motivation and higher achievement?

Other examples of meaningful research questions are provided in Table 4.3. These research questions have had great meaning to most people involved in education since they have influenced the thinking of many educators and have resulted in significant changes in the focus of many educational researchers.

Research questions do not, of course, have to be groundbreaking or highly influential to be "meaningful." Most educational research, in fact, appears to follow a *replication and extension* model. This means that a great deal of research is conducted to test the limits and extend the general work already done. *Replication* suggests that the research is basically a "repeat" of earlier work—essentially the same hypothesis is tested or the same research question is asked but with a design that provides for an additional piece of information. For example, recall from the guided tour of published research in Chapter 3 that researchers tested whether students who use a matrix type of study notes before a test outperform those who use the more traditional outline study notes (Kiewra, DuBois, Christian, & McShane, 1988). This study was done with a nineteen-minute videotaped lecture on types of creativity with college students who were not allowed to take notes themselves (they could only review the notes supplied by the researchers one week later prior to the test). An example of the replication and extension model would involve a replication in the sense that the research hypothesis

TABLE 4.3 Examples of Meaningful Research Questions in Education

How are early childhood education programs related to later achievement in school?

How are qualities of the home environment related to childrens' achievement in school?

What is the relationship between children's excessive viewing of television and their academic achievement?

What is the relationship between school expenditures and students' achievement?

What teaching behaviors are most strongly associated with high achievement in mathematics?

How do American students compare to students from other industrialized nations in terms of achievement?

How do changes in self-esteem relate to educational outcomes?

How do socioeconomic status, ethnicity, race, and sex affect students' school experiences?

How does prior knowledge affect new learning?

How does a student's cultural background influence the school experience?

What factors are most strongly associated with high school dropout rates?

Is teachers' use of constructivist techniques of teaching related to ease of learning?

How does ability grouping affect students' outcomes?

How does the practice of mainstreaming influence students' achievement?

would still maintain that matrix notes are superior to traditional notes. It would involve an extension in the sense that the followup study might use a forty-minute videotape on a different topic, or a live lecturer as opposed to a videotape, or high school students instead of college students, or a three-week test interval instead of one week. Notice that these extensions will test the general application of the original finding, or the extent to which the finding holds up under somewhat different situations using different participants.

Another logical followup to matrix notes study described earlier would involve training students to take matrix study notes, then comparing their test scores with those who take traditional notes. This research is probably regarded as being beyond the limits of replication and extension, because the original hypothesis tested whether students' *review* of matrix notes yielded higher test scores (recall they were written by the researcher and simply given to students for review). The follow-up study, on the other hand, tested the effect of matrix notes as *written* and reviewed by students. This study would test a different, albeit related, research hypothesis and would be considered more "extension" than "replication."

The important point is that educational research is nearly always linked, more or less, to research that has already been done. In this sense, each research study provides a small piece to a much larger puzzle and should, in some way or another, fit into a larger scheme. This leads us to yet another question.

HAS IT ALREADY BEEN ANSWERED?

This question is answered by what is called the *review of literature*. This is a description of the prior research that is related to the study (what other researchers have done) and its conceptual basis (relevant theories and constructs). The theoretical underpinning or conceptual framework of a study provides a context for the findings and helps orga-nize all the empirical information that is known about a particular phenomenon.

The obvious source of information in the review of literature is the library. Libraries on many college and university campuses can change dramatically (and very quickly) in response to technological advances in information science. In fact, universities may soon be built without a library building, since many library holdings can be accessed electronically from the desktop or laptop of researchers from almost any location.

Reports of published research are most often found in periodicals—the profes-sional journals in the field of education which are organized around common inter-ests, such as learning, motivation, assessment, etc. Some journals are specialized (e.g., *Journal of Educational Psychology*) while others are more general or broad in scope (e.g., *American Educational Research Journal*). Some are considered to be very scholarly (e.g., *Educational Researcher*) and others less so (*Educational Leadership*). There is a daunting, nearly overwhelming, amount of educational research published in schol-arly journals. Fortunately, there are educational indexes available which enable re-searchers to locate from the vast amount of educational research those studies which are of particular interest to the researcher describing the context for research. The *Edu-cation Index* is one such resource, allowing researchers to search for (by topic and au-thor) empirical research reports published in nearly 400 journals since 1929. Skill in using the *Education Index* comes only with first-hand practice, requiring a consultation with a reference librarian.

Another resource is the *Current Index to Journals in Education (CIJE)* published by a national information center and clearinghouse known as ERIC (Educational Re-sources Information Center). *CIJE*, dating back to 1969, is especially useful since it pre-sents a summary of the research in addition to its location within the hundreds of journals. The most efficient way of searching for relevant research reports is through the use of computers. Computer searching of *CIJE* is made possible by searching with *ERIC descriptors*, or key words and phrases that allow rapid scanning of topics. These descriptors are found in the publication *Thesaurus of ERIC Descriptors*. A learn-by-doing visit to the reference section of your library is the best way to understand *CIJE* and the ways of accessing it. Searching is quick, painless, probably free, and often done for the first time without any assistance, thanks to technological advances such as CD-ROM.

Many researchers make valuable contributions to education by reviewing the vast amounts of research done in an area, making sense of it, and presenting it in a useful, newly organized (synthesized) format. These reports can be found in some journals (e.g., *Review of Educational Research*) and comprehensive, scholarly books such as *Re-view of Research in Education, Handbook of Research on Teaching, Handbook of Educational Psychology*, and *Encyclopedia of Educational Research*. Examples of widely circulated ed-ucational journals are found in Table 4.4.

Appearing with increasing frequency are published reports of *meta-analysis* stud-ies, a type of *quantitative* summary of the literature in one field. Meta-analysis is a *statis-tical* summary of a body of empirical studies, all of which were conducted to answer one research question (or test one research hypothesis). These summaries are very helpful for researchers wanting to learn what research has already been conducted on a topic since the meta-analyst must compile (and usually cite) all of the studies before meta-analysis can be performed. Meta-analysis is best suited for research questions that can be answered "yes" or "no." For example, one of the earliest meta-analyses was done in psychology trying to answer the question, "Does psychotherapy work?" Each study conducted earlier by researchers trying to answer this question now becomes a "data point" in a meta-analysis. Of course, each of the hundred or more individual studies was not a perfect replication of any other; researchers may have studied differ-ent outcomes, types of therapy, length of therapy, types of patients, and the like (in the same mode as replication and extension, described earlier). Nevertheless, all of the studies have one important quality in common: they all searched for an answer to the

TABLE 4.4 Examples of Widely-Cited Journals in Education (after Smart & Elton, 1981)

American Annals of the Deaf	Journal of Educational Research
American Educational Research Journal	Journal of Experimental Child Psychology
American Journal of Mental Deficiency	Journal of General Psychology
British Journal of Educational Psychology	Journal of Genetic Psychology
Child Development	Journal of Learning Disabilities
Developmental Psychology	Journal of Legal Education
Educational and Psychological Measurement	Journal of Personality Assessment
Educational Leadership	Journal of School Psychology
Educational Researcher	Language Learning
Exceptional Children	Measurement and Evaluation in Guidance
Harvard Educational Review	Mental Retardation
Human Development	Monograph of the Society for Research in Child
Instructional Science	Development
Journal of Applied Behavioral Analysis	Personnel and Guidance Journal
Journal of Applied Behavioral Sciences	Psychology in the Schools
Journal of Child Psychology and Psychiatry and	Reading Research Quarterly
Applied Disciplines	Reading Teacher
Journal of Counseling Psychology	Review of Educational Research
Journal of Curriculum Studies	School Review
Journal of Educational Measurement	Social Education
Journal of Educational Psychology	Teachers College Record

same basic question. Meta-analysis, when applied to a large collection of studies, is an overall test in the sense that it attempts to report the "big picture." Meta-analysis also is able to uncover relationships across studies that would not be apparent to the single researcher testing one relationship. For example, a meta-analysis might reveal that therapy *is* effective, but only if administered over sixteen weeks or more using one specific approach with only one particular type of illness. Meta-analytic counterparts in education might be: "Does retention help students?" or "Is bilingual education effective?" or "Does corporal punishment reduce misbehavior?" or "Do mainstreamed students hinder the progress of other students?" Needless to say, the report of a carefully executed meta-analysis would be a welcome finding for anyone needing to review the literature in a particular area. Examples of published meta-analysis reports are provided in Table 4.5.

WHAT TYPE OF DATA WILL ANSWER IT?

This question is concerned with the nature of educational data and whether it is even possible to collect data that is relevant to the research question or hypothesis. There are many different types of educational data and many different methods used to gather it. Probably the best known type of educational data is standardized achievement test scores. These are well known because of their widespread use in this country and because their results are usually made public, sometimes in the form of international rankings on the evening news. But there are many other important outcomes, and they may be assessed with questionnaires, essay tests, oral interviews, behavioral observations, portfolios, performance measures and many others. These assessments may be used to measure, for example, attitudes, motivation, persistence, creativity, optimism, emotional adjustment, ability to form an argument, think critically, or form character. All of these outcomes are measurable, although some may not measure up to the stan-

TABLE 4.5   Examples of Published Titles Using Meta-Analysis in Educational Research

The efficacy of computer assisted instruction (CAI): a meta-analysis (Fletcher-Flinn, C. M., & Gravatt, B., 1995)

Gender differences in student attitudes toward science: a meta-analysis of the literature from 1970–1991 (Weinburgh, M. H., 1995)

Gender differences in learning styles: a narrative review and quantitative meta-analysis (Severiens, S. E., & Geert T. M., 1994)

An investigation of the effectiveness of concept mapping as an instructional tool (meta analysis of research) (Horton, P. B., McConney, A., & Gallo, M. A., 1993)

Effectiveness of mastery learning programs: a meta-analysis (with discussion) (Kulik, C. C., Kulik, J. A., & Bangert-Drowns, R. L., 1990)

The nature, effects, and relief of mathematics anxiety (meta-analysis of research) (Hembree, R., 1990)

A meta-analysis of the relation between class size and achievement (McGiverin, J., Gilman, D. A., & Tillitski, C., 1989)

A meta-analysis of the effects of direct instruction in special education (White, W. A., 1988)

Research on group-based mastery learning programs: a meta-analysis (Guskey, T. R., & Pigott, T. D., 1988)

A meta-analysis of research on the relationship between educational expenditures and student achievement (Childs, T., & Shakeshaft, C., 1986)

Teaching test-taking skills to elementary-grade students: a meta-analysis (Scruggs, T. E., White, K., & Bennion, K., 1986)

Drugs, academic achievement, and hyperactive children (meta-analysis of research) (Byrd, P. D., & Byrd, E. K., 1986)

Effects of hand-held calculators in precollege mathematics education: a meta-analysis (Hembree, R., & Dessart, D. J., 1986)

The efficacy of early interventions programs: a meta- analysis (Casto, G., & Mastropieri, M. A., 1986)

Does moral education improve moral judgment? A meta-analysis of intervention studies using the Defining issues test (Schlaefli, A., Rest, J. R., & Thoma, S. J., 1985)

A meta-analysis of selected studies on the effectiveness of bilingual education (Willig, A. C., 1985)

Homework: a meta-analysis (Otto, 1985)

The effects of nonpromotion on elementary and junior high school pupils: a meta-analysis (Holmes, C. T., & Matthews, K. M., 1984)

Effects of ability grouping on secondary school students: a meta-analysis of evaluation findings (Kulik, C. C., & Kulik, J. A., 1984)

dards using the criteria of reliability and validity (see Chapter 7). Examples from the myriad of educational measures that can be applied in research studies can be found in Table 4.6.

The type of data used by researchers often reflects an orientation (or philosophy) about education and how to best proceed toward meeting common goals. An example may be found in the debate about teaching reading. Should children be taught using a phonics approach (an emphasis on letter sound correspondence with bit-by-bit skills building on each other) or a whole language approach (immersion in meaningful literature with an emphasis on discovery)? This debate, one might think, would be resolved by examining the research on the issue. The problem is that advocates of *both* approaches point to research that supports their view. How can educational research

TABLE 4.6 Examples of Common Sources of Educational Data Used in Research

Standardized Performance Test Scores
- intelligence (e.g., Otis-Lennon School Ability Test)
- achievement
  —norm-referenced (e.g., Stanford Achievement Test)
  —criterion-referenced (e.g., General Educational Development or GED Test)
- aptitude (e.g., Seashore Measures of Musical Talent)
- diagnostic (e.g., Diagnostic Math Inventory)

Standardized Affective Measures
- general personality (e.g., Adjective Checklist)
- interest (e.g., Strong-Campbell Interest Inventory)
- self-concept (e.g., Piers-Harris Children's Self-Concept Scale)
- attitudes (e. g., Attitudes Toward Mathematics)
- styles or preferences (e.g., Learning Style Inventory)

Teacher-made or Researcher-made Achievement Tests
- essay tests
- objective tests (multiple choice, true-false, matching, completion, short-answer, etc.)

Portfolio Assessments (e.g., judgments of learning gain, attitude shifts, etc.)

Questionnaires or Surveys (often with rating scales or rankings)

Interviews (often unstructured, open-ended)

Observational Measures (e.g., tallies, frequencies)

Unobtrusive Measures (e.g., "hidden" record keeping such as attendance rates)

Field Notes and Logs (e.g., perceptions, reactions, accounts)

Content Analysis (e.g., narrative themes within documents)

---

produce two sets of findings that are inconsistent, in the sense that both support opposing approaches? Simply, each approach favors different types of data that would be useful in the evaluation of the approach. Phonics advocates may point to decontextualized skills that are assessed easily by standardized multiple-choice tests. Whole language advocates tend to believe that more global, qualitative measures of meaning and comprehension (not multiple-choice tests) are most appropriate in the study of emerging literacy in language-rich environments. Because their focus is not subskill instruction, tests that are designed to determine how well beginning readers break language into its components, more common in standardized tests, are simply not appropriate. In this way, the choice of one particular type of data does not represent a search for "the truth" as much as it does an inclination toward one preferred method of teaching. It would be no surprise, therefore, that when phonics is compared with whole language using standardized multiple-choice tests, phonics would appear better, but when the two approaches are compared using students' reading diaries, the whole language approach would appear better. To be sure, the choice of a particular type of educational data is one reason for the proverbial weak conclusion that research shows "mixed results."

CHAPTER SUMMARY

Because of its central importance, much attention is focused on the research hypothesis (or question) so that it is researchable, legal and ethical, and meaningful. The research hypothesis is tested within the context of prior research (or literature) in the area using numerous types of educational data. Two researchers testing the same hypothesis may arrive at different conclusions, explained in part by differences in methodology and the inclination to use different types of data.

GUIDED TOUR

Let's turn our attention now to a guided tour of published educational research. This will help solidify important terms and concepts described in this chapter.

Brief Reports

SELF-ESTEEM, NEED FOR APPROVAL, AND CHEATING BEHAVIOR IN CHILDREN

Thalma E. Lobel and Ilana Levanon

Tel-Aviv University

Tel-Aviv, Israel

We investigated the effects of personality and situational variables on children's cheating behavior. Two hundred twenty-eight 10- to 12-year-old boys and girls completed the Children's Social Desirability Questionnaire and the Coopersmith Self-Esteem Inventory and were given unsolvable problems at which they could "succeed" only by cheating. One group was offered a tangible prize for success, the second group was told that its performance would be made public, and the third group served as a control group. The children with high self-esteem and low need for

Correspondence concerning this article should be addressed to Thalma E. Lobel, Department or Psychology, Tel-Aviv University, Ramat Aviv, 69978, Israel.

approval cheated significantly less than the children with high self-esteem and high need for approval, who behaved similarly to the children with low self-esteem. In addition, boys cheated more than girls, and all children cheated most when they expected a tangible prize. We discuss two kinds or high self-esteem: "true" high self-esteem and defensive high self-esteem.

We investigated children's cheating behavior in three situations as a function of their self-esteem and need for approval. Copying answers and cheating behavior in the classroom have been shown to be affected by situational variables such as previous success or failure, knowledge of peer performance, or reception of a tangible prize for success (e.g., Houston, 1978; Mills, 1958). Children's cheating behavior was investigated in three different situations. In one situation, a tangible prize was promised to the 20% best performers; in the second situation the children were told that their performance would be made public; and in the third situation, which served as control, subjects were told that their performance would be known only to the researchers. [1] We predicted that children would cheat significantly less in the control situation than in the other two situations.

Less consistent results have been obtained in studies of the relation between cheating behavior and need for approval (NA) or self-esteem (SE; e.g., Eisen, 1972; Millham, 1974). [2] One of the reasons for this inconsistency might be the fact that the relation between SE and NA is not clear. On the one hand, because both types of constructs require the subject's positive assessments of himself or herself, they should be positively correlated. On the other hand, because high self-esteem (HSE) is assumed to be related to low defensiveness, whereas high need for approval (HNA) is assumed to be related to high

[1] *Many research studies test more than one research hypothesis, as is the case with this study. The first research hypothesis is derived from past research, and appears to be a type of replication. Researchable ideas are not born in a vacuum, nor do they arise from dream-like states (usually). They typically follow a replication and extension model and are closely tied to research literature and personal observation, or are derived logically from theoretical underpinnings. Prior research has shown that cheating is affected by situational variables, hence they plan to substantiate this claim by measuring cheating under three different situations (conditions). Sometimes researchers include a hypothesis that is far stronger than a hunch; indeed, it would be surprising to find that cheating was not affected by these situational variables. This hypothesis functions more like a double check (or manipulation check), a way of assuring that their procedures and instrumentation are functioning as they should be. If cheating was not found to be greater in the public performance condition, as the literature suggests it should be, then the results of the more interesting hypothesis described in #2 below would probably be put in doubt. By contrast, if the hypothesis relating to situational factors were supported as expected, then the test of the second hypothesis would be more believable. My general sense, then, is that this hypothesis is a type of "circuit test" to make sure that all is functioning properly before modifications are made or extensions are added.*

[2] *Here is the more interesting portion of this study, and a common reason for conducting research in the first place: inconsistencies in the literature. In this case, these researchers believe that the constructs of self-esteem and need for approval might be related to cheating in a complex way. This idea was developed by personality theories as well as prior research in this area. It appears that this idea was the primary reason for conducting the research, and the support for such a relationship would be the unique contribution of this study.*

defensiveness, these two constructs should be negatively correlated. Indeed, both positive (e.g., Pervin & Lili, 1967) and
negative (e.g., Fleming & Courtney, 1984) correlations between
NA and SE have been obtained. Hewitt and Goldman (1974)
argued that there may be two types of individuals with HSE,
those with "true" self-esteem, who truly believe that they possess positive characteristics and are not motivated to gain approval, and those who obtain high scores on both SE and NA
and whose behavior is therefore actually defensive. Consequently, HSE individuals may be expected to exhibit two opposing patterns of behavior depending on their NA,
particularly in behaviors that are defensive in nature, such as
cheating (e.g., Millham, 1974). Therefore, we predicted that
HSE/LNA (low NA) children will cheat significantly less than
HSE/HNA children and LSE (low SE) children. **[3]**

Method

Subjects

The subjects were 228 children (120 boys and 108 girls),
aged 10–12, in the fifth and sixth grades.

Instruments

We used the Children's Social Desirability (CSD) questionnaire (Crandall, Crandall, & Katkovsky, 1965), which consists of
48 true/false items, to measure the children's need for approval.

We assessed self-esteem with Version A or the Coopersmith Self-Esteem Inventory (SEI; Coopersmith, 1967), which
consists of 50 true/false items. **[4]**

We assessed cheating behavior in the following way: The
children received five forms that they had to copy without lifting their pencils from the paper and without passing over the
same line twice. The first two figures were quite easy, as
shown in a pretest, whereas the last three figures were impos-

[3] *Here they state very clearly their prediction, or what most would call their research hypothesis. Recall that good hypotheses are not vague or without direction. There should be no doubt, given the outcome, whether or not the hypothesis was supported.*

[4] *Research hypotheses, of course, must be researchable. This means that it must be possible to collect data that will answer the question. Self-esteem and need for approval, then, must be measurable in order to collect data. In this section, we see how the researchers have operationally defined these constructs. This enables them to collect the data directly relevant to their second hypothesis. You will see in Chapter 7 that these operational definitions may not necessarily be reliable and valid measures of the underlying construct; if they are not, then a serious problem with the study becomes obvious.*

sible to copy without lifting the pencil or passing over the same line twice. Hence, any child who copied the figure had either lifted the pencil or gone over some of the lines. Subjects had to write down at the bottom of the page the number of figures that they succeeded in copying.

Procedure

In accordance with the Israeli regulations, we obtained the approval of the chief scientist of the Ministry of Education and the school's consent before conducting the study. The study was conducted in two stages. **[5]** In the first stage, children completed the CSD and the SEI questionnaires. The order of the two questionnaires was counterbalanced. A few weeks later, we measured cheating behavior. Children were taken in groups of 15–20 to a vacant classroom, where they were administered a "test for children your age." The children were told that they had to copy the five forms without lifting the pencil or going over any of the lines. The instructions were printed inside the booklet and were also read aloud to the children. Children were assigned randomly to one of three conditions. In the first, they were told that their scores would be posted on the notice board at the end of the day. In the second condition, the children were told that performers scoring in the top 20% would receive a prize. In the third (control) condition, the children were told that their performance would be known to no one but the experimenter, who needed it for research purposes only. At the end of the experiment, the children were debriefed.

Results

Because the first two figures were easily solved and the last three were unsolvable, any reported score above 2 was considered a lie, and the lie score was the number of unsolvable

[5] *We know from this chapter that p_____d research must conform to standard legal, ethical, and moral guidelines. Approving boards (committees, panels, etc.) have been set up for this purpose, and they guard against unethical practices such as coercion and harm. They are usually centralized and local; therefore, permission must often be obtained at several levels, as was the case in this study. Many studies in education warrant an "expedited" review, a speedy one when the procedure leaves no doubt that ethical guidelines are in place. Studies which use tests that are, for example, a regular part of the classroom routine (especially when students' identity cannot be revealed to the researcher) are usually sped through the review process. Many studies in education, however, raise more interesting ethical dilemmas. The practice of deception is one such dilemma. When you read this section of the report closely, you see that subjects were indeed tricked to some extent. They were led to believe that they could copy five forms, when in fact they could only copy two. Any score reported by the students that was greater than two was clear evidence of cheating. One could argue that these children were deliberately encouraged to cheat, hardly compatible with goals of character education. Most reasonable people would see no harm resulting from this experimental setup and would grant approval to study cheating in this benign and inoffensive manner. By contrast, leading subjects to believe they have failed a high-stakes test or lost a loved one in order to study their reactions would clearly be ethically controversial. This outrageous type of harmful deception must be avoided.*

Examine the last sentence in this section. You see that students were debriefed—as they should have been according to ethical guidelines—so that they could learn about the study after the fact. This debriefing process could not have been too pleasant for many students; some had clearly been caught cheating. This might arouse fear of reproach; some may worry this will become part of their record, despite what the researchers told them. Measuring high on a cheating task may be embarrassing for some and clearly not compatible with one's sense of self-respect. Others, most likely, may not care and be totally unaffected. What makes the study of ethics so interesting is the complex weighing of pros and cons. Deception and its potential to harm as practiced by researchers should always be weighed against the potential benefits accrued by the research. Will our understanding of this problem be sufficiently advanced so as to offset any embarrassment or harm experienced by subjects? Could the very act of debriefing, an important ethical guideline, itself be responsible for negative reactions among students? Might it be more ethical not to debrief students in some situations? These are not easy questions to answer. (It is unclear from

figures that the child reported copying; that is, we calculated the lie score by subtracting 2 from the number of figures that the child reported copying correctly. For example, if a child reported copying 3 figures, his or her lie score was 1.

A 2 (high/low NA) × 2 (high/low SE) × 3 (type of situation) × 2 (sex) analysis of variance (ANOVA) was conducted on the lie scores. The ANOVA yielded a significant main effect of NA, $F(1, 204) = 10.78$, $MS = 13.416$, $p < .001$, which reflected the fact that high-NA subjects cheated significantly more ($M = 2.04$, $SD = 1.18$) than did low-NA subjects ($M = 1.59$, $SD = 1.20$); a marginally significant main effect of sex, $F(1, 204) = 3.67$, $MS = 4.571$, $p < .06$, indicated that boys ($M = 1.90$, $SD = 1.19$) cheated more than girls ($M = 1.70$, $SD = 1.20$), and there was a significant main effect of situation, $F(2, 204) = 12.676$, $MS = 15.775$, $p < .001$.

Duncan post hoc comparisons revealed that subjects cheated significantly more in the tangible prize condition ($M = 2.29$, $SD = 1.06$) than in either the control condition ($M = 1.38$, $SD = 1.18$) or the announcement condition ($M = 1.70$, $SD = 1.18$).

In addition, the NA × SE interaction was significant, $F(1, 204) = 4.702$, $MS = 5.85$, $p < .05$. We conducted t tests based on the error term of the ANOVA to compare the lie scores; these tests revealed that HSE/LNA subjects cheated significantly less ($M = 1.32$, $SD = 1.20$) than HSE/HNA subjects ($M = 2.10$, $SD = 1.07$), $t(204) = 2.96$, $p < .01$, less than LSE/HNA subjects ($M = 1.93$, $SD = 1.20$), $t(204) = 2.04$, $p < .05$, and less than LSE/LNA subjects ($M = 1.76$, $SD = 1.21$), $t(204) = 2.11$, $p < .05$. HSE/HNA subjects tended to cheat more than LSE/LNA subjects, $t(204) = 1.80$, $p < .10$, and there were no significant differences between HSE/HNA and LSE/HNA subjects.

Discussion

Boys in this study tended to cheat more than girls. This result might stem from the fact that boys are expected to succeed

this brief report whether subjects were fully debriefed. I suspect they were told about the cheating task but were debriefed in a sensitive manner, hence not negatively affected.) Deception in research should never be practiced without thoughtful discussion of ethical issues; deception that results in harm should be avoided. (Note: I do not consider this study to be ethically controversial. Highly reputable journals, such as the Journal of Educational Psychology, in which this study appeared, do not publish studies unless the editors believe that the researchers adhere to the highest ethical as well as methodological standards. This study was not chosen for its ethical dilemma but rather to illustrate other important facets of the research hypothesis. It does, however, provide a context to discuss the importance of ethics.

in academic tasks more than are girls (e.g., Skaalvik, 1983) and therefore cheat more often when facing failure.

In addition, children cheated most when they believed that they would receive a tangible prize for good performance, regardless of their self-esteem or need for approval. These results complement Mills's (1958) results, who also found that sixth-grade children cheated more when they could receive a tangible prize than when they knew that the names of successful performers would be read aloud in class. It is reasonable to assume that for preadolescent children (11–12 years old), a tangible prize has greater motivational power than does the knowledge that their performance would be made public. It is possible, however, that older subjects would have yielded different results.

Of most interest was that HSE/LNA children cheated significantly less than the other three groups and that the behavior of the HSE/HNA subjects was similar to that of the LSE subjects. In fact, although the differences did not reach significance, the HSE/HNA group cheated the most. These results provide further support for the proposition that there are two types of high self-esteem scorers, the HSE/HNA children, who are defensive, and the HSE/LNA children, who possess "true" self-esteem. Moreover, the results indicate that cheating behavior provides a sensitive tool for differentiating between these two types. It appears that in situations involving a threat of failure, the HSE/HNA children resort to behaviors that preserve their positive public image. Thus in the situation tested in this study, in which cheating was instrumental for success and the risk of detection seemed low, these children cheated more than did HSE/LNA children, who were probably less concerned about their public image. These results suggest that encouraging children to rely more on internal reinforcement and to believe in their positive characteristics could perhaps reduce the incidence of cheating in the classroom.

References

Coopersmith, S. (1967). *The antecedents of self-esteem*. San Francisco: Freeman.

Crandall, V. C., Crandall, V. T., & Katkovsky, W. (1965). A children's social desirability questionnaire. *Journal of Consulting Psychology, 29,* 27–36.

Eisen, M. (1972). Characteristic self-esteem, sex, and resistance to temptation. *Journal of Personality and Social Psychology, 24,* 68–72.

Fleming, J. S., & Courtney, B. E. (1984). The dimensionality of self-esteem: II. Hierarchical facet model for revised measurement scales. *Journal of Personality and Social Psychology, 46,* 404–421.

Hewitt. J., & Goldman, M. (1974). Self-esteem, need for approval, and reactions to personal evaluations. *Journal of Experimental Social Psychology, 10,* 201–210.

Houston, J. P. (1978). Curvilinear relationships among anticipated success, cheating behavior, temptation to cheat, and perceived instrumentality of cheating. *Journal of Educational Psychology, 70,* 758–762.

Millham, J. (1974). Two components of need for approval score and their relationship to cheating following success and failure. *Journal of Research in Personality, 8,* 378–392.

Mills, J. (1958). Changes in moral attitudes following temptation. *Journal of Personality, 26,* 517–531.

Pervin, L., & Lili, R. (1967). Social desirability and self-ideal self-ratings on the Semantic Differential. *Educational and Psychological Measurements, 27,* 845–853.

Skaalvik, E. M. (1983). Academic achievement, self esteem and valuing of the school—Some sex differences. *British Journal of Educational Psychology, 53,* 299–306.

Received November 24, 1986

Revision received August 12, 1987

Accepted September 7, 1987

APPLICATION EXERCISES

1. Decide whether you think each of the following questions is researchable:
   a. Should the school year be lengthened to include most of the summer months?
   b. How should the history of the Nazi Holocaust be taught in high schools?
   c. Are students more creative in groups or working alone?
   d. How can students' creativity be maximized?
   e. Does research prove students learn to read best by phonics instruction?

2. For each of the following research proposals, make a judgment about whether or not you think it would pass an ethics review committee. If not, state what ethical violation is apparent.
   a. A random sample of students at Carver Junior High School will be told that their performance on an intelligence test was far below average; then their achievement one year later will be compared to a control group to see how beliefs about intelligence affect learning.
   b. Students will be required to wear beepers; when beeped by the researchers, they will write down their private thoughts.
   c. Students will each be given $2500 for their participation in a year-long study; to decrease the chance of dropping out, they will be paid after their participation is complete.
   d. Students will not be told before or after the experiment that the study is related to cheating in order to minimize their embarrassment.
   e. College students who volunteered to participate will *not* be told that the "brain food" diets may cause impotence in rare situations, since the very suggestion may cause the problem.
   f. Tiny hidden cameras will be installed in the rest rooms to see if the educational program actually reduced smoking between classes.
   g. Researchers will use one hundred schools to statistically assess a new achievement test; names of the lowest scoring one-third will be sold to private tutoring companies with the highest bid.
   h. SAT scores with names will be used by the researchers; they will contact each test taker for permission to use the scores in a test of the relationship between achievement and month of birth.

MULTIPLE CHOICE QUESTIONS

1. Research hypotheses can be reasoned _____ from general theories or _____ from specific observations
   a. spiritually; holistically
   b. formatively; summatively
   c. summatively; formatively
   d. deductively; inductively
   e. inductively; deductively

2. Which of the following is *not* researchable?
   a. Do girls read emotional cues better than boys?
   b. Is there a link between IQ and happiness?
   c. Is there a link between astrological sign and GPA?
   d. Should all children learn a foreign language?
   e. How do teachers feel about the K–16 movement?

3. Which of the following is regarded as an important ethical principle by educational researchers?

    a. prompt reporting

    b. informed consent

    c. detailed logs

    d. avoiding mass media

    e. affirmative action

4. Most educational research appears to test the limits and generalizability of work already done using a common model known as:

    a. replication and extension
    b. description and deduction
    c. empirical proving
    d. meaningful empiricism
    e. quantitative blinding

5. Computer searches of retrievable educational research is made possible by a clearinghouse known as:

    a. CORE

    b. EDUcate
    c. SAMsearch
    d. BETA
    e. ERIC

6. A statistical summary of a collection of research studies—all designed to answer the same general question—is known as:

    a. beta-searching
    b. meta-analysis
    c. alpha testing
    d. CIJE indexing
    e. Interneting

7. The fact that advocates of two different (even opposing) instructional methods can point to supporting research often can be explained by differences in:

    a. computers analyzing the data
    b. ethical guidelines
    c. types of data collected
    d. reporting formats
    e. sample sizes

8. An example of a widely used standardized test of intelligence in schools, often referred to by the names of its developers, is the:

    a. "Piers-Harris"
    b. "Otis-Lennon"
    c. "Strong-Campbell"
    d. "Seashore-Gardner"
    e. "Glass-Kuder"

9. Which of the following best describes the types of data used by educational researcher?

    a. vast
    b. limited
    c. simplistic

d. fleeting
e. error-free

10. The 1974 Buckley Amendment assured which of the following for research participants:

a. non-English translations
b. payment of minimum wage (at least)
c. confidentiality and anonymity
d. blinding and debriefing
e. alternative service

Answers: 1) d   2) d   3) b   4) a   5) e   6) b   7) c   8) b   9) a   10) c

TYPES OF EDUCATIONAL RESEARCH

OVERVIEW

Recall from the last chapter that once a researcher focuses on a research hypothesis (or research question), there are answers to several questions which determine whether to proceed. If so, another major question—deserving the focus on an entire chapter—must be answered. Which type of research is best suited to test the hypothesis or answer the research question? The research approach is crucial, since it directly affects the type of conclusions which are warranted after the data are analyzed. There are literally hundreds of different types of educational research, but this chapter will not belabor all of the fine distinctions. It will focus on the major research classifications, those which have implications for the researcher's conclusions.

RESEARCH PERSPECTIVES

Educational researchers approach their work from many different perspectives using many different methods. How researchers manage the independent, dependent, and extraneous variables—and even whether they manage them at all—configure to form complex patterns. It is a misleading oversimplification to pigeonhole the vast array and complexity of educational research and discuss only five different types of research. Thus, instead of oversimplifying and compartmentalizing educational research, we will present the most important *distinctions* that occur in educational research. Labelling educational research as a "type" is not as important as understanding the implications of a study's most distinctive features. I believe that describing the distinctive features of educational research, and thus avoiding contrived artificial typologies, captures its complexity and does not place imposing restraints on researchable questions that may be answered by you or by others. This implies that a research question need not be rejected because it does not conform to a standard classification of research.

The six distinctions to be described are:

- Quantitative versus Qualitative
- Descriptive versus Inferential
- True Experimental versus Quasi-experimental
- Causal Comparative versus Correlational
- Single-Subject versus Group
- Teacher versus Traditional

QUANTITATIVE VERSUS QUALITATIVE

This distinction, risking oversimplification, is concerned with "numbers" versus "words." A quantitative study tests specific hypotheses, usually stated in advance, and incorporates measures which can be analyzed statistically. This type of research uses tables or charts to display findings which can (hopefully) generalize beyond the sample to a wider population. The researcher is distant in a sense, and guards against researcher bias and other influences which may skew the results. Qualitative studies, by contrast, often allow a hypothesis to emerge after careful exploration, observation, or interaction. They often use narratives to describe their observations. These stories capture a rich understanding which may not generalize beyond the research setting and unique characteristics of the sample. Researchers often opt for this approach when they believe that the educational outcomes are too complex to reduce to a number. They might argue that pinning numbers on students and applying statistical maneuvers is akin to averaging musical notes. Qualitative researchers are inclined to "paint a portrait" or describe teaching as "orchestration," whereas quantitative researchers are more inclined to "plug in the numbers," simplify the results, and describe effective teaching in terms of percentages, ratings, and students' percentile scores on achievement tests.

Once again risking oversimplification, if you agree with the statement, "Teaching is a science" you are probably more inclined toward quantitative research. By contrast, if you agree with the statement, "Teaching is an art" you are probably more inclined toward qualitative research. A quantitative study of teacher style might describe effective teachers in the following way: They waited an average of six seconds before answering, asked 7.2 questions per five-minute interval, and deviated from the prescribed model only once or twice during each lesson." A qualitative study of teacher style might describe an effective teacher in the following way: She almost appeared to have eyes on the back of her head, all the while maintaining a quick tempo and displaying an artistry not usually seen in beginning teachers.

It is not true that all educational research is either quantitative or qualitative in nature. Increasingly, researchers are incorporating both approaches in a single study, and as a consequence, current educational research is as valuable as it has ever been. Blending the two approaches might, for example, involve a study of the *scientific* basis of the *art* of teaching. Today, a purely quantitative study may be criticized for its lack of attention to qualitative analysis. Examples of quantitative versus qualitative research findings in published reports are presented in Table 5.1.

DESCRIPTIVE VERSUS INFERENTIAL

This distinction is concerned with the generalization of research findings. If data are collected for the single purpose of describing a specific group with no intention of going beyond that group, then the study is considered to be *descriptive*. Examples here would include a study of teachers' attitudes toward the integration of computers in the curriculum at Polytechnic High School or a study of how students in Mr. Alonzo's class use probability to solve everyday problems. Such descriptive studies could be undertaken for very practical reasons, like how to best prepare teachers for computers in their classrooms, or how to best introduce a lesson that builds on students' prior knowledge. Clearly, data from these studies do not test any theory, nor are they used to learn about teachers or students in general. No attempt is made to infer what other teachers might think or what other students might know. This distinction is important because, among other reasons, it determines the type (and even the calculation) of statistics used in the analysis of data.

In contrast to descriptive studies, *inferential* studies attempt to go beyond those people and settings studied by making generalized statements about a larger population—specifically, the one that supplied the people for the sample. Such generalized

TABLE 5.1 Examples of Quantitative and Qualitative Research Findings in the Published Literature

Quantitative findings

"The statistical analysis of data supports the four hypotheses. Subjects instructed in the Model of Generative Teaching comprehended more economics ($p < .0001$)...(Kourilsky & Wittrock, 1992, p. 873)

"The means presented in Table 1 suggest that 4-year-olds in same-sex classrooms were more likely to engage in solitary dramatic play..." (Roopnarine, 1992, p. 765)

"Abecedarian children earned higher average scores than did the Perry Preschool Project subjects: Mean CAT percentile scores ranged between 38 and 41..." (Campbell & Ramey, 1995, p. 764)

"Altogether, readers made 3,003 oral reading errors in the 72 lessons. Table 1 presents error rates by story for students in low, middle, and high groups..." (Chinn, Waggoner, Anderson, Schommer, & Wilkinson, 1993, p. 372)

"The results of the multivariate and univariate analyses of the reading data are summarized in Tables 2–4. In the tables, grade equivalents are shown for each outcome measure...In addition, effect sizes are shown for each experimental-control comparison." (Madden, Slavin, Karweit, Dolan, & Wasik, 1993, p. 132).

Qualitative findings

"Our subsequent interviews show that naive but imaginative accounts persisted in some children even after direct instruction designed to change them. Thus, despite their fanciful qualities, these ideas apparently acquire a 'ring of truth' for those children who are prone to construct and believe in them." (VanSledright & Brophy, 1992, p. 854)

"Our analysis of field notes and videotapes suggested that all students did in fact participate meaningfully in science activities and class discussion..." (Scruggs & Mastropieri, 1994, p. 794).

"Thus, interactions from a transactional perspective seemed to emphasize the processes important for children to learn, rather than particular products or skills." (Neuman, Hagedorn, Celano, & Daly, 1995, p. 814)

"Interview transcripts were coded as categories emerged from the data.... Each classification is explained in depth, and illustrative teacher comments are provided.... The majority of teachers were classified as remediationists..." (Tomchin & Impara, 1992, p. 210, 213–214)

"...the microanalysis revealed five interactive strategies that seemed to be used quite naturally by African-American parent-teachers to assist and extend children's literacy activity." (Neuman & Roskos, 1993, p. 115)

"A third theme that emerged from the interviews was the juxtaposition of two cultures: that of the elementary school and that of the university." (Kagan, Dennis, Igou, Moore, & Sparks, 1993, p. 439)

statements are warranted only to the extent that the sample is representative of the larger population from which it was drawn. These generalized statements are known as *inferences*, hence the name inferential. Political pollsters provide an example of research that is clearly inferential. The pollsters are not so much concerned with the responses of the sample—their primary focus is the population that is represented by the sample. A typical research finding in this case might be that seventy-five percent (+ and – three percent) of parents support the idea of year-round schooling. The plus and minus three illustrates an inference about the population, in the sense that the true percentage in the population of all parents is most probably between seventy-two percent and seventy-eight percent.

Inferential studies are also identified by statements regarding *statistical significance*. For example, assume a researcher wanted to know whether sixth grade girls have a larger vocabulary than sixth grade boys. To test this hunch, 500 boys and 500 girls were randomly selected from a large school district in Los Angeles and were given a test of spelling ability. Let's assume that the girls scored an average of eighty-six percent while boys scored an average of eighty-one percent. The researcher reported that this difference was "statistically significant." This means that there is most likely a true difference in the spelling ability of girls and boys in the population represented by the sample. (The population in this case would be all sixth graders in the Los Angeles School District. These findings may also apply to sixth graders in general across the nation, but this would have to be confirmed by a nationwide sample.)

In summary, the most salient feature of inferential studies is the use of a sample in order to make generalized statements about a larger population. Descriptive studies, by contrast, merely describe a characteristic of a group with no intention of making statements that extend beyond the group being studied. Other examples of descriptive versus inferential studies are presented in Table 5.2.

TRUE EXPERIMENTAL VERSUS QUASI-EXPERIMENTAL

True: Manipulation + Random Assignment

True experimental research is characterized by a *manipulation* (creation) of an independent variable coupled with *random assignment* to groups. Recall from Chapter 2 that a true independent variable is defined in terms of a manipulation with random assignment; hence its use in research qualifies it as true experimental research. This type of research is strongest for ferreting out cause-and-effect relationships, and for this reason experimental research is the first choice—if practical—when the research question concerns relationships. For example, let's assume, once again, that a researcher wanted to

TABLE 5.2 Examples of Descriptive and Inferential Research

Descriptive

A researcher interviews all recent graduates of a teacher education program to learn more about their perceptions of program quality.

A researcher develops a new test of computer literacy and administers it to ninth graders in one school district to determine their level of background knowledge.

A researcher measures the school climate at Evergreen High and makes recommendations for improving teachers' morale.

A researcher in special education observes Cindy for one week in an attempt to understand her reading difficulties.

Inferential

A researcher samples 1300 adults to learn more about the nation's attitudes toward public education.

A researcher samples one-hundred boys and one-hundred girls and tests them to learn about gender differences in emotional intelligence in the population

A researcher samples sixty schools in the state for three years to see whether the student absenteeism rate has significantly shifted over time.

A researcher samples one-hundred top scoring high school students on the Advanced Placement tests to learn more about the study habits of high achievers in general.

determine whether learning how to spell with the use of a computer or by handwriting resulted in higher spelling achievement. To this end, she sampled 120 third-graders and randomly assigned them to one of two created groups: a computer group or a handwriting group. The computer group learned and practiced the spelling of words with a computer three times a week for ten weeks. The handwriting group learned and practiced the same words for the same amount of time. Then both groups were tested on the same sample of words chosen from the pool of words that were practiced during the ten weeks. Let's pretend the results revealed the handwriting group scored significantly higher than the computer group. Assuming that all extraneous variables were controlled and that there existed no alternative hypotheses (rival explanations), this researcher would be entitled to conclude that learning to spell via handwriting results in higher spelling achievement (at least among students similar to those in this study). This type of cause-and-effect interpretation is possible only because the research is truly experimental; the independent variable (computer versus handwriting) was manipulated (groups were created by the researcher) and subjects were assigned randomly to groups.

Consider another example. A researcher suspects that excessive fat in a diet is linked to lowered cognitive functioning. As a test of this idea, 300 high school students are randomly assigned to one of three diet groups: high fat, low fat, and control. Students in the high fat group are required to eat a balanced diet consisting of a minimum of one hundred grams of fat per day. Students in the low fat group are required to eat a balanced diet of a maximum of ten grams of fat per day. Control students function as a type of baseline by eating what they normally eat. The prescribed diets are followed for six months before several tests of cognitive functioning are collected (these include simple measures of reaction time in an associative learning task to more complex tasks such as solving logic problems). After tabulating the results, the researcher finds enhanced performance across the board for the low fat group (relative to the controls) and lowered performance for the high fat group (relative to the controls).

The study described above qualifies as a true experiment because an independent variable was *manipulated* (the investigator created the three conditions) and students were *randomly* assigned to the three conditions. If the researcher were certain that extraneous influences were neutralized and there were no competing alternative explanations, then the researcher is entitled to a causal interpretation. In this case, a reasonable interpretation of the data might be that fat in the diet affects our ability to remember, think, and reason.

Group comparability formed by random assignment even applies to variables that have not yet been discovered. Imagine randomizing two groups right now, then peer into your crystal ball to discover that Factor Q, discovered in the year 2020, is believed to be the most important determinant of school success. This doesn't even present a problem today, because these two random groups would have roughly equivalent levels of Factor Q.

Quasi: Manipulation Without Random Assignment

Quasi-experiments are so named because they resemble experiments to some degree (*quasi* in this sense means "somewhat"). They employ some type of manipulation, but a critical feature, however, is lacking: *random assignment*. Recall from Chapter 2 that a quasi independent variable lacks random assignment to manipulated conditions, hence studies that use quasi independent variables are named quasi-experiments. Because of this limitation, quasi-experiments are not especially strong with regard to uncovering cause-and-effect relationships. For example, a researcher wanted to learn about the achievement effects of year-round schooling. Many schools were contacted to learn whether they would be interested in participating in the study; ten schools having the resources and commitment needed to fairly answer this research question were found. As a comparison, ten other schools were selected to function as a control group. Note that the schools were not assigned randomly to the two groups. Follow-up testing revealed that the year-round schools achieved significantly higher than the control (nine-month) schools. The researcher must carefully temper the interpretation of these data because schools comprising the two groups may have been different from the start—perhaps the year-round schools would have achieved higher *without* the year-round intervention. Recall that these schools were unique in the sense that they were able to participate in the first place. Might some other factor co-occur with the year-round calendar? Might they have better facilities, teachers with higher morale, or different student populations?

It is important to remember that without random assignment, one can never assume that two or more groups are comparable. This problem could be offset, however, if the control schools were *matched,* or equated, with the year-round schools. Matched schools would be chosen for their similarity based on one or more characteristics, such as facilities, teacher morale, student backgrounds, and so forth. Matching falls short of randomization, however, since there always exists the possibility of a difference on a critical, unmatched variable—one that "explains away" the presumed effects. (There is another type of matching, a statistical maneuver used in the analysis of data called the *analysis of covariance,* that can also offset some of the problems due to lack of randomization.) When individual students cannot be assigned randomly, as is frequently the case, researchers often invoke alternative types of randomization. They may, for example, randomly select entire classrooms to receive a treatment while others are reserved as controls. Simply, the power of random assignment, the cornerstone of true experiments, lies in its ability to equate groups.

Consider another example of a quasi-experiment, a *time series design*. As is true with all quasi-experiments, a time series study uses an intervention or treatment without random assignment. With this design, a group is observed (or some measure collected) over a period of time followed by an intervention. Observation or measurement continues, and a treatment effect is presumed if the post-treatment observations differ significantly from the pre-treatment observations. For example, assume that a researcher tracked a school's student absenteeism rate daily for sixty days and found a fairly steady rate of .15 over this time period. Next, the researcher implemented an automatic computer-controlled home telephone calling device. The rate of absenteeism was then tracked for sixty days after the installation of the new system. The researcher observed a steadily decreasing rate which appeared to level off at about .06 and concluded that the new system of home calling was responsible for the decline. Notice that researchers who use quasi-experimental designs are intent on making cause-and-effect claims (they often conclude that their treatment or intervention resulted in a change in the trend). Such cause-and-effect claims, however, are more risky without the use of a randomized control group. How can the researcher be certain that the computer calling system, not some other factor, was responsible for the effect? Maybe the calling system was put into effect in early February, and absenteeism might have improved without any intervention during March because of better weather. Or possibly a new principal was hired in February, one that vowed to lower absenteeism. Or maybe new computers were introduced in the school in February, enhancing student interest, and consequently lowering absenteeism. Or maybe the pre-intervention rate of .15 in the preceding months was unusually high due to a flu epidemic, so the improved rate of .06 represented a return to normal during February and March (hence there was no treatment effect at all). The point is that other interpretations are plausible without a randomized comparison group, one that would be affected similarly by weather, flu, new policies, new computers, and the like. Ideally, one would also want to track a randomized control group within the same school to be used as a basis for comparison (in other words, redesign the quasi-experiment into a true experiment).

Educational research that is quasi-experimental is not flawed simply because it is quasi-experimental, for it may be that techniques such as group or case-by-case *matching* successfully produced comparable groups. Group matching involves selecting a comparison *group* that is similar on average to a treatment group on the matched variables; case-by-case matching involves repeatedly selecting a comparison *subject* who is similar to a treatment subject on each of the matched variables. (More will be said about matching in Chapters 8 and 9.) It may be that nonrandom groups are, for all practical purposes, essentially similar and do function as good controls in the same way as randomized groups. It is unwarranted to automatically assume, however, that they are similar. Quasi-experimental research is common in education, and good quasi-experimental research is marked by the use of clever control procedures to circumvent some of the problems associated with lack of randomization. Several common applications of true experiments and quasi-experiments are shown in Table 5.3.

CAUSAL COMPARATIVE VERSUS CORRELATIONAL

Causal comparative and correlational research both stand in stark contrast to true experimental and quasi-experimental research. As we have seen, experimental research involves some type of manipulation or intervention in order to reliably make cause-and-effect statements. Causal comparative and correlational research involve *no intervention, manipulation, or random assignment* of any sort and, consequently, pose challenges for researchers intent on discovering cause-and-effect relationships. These research approaches involve the examination of relationships that exist naturally. Let's first examine causal comparative research.

Causal Comparative Research

Group Classifications. A researcher might explore the relationship between the amount of television watching and academic achievement in a causal comparative study. Stu-

---

TABLE 5.3 Examples of True and Quasi-Experimental Research

True

A researcher randomly assigns one-hundred students to either an experimental group (exercise four times a week) or a control group (no exercise) and after six months tests their memory spans.

A researcher pretests students' ability to reason with logic and then randomly assigns one-hundred to a group that receives a daily dose of ginseng or a control group which receives placebo. They are all posttested six months later.

A researcher measures the baseline level of hyperactivity in one-hundred hyperactive third graders. The two highest (one pair) are randomly assigned to either an experimental group (which receives a drug hypothesized to reduce hyperactivity) or to a control group (which receives a placebo). The next pair is similarly assigned; likewise, until the pair with the lowest level of hyperactivity is randomly assigned. The researcher collects hyperactivity measures after three months.

Quasi-

A researcher implements year-round schooling in one district and finds a similar one to serve as a control. After three years, students' average achievement scores are compared.

A researcher finds fifty seven-year-old identical twins who are all tested in their mathematical reasoning aptitude. One member of each pair volunteers to have piano lessons weekly for two years (the other member does not). Eight years later, all twins are then tested in their math ability.

A researcher measures the dropout rate in a large urban school district for four years before implementing a mentoring program in the district. The dropout rate is monitored for another four years.

dents might be classified into one of four groups (zero to five hours per week, six to fifteen hours per week, sixteen to twenty-five hours per week, and twenty-six or more hours per week). Then academic achievement scores would be collected and compared across the four classifications. Notice that students were *classified* (not manipulated) in accordance with their television habits; they were not assigned randomly to watch a prescribed number of hours per week. This classification procedure is the hallmark of causal comparative research, and as such involves studying "the world the way it is." Causal comparative research might be better renamed "group classification" research.

Another example of this approach would involve exploring the relationship between early music lessons and later math achievement. Two groups of sixth-grade children might be formed: those who had piano lessons prior to age seven and those who did not. Then the math achievement would be compared between the two groups. There is no intervention here; no random assignment to music conditions. This type of causal comparative study is more like a natural experiment. Even if the children who had piano lessons were higher achievers in math, the explanation could be related to some other extraneous factor, for example, socioeconomic status (wealthier families could afford music lessons *and* Math Camp).

Many issues in educational research can only be studied in this passive (non-experimental) manner because to do so in any other way would be impractical or unethical. The influence of divorce on children's achievement, interests, and aspirations could only be studied with the causal comparative method. (Can you imagine assigning parents randomly to the "bitter divorce group"? Of course not.) Another example of causal comparative research might be the link between style of parenting and outcomes such as academic achievement, self-esteem, and disruptive behavior. In this case, parents would be classified (not assigned) into one of several groups based on their parenting style. Then measures of achievement and self-esteem would be compared across the parenting styles.

Tempered Conclusions.   In the above examples concerning television, music, divorce, and parenting it is important to realize that researchers must temper their interpretations about cause and effect. If frequent television watching is associated with lower achievement, one would not know whether television was responsible for the decline in achievement; possibly, the low achievement was a consequence of lower scholastic ability, which led to a lack of interest in school, and more television watching to fill the void left by that lack of interest (not doing homework and the like). Similarly, if children of divorced parents have more behavior problems at school, one would not know what caused what (or even whether one caused the other). Maybe the behavior problems were a result of the divorce; maybe the divorce was the result of behavior problems. Quite possibly, both the divorce and behavior problems were a consequence of some other cause entirely (like socioeconomic factors). Furthermore, if an authoritarian style of parenting is associated with more disruptive behavior at school, could it not be the case that children who are disruptive to begin with might foster a specific type of authoritarian parenting? This problem is akin to the old chicken and egg problem—which comes first?

Consider another hypothetical study aimed at comparing the IQs of adolescents who were breast fed versus bottle fed as infants. This would qualify as a causal comparative study because groups were formed on the basis of some pre-existing attribute (they could not be randomly assigned, and, in a sense, the adolescents assigned themselves). Let's presume that the IQs of breast-fed infants were significantly higher than their bottle-fed counterparts. It can be concluded, quite correctly, that there exists a relationship between type of feeding and IQ measures. It may not be warranted to conclude that breast feeding *results* in higher IQs because of the inherent limitations imposed by causal comparative research. This is because breast-feeding mothers may be different in other important ways. For example, breast-feeding mothers might be older with higher socioeconomic status. They might be healthier, less likely to have consumed alcohol while pregnant, less likely to live in homes with lead paint (assuming this is linked to socioeconomic status), or more likely to expose their pre-school children to music. All of the these reasons, plus hundreds more, could easily be the causal mechanism underlying the type-of-feeding and IQ connection.

Causal comparative studies are common in other fields, and their interpretations are also fraught with difficulties. Consider a hypothetical finding that vegetarians live longer than meat eaters. Is this longevity the result of diet? We simply would not know because the vegetarians may also exercise more, and this exercise might be the direct cause of longer lives. Or maybe the vegetarians also smoked less, and the smoking difference is the real cause of longevity effect. If this is true, then smokers who become vegetarians would not increase their longevity in any way. (I am reminded of early reports that premature male baldness is linked to heart attacks among the middle aged. If one were balding, would he have hair transplants to ward off heart attacks?)

Consider one more example. Let's assume that it is discovered that those who have headaches also have high levels of muscle tension in their neck and shoulders. Would you interpret this to mean that muscle tension in the neck and shoulders causes headaches? Isn't it just as likely that headaches lead to muscle tension in response to pain? Or might a third factor, like pollen, cause both the headache and the "achy all over feeling" that triggers muscle tension? Clearly, causal comparative studies, despite the name, are not as well suited to study cause and effect as are experimental studies.

Search For Causes.   Causal comparative studies are valuable, though, because they do uncover relationships which then could be studied with different, preferably experimental, methods to learn more about the basis (cause) of the relationship. If experimental methods are not possible (e.g., studying the influence of divorce on children) or impractical (e.g., studying the effects of different styles of parenting), then clever researchers who use causal comparative methods must rely on other techniques to help illuminate uncovered relationships. One technique is the investigation of *time sequence*. For example, if it is found that divorce is related to misbehavior at school, a time sequence could differentiate the divorce-causes-misbehavior interpretation from the misbehavior-causes-divorce interpretation. Since the cause of an effect must occur first, the divorce should *precede* the misbehavior if it is the causal mechanism. But if divorce is the effect of a misbehavior cause, then the misbehavior should come first. The reality, of course, is certainly not that simple. Both divorce and behavior problems at school may themselves be the complex effects of many other complex causes.

Causal comparative researchers use other strategies to infer cause. One might be called the method of *common prior antecedents*. This method involves focusing on a presumed effect, say, skill at teaching. After groups of highly skilled and less skilled teachers have been identified, one begins a systematic search for prior differences that distinguish the two groups. For example, one might find no differences between the two groups based on college GPA, highest degree (bachelors versus masters), educational philosophy, whether or not they have children in their own family, and many other prior variables. By contrast, it might be found that the highly skilled teachers regularly enrolled in continuing education courses and attended workshops, whereas the less skilled teachers did neither. If such dramatic differences did exist (and they seem to make sense), then one would have some degree of assurance that the variable on which the two groups differ (continuing education) is probably related in some causal way to the difference which formed the basis of the two groups in the first place (more versus less skilled teachers). One alternative hypothesis is that skilled teachers are simply born that way. And they are also more interested in education issues because of their skills, and their continuing education merely reflects that interest. Establishing cause is clearly not all-or-none. It is, so to speak, more-or-less, and so it is with different approaches to research: some approaches are better suited for establishing cause. A well designed and executed causal comparative study, to be sure, may establish stronger causal connections than a weak experiment. Also, it makes little sense to establish *the* cause, as if there were one and only. It seems reasonable to conclude that most relationships in the teaching and learning process are complex; an experiment could shed light on one aspect of a multi-faceted causal chain and a causal comparative study could illuminate another facet.

Correlational Research

Correlational research is also a type of non-intervention research, one that measures the world the way it is in search of relationships. But correlational studies differ from causal comparative ones in several ways. Let's examine these more closely.

Individual Differences.   The most salient difference between causal comparative and correlational research is whether or not subjects are classified into groups (causal comparative) or measured as individuals (correlational). Consider a typical correlational study, one examining the relationship between television watching and scholastic achievement. (Recall that the same relationship was assessed earlier as an example of a causal comparative study.) Assume a sample of one hundred students was available for this study. Each one would be measured and scaled on a continuum revealing the number of hours per week (on average) spent watching television. All subjects would also be measured on a scale designed to assess scholastic achievement. Finally, a statistical maneuver would be applied to the data and would reveal the extent to which the two variables are related. (We will say more about this statistic, called the correlation coefficient or r, in Chapter 7.) Notice that no groups were formed with the correlational approach; the individual scores were not clumped in any way. They were analyzed statistically as individuals.

Correlational researchers are keenly interested in the vast array of people differences that need explanation, such as the differences in intelligence, personality, home environments, teaching styles, learning styles, leadership styles, or temperaments, to name just a few. Differences in constructs like these cry out for explanations. Consider the complex variation in "happiness," a focus of correlational researchers. (Psychologists who study individual differences via correlations are often called "differential psychologists.") In order to explain differences in people's levels of happiness, one might begin by determining what other differences happiness is correlated (and *un*-correlated) with. Correlational researchers, such as psychologists David Lykken and Auke Tellegen of the University of Minnesota, are finding that it is related to individual differences in optimism but apparently *not* correlated with logical factors such as wealth, education, family, job status, or professional achievement. Happiness is apparently best understood as another trait, probably genetically based (in part), whose level is predetermined seemingly randomly and relatively immune to the vicissitudes of daily life. Like a biological set point that determines weight, people tend to hover around a constant happiness level that may only temporarily shift (for maybe three to six months at most) after winning lotteries or losing loved ones. This theory suggests that someone with many problems may be happier than someone who "has it all." The point being that individual differences need explaining, and they are best explained by determining what other differences they are correlated with. These correlational researchers welcome differences, and they design their measuring instruments to be sensitive to very small differences. This is because in a correlational study, greater variation (a larger spread in scores) is more likely to correlate with other measured differences. Simply, if you want to show that happiness is correlated with optimism, you want the full range of people, happy and sad, optimistic and pessimistic, and those in the middle.

Correlation Is Not Causation.   Virtually all of the cautionary statements made about causal comparative research with regard to cause and effect are equally applicable and important with correlational research. When a correlation is found between the amount of sugar consumed by first graders and their level of hyperactivity, it might be tempting to conclude that sugar causes hyperactivity. This type of reasoning is flawed because *associations do not prove cause*. The sugar and hyperactivity correlation could be explained by some other causal mechanism, for example, high sugar consumption itself might be linked to a poor diet, and a lack of Vitamin D (as you might find in poor diets) might be the real trigger for hyperactivity. If so, then simply reducing sugar by itself would have no affect on hyperactivity. Consider reports from Sweden that reveal a correlation between the number of babies born and the population of storks around the calendar year. We would not conclude that storks cause babies! (The causal mechanism is likely related to climate.) Or consider a correlation between the speed of test taking and scores on a test (let's pretend that faster speed is associated with higher scores). Does this correlation suggest that speed causes better performance? If so, then simply encouraging the lower scorers to go faster should raise their scores. (This is unlikely.) Or the correlation between foot size and spelling ability among elementary school children. One does not cause the other; development explains both (older children have bigger feet and they are better spellers). Finally, what about the correlation between the number of churches and the number of liquor stores in a sampling of American cities? Does church drive you to drink? Hardly. The causal mechanism is simply city size—larger cities have more churches and more liquor stores as a function of population.

Summary

Causal comparative research is differentiated from correlational research because subjects are *grouped* on the basis of a shared or common characteristic (e.g., whether they had early training in music). The classification (not random assignment) into groups and their comparison on some other measure (e.g, math aptitude) are the defining characteristics of causal comparative research. They are focused on the effects or causes of these "clumped" group differences. They do not ignore individual differences, to be sure, but their research questions are directed at cause-and-effect relationships and answered with group contrasts (hence the name "causal comparative"). The effects of authoritarian versus permissive styles of parenting, for example, would be answered by contrasting groups of children with parents of both styles while searching for influences on behavior, occupational aspirations, self-esteem, or whatever the researchers' hunches might be. Both causal comparative and correlational research reveal associations, and because of the non-manipulated nature of their variables, cannot conclusively establish cause and effect. Cause-and-effect relationships are best discovered with experimental research.

Correlational research, by contrast, measures individual differences on two or more variables, and describes their linkage with a statistical summary. Correlational researchers are often interested in the full range of people's differences and their explanations. They may seek to explain variation in occupational aspirations, for example, by correlating it with measures of tolerance to frustration or even height. Their focus is the explanation of human variation; they are less interested in isolating the cause or the effect. Examples of causal comparative versus correlational research are shown in Table 5.4.

SINGLE-SUBJECT VERSUS GROUP

In some fields of education, such as special education, researchers often use designs that require a single subject (or a small group). The goal of single-subject research is to determine if interventions designed to change some aspect of behavior are effective (at least for this single individual). Single-subject research designs achieve their control through a system that uses the individual as their own control if a control group is not available. For example, let's assume that Sam shows clear signs of hyperactivity,

TABLE 5.4　Examples of Causal Comparative and Correlational Research

---

Causal comparative

A researcher measured the mathematical reasoning ability of young children who had enrolled in Montessori schools and compared the scores with a group a similar children who had not been to Montessori schools.

A researcher measured the frequency of students' misbehavior at schools which use corporal punishment and compared that to schools which did not use corporal punishment.

A researcher compared the high school dropout rate between students who had been retained (held back) in elementary school versus similar students who had not been retained.

A researcher formed three groups of preschoolers—those who never watched Sesame Street, those who watched it sometimes, and those who watched it frequently—and then compared the three groups on a reading readiness test.

Correlational

A researcher measured students' self-esteem and linked these scores to ratings of their physical attractiveness.

A researcher measured how quickly students complete a test to see if their speed was associated with test scores.

A researcher investigated the relationship between age and reaction time in a simple task (push the left button to a red light, the right button to a green light).

A researcher studied a group of twenty-year-olds by examining the association between height and the age (in weeks) when they first began walking.

---

and his teacher wants to experiment in an attempt to find the best strategy (at least for Sam) for bringing about behavior that is more conducive to learning. The teacher may record the frequency of hyperactivity by sampling behavior every hour (several five-minute blocks could be randomly chosen each hour). This systematic observation functions as a baseline against which treatments may be compared. Next, the teacher introduces a system for praising instances of behavior judged to be counter-hyperactive. Praise may continue for a period of time while careful observations of hyperactivity are recorded. If hyperactive behavior does decline during the praise sessions, then this is taken as evidence that the treatment is effective. Greater support for its effectiveness would be found if hyperactivity increased when the treatment (praise) was withdrawn (this is usually called a *return to baseline*). Furthermore, when the treatment is reinstated, one would expect to find a concomitant reduction in hyperactivity. These return-to-baseline and reinstated-treatment phases may continue until the evidence for the treatment's effectiveness is so strong that a return to baseline is no longer needed as evidence.

The design described above is relatively simple, but this is not representative of all single-subject designs. Some are very sophisticated indeed, and these will be described in Chapter 9. Single-subject research, as you may suspect, is not appropriate when a researcher intends to make widely generalized statements about the relative effectiveness of educational interventions.

Group research in education is far more common than single-subject research, since many researchers want to test broadly generalizable theories about school learning. Group research designs, as we will see in Chapters 9 and 10, appear in many different configurations, all intended to produce meaningful interpretations of the data that have been gathered according to a specific plan (design). The number of subjects are required to form a group is discussed in Chapter 6.

To summarize this distinction, a finding from a single-subject research design might be "Paul's social interactions increased, compared to baseline, when these behaviors were reinforced with tokens." By contrast, a group research finding might be "The thirty classes that were taught rules for sharing had fewer conflicts than the thirty control classes." Other examples of single-subject versus group studies are shown in Table 5.5.

TEACHER VERSUS TRADITIONAL

Teacher research is often described as self-reflective inquiry and, as such, refers to classroom teachers who study their own practice of teaching. (Recall from Chapter 3 that this general concept was referred to as *action research*. Teacher research can be viewed as a type of action research.) Teachers who favor this approach to research understand the complex nature of the teaching and learning process in the classroom, but at the same time, are intent on studying their professional craft in a personalized, intimate, empowering way. Teacher research is an attitude. Such teachers often question the value of outside experts who collect data without any personal experience, then issue directives to the passive implementers (lowly teachers) about the best pedagogical methods. Teacher research assumes that teachers are reflective practitioners who have an obligation to study their own work, in spite of the institutional bureaucracy that may appear to deny teachers some of their intellectual and professional rights. Teacher-researchers are more likely to use their field notes, work samples, or journals instead of standardized test scores. They may use shared teacher stories and metaphors as a way of understanding classrooms.

Some may call teacher research a "movement," and it is clearly gaining momentum, most likely because it recognizes that "teaching belongs to teachers, and that, as experts about their own practice, teachers are the ones most able to understand and refine their work" (Oberg & McCutcheon, 1987). It would be ill-advised to think of

TABLE 5.5   Examples of Single-Subject and Group Studies

Single-Subject

Jim's frequency of stuttering was observed for one week, followed by weekly observations during which classical music was played quietly in the background. Observations were then made for one week with no music in the background; finally, music was reinstated for one week before final observations.

Sam and Ted were very aggressive fifth graders who were placed on special diets and observed intensely for six one-week sessions to determine if their diet was related to their behavior. The design was as follows, where D = diet and C = control.

	Week 1	2	3	4	5	6
Sam	C	D	C	D	C	D
Ted	D	C	D	C	D	C

Group

200 low-achieving third graders were tutored for one hour after school by high school volunteers. After six months, their achievement was compared to a random control group which did not receive training.

Three groups of 500 high school seniors—first born, second born, and later born—were tested to determine their level of occupational aspiration.

TABLE 5.6   Examples of Teacher Research and Traditional Research

Teacher

Mrs. Goetz wondered whether cooperative learning strategies would help students learn about division using fractions. She arranged for her third period math class to complete the exercise sheets while working together in groups of four to five. She compared their final test scores with her fourth period control group which worked on the exercises individually. Because the cooperative group did so well, she took "action" and used cooperative learning strategies in her other math classes.

Upon reflection, Mr. Shepherd realized that seventh graders would learn German faster if only German (no English) were spoken in his classes after the midterm. He tried this for a semester and compared students' test scores against the scores in his classes the previous semester. The results favored the German-only method, the method he now uses.

Traditional

In order to test the effectiveness of computer-assisted instruction in physics (developed from generative models of learning), sixty schools were selected to use the courseware for one year. A randomized control group of sixty schools which used traditional "talk-and-chalk" methods was used as a comparison.

In a multi-site longitudinal study of the effects of early childhood education, 200 "at-risk" preschoolers participated in a special intervention program from the ages of one to four. They were tracked for ten years and assessed yearly on a battery of different measures. A control group not receiving any intervention was also tracked and measured as a comparison.

this approach to research as substandard. Newer standards for the validity of classroom research (e.g., Eisenhart and Borko, 1993) are in fact more inclusive than conventional ones and in many ways create a more level playing field. It offers an alternative method for gaining knowledge and reforming our schools, and should not be perceived as merely a small-scale version of traditional research.

Traditional research, by contrast, is far more formal. Traditional researchers strive toward theory building and generalized knowledge. It is "colder" in the sense that data–gathering is detached, standardized, and relatively free from bias. Traditional research usually builds on prior research, as revealed by a review of the literature, and findings are more remote, often hidden in journals and couched in statistical terms. Standardized test scores may be transformed in arcane ways. Critics say that the academic authors writing such reports may be promoted to full professors within their institutions, but classrooms may be left in the dark. Examples of teacher research and traditional research appear in Table 5.6.

It is probably not too productive to think in either–or terms, as the above six dichotomies might suggest. (These six dichotomies functioned to organize the chapter, but they may break down somewhat when applied to published research.) I believe that the most valuable educational research is a blend, as needed, across these distinctions to increase our understanding of the teaching and learning process in ways that favorably affect individual classrooms.

CHAPTER SUMMARY

The research hypothesis is tested within the context of prior research (the literature) in an area using many different approaches. These alternative forms of educational research can be differentiated in terms of *quantitative* orientation (analyzed with numbers) or *qualitative* orientation (analyzed with words). They can *describe* characteristics within the sample, or use the sample in order to make *inferences* about a larger population. They may use *experimental* or cause-and-effect methods (manipulation, or creation, of an independent variable with the use of random assignment) or *quasi-experimental* methods (a manipulated intervention without random assignment). Furthermore, research may involve comparing groups that already differ (e.g., children with single versus dual parents) with the hope of learning about cause and effect, as in *causal comparative* research; it may also involve measuring individual characteristics and statistically linking them to other measures with the hope of discovering and explaining relationships, as in *correlational research*. Researchers may also study *single cases* or (more typically) larger *groups*. Finally, teachers may conduct "action" research for the purpose of learning more about their practice, as in *teacher research*; others may carry out more formal research, often guided by theory with the intent of generalizing to a larger population, as in *traditional research*.

This chapter includes two guided tours; both illustrate the wide variation in approaches to educational research.

GUIDED TOUR #1

Let's turn our attention now to a guided tour of published educational research. This will help solidify important terms and concepts described in this chapter.

Brief Reports

CONTINUED HIGH OR REDUCED INTERPARENTAL CONFLICT FOLLOWING DIVORCE: RELATION TO YOUNG ADOLESCENT ADJUSTMENT

Nicholas Long

University of Kansas Medical Center

Elisa Slater

University of Maryland School of Medicine

Rex Forehand and Robert Fauber

University of Georgia

Three groups of young adolescent subjects were compared on several measures of adjustment in the school

This research was supported, in part, by the William T. Grant Foundation and by the University of Georgia's Institute for Behavioral Research.

Correspondence concerning this article should be addressed to Nicholas Long, who is now at the Department of Pediatrics, Slot 512, University of Arkansas for Medical Sciences, 800 Marshall Street, Little Rock, Arkansas 72202.

setting. The three groups or subjects included (a) a group from recently divorced families in which high levels of interparental conflict prior to parental separation and after the divorce had been reported, (b) a group from recently divorced families in which high levels of interparental conflict prior to parental separation but low levels after the divorce had been reported, and (c) a comparison group from intact families. Adolescents from the first group were found to be functioning at a lower level than those from the other two groups.

Although most studies suggest that parental divorce is associated with child problems, some studies have reported that parental divorce has no effect or even a positive effect on child adjustment (see the review by Atkeson, Forehand, & Rickard, 1982). [1] Conflicting findings in this area may result because the adjustment of children to parental divorce is dependent on the numerous mediating variables for which most studies have not controlled (Long & Forehand, 1987). Several investigators believe that the most important mediating variable associated with divorce and child adjustment is interparental conflict (Atkeson et al., 1982; Emery, 1982; Lupenitz, 1979). Recent empirical studies support the notion that interparental conflict is an important mediating variable (Block, Block, & Gjerde, 1986; Long, Forehand, Fauber, & Brody, 1987). However, it is not known how changes in interparental conflict after divorce relate to child adjustment. This issue must be studied empirically if mental health professionals are to address questions such as, should parents who are unhappy and engage in frequent conflict divorce, or should they remain married "for the sake of the children?" The present study examined the relation or continued high interparental conflict following divorce and reduced interparental conflict following

[1] *It is clear from this chapter that "conflicting findings" in any area of research may be due, in part, to the many different types of educational research that may be used to answer a research question. The researchers' use of the term* mediating variable *is closely related to* extraneous variable *described in Chapter 2. Some types of research may be able to control for these mediating, or extraneous, variables while other types may not. Experiments, for example, are able to control for mediating variables through the mechanism of random assignment. Some studies, of course, cannot use random assignment because it is not possible, as randomly assigning students to a divorce group or a control group would not work for this study. Other types of research may single out a mediating variable statistically (as in a correlational study), build it into the design (as in causal comparative research, illustrated by this study), or maybe even describe it in a story or metaphor (as in a qualitative study).*

divorce with the adjustment of young adolescents. Measures were collected from the school setting in the areas of: (a) academic achievement, (b) externalizing problems, and (c) internalizing problems in order to obtain an independent assessment of adolescent functioning.

Method

Subjects

Thirty-five White adolescents, their mothers, and their social studies teachers participated in this study as part of a larger project. The adolescents ranged in age from 11 years and 3 months to 15 years and 3 months (M = 13 years, 4 months). Twenty-three of the subjects were from recently divorced families (biological parents divorced within the last 12 months), and the remaining 12 subjects were from intact families (biological parents still married). The average time since parental divorce was 6.6 months, and the average time since parental separation was 22.1 months. All of the adolescent subjects from divorced families were in the custody of their mothers. Divorced families were not recruited for the project if either parent had remarried.

Subjects were recruited for the larger project through notices posted in local communities, fliers distributed at public schools, advertisements placed in local newspapers, and public service announcements broadcast on local radio stations. In addition, recently divorced parents of young adolescents were identified through local courthouse records and contacted by mail or by telephone. Participants were told that the project was an investigation of parent–adolescent adjustment.

Design

From a sample or 55 recently divorced families who were participating in a larger project, 23 adolescents were selected based on their mothers' reports of preseparation and post-

[2] *The design section helps us classify the study as a causal comparative type of research. The distinguishing feature of causal comparative research is the classification of subjects into groups based on some attribute, and then a search for the causes or consequences of differences across the groups. In this causal comparative study, the concern was focused on the consequences of divorce (especially with continuing conflict) on the adjustment of young adolescents. (Investigating the causes of divorce is a completely different study.)*

A close cousin to causal comparative research is correlational research. Correlational research, however, does not study group contrasts. It examines linkages between variables (reflecting pre-existing attributes) using statistical techniques that retain subjects' scores at the

divorce interparental conflict. The adolescents selected did not differ significantly from the larger group in family socioeconomic status (SES) or adolescent age. [2] Adolescents were eligible for inclusion in the study if their mother reported high interparental conflict both before separation and after the divorce or if their mother reported high interparental conflict before separation but low conflict after the divorce. Interparental conflict prior to parental separation and after the divorce was assessed using the Divorce Conflict Measure (DCM), which was developed for this study. Eleven adolescents (9 boys, 2 girls) met the criteria for the continued high conflict group (DCM ratings of 4 or 5 before separation and after divorce), whereas 12 adolescents (11 boys, 1 girl) met the criteria for the reduced conflict group (DCM ratings or 4 or 5 before separation and of 1 or 2 after divorce). [3] A matched comparison group of 12 adolescents (11 boys, 1 girl) from intact families was selected from a pool of 69 intact families who were participating in the larger project. The adolescents from intact families were matched to the adolescents from divorced families on adolescent age, adolescent sex, and family SES. The SES of each family was determined using Myers and Bean's (1968) two-factor index of social position.

Measures

O'Leary-Porter Scale (OPS). The OPS is a parent-completed scale that assesses the frequency of overt parental conflict that occurs in the child's presence (Porter & O'Leary, 1980). [4] Scores can range from 0 to 40, with high scores indicating low levels of interparental conflict.

Divorce Conflict Measure (DCM). The DCM was developed for the present study to obtain a rating of the change in interparental conflict following divorce. The OPS could not be used for this purpose because it was designed solely to assess the current level of interparental conflict. Divorced mothers

individual level (no groupings). For example, these researchers could have investigated the correlational link between conflict scores and adjustment scores. To do this, each student would be scored (or "scaled") on the level of reduced conflict between their divorced parents, say, on a score of one to twenty (from greatly reduced to hardly reduced at all). The adjustment scores would then be correlated with conflict reduction scores to see whether a connection exists between them. If they are related, say, better adjustment is linked to less conflict, then the researcher (as in causal comparative studies) is still uncertain about the basis of the relationship. This is because less conflict could cause better adjustment, better adjustment could cause less conflict, or some third variable, like poverty level, could cause both poor adjustment and greater conflict.

[3] *Notice the description of the matched "intact" group in this study. This is closely akin to a control group as used in experimental research. This group is necessary for use as a type of baseline comparison since the researchers wanted to know whether the adjustment of children from divorced families was negatively affected in relation to a nondivorced or intact family. These researchers used matching as a method to equate the groups so that they were not comparing apples and oranges. Only when the intact and divorced groups are considered comparable, except for the obvious intact/divorce dimension, can the researchers be comfortable concluding that the differences in adjustment are due to the divorce. Notice that they matched the groups on the basis of age, sex, and family socioeconomic status (SES), or the "Big Three" in educational research. These are common matching variables because they tend to create comparability better than any other set of three variables. (Knowing a person's age, sex, and SES probably tells you more about a person than any other three variables.) Matching tries to accomplish in causal comparative studies what random assignment does so well in true experimental studies. Matching is described further in Chapter 8 and 9.*

[4] *Causal comparative studies, naturally, have to confront head-on the challenges associated with the operational definitions of constructs. In fact, they often have greater challenges if the basis of the group classification itself is related to a construct, as in this study. Recall that "conflict" was a primary concern of these researchers, and it was operationally defined by scores on the O'Leary-Porter Scale and the Divorce Conflict Measure, specifically designed for this study. Incidentally, do you see how the construct of adjustment was operationally defined? The anxiety-withdrawal scores and the conduct disorder scores (from the Revised Behavior Problem Checklist) were used as measures of "internalizing" and "externalizing" problems, respectively.*

retrospectively rated the frequency of interparental conflict for the 6 months prior to parental separation and for the period (range = 1–12 months) since the divorce. Ratings were made on 5-point Likert-type scale with end points labeled *rarely* (1) and *frequently* (5).

To assess the concurrent validity of the DCM, a Pearson product-moment correlation between maternal ratings of post-divorce interparental conflict on the DCM and maternal scores on the OPS was calculated. Maternal reports (N = 23) on these two measures were significantly correlated, $r(21) = -.70$, $p < .001$.

Revised Behavior Problem Checklist (RBPC).   This measure consists of 89 items regarding the child/adolescent that can be rated by parents or teachers (Quay & Peterson, 1983). In the present study, teacher-completed forms were used, and two of the six subscales were examined. The two subscales selected were chosen because together they represent both internalizing and externalizing problems. The Anxiety-Withdrawal subscale was utilized as a measure of internalizing problems, and the Conduct Disorder subscale was utilized as a measure of externalizing problems. The remaining subscales were not examined due to their questionable appropriateness for this study.

[5] *This table reveals that the research is clearly quantitative, not qualitative, in nature. Numbers, not words, summarize these findings, and it is the researchers' belief that adjustment is best measured empirically. Other researchers, however, might have answered this research question by examining the qualities of adjustment, possibly through interviews, interpretations from observations, or therapists' notes.*

TABLE 1   Group Means, Standard Deviations, and Analyses of Variance

| | Group | | | | | | | |
| | Intact | | Reduced conflict | | Continued conflict | | | |
Variable	M	SD	M	SD	M	SD	F	df
GPA	3.19	0.70	3.42	0.76	2.49	0.93	3.99	2, 34**
CD	3.08	5.27	2.56	2.65	10.20	12.12	3.05	2, 28*
AW	2.58	2.78	1.22	1.92	5.70	3.47	6.43	2, 28**

Note. CD = Conduct Disorder subscale; AW = Anxiety-Withdrawal subscale. Subscales are from the Revised Behavior Problem Checklist.
*p = .06.   **p < .05.

Grade Point Average (GPA). Each adolescent's GPA (4-point scale) was calculated based on grades in math, English, science, and social studies from the adolescent's most recent report card.

Procedure

Maternal data for this study were collected while the mother-adolescent dyads were attending a 2-hr data collection session on a university campus. After informed consent was obtained, mothers completed their questionnaires, which were presented in randomized order. The adolescents' social science teachers completed their questionnaires through the mail. A total of 31 of the 35 teacher questionnaire packets were completed and returned.

Results and Discussion

One-way analyses of variance (*anovas*) were calculated to determine whether the groups differed on certain important variables. Univariate tests were utilized because they allowed individual examination of several potentially confounding variables. Results indicated that there were no significant differences between the three groups on adolescent age. There were also no significant differences between the two divorced groups on frequency of contact between the parents, frequency of adolescent visitation with the noncustodial parent, time since parental separation, or time since parental divorce. As expected, the two groups did not differ on the DCM rating of interparental conflict prior to separation ($p > .1$) but did differ on the rating of interparental conflict after divorce, $F(1, 21) = 209.00$, $p < .01$. **[6]**

In terms of interparental conflict, a one-way *anova* on maternal OPS scores was significant, $F(2, 32) = 9.14$, $p < .01$. Newman-Keuls tests indicated that the continued high conflict group ($m = 19.9$) reported significantly more conflict than the reduced conflict group ($m = 31.6$) or the intact group ($m = 28.1$).

[6] *The results section tells us that this study is inferential in nature, not merely descriptive. We know this because of the levels of statistical significance reported in the analysis (as p values). This tells us that the researchers wish to generalize beyond their sample and make statements about relationships that are likely to exist in the population of students like those studied. Without statistical significance (p values), researchers are restricting their statements (descriptions) to the sample itself.*

Let's look at the remaining distinctions described in this chapter and see how they relate to this study. The experimental versus quasi-experimental distinction is not relevant in this study since it was not experimental in nature. How could they manipulate divorce and ensuing levels of conflict? With regard to the single-subject versus group distinction, we can see that this research is clearly group oriented. And as far as teacher versus traditional research is concerned, this study appears to be an example of traditional research. Recall that teacher research, by contrast, is very local and conducted for the purpose of answering a specific applied problem within a single classroom (or similar context). Teacher research does not seek to generalize beyond the confines of the study, nor is it concerned with a general understanding of a broader phenomenon. It is, though, very "action" oriented.

In summary, we have seen that this published research is quantitative, inferential, causal comparative, group, and traditional (and is neither true nor quasi-experimental).

There was not a significant difference between the intact group and the reduced conflict group on maternal OPS scores.

A one-way multivariate analysis of variance with three groups was performed on the dependent variables listed in Table 1. Using the Hotelling-Lawley trace criterion, we obtained a significant group effect, $F(6, 50) = 2.36$, $p < .05$. Subsequently, one-way ANOVAS were calculated to determine whether there were significant differences between the three groups on each of the dependent variables. The results of these analyses are presented in Table 1. There were significant group differences ($p < .05$) on GPA and the Anxiety-Withdrawal subscale, whereas the group difference on the Conduct Disorder subscale approached significance ($p = .06$). To determine which groups were significantly different from each other on GPA and the Anxiety-Withdrawal subscale, post hoc comparisons were made using Newman-Keuls tests. The continued high conflict divorced group had significantly lower GPAs than both the reduced conflict divorced group and the intact group. The reduced conflict divorced group and the intact group did not differ significantly on GPA. The continued high conflict group had significantly higher scores than both the reduced conflict divorced group and the intact group on the Anxiety-Withdrawal subscale. The reduced conflict divorced group and the intact group did not differ significantly on this variable.

The results suggest that young adolescents from divorced families in which high interparental conflict continues following divorce are less well-adjusted than adolescents from divorced families in which interparental conflict is reduced following divorce. The nature of these adjustment difficulties appears to be rather general and includes academic problems, internalizing problems, and externalizing problems (although it must be remembered that the measure of centralizing problems only approached significance). Given that the majority of the young adolescent subjects were boys, the finding that continued interparental conflict was more strongly related to internalizing problems than externalizing problems was somewhat surprising. Because the vast majority of young adolescent subjects in this study were boys, it is not clear whether these findings will generalize to young adolescent girls.

The mechanism by which interparental conflict and young adolescent adjustment are related is unclear. A continued high level of interparental conflict may interfere with the functioning of adolescents by creating a tense and stressful home environment, by exposing the adolescents to dysfunctional models or interpersonal conflict resolution, or by creating an atmosphere or neglect (e.g., reduced monitoring of adolescent behavior or assisting with homework) due to poor parent adjustment. Adolescent adjustment problems can also lead to increased levels of interparental conflict. [7] The present study cannot address which of these factors may be the active mechanism; however, the results do indicate that interparental conflict is an important mediating variable in young adolescent response to divorce. This issue should be considered by clinicians who work with parents and young adolescents when divorce is being considered or has already occurred.

[7] *Here is a good reminder of the need for tempered conclusions with causal comparative research.*

References

Atkeson, B. M., Forehand, R., & Rickard, K. M. (1982). The effects of divorce on children. In B. B. Lahey & A. E. Kazdin (Eds.), *Advances in clinical child psychology* (Vol. 5, pp. 255–281). New York: Plenum Press.

Block, J. H., Block, J., & Gjerde, P. F. (1986). The personality of children prior to divorce: A prospective study. *Child Development, 57,* 827–840.

Emery, R. E. (1982). Interparental conflict and the children of discord and divorce. *Psychological Bulletin, 92,* 310–330.

Long, N., & Forehand, R. (1987). The effects of parental divorce and parental conflict on children: An overview. *Journal of Developmental and Behavioral Pediatrics, 8,* 292–296.

Long, N., Forehand, R., Fauber, R., & Brody, G. (1987). Self-perceived and independent-observed competence of young adolescents as a function of marital conflict and divorce. *Journal of Abnormal Child Psychology, 15,* 15–27.

Lupenitz, D. A. (1979). Which aspects of divorce affect children. *Family Coordinator, 28,* 79–85.

Myers, J. K., & Bean. L. J. (1968). *A decade later: A follow-up of social class and mental illness.* New York: Wiley.

Porter, B., & O'Leary, K. D. (1980). Marital discord and childhood behavior problems. *Journal of Abnormal Child Psychology, 8,* 287–295.

Quay, H. B., & Peterson, D. R. (1983). *Interim manual for the revised Behavior Problem Checklist.* Unpublished manuscript, University of Miami.

Received February 13, 1987
Revision received August 11, 1987
Accepted October 5, 1987

GUIDED TOUR #2

Let's turn our attention now to a guided tour of published educational research. This will help solidify important terms and concepts described in this chapter.

Does the "Art of Teaching" Have a Future?

WE NEED TO BROADEN OUR IMAGE OF PROFESSIONALISM TO INCLUDE THE ARTISTIC DIMENSIONS TEACHERS CONSIDER CENTRAL TO THEIR WORK.

David J. Flinders

Penelope Harper quickly takes roll, steps out from behind her desk, and glances around the classroom. Her eyes meet those of her students. Standing with her back to the chalkboard, she clasps her hands close in front of her, a ballpoint pen intertwined between her fingers. She holds her arms close to her sides and shifts her weight onto the heels of her shoes. This posture signals the beginning of class. **[1]**

The students quiet down. Harper shakes back her dark hair and then addresses the class: "OK, today we need to discuss chapter two. Who would like to share something from your reading notes?" Silence. Harper breathes out, assuming a more casual and relaxed attitude. She is smiling softly now, confident that her students have read the assignment and that the silent classroom alone will motivate someone to risk putting forth an idea. Someone does. Harper listens intently and nods her head. "Good," she replies. "I really hadn't thought of it that way, but it tells us something, doesn't it? What's the author getting at here?" Harper steps forward, closer to her students, as their discussion begins to unfold.

Artistry in Professional Life

Penelope Harper (the name is a pseudonym) is good at what she does. **[2]** She's a professional. But in Harper's line of work, what exactly does it mean to be a professional? Does it mean simply possessing a body of expert knowledge and a repertoire of technical skills? Climbing a career ladder toward greater autonomy and increased occupational rewards? Or, for classroom teachers, does professionalism mean something more?

These questions were the focus of a qualitative study I conducted on the nature of professional life in schools (Flinders 1987). Penelope Harper was one of six high school English teachers I observed and interviewed as part of this study. My purpose was to identify what Harper and her colleagues regard as the salient concerns of their day-to-day work experience. I hoped to view professional life through the eyes of classroom teachers.

[1] *You have undoubtedly noticed already how the reporting of a qualitative study can differ from a quantitative one. Instead of describing relevant theory or summarizing reviews of the research literature, Flinders chose to tell a story. In fact, Flinders (1993) reported that he found his inspiration for this research by "going 'back to school.'"*

[2] *Many qualitative researchers use the metaphor as a mechanism for sharing findings. Flinders has chosen the "teacher as artisan" metaphor and in the following section refers to a "beautiful lesson" or "well-orchestrated class discussion."*

I began my research with an understanding of professional life strongly influenced by the "new reform" (Shulman 1987). Two prominent examples of this reform are the reports by the Carnegie Task Force (1986) and the Holmes Group (1986). These reports share a common theme: the need to increase the professional status of teaching. In particular, they call for strengthening the career advancement opportunities, the subject-matter knowledge, and the technical expertise of all classroom teachers.

This focus on career development and expert knowledge reflects a widely shared and commonsense image of professionalism (Schon 1983). However, in listening to teachers talk about their work and in observing their teaching day after day, I soon realized that this image did not match their daily routines and their concerns. This image of professionalism failed to capture the artistry that these teachers often spoke of and demonstrated as central to their work.

Perhaps I can clarify this point by referring to my description of Penelope Harper. Consider, for example, her ability to signal the beginning of class through body language or her use of silence to motivate student participation. These skills reveal something of the grace, subtlety, and drama of Harper's day-to-day teaching. Granted, these deft moves cannot be evaluated solely by conventional testing procedures or through the use of systematic rating scales. Yet they are no less important than Harper's technical expertise or subject-matter knowledge. As my study progressed, the challenge became to understand this other side of teaching—the artistic side.

The Arts of Teaching

Elliot Eisner (1983) has examined at a theoretical level various ways in which teaching can be regarded as art and craft. He calls attention, for example, to the dynamic and emergent qualities of classroom life, as well as to the intricate skill and grace that can characterize the teacher's classroom performance. In this context, Eisner uses the term *art* in its broad sense to signify engaging, complex, and expressive human activity. It is this sense that allows us to speak of a beautiful lesson or of a well-orchestrated class discussion.

If we want to observe artistry in teaching, where might we look in order to find it? [3] My research suggests several possible outcomes. The first I have already touched on in my brief description of Harper's work: the art of communication.

Communication. On a day-to-day basis, classroom teachers rely heavily on interpersonal forms of communication. Philip Jackson's (1965) early research, for example, suggests that teachers engage in as many as a thousand interpersonal interactions each day. This is an impressive number, particularly if we consider the intricate nature of even the most routine instances of face-to-face communication. Such communication, as Harper's teaching reveals, goes far beyond the spoken and written word—it also encompasses the use of space (what sociolinguists call *proxemics*), body language, and paralinguistics (voice tone and rhythm). One teacher I observed, for example, consistently demonstrated uncanny responsiveness toward her students. When a student asked a question or made a comment, that student could feel the teacher's undivided attention. In talking with students, the teacher would face them directly, lean or step in their direction, and maintain eye contact. At appropriate moments she would raise her eyebrows, nod her head, smile, and bring the index finger of her right hand up to her lips in a gesture of serious concentration. All of these nonverbal cues were coordinated to signal a coherent message: *I care about what you have to say.* This unspoken message was often as important to the students as the substantive meaning of her verbal responses.

[3] *Flinders collected a large amount of data, mostly in the form of interviews, extensive field notes from observations (in which he followed teachers for entire days), and written documents. What follows is a description of Flinders's conclusions after examining all his data. His findings, in part, take the form of four artistic dimensions. These findings, or focused themes, did not spring from a computer after statistical analysis. Rather, like most qualitative findings, they more likely emerged from Flinders' system of categorizing and making connections between all types of data. He could not simply enter interviews, observations, and written documents into a computer, sit back, and watch his findings on a screen. The analysis of such complex forms of qualitative data, such as extracting prominent themes, is a daunting intellectual experience for many beginning researchers. Flinders' artistic dimensions of teaching were the result of his insight and keen perception more than from a crunching of numbers.*

Nonverbal cues serve primarily as a form of metalanguage (Tannen 1986). That is, they help teachers establish a context for communication. Consider yet another, somewhat different example. During a literature class, one teacher I observed lighted a kerosene lamp, asked his students to sit in a circle, turned on a recording of the sound effects of a storm, and read passages from Dickens' *Bleak House,* just as a Victorian father might have read the novel to his family. This teacher's well-calculated nonverbal cues provided a context for his students to gain insight into the novel that could not be "explained to them" using words alone. Creating a setting—this too is part of communication.

Perception.   It would be difficult to imagine good teachers who could not communicate well with their students. Yet effective communication does not begin with formulating a message or selecting a medium, but rather with the process of learning to see and to hear. This notion suggests another, perhaps more fundamental art relevant to classroom teaching: the art of perception.

The teachers in my study often alluded to this art in describing their work. During an interview, for example, one teacher casually mentioned that she adapts her daily lesson plans depending on "how the group comes in at the beginning of the period." Such a comment underscores the ability to read those subtle cues in student behavior that signal the changing mood and tone of a class. Another teacher, when I asked how he evaluated his work, replied: "The real test in teaching is how the kids feel about you, and it's the vibrations that you pick up from them that tell you the most." Again, this comment suggests that perceptiveness—the ability to pick up on student attitudes, motives, beliefs, and so forth—lies at the heart of this teacher's professional expertise.

The type of perceptiveness and sensitivity to which these examples refer is a largely tacit dimension of social life. It depends on the ability to make complex and fine-grained distinctions between, for example, a wink and a blink, or between a sigh of relief and a sigh of frustration. All of us learn to make such discernments, at varying levels of sophistication, through social interaction. The point, however, is that this learning reflects an intuitive receptivity that Noddings (1984) has identified as critical to sound pedagogy. At a practical level, learning to operate in a receptive mode is basic to getting to know the students, and I was not surprised to find that all of the teachers in my study mentioned this process as central to their work.

Cooperation. Knowledge of students, of "what they are like as people," as one teacher described perception, serves as the foundation for a third art that is salient in the professional lives of teachers: cooperation. For classroom teachers this means negotiating an alliance with their students. As one teacher commented, "You have to get the students on your side with honesty and a certain amount of candor, so they understand you, and you understand them." This teacher continued, "I'm here to work *with* the kids; I'm not here just to shovel out stuff and let them grab it." The other teachers were also quick to stress the practical value of student-teacher cooperation. One teacher summed it up simply: "You can't force students to do what you want them to do, but if they know you're working hard and care about 'em, from there on it's gravy."

The teachers I observed displayed various strategies for negotiating cooperative relationship with their students. Some of these strategies include: (1) using humor and self-disclosure to promote teacher-student solidarity, (2) allowing students to choose activities, (3) occasionally bending school and classroom rules in the students' interest, (4) providing opportunities for individual recognition, and (5) creating pockets of time that allow teachers to interact one-to-one with students.

An example of this last strategy, creating pockets of time, is illustrated by a teacher who set aside every Thursday for mini-conferences. On this day, while his students worked independently, he went around the classroom to speak individually with as many students as possible. He justified this routine by insisting that "it helps break the mannequin-like image of me standing up in front of the room. It pays tremendous dividends. It allows the students to ask questions, and I find out a lot."

Appreciation. The final art of teaching is appreciation. Unlike communication, perception, and cooperation, the art of appreciation is not primarily something that teachers *do*. Instead, it is a product of their artistry and, thus, cannot always be directly observed. Nevertheless, I found it readily apparent in how teachers describe the types of satisfaction they derive from their teaching. As Harper explained: "In almost any job you do, if you do it well, you get a certain ego-satisfaction from it. It's a really good feeling—when I run a discussion—to know that I did it well." **[4]** Eisner (1983) describes the same idea in another way: "The aesthetic in teaching is the experience secured from being able to put your own signature on you own work—to look at it and say it was good" (p. 13). Both the classroom teacher and the scholar are describing the intrinsic sense of worth that comes from having done a difficult job well. This idea is central to the daily work of classroom teachers.

A Challenge to Educational Leaders

The artistic dimensions that teachers recognize as basic to their profession stand in sharp contrast to the priorities of the new reform movement. Of course, professionalism is about opportunities for career advancement, the expert knowledge

[4] *Herein lies one advantage of the qualitative approach to research taken by Flinders. Behavioral observation scales (like the type found in quantitative studies whereby observers rate the frequency of occurrence of specific behaviors), or stopwatches (used to measure how long teachers wait before answering their own questions), or structured personality inventories (used to measure already established dimensions of personality) would not likely capture the essence of the art of appreciation in the classroom. Of course, Flinders's reference near the end of this paragraph to the idea of teachers putting signatures on their work typifies his model of teaching as an art or craft.*

teachers possess, and the types of learning that can be easily tested. Yet the day-to-day experience of teachers reminds us that teaching is also about much more. It is about subtle interpersonal skills, discernment, caring, and "ego-satisfaction." These artistic aspects reflect highly complex forms of human expression that may well influence teacher effectiveness more than career ladders and fifth-year preparation programs.

If the art of teaching is to have a future, we must enlarge our understanding of professionalism to include the artistic skills and judgment that good teaching demands. This task presents a challenge to educational leaders for at least two reasons. First, artistry cannot be mandated by the central office. Neither can it be fostered by an afternoon of inservice training once or twice a year. Therefore, we have to think more deeply about the conditions under which teachers work, their opportunities for interacting with each other, the amount of discretionary time in their daily schedules, the number of students they see each day, and the resources with which they have to work. Second, the art of teaching is simply less well understood than technical aspects of instruction. We know more, for example, about the mechanics of lesson planning, test construction, and curriculum development than we do about how Penelope Harper is able to gracefully orchestrate a class discussion.

The profession can learn much about the complexity and artistry of teaching from colleagues like Penelope Harper. [5] We might begin by cultivating our own abilities to engage teachers in genuine dialogue. Basic to this dialogue is our perceptiveness—learning to see and hear teachers in ways that take us beyond stereotypical images. Like teachers, we must operate in a receptive mode. We might also promote a cooperative alliance both with and between classroom teachers, for example, by occasionally bending rules for their professional well-being and by involving them in decision making. Finally,

[5] *Qualitative researchers may not close their report with a simple summary. They often punctuate their reports in a provocative way, maybe by asking challenging questions or upsetting our traditional thinking about something. One mark of a good qualitative study is its persuasiveness, in addition to how well it stimulates the reader's thinking. Does Flinders's report influence the quality of your thinking?*

we might strive to fully appreciate the multifaceted nature of this collaborative effort as an art and craft in its own right.

References

Carnegie Task Force on Teaching as a Profession. (1986). *A Nation Prepared: Teachers for the 21st Century.* Washington, D.C.: Carnegie Forum on Education and the Economy.

Eisner, E. W. (January 1983). "The Art and Craft of Teaching." *Educational Leadership* 40: 4–13.

Flinders, D. J. (June 1987). "What Teachers Learn from Teaching Educational Criticisms of Instructional Adaptation." Doctoral dissertation submitted to the Graduate School of Education, Stanford University.

The Holmes Group. (1986). "Tomorrow's Teachers, A Report of the Holmes Group." East Lansing, Mich.: The Holmes Group, Inc.

Jackson, P. W. (1965). "Teacher-Pupil Communication in the Elementary Classroom: An Observational Study." Paper presented at the American Educational Research Association Annual Meeting, Chicago.

Noddings, N. (1984). *Caring: A Feminine Approach to Ethics and Moral Education.* Berkeley: University of California Press.

Schon, D. A. (1983). *The Reflective Practitioner.* New York: Basic Books.

Shulman, L. S. (February 1987). "Knowledge and Teaching: Foundations of the New Reform." *Harvard Educational Review 57*, 1: 1–22.

Tannen, D. (1986). *That's Not What I Meant!* New York: Ballantine Books.

David J. Flinders is Assistant Professor, University of Oregon, Division of Teacher Education, Eugene, OR 97403-1215.

Flinders, D. (1989). Does the 'art of teaching' have a future? *Educational Leadership, 46,* 16–20. Reprinted by permission of the Association for Supervision and Curriculum Development. Copyright © 1989 by ASCD. All right reserved.

Note: This study received the Outstanding Dissertation of the Year award bestowed by the Association for Supervision and Curriculum Development in 1987. It also contributed to a conceptualization of "responsive teaching" (Bowers & Flinders, 1990) whereby the context of teaching and learning is best viewed as a complex ecology of inseparable language, culture, and thought.

APPLICATION EXERCISES

For each of the research summaries below, decide whether it is a better example of research that is:

1. Quantitative versus Qualitative
   a. The researchers concluded that students often perceive of school as The Big Game.
   b. The researchers found that standardized achievement measures have steadily declined.
   c. The researchers found that students' stories reflected strong achievement motivation.
   d. The researchers concluded that the time spent on homework predicted final examination performance.

2. Descriptive versus Inferential
   a. Researchers found that teachers at Henderson High favored the concept of year-round schooling.
   b. Researchers concluded that males had less electrical activity in the emotional centers of the brain.
   c. Researchers concluded that the general public perceives teaching to be one of the most important occupations.
   d. Researchers found that very few students in Chicago schools studied Latin as a foreign language.

3. Experimental versus Quasi-Experimental
   a. Researchers compared the treatment group receiving low-fat meals with a randomized control group and found faster mental processing in the low-fat group.
   b. Researchers compared students' scores under the "less is more" curriculum with a matched comparison group and found better achievement under "less is more."
   c. Researchers observed the trends in teenage smoking before and after the advertising ban and concluded that the ban effectively reduced the incidence of smoking.
   d. Researchers manipulated the length of lecture time in six randomized groups and concluded that the optimum length is twenty minutes.

4. Causal Comparative versus Correlational
   a. Smokers were compared with non-smokers and it was found that smokers have shorter attention spans.
   b. Delinquents were compared to non-delinquents and it was found that delinquents were less likely to grow up with fathers.
   c. Students' scores on the Inference Ability Test were significantly linked to hours of sleep.
   d. Weight at birth was found to be unrelated to IQ ten years later.

5. Single-Subject versus Group
   a. It was found that music influenced John's behavior more than other treatments.
   b. Respondents' test scores were positively related to length of time allowed.
   c. Females recognized the subtle expressions more than males.
   d. It was found that the key to Mrs. Smith's outstanding class performance was the frequent use of metaphor.

6. Teacher versus Traditional

    a. Mr. Smith discovered that his students greatly benefitted from brain-storming before writing.
    b. The researchers found that the evolutionary theory of happiness was supported.
    c. Professor Ortega found that students' understanding was enhanced with the use of two, not ten, concrete examples.
    d. The researchers found that extroversion as a trait was largely inheritable.

MULTIPLE CHOICE QUESTIONS

1. To validate a claim that "teaching is an art," which of the following types of research would be most appropriate?

    a. true experimental
    b. quasi-experimental
    c. meta-analytic
    d. quantitative
    e. qualitative

2. If a study reports that a difference was "statistically significant," then we know that the study was:

    a. inferential
    b. descriptive
    c. single-subject
    d. qualitative
    e. replicated

3. Which of the following types of research is strongest for establishing cause-and-effect relationships?

    a. descriptive
    b. quasi-experimental
    c. true experimental
    d. qualitative
    e. correlational

4. Research that uses time series observations or matched control groups are examples of research that is regarded as:

    a. descriptive
    b. single-subject
    c. qualitative
    d. true experimental
    e. quasi-experimental

5. Researchers who study the impact of divorce on children would most likely be using research designs that are regarded as:

    a. true experimental
    b. descriptive
    c. quasi-experimental
    d. causal comparative
    e. single-subject

6. Researchers who study the linkage between students' existing level of the hormone DHEA and SAT scores would most likely be using designs that are regarded as:
   a. qualitative
   b. correlational
   c. true experimental
   d. quasi-experimental
   e. descriptive

7. Studies that compare treatment phases against baseline phases are most likely:
   a. correlational
   b. single-subject
   c. descriptive
   d. qualitative
   e. inferential

8. Research that involves self-reflective inquiry as part of a "movement" is known as which of the following types of research?
   a. teacher
   b. traditional
   c. quasi-experimental
   d. single-subject
   e. group

9. A great deal of research that might make headlines, like people who drink moderately live longer, is _____ and cause-and-effect interpretations are often _____.
   a. experimental; safe
   b. descriptive; logical
   c. causal comparative; suspect
   d. qualitative; wordy
   e. inferential; impossible

10. Which of the following types of research is a hypothesis most likely to "emerge" and the results are most likely to tell a story?
    a. qualitative
    b. group
    c. inferential
    d. correlational
    e. quantitative

Answers: 1) e   2) a   3) c   4) e   5) d   6) b   7) b   8) a   9) c   10) a

SAMPLES AND SAMPLING

OVERVIEW

One of the most frequently asked questions in the conduct of educational research is: "How many subjects do I need?" In fact, this question undoubtedly prompted researchers Helena Kraemer and Sue Thiemann to write a fine book titled, not surprisingly, *How Many Subjects?* (Kraemer & Thiemann, 1987). The answer to this question is straightforward, but it does require the asker to know about a statistic called the *effect size.* To understand this important statistic in a truly meaningful way, you must first be familiar with the all-important *standard deviation.* We now turn our attention to how scores (or other measures) are described. Then we can better answer the question, "How many subjects do I need?" and "How do I acquire my sample of subjects?" These two questions form the basis of what is usually called the researcher's *sampling plan* or *sampling design.*

DESCRIBING DATA[1]

Central Tendency

In order to make sense out of what may seem an unmanageable array of scores collected during a research project, researchers often list them from highest to lowest and tally the number of times each score occurs. As an illustration, consider twenty-five test scores in reading achievement that researcher Kim recorded. These are shown in Table 6.1.

If we rank order these scores from highest to lowest, we will find that they fall into the pattern shown in Table 6.2 under the column labeled "Scores Ranked Ordered." Next to each ranked-ordered score in Table 6.2, we find tally marks that reflect the number of students who made each score. The last column in Table 6.2, labeled "Frequency" is simply the number of tally marks next to each score. The result of this reorganization of scores is a *frequency distribution,* which is simply one way of organizing a larger set of scores into a form that enables us to determine where most scores fall and how they distribute themselves at and around a midpoint. This pattern of tallies shown in Table 6.2 is typical of ability, achievement, and many other measured traits. This characteristically bell-shaped curve is known as a *normal shape,* simply be-

---

[1]The material on pp. 120–122 and Tables 6.1, 6.2, and 6.3 were adapted from *Educational Psychology in the Classroom,* (7th ed.), by H. C. Lindgren and W. N. Suter. Copyright © 1985 Brooks/Cole Publishing Company, Pacific Grove, CA, a division of International Thompson Publishing Inc. By permission of the publisher.

TABLE 6.1   Reading-Test Scores from Kim's Research Project

Name	Score	Name	Score
Daniel	70	Susan	84
Marsha	70	Juan	73
Rujal	89	Bill	73
Steve	76	Karyn	61
Stan	91	Bobbie	73
Rita	69	Stella	73
William	70	Marco	61
Georgette	98	Thom	73
Nabodiri	90	Nancy	76
Maggie	78	Kathy	89
Sam	59	John	78
Gretchen	78	Peter	54
		Linda	69

cause it is so common. Many scores bunch up near the middle, and few scores are in the extremes (called *tails*).

Although the frequency distribution gives us a rough picture of the performance of those who have taken a test and is an efficient method of organizing and summarizing an array of scores, we usually need more information to describe the distribution itself. What, for example, is the score that best represents the group's performance? Logically, the most representative score is to be found where most scores tend to center. The most

TABLE 6.2   Frequency Distribution of Scores from Table 6.1

Scores Rank Ordered	Tally	Frequency
98	I	1
91	I	1
90	I	1
89	II	2
84	I	1
78	III	3
76	II	2
73	IIIII	5
70	III	3
69	II	2
61	II	2
59	I	1
54	I	1

frequently used index of this tendency is the *mean,* or arithmetic average. The mean is computed simply by adding up all scores in the distribution and dividing by the total number of scores. The mean is usually symbolized as M, and its computation is summarized by $\Sigma X/N$, where Σ refers to "sum up," X refers to scores, and N refers to the number of scores. (There are other measures of central tendency, such as median and mode, but the mean is by far the most widely used, and is the logical companion to the standard deviation, described next.) Your calculator will confirm that the sum (ΣX) is 1875, and since there were twenty-five scores ($N = 25$), the mean (M) = 75.

Dispersion

Although the mean of a set of scores is very helpful for describing the midpoint or central tendency of scores, it tells us nothing about how widely scattered the scores are from the mean. Did all the students in the sample score about the same on the test, or were there great differences among them? In order to answer this question, we need another statistic that tells us the degree of dispersion, or spread, of the scores around the mean. One such index of this spread is called the *standard deviation,* which is computed by subtracting the mean from each score, squaring the resulting differences, totaling those differences, dividing their sum by the number of scores, and finding the square root of the result. The standard deviation is usually symbolized SD, and we can see how $SD = 10.52$, given the calculations in Table 6.3.

Once we know the standard deviation, we are able to say a great deal about the spread of scores. When scores are distributed normally (bell-shaped, or close to it), scores tend to fall within certain limits or boundaries around the mean. About two-thirds or sixty-eight percent of the scores fall within the limits formed by the mean plus 1 standard deviation and minus 1 standard deviation. About ninety-five percent of the scores fall within the limits formed by the mean plus and minus 2 standard deviations. Finally, about ninety-nine percent (or nearly all) of the scores fall within the limits formed by the mean plus and minus 3 standard deviations. This suggests that about sixty-eight percent of Kim's scores fall between 65–85 (which they do) and about ninety-five percent the cases fall between 55–95 (which they do). To check your understanding of this concept, consider the following: If the average weight of adult females were 135, what would be a reasonable standard deviation? Twenty? This means that two-thirds of all women weigh from about 115–155; Ninety-five percent would weigh between 95 and 175. What about the standard deviation of rainfall in inches in your city, if the average were fifty inches? Six? You simply form boundaries, and then make a judgment.

With these ideas about normal distributions, means, standard deviations, and percentages within normal distributions, you can see how easy it is to imagine what a distribution of scores might look like if someone told you, for example, that the mean was 83 and the standard deviation was 4. I can envision a bell-shaped distribution with the "hump" above 83, a downward curve toward 79 and 87, and "tails" beginning around 75 and 91.

Effect Size

One value of the standard deviation is its use in the calculation of what is known as an *effect size*. The effect size is best understand when it can be applied to a simple experiment. For example, let's consider a study testing the effectiveness of a new method to boost reading comprehension scores. (The treatment was concerned with teaching young readers how to read metacognitively, that is, by asking questions, making predictions, and using other active mental tasks). Let's assume that the experimental group scored an average of 85 on a reading comprehension test, and the control group

TABLE 6.3 Calculation of the Standard Deviation (SD) for Kim's Research Project

Score	Mean	Difference	Difference Squared
70	75	−5	25
73	75	−2	4
70	75	−5	25
73	75	−2	4
89	75	14	196
61	75	−14	196
76	75	1	1
73	75	−2	4
91	75	16	256
73	75	−2	4
69	75	−6	36
61	75	−14	196
70	75	−5	25
73	75	−2	4
98	75	23	529
76	75	1	1
90	75	15	225
89	75	14	196
78	75	3	9
78	75	3	9
59	75	−16	256
54	75	−21	441
78	75	3	9
69	75	−6	36
84	75	9	81

$$\Sigma = 2768$$
$$2768/25 = 110.72$$
$$SD = \sqrt{110.72} = 10.52$$

scored 75. The standard deviation of the control group was 20. The effect size called *delta* (usually written as d) is calculated in the following way:

$$d = \frac{\text{Treatment Mean} - \text{Control Mean}}{\text{Standard Deviation of Control}}$$

In this case,

$$d = \frac{85 - 75}{20} \text{ or } d = .5$$

This *d* value of .5 tells us how far the treatment group moved in standard deviation units relative to the control (comparison) group. So, we can say that the average treatment reader scored one half of a standard deviation above the mean of the untreated control group. This idea is shown in Figure 6.1.

The *d* statistic is usually converted to a *percentile-shift* measure by consulting a statistical table known as the standard normal curve (called the *Z table*). (Note: The details of the conversion of *d* to a percentile is appropriate for a first course in statistics. The *Z* table can be found in any statistics text; for our purposes, simply be aware that a simple conversion is accomplished with a statistical table.) For example, the *d* of .5 (one-half of a standard deviation) in the reading experiment converts to a value at the sixty-ninth percentile. We can say, therefore, that the treatment group on average shifted to the sixty-ninth percentile of the untreated control group. The baseline measure in this sense is the fiftieth percentile of an untreated control group, and the treatment's effect is expressed as a shift from this initial starting position.

Think of the *d* as the force or pressure that can boost an entire distribution; think of the percentile shift as the position in the control group where the average of the treatment group has landed after its shift. If a shift corresponds to the eighty-fourth percentile, for example, you might imagine picking up the entire treatment distribution and placing it over the control distribution so that its average falls to the right at the eighty-fourth percentile. Figure 6.2 illustrates the force needed to shift a treatment group to the right, hence scoring considerably higher than the control group on average.

The *d* statistic can also be negative, indicating an average treatment group shift *below* the mean of a control group. As an illustration, think about a weight loss group (the treatment is group hypnosis) compared to an untreated control group. Let's assume the treatment group after the hypnosis sessions weighed 120 and the control group weighed 130 with a standard deviation of 15. The effect size would be 120 – 130/15 = –.67. This converts to a percentile of 25, suggesting that the *average* hypnosis group fell at the twenty-fifth percentile of the untreated control group. Table 6.4 lists several effect sizes, along with their associated "percentile shifts."

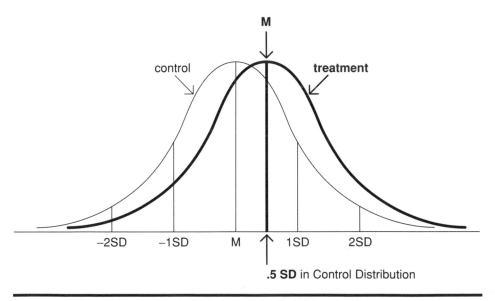

FIGURE 6.1   The treatment group (**bold**) scores higher than the control group, shifting to the right and overlapping so that its mean (**M**) falls at the .5 standard deviation (SD) mark of the control group. The effect size of .5 reveals where the average of the treatment group falls *in relation to the untreated controls* using a standard deviation scale.

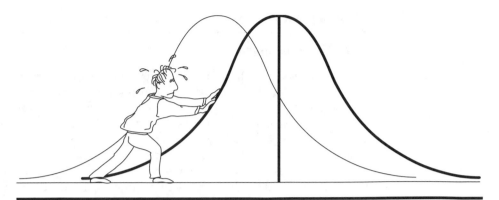

FIGURE 6.2   The treatment group (**bold**) has been pushed to the right. Its mean falls closer to the tail of the control group (at the eighty-fourth percentile), suggesting a large effect size.

Notice that the percentile shifts are symmetrical above and below the average ($d = 0$). The d values which fall between those values listed in Table 6.4 have percentile shifts which could be approximated by an interpolation. It should be noted, however, that the interpolated percentile is not a simple linear interpolation (e.g., half way between d values of .50 and .80 is not exactly half way between percentiles 69 and 79). A standard Z table should be consulted for exact values associated with each d.

Various effect sizes have been given somewhat arbitrary labels. There is general agreement that a small effect size is **.20** (percentile shift from 50 to 58), a medium effect is **.50** (percentile shift from 50 to 69), and a large effect size is **.80** (percentile shift from 50 to 84). These values of d for small, medium, and large effects may be used in several ways. One important way is described in the following section.

TABLE 6.4   Effect Size Measures (d) and Related Percentile Shifts

d	Approximate Percentile Shift (Compared to Control Group)
−2.00	2
−1.50	7
−1.00	16
−.80	21
−.50	31
−.20	42
00	50
.20	58
.50	69
.80	79
1.00	84
1.50	93
2.00	98

SAMPLE SIZE DETERMINATION

Group Comparison Studies

We have explained the effect size measure *d* because, as it turns out, the appropriate sample size in many types of educational research is determined in large part by *d*. Sample size is also determined by other factors, but fortunately, these factors have standard values which can be preset to generally accepted levels. We will discuss these factors in greater detail in Chapter 11, but for now, these factors will be preset to the following values: alpha = .05, power = .80, tails = 2. *Alpha* refers to the probability that a mean difference could arise by chance; .05 is the agreed-upon standard for this value. *Power* refers to the probability of finding a difference when in fact a true difference exists; .80 is considered a desirable standard for power. *Tails* refers to the direction of a mean difference. Two tails allow for an experimental group to be higher or lower than a control group; one tail allows for one specific direction of a difference, such as the experimental group scoring higher, not lower, than a control group. Nearly all statistical tests have two tails if two directions are possible, so this has become the standard.

Given these preset values and knowledge of small, medium, and large effect sizes, one can use the chart in Table 6.5 to arrive at the required number of subjects to uncover a significant difference, if in fact one exists in the population. It should be obvious from this chart that more subjects are needed if the effect size is small. (If an effect size is zero in a population, meaning that there is no difference between groups, then a researcher, of course, would not find a true difference even with an enormous sample size).

The effect sizes and required sample sizes shown in Table 6.5 are appropriate whenever a research question pertains to two contrasted groups, for example, experimental versus control, male versus female, second graders versus third graders, Teaching Method I versus Teaching Method II. This table can be useful in many different contexts. If a research hypothesis posits a large difference (effect) between males and females in their self-perceived math competency, then it is clear that only twenty-five males and twenty-five females would be needed to uncover this difference. Or, presume that prior research suggests that students taught to read via whole language (experimental group) will read with greater comprehension than the standard basal group (control group) but that this difference (effect) is small, then the researcher would know that 392 students in each group would be needed. Or, perhaps a researcher is interested in an unexplored relationship, say the effect of exercise on memory span, but only if it is at least medium in strength. It would then be known that sixty-three subjects would be needed in each group (exercise versus control).

Without the information conveyed in Table 6.5, researchers would not know how a finding of no significant difference should be interpreted. For example, suppose a

TABLE 6.5. Sample Sizes Needed for Finding a Significant Difference in a Two-group Study, assuming alpha = .05, power = .80, and tails = 2

Effect size *d*	Required Sample Size in Each Group
.20 (Small)	392
.50 (Medium)	63
.80 (Large)	25

(After Howell, 1982, p. 167)

researcher tested the hypothesis that sugar causes hyperactivity and found that there were no significant differences in hyperactivity between the sugar group and the control group. This finding may reflect the truth: sugar in fact does not cause hyperactivity (let's just presume this is the truth for this example). Or, maybe sugar *does* cause hyperactivity but the research could not uncover this relationship because of insufficient sample size. *A finding of no difference is ambiguous without an adequate sample size.* A finding of no difference with an appropriate sample size, by contrast, is fairly easy to interpret—the variables are probably *not* related in the population. In the hyperactivity example, if 400 sugar students were compared with 400 control students and no influence on hyperactivity were found, then the researcher could more comfortably conclude that sugar does not cause hyperactivity. (Note: This conclusion would be warranted only if other aspects of the study were in order, such as utilizing proper control techniques as described in Chapter 8.)

Before closing our description of the effect size measure d, we should note that d has uses other than determining sample size. It is also one common measure employed in meta-analysis, a technique described in Chapter 4. Meta-analysis uses d in order to summarize the strength of a treatment effect across many studies. Hundreds of separate studies, each one providing a single d, can be summarized by one overall effect size.

Correlational Studies

Correlational studies are not immune from statistical guidelines relating to the proper sample size. Weak, moderate, and strong relationships, defined as $r = .20$, $r = .50$, and $r = .80$, respectively, have proper sample sizes (total number of subjects) of about 197, 33, and 14 with power = .80, alpha = .05, and tails = 2 (Howell, 1982, p. 167). The effect size measure in correlational studies is usually indexed by r itself, called the *correlation coefficient*.

Rules of Thumb

The sample sizes described above for group comparison studies (25, 63, 392 per group for small, medium, and large effects, respectively) may be thought of as *statistically validated*. By contrast, there are frequently invoked "rules of thumb" for determining sample size. There is widespread consensus (at least in education and the behavioral sciences) that research involving the comparison of two groups should be based on a *minimum per group* size of thirty. (Note: You'll notice from Table 6.5 that this value assumes a fairly large effect size.) Although a sample size of thirty is a very a common recommendation in reference sources about educational research, it may as well be called a "magic number," since it is a mystery how this number came to be. Having forty participants per group is also frequently recommended, particularly in the sense of creating comparable groups after random assignment. (Randomly dividing eighty people into two groups should create roughly equivalent groups since individual differences should "wash out." There would be far less confidence about group comparability after randomly assigning, say, ten people to two groups.)

There is another rule of thumb that can be applied to complex correlational research designs. One such correlational design used commonly in educational research is multiple regression, whereby more than one variable is correlated with an outcome (called a *criterion variable*). For example, a researcher might investigate how logical reasoning scores are related to a host of personal attributes such as the amount of vigorous exercise, early music training, vitamin B6 in the diet, level of second-hand smoke, and even the month of birth. This rule suggests one should have significantly more cases (subjects) than variables (Tabachnick & Fidell, 1983, p. 379). This means, at the very minimum, having at least four to five times more people than variables. Other sources suggest twenty times more cases than variables. The most common recommendation seems to be at least *ten times as many cases as variables*. The logical reasoning example would therefore require at least fifty subjects (since there are five attribute variables).

Sample Size and Precision in Scientific Surveys

A good example of a scientific survey is the 28th Annual Phi Delta Kappa/Gallup Poll of the Public's Attitude Toward the Public Schools by Elam, Rose, & Gallup (1996) published in the September 1996 *Phi Delta Kappan*. Their "magic number" is 1,329. This is admittedly large, but their intended population—the group that they wish to make generalized statements about—is essentially all adults in households with telephones. In surveys, the overriding statistical concern is precision, or the accuracy of the results. Survey findings are precise when the findings in the sample closely match the real value in the population. Precision is often referred to as *sampling tolerance*. Tolerance is directly a function of sample size, and, to a lesser degree, the value of population parameters (e.g., Is the percentage of respondents in the population who support an issue closer to eighty percent or fifty percent?) This precision or tolerance in a survey is usually referred to as the *margin of error*. For example, if sixty percent of the respondents support the idea of home schooling with a margin of error of +/–3 percent, we would know that the true percentage in the population is most probably between fifty-seven percent to sixty-three percent, derived simply by subtracting and adding the margin of error to the sample result. These limits, which most likely span the true value in the population, are also referred to as *confidence intervals*. "Most likely" in this case refers to ninety-five out of one hundred times.

Sample sizes for scientific surveys, therefore, are largely determined by how much error you are willing to tolerate. Table 6.6 shows the required sample sizes for varying levels of sampling error (or margin of error) for the standard level of confidence (.95, or ninety-five out of one hundred as described above). It also maximizes the sample size ("worst case scenario") by assuming the true split in the population is 50/50 (the required sample sizes are smaller for splits like 80/20 or 60/40).

A simple formula, 1 divided by k squared, will also provide a ballpark estimate, where k is the desired confidence interval. For example, if a margin of error of .04 is acceptable, then 1 divided by .04 squared would equal 625. You can see that this estimate is low, but the tabled values are maximized, as described above. If you are conducting a survey, then, a recommended sample size would fall, most probably, between 600 and 1,000 if you wanted your precision to be within reasonable limits. This may sound like a huge undertaking, but keep in mind that in some surveys, such as the Gallup, the size of the population is enormous, consisting of 150 million people.

There is no strategy for determining sample size in a survey that involves only a specific percentage of the population (e.g., ten percent of the population of size 500 is fifty). If this were true, then, the sample size of the Gallup surveys would be fifteen million, assuming a ten percent sample selection rate.

SAMPLING METHODS

Random Selection

Now that you understand the importance of sample size and how to determine the appropriate number, we turn our attention to *sampling methods* (sometimes called sampling designs). The concern here is how you select research participants from a

TABLE 6.6 Required sample sizes for scientific surveys as a function of sampling error

Margin of Error	Required Sample Size
13%	100
9%	200
6%	400
5%	750
4%	1000
3%	1500

(from Elam, Rose, & Gallup, 1996, p. 53).

larger group. The larger group is called a *population;* it is the entire group which you hope to make generalized statements about. A sample, by contrast, provides data and is a subset of the population, one that presumably mirrors it. The overarching principle of sampling is concerned with *representativeness,* or the similarity between the sample and the population. Researchers are entitled to generalize their sample findings to a larger population if the sample is representative of the larger population. One of the best methods for assuring that the sample is representative is to select the sample *randomly* from the larger population. Random sampling is accomplished with a table of random numbers, like the one shown in Table 6.7. Random sampling is not accomplished with coin flips or numbers in a hat. The use of a random number table assures that each member of the population has an *equal and independent chance* of being selected. To understand this, simply imagine a list of the 5,000 (let's assume)

TABLE 6.7 Portion of a Table of Random Numbers

69513	93372	98587	64229
24229	23099	96924	23432
45181	28732	76690	06005
75279	75403	49513	16863
89751	63485	34927	11334
06282	75452	26667	46959
69714	28725	43442	19512
10100	43278	55266	46802
08599	32842	47918	40894
93886	57367	78910	38915
94127	99934	35025	50342
97879	92921	68432	68168
43382	28262	10582	25126
91218	49955	01232	55104
89495	00135	27861	39832

teachers in your state. *Equal and independent* means that Person #1 in the population has exactly the same chance of being selected as Person #5000 who has the same chance as Person #2500 who has the same chance as Person #25 who has the same chance as Person #2501. Furthermore, if Person #200 is selected, then Person #201 has the same chance as Person #4592. In a sense, random selection has no "memory," so to speak, and the selection is just as likely to target the neighbor from the previous selection as, say, Person #5000. (Likewise, a slot machine which has just hit the jackpot is as likely to hit the jackpot on the very next turn as it is on, say, pull #777.)

Let's select a sample randomly from a larger population to see how this is done. We will use a small scale for efficiency, with the understanding that the same procedures would be applied on a much larger scale. A current list of numbered students (first names only) in my Introduction to Research course appears in Table 6.8. Assume they represent the population, and my task is to select a random sample consisting of five.

You can enter the Table of Random Numbers (at least a portion, as shown in Table 6.7) anywhere you would like. (I know this doesn't sound scientific, but you really can simply close your eyes and point your finger anywhere in the table.) Let's say that you chose the second column from the left, third row down, last two digits—32. (You need two digits since there are ten or more people in the "population." If there were one hundred or more people in the population, you would simply choose three digits.) Person #32 does not exist in the population, so I choose a direction (down, let's say) and continue until I find numbers which are valid. The next two digits down are 03, hence Harriet is in my random sample. Continuing down, we see Person #85 is not valid, likewise Person #52. Continuing, we find Person #25 (Leslie) is in the sample, so is Person #21 (George). If we continue, we'll reach the bottom of the column before finding valid numbers. So we'll continue in the same spot (last two digits) at the top of the next column to the right (87, do you see this?). Continuing down, we find Person #24 (Diana) and Person #13 (Cynthia). These five students, then, comprise my random sample from the population.

It is important to note that random selection is a *process,* not an outcome. When it is accomplished with the aid of a random number table (the process), we can say that the resultant sample is random, period. It makes no sense to check the randomness af-

TABLE 6.8   Population of UALR Students Enrolled in Introduction to Research

1. Carolyn	15. Linda
2. Martha	16. Sara
3. Harriett	17. Margaret
4. Janet	18. Rhanda
5. Joyce	19. Angela
6. Brenda	20. Shirley
7. Ledys	21. George
8. Shannon	22. Tammy
9. Robbin	23. Joyce
10. Brenda	24. Diana
11. Carmen	25. Leslie
12. Loretta	26. Mary
13. Cynthia	27. Carol
14. Karen	28. Zhichao

ter the fact to make sure it is representative. Use the table and then forget about it! This process of random selection is easy, but there is one catch: the members of the population must be numbered so that the table of random numbers can be linked to them. This usually does not present a problem, however, since many lists (either paper or electronic) are routinely numbered. (There is another very important type of randomization called *random assignment*, but we will postpone a further description of this until Chapter 8 where we discuss control procedures and their role in neutralizing the potential contaminating influences of extraneous variables.)

We should point out that one common form of sampling uses the "every *n*th" system, whereby every seventh (or tenth or two-hundredth) person on a list is selected. This type of sampling is a form of *systematic* (opposed to random) sampling. This method clearly does not conform to the definition of random (each member has an equal and independent chance of being selected). Once the seventh (or *n*th) person is chosen, the eighth person has zero chance, but the fourteenth has absolute certainty of being selected. In reality, it is unlikely that systematic sampling plans such as this introduce serious bias (but they could, in theory). It appears to be used for reasons of practicality and efficiency when no serious bias is suspected with its use (i.e., it is much easier to direct others to choose every seventh name than to explain what a random number table is and how to use it). This form of systematic sampling is also used when the accessible population is not known (or not truly accessible) or when random selection is not possible. Consider a population of consumers, for example. Surveying every fiftieth shopper who enters a mall may be the only plausible sampling method, for there could be no list of the population of all shoppers that day from which to randomly select. Although not strictly random, this type of *n*th person sampling is often considered the "next best thing."

Variants of Random Sampling

Clusters. Researchers frequently encounter intact groups which cannot easily be chopped into small units (or individual students). These unbreakable units are often called clusters, and typical clusters in educational research include classrooms, schools, or even districts. (In other disciplines, clusters may be wings of a hospital, city blocks, or counties.) Clusters can be randomly selected in the same way that individuals are randomly selected. Classrooms or schools may be numbered using any logical sequence, and then selected randomly with the use of a random number table. Such a sampling design is referred to as a *randomized cluster.*

Multiple-Stage. Sometimes researchers find it easier to select randomly at two or more stages. For example, sixty schools may be selected randomly in a state, followed by the random selection of twenty classes within each of the sixty schools. This plan would be described as *two-stage random.* Three-stage random may start with the selection of 200 large school districts across the nation, followed by the random selection of twenty schools within each district. A third stage could involve the random selection of ten classes within each of the twenty schools, thus qualifying as a *three-stage random.*

Strata. Many random sampling designs incorporate subgroups formed on the basis of categories believed to be especially influential. For example, the nationwide Gallup Poll which measures adult's opinions about issues in education will use strata based on four regions of the country and three sizes of community. The decision to stratify on these factors suggests that attitudes about education vary as a function of geographic region and size of community. Researchers using these *stratified random* sampling designs often arrange for their sample to mirror the entire population on these stratified factors. For example, if twenty-one percent of the nation's population resides in the South, then the sample will comprise twenty-one percent Southerners. If forty percent of the population lives in large cities, then the sample will comprise forty percent large-city dwellers. These population values are usually learned from the latest census data. Also, stratified sampling of a large population is more likely to yield a sample group that is representative of the population than is simple (not stratified) random sampling—unless the simple random sample is very large.

EXTERNAL VALIDITY

Educational researchers reserve the term *external validity* to refer to how well the findings in a sample can be generalized to a larger population. If a study lacks external validity, then one is not confident that the findings can be applied beyond the narrow confines of the study. One especially common threat to external validity is, to no surprise, lack of random selection. When the sample does not fairly represent the population, external validity is lacking. This is most likely to happen when samples are chosen on the basis of convenience rather than representativeness. For example, assume you wanted to learn about the opinion held by students at your college or university regarding weekend classes. To this end, you select only those students enrolled in one of your night courses. The findings would almost certainly not apply to students in general. The sample may have been easy to obtain, but it would not be generalizable, threatening the external validity of the survey and rendering it useless.

The same problem occurs when opinion surveys are solicited, not randomly selected. For example, radio programs may ask their listeners to call a specific number if they agree with a position and a different number if they disagree. Those who choose to call may bear little resemblance to the population at large. Maybe those who agree feel stronger than those who disagree, hence are more motivated to call in. Or consider magazines that print questionnaires and ask readers to return it upon completion. Only those who have a high interest in the purpose of the survey may be motivated to return it. Such procedures should be considered marketing or entertainment, not science.

POPULATION AND ECOLOGICAL GENERALIZATION

We have seen that the term *external validity* refers to generalization. It is useful to define two types of generalization: *population* and *ecological*. *Population generalization* refers to people; *ecological generalization* refers to settings—all aspects of the setting, including the physical environment. The type of generalization that focuses on the research participants themselves—apart from the setting—is called population generalization. It is concerned with how well people in the sample mirror those people in the population, or the representativeness of the sample participants in relation to the population. Ecological generalization is no less important, since problems here can also threaten external validity.

Consider the following study based on educational "seduction" (an idea first described by Naftulin, Ware, and Donnelly, 1973 and later extended by Perry, Abrami, and Leventhal, 1979). Researchers wanted to know if college students' ratings of their professors (in terms of knowledge gain) was affected by factors such as enthusiasm. The researcher arranged for an actor on videotape to deliver a thirty-minute lecture on some obscure topic. Two versions of the *identical* lecture were given, an enthusiastic one and a boring one. In the enthusiastic presentation, the lecturer was dynamic, eager, excited, and entertaining; in the boring condition, the same lecturer was, well, boring. After the lecture, students in both groups rated how much they thought they learned. The results showed that students attending the enthusiastic lecture rated their knowledge gain greater than those in the boring one. The researchers concluded that college students' ratings of their professors are biased since they can be "seduced" by highly entertaining professors into believing they have learned more than they actually have.

Even if the sample in the research described above was large and randomly selected from a population, many people would question its applicability to actual college classrooms. College courses are taught by professors, not actors; lectures are most frequently delivered by live professors, not video screens; and courses last maybe fifty hours, not thirty minutes. And students are students, so to speak, not subjects who signed up for an experiment to earn course credit. One might question both the ecological and population generalization of a study such as this.

Consider another hypothetical example. A researcher studied how young children make sense of reading. In a campus laboratory built especially for this purpose, the subjects in small groups read an experimenter-prepared passage about a summer vacation. A research assistant in each group asked funny questions as they read to those in the experimental group and said very little to the control group. Results revealed that the experimental group scored higher on reading comprehension tests than the control group. The researcher concluded that school teachers should make greater use of humor when teaching children how to read. This study may be questioned on grounds that its setting does not match real-world, noisy classrooms, staffed by certified teachers using standard materials. Children simply don't learn how to read in sterile learning laboratories within ivory towers staffed by research assistants who use experimenter-prepared reading passages.

It should be emphasized that the concept of ecological generalization encompasses virtually all aspects of the research setting except the subjects themselves. The method of data collection, for example, is part of the "ecology." Do the opinions expressed over the phone generalize to other settings such as face-to-face interviews? Or paper-and-pencil formats? While most of us would recognize the size, color, and temperature of a room as part of its ecology, many of us wouldn't readily think of the sex of the experimenter (interviewer) or the readability of materials as part of the ecology (which they are).

SAMPLING BLUNDERS AND SHORT CUTS

An appreciation of representative sampling might be gained from a brief description of improper sampling. Probably the most famous sampling blunder (at least in politics) occurred in the 1936 Landon and Roosevelt Presidential runoff. This was described in Chapter 1. There are plenty of other examples.

One notorious case is the 1970 draft lottery. Some of you may have a vivid image of this, for it was televised nationally amid widespread tension. The lottery involved choosing "random" birth dates (366 dates, including February 29) from a large barrel. The first date selected would receive lottery number 1; the second date selected, lottery number 2, etc. This would be a fair sampling procedure if it were truly random (each date having an equal and independent chance of being selected). Clearly, random number (or date) generators were available in 1970, but the military opted for an old-fashioned "drawing-numbers-from-the-hat" system (probably for public relations). Birth dates were placed in plastic capsules, and then dropped into a barrel. Starting with January 1 and systematically working around the calendar, each capsule was added to the others in the barrel and presumably mixed together. This system, of course, guaranteed that December dates would go into the barrel last. But when the lights came on and the television cameras started rolling, the system also guaranteed that the December dates would be the first to come out. December dates, therefore, had low numbers simply because they were the last to go in and the first to come out.

Far too many December babies went off to Vietnam as a result, and the military learned a lesson about random sampling: Do it properly with a table of random numbers and forget about displays for public relations.

To borrow an example from medicine, it turns out that we were about a decade late in learning about the dangers of asbestos, in particular the unique form of lung cancer associated with it. A 1973 survey of asbestos workers in scores of asbestos plants found only one worker out of thousands who had the asbestos-caused lung cancer. The survey, however, was terribly biased because only retirees were surveyed! These people, by definition, had to be reasonably healthy since they lived to retirement age. It turns out that most of the workers who got asbestos-caused lung cancer died before retirement, hence could never be part of the study! Of course, a random selection of people who had ever worked with asbestos (within a specific time frame) would have revealed a mortality rate much higher and closer to the truth.

The Lewis Terman longitudinal study of geniuses, though not considered a blunder, also provides an example of unrepresentative sampling. (The late Lewis Terman of Stanford University is credited with revising and standardizing the original test of intelligence developed by Alfred Binet of France for use in this country, hence the *Stanford-Binet* scale of intelligence.) In the 1920s, Lewis Terman initiated a lifespan study of geniuses, tracking their development as children and watching their progress as adults until old-age. Only about two percent of the population can be labelled "genius" using the traditional Stanford-Binet intelligence quotient of over 132. The test may take an hour to administer and score, so hundreds of hours of testing would have to be done before a handful of geniuses could be found. And Terman wanted to study 1000 of them! Terman would have to spend his entire life testing! The solution involved asking teachers to nominate those few students in their classes who appeared to be geniuses. Then possibly one true genius could be found for every two children who were tested. It worked! The testing was greatly reduced, and about 1000 geniuses were selected for study through their lifespan. What is the sampling problem, you ask? Teachers were likely inclined to nominate those children who fit a stereotyped images of genius—well behaved, studious, quiet, conforming, high achieving, etc. Quite possibly, another type of genius would be more interesting to study—the creative, funny, bored, trouble-maker type who probably never made it to the sample.

The Lawrence Kohlberg study of moral development also provides an interesting example of nonrepresentative sampling (but also not considered a blunder). Kohlberg tracked how children's moral reasoning changes as they progress through developmental stages (i.e., from "Don't do it because you might get caught and spanked" to "Don't do it because good boys don't do it" to "Don't do it because it's the law"). Kohlberg was able to developmentally categorize many children's rationales for particular behaviors. The problem arose when his early research revealed that girls were somewhat behind boys in their moral thinking. As it turned out, Kohlberg's system of classifying moral responses developmentally was based on boys only! Girls, it was later revealed, are not *slower*; they are simply *different* (and, some would argue, more advanced). Whereas boys are concerned about not interfering with the *rights* of others, girls appear to be more concerned about the *needs* of others.

Finally, the study of personality in psychology affords at least one interesting sampling blunder. Consider the *Minnesota Multiphasic Personality Inventory (MMPI)*. This test was designed to assess abnormal deviations in personality, such as paranoia and schizophrenia. For a scale on this test to successfully identify schizophrenics and so-called "normals," a sample of schizophrenics must answer a set of questions differently than a representative sample of normal personalities. The sample of hospitalized schizophrenics was obtained from a university hospital in Minnesota. And how was part of the sample of "normals" obtained? From visitors to the hospital! (You might recognize this as a convenience sample.)

CHAPTER SUMMARY

Most researchers want to learn something that extends beyond the sample of subjects to a larger, more generalized population. The process of sampling, or how many subjects are sampled and by what method, often determines whether or not this extension is warranted. Central to the notion of sample size is a statistic called an *effect size,* or *d*. This measures the strength of a relationship; weaker relationships require larger sample sizes to be detected. A medium effect size, defined as a percentile shift from fifty to sixty-nine, requires about sixty-three subjects per group. Common rules of thumb, however, suggest that thirty to forty subjects per group is appropriate. The size of sample also determines precision, or *margin of error,* in a survey study. Large-scale surveys with acceptable precision often require 1000–1500 respondents.

How subjects are selected often determines the external validity, or the general applicability of the study. Random sampling is one good method of assuring that the sample is representative of the population from which it was drawn. Other methods often introduce bias that can threaten the *population generalization,* which jeopardizes statements about people in the population. The use of unreal settings or materials can threaten the *ecological generalization,* which jeopardizes statements about environmental conditions in the population (such as classrooms, materials, tasks, etc.).

GUIDED TOUR

Let's turn our attention now to a guided tour of published educational research. This will help solidify important terms and concepts described in this chapter.

Sociometric Differences Between Mildly Handicapped and Nonhandicapped Black and White Students

Frank M. Gresham

Louisiana State University

Daniel J. Reschly

Iowa State University

We investigated sociometric differences between mainstreamed mildly handicapped and nonhandicapped

Correspondence concerning this article should be addressed to Frank M. Gresham, Department of Psychology, Louisiana State University, Raton Rouge, Louisiana 70803.

black and white students in a factorial design by using three indexes of peer acceptance. Results indicated differential patterns of peer acceptance between black and white mildly handicapped children. We noted no main effects for race or sex; there was, however, a significant multivariate Sample × Race interaction effect. Race accounted for little variance in the sociometric status of mildly handicapped and nonhandicapped students. We discuss the implications of this study in terms of the degree of disparity between white and black mildly handicapped and nonhandicapped students.

One or the most consistent findings concerning the education of mildly handicapped children in regular classrooms is that they are poorly accepted by their nonhandicapped peers. The authors of several major reviews of this literature have concluded that mildly handicapped students experience lower sociometric status than their nonhandicapped counterparts in regular classrooms (Gottlieb, 1981; Gresham, 1981; Madden & Slavin, 1983).

Although the poorer sociometric status of mildly handicapped children in regular classrooms is a well-established finding, there is relatively little information regarding the effects of race on the sociometric status of mainstreamed mildly handicapped students. Singleton and Asher (1977) investigated the effects of race and sex on sociometric ratings by using a sample of black and white nonhandicapped children in an integrated school district. This study showed that race accounted for only 1% of the variance in sociometric ratings of nonhandicapped schoolchildren.

The purpose of the present study was to investigate the effects of race on the sociometric ratings of mildly handicapped and nonhandicapped students in regular classrooms. Given the independent variables of sample (mildly handicapped vs.

nonhandicapped), race (black vs. white), and sex, we hypothesized a main effect for sample in the light of past research findings reviewed earlier. We did not hypothesize any such effect for sex because, unlike Singleton and Asher (1977), we used same-sex sociometric ratings. We did not expect a race main effect in view of Singleton and Asher's findings. We did not make any hypotheses regarding interaction effects, given the absence of an empirical basis from past research.

Method

Participants in the study were 199 nonhandicapped (NH) and 103 mildly handicapped (MH) students from a midwestern state and a south central state. The 302 subjects were enrolled in urban, suburban, and rural school districts throughout the two states. Table 1 contains the demographic, intellectual, and academic achievement characteristics of the sample. **[1]** All MH students were classified as learning disabled, educationally handicapped, or mildly mentally retarded according to state guidelines in effect at the time of the investigation. We deemed efforts to differentiate the MH sample into specific exceptional categories for data analysis unnecessary and potentially hazardous because of the variability in children's receiving specific labels. Previous investigators have presented a similar logic (Morrison, 1981; Morrison, Forness, & MacMillan, 1983).

All MH students were receiving special-education services in a resource room but were mainstreamed into a regular classroom in academic subjects (e.g., reading, math, and language arts) for the majority of the school day (i.e., greater than 50% of the day). The NH sample consisted of students who had never been referred to or enrolled in special education. These students were enrolled in the same regular classrooms as the MH students.

[1] *Notice that these researchers make it a point to describe the characteristics of their sample. This is important so that readers may judge the external validity of the study, or the extent to which the findings may generalize to a larger population. This is a judgment call; there is no statistical formula that reveals how widely applicable these findings might be.*

Sample Selection

We asked school psychologists representing school districts throughout the two states to randomly select from their caseloads five children who were receiving services in a resource room for the mildly handicapped.[2] Random selection was effected by the psychologists' selecting every fifth child from their caseloads until they had five. Children were between the ages of 7½ and 11½ years because of the age requirements of the dependent measures.

NH students were randomly selected from schools that the school psychologists were assigned to, with the restriction that the students be between 7½ and 11½ years old. A total of 45 classrooms in 20 schools were used to select the NH sample. In each classroom, the teacher randomly selected six NH students from the class roster. We asked teachers to select three boys and three girls randomly from their rosters by selecting every fourth child. A total of 71 subjects were not selected because some teachers failed to select six students.

Dependent Measures

We used three sociometric measures as dependent variables in the present study—(a) Play With Rating Scale (PWRS), (b) Work With Rating Scale (WWRS), and (c) Structured Peer Assessment (SPA). The PWRS and WWRS are 5-point rating scales on which children rate each of their classmates according to how much they like to play with and work with each other (1 = *not at all*, 2 = *not much*, 3 = *doesn't matter*, 4 = *a little*, and 5 = *a lot*). A face corresponding to each number was placed on each child's rating scale to better communicate the meaning or the scale. The PWRS and WWRS have been used extensively in research concerning peer acceptance of both handicapped and nonhandicapped children (Asher & Hymel, 1981; Gresham, 1981; Singleton & Asher, 1977).

[2] *Here is a very interesting description of random selection. Recall that this important sampling technique has strong implications for generalizing beyond the sample, if it is accomplished correctly. The random selection process relies on a random number table, plain and simple. But look how these researchers selected their sample—choosing every fifth child. (This would be random only if the names were laid down on the list with a random number table.) In a strict sense, then, this method of sampling by choosing every "nth" name is a systematic sampling technique, not a random selection technique.*

Recall that the definition of random requires that each member of the pool has an equal and independent chance of being selected. Selection of every fifth name does not satisfy the equal criterion since the first name has zero chance of being selected and the fifth name has a 1.00 chance (certainty). Also, the independence criterion is not satisfied since the remaining names chosen depend on which name was chosen at the outset—the fifth. The next name chosen will be the tenth; the sixth was not free to be chosen. In truth, the "every nth name" technique, in this case, probably did not introduce a serious bias. It was done, I surmise, for practical reasons. I can imagine the difficulties encountered if they had instructed psychologists and teachers to select names using a random number table. (Names would have to be numbered, random number tables provided, instructions given, etc.) By contrast, selecting every fifth name is easy to accomplish (well, probably not that easy, for you can see at the end of the sample selection section, seventy-one students were not sampled because teachers did not follow instructions). It must be emphasized, however, that true random sampling is accomplished with a table of random numbers (or a computer programmed to deliver random digits.) Many researchers, however, do employ the systematic nth technique since it may be the only practical method and probably yields a sample that is free of bias. Many researchers in fact refer to the nth method as random or "quasi-random." I am simply pointing out that it does not satisfy the definition of random in the strict sense.

We have seen that the researchers opted for the most practical method of sampling. A strength of their sampling design was the rather extensive pool from which subjects were drawn. Instead of sampling from just one school (surely limiting the generalization), these researchers sampled "throughout the two states" for a total of forty-five classrooms and twenty schools in the sample of nondisabled students. This is clearly not a convenience sample and, as such, increases the accuracy of the generalization to the population.

TABLE 1 Sample, Age, Intellectual, and Academic Achievement Characteristics

Variable	White nonhandicapped (n = 100)		White mildly handicapped (n = 59)		Black nonhandicapped (n = 99)		Black mildly handicapped (n = 44)	
	M	SD	M	SD	M	SD	M	SD
Age in years	9.33	0.97	9.15	1.49	9.22	0.68	9.28	1.32
Intellect (WISC–R)								
Verbal IQ	109.06	13.17	87.64	10.68	90.57	12.95	77.10	9.18
Performance IQ	111.35	12.84	90.13	12.39	93.81	12.33	78.89	11.93
Full-scale IQ	111.09	13.08	87.59	10.32	91.19	11.59	76.18	9.94
Academic Achievement (PIAT total)	105.56	9.12	87.14	8.11	92.18	11.81	76.82	10.43

Note. WISC–R = Wechsler Intelligence Scale for Children–Revised (Wechsler, 1974); PIAT = Peabody Individual Achievement Test (Dunn & Markwardt, 1970).

Each child's scores on the PWRS and WWRS were based on the averages of the ratings received from same-sex peers, which were converted to z scores based on the means and standard deviations of the ratings for the child's class. These scores made reference to children's relative standing in their own classrooms because the purpose of the measures was to index peer-acceptance status of children to children in their own classrooms.

The SPA is a 13-item scale on which children rate each other according to the Frequency with which the child exhibits the 13 behaviors (0 = *don't know the person*, 1 = *never*, 2 = *sometimes*, and 3 = *a lot*). This measure is similar to Guess Who?, a scale that has been used extensively in past research with mildly handicapped children (Gottlieb, Semmel, & Veldman, 1978; Morrison, 1981; Morrison et al., 1983). Items on the SPA concern social behaviors, for example, sharing with others, helping others, following rules in games, and smiling at others.

A child's SPA score was based on the average sum of the ratings for the 13 behaviors he or she received from same-sex

[3] *Let's examine sample size as revealed by this table. The group sizes (range forty-four to one hundred) are sufficient as far as most rules of thumb are concerned (e.g., thirty to forty subjects per group). They are also sufficient, generally, to detect a medium effect size. Recall this requires a per-group sample size of about sixty-three. (They are insufficient, though, to detect small effects, which require about 400 subjects per group.) These group sizes are a strength of this study, for it is rather common to see published reports of group sizes in the range of fifteen or even less, which assume that extra large effects are being sought. More commonly, educational effects are much smaller, hence research often fails to uncover significant relationships.*

This table also employs two very common statistics, the mean (M) and standard deviation (SD). Let's focus on one measure and one group, the full-scale IQ of white handicapped students. The average is 111.09, which we know is above the general population (which hovers around 100). The standard deviation as a measure of dispersion (13.08) tells us that the spread or scatter of IQ scores in this group is about the same, or a little less, than the spread you find in the general population (about 15 or 16).

peers in the classroom. The ratings were transformed to *z* scores in the same manner as were ratings for the PWRS and WWRS.

Results and Discussion

We completed a 2 × 2 × 2 (Sample × Sex × Race) fixed factorial multivariate analysis of variance (*manova*), using the PWRS, WWRS, and SPA as dependent variables. We used a general linear model that yields a more exact solution to unbalanced designs (Cohen & Cohen, 1983). A *manova* was used instead of three separate *anovas* because the three dependent variables were highly intercorrelated. The intercorrelations between the measures were as follows: (a) PWRS/WWRS, $r = .81$; (b) PWRS/SPA, $r = .85$; and (c) WWRS/SPA, $r = .83$. Table 2 contains the means as a function of the levels of each independent variable.[1]

There was a significant main effect for sample when using Wilks's lambda criterion, $F(3, 292) = 20.40$, $p < .0001$, The canonical correlation between sample and the dependent measures was .416, indicating that this effect accounted for 17.3% of the variance (lambda = .827). The sample main effect indicated that NH students had higher acceptance scores across the three dependent measures than did MH students. We calculated effect size for the sample main effect on the average score across the three dependent measures by using Glass's (1977) delta. This statistic is based on the mean of the NH group minus the mean of the MH group, divided by the standard deviation of the NH group. The effect size was .84, sug-

---

[1]We did not conduct a covariance analysis using intelligence level as a covariate because of the inequality of covariate means (i.e., the covariate is correlated with the "treatment" levels of sample, $r = .59$, and race, $r = .54$; see Table 1.) Moreover. intelligence level was not correlated with the dependent variables of PWRS ($r = .08$). WWRS ($r = . 14$), and SPA ($r = . 17$).

gesting that on the average, MH children are .84 of a standard deviation below the average acceptance of NH students. No other main effects reached significance. **[4]**

[4] *Did you recognize the effect size as being large?*

There was a significant Sample × Race interaction, *F*(3, 292) = 3.38, *p* < .05. The canonical correlation was .183, indicating that this effect accounted for 3.3% of the variance (lambda = .967). The means in Table 2 show that white NH students had higher acceptance scores than black NH students, whereas black MH students had higher acceptance scores than white MH students. No other interaction effects were significant.

The finding that MH children had lower sociometric status than their NH peers was not unexpected and is consistent with the previous literature reviewed earlier. The present data agree with Singleton and Asher's (1977) finding that race accounted for little variance in cross-race ratings of peer acceptance.

We did not expect the interaction between sample and race. As Table 2 suggests, white MH students were more poorly accepted than black MH students, and black NH students were more poorly accepted than white NH students. Two explanations of this effect seem plausible. First, Table 2 indicates that the white MH sample was more discrepant in terms of intellectual and academic performance than the black

TABLE 2 Sociometric Characteristics, Race, and Gender of Sample

	Nonhandicapped (*n* = 199)				Mildly handicapped (*n* = 103)			
	Male		Female		Male		Female	
	White (*n* = 52)	Black (*n* = 45)	White (*n* = 48)	Black (*n* = 54)	White (*n* = 31)	Black (*n* = 32)	White (*n* = 28)	Black (*n* = 12)
Measure	M SD	M SD	M SD	M SD	M SD	M SD	M SD	M SD
PWRS	103.4 16.5	92.4 14.9	108.4 14.6	106.2 14.4	90.6 16.8	96.3 6.5	87.0 12.2	90.6 8.86
WWRS	102.8 13.5	87.9 15.6	110.4 14.9	102.6 15.1	85.9 14.8	93.1 8.5	85.2 12.4	92.5 9.18
SPA	102.6 14.3	99.8 13.5	110.4 14.7	103.6 14.9	85.2 12.5	94.0 11.7	87.0 14.3	94.0 10.10

Note. PWRS = Play With Rating Scale; WWRS = Work With Rating Scale; SPA = Structured Peer Assessment.

MH sample in relation to their same-race NH peers. White MH children may experience greater academic problems in regular classrooms than black MH students. Support for this interpretation can be found in the Gottlieb et al. (1978) study, which demonstrated that peer- and teacher-perceived academic competence was associated with the social acceptance of mainstreamed educable mentally retarded pupils. Additional support for this interpretation can be found in the Morrison et al. (1983) investigation, which showed that peer and teacher perceptions or cognitive competencies act as mediating variables between observed behavior and academic achievement and sociometric status of MH students. The second explanation for this effect is that there may be racial and cultural differences in how children react to mild handicaps in educational settings. Foster and Ritchey (1979) suggested this, and it requires further study.

References

Asher, S. R., & Hymel, S. (1981). Children's social competence in peer relations: Sociometric and behavioral assessment. In J. D. Wine & M. D. Smye (Eds.), *Social competence* (pp. 125–157). New York: Guilford Press.

Cohen, J., & Cohen, P. (1983). *Applied multiple regression/analysis in the behavioral sciences.* Hillsdale, NJ: Erlbaum.

Dunn, L., & Markwardt, F. (1970). *Test.* Circle Pine, MN: American Guidance Service.

Foster, S., & Ritchey, W. (1979). Issues in the assessment of social competence in children. *Journal of Applied Behavior Analysis, 12,* 625–638.

Glass, G. V. (1977). Integrated findings: The meta-analysis of research. *Review of Research in Education, 5,* 351–379.

Gottlieb, J. (1981). Mainstreaming: Fulfilling the promise. *American Journal of Mental Deficiency, 86,* 115–126.

Gottlieb, J., Semmel, M., & Veldman, D. (1978). Correlates of social status among mainstreamed mentally retarded children. *Journal of Educational Psychology, 70,* 396–405.

Gresham, F. M. (1981). Social skills training with handicapped children: A review. *Review of Educational Research, 51,* 139–176.

Madden, N., & Slavin, R. (1983). Mainstreaming students with mild handicaps: Academic and social outcomes. *Review of Educational Research, 53,* 519–569.

Morrison, G. (1981). Sociometric measurement: Methodological consideration of its use with mildly handicapped and nonhandicapped children. *Journal of Educational Psychology, 73,* 193–201.

Morrison, G., Forness, S., & MacMillan, D. (1983). Influences on the sociometric ratings of mildly handicapped children: A path analysis. *Journal of Educational Psychology, 75,* 63–74.

Singleton, L., & Asher, S. (1977). Peer preferences and social interaction among third-grade children in an integrated school district. *Journal of Educational Psychology, 69,* 330–336.

Wechsler, D. (1974). *Wechsler Intelligence Scale for Children–Revised.* New York: Psychological Corporation.

Received September 2, 1985

Revision received October 9, 1986

Accepted December 1, 1986

APPLICATION EXERCISES

1. Assume that the amount of time in minutes-per-week high school students spend reading for pleasure is normally distributed with $M = 300$ and $SD = 60$. What can you conclude about the middle two-thirds of the distribution, with regard to time spent reading? What about ninety-five percent of the students? What percent read more than 360 minutes? (Hint: Draw a distribution with areas marked off in standard deviation units, and remember that the distribution is symmetrical.)

2. If a researcher found that a treatment designed to boost students' reading for pleasure was described with an effect size $d = 1.00$, what can you conclude about the treatment group's percentile shift? What if $d = .75$? (Hint: You will probably have to approximate this answer.)

3. Let's presume that a researcher attempted to uncover a treatment effect of "brain food" on students' memory span. Pretend that we know the concocted meal has a true effect with $d = .20$.

   a. If memory span averages 7 (with $SD = 2$), what can you conclude about the food-boosted memory span?

   b. If a researcher tested this effect with forty students in the "brain food" group and forty students in the control group, what type of conclusion would this researcher invariably make?

c. What conclusion would most likely be made if $d = .50$ and seventy-five students were in each group?

4. Assume you have a friend who wants to compare males' and females' levels of math anxiety. How would you answer her question "Is there a usual and customary number of people I'll need in each group for this comparison?"

5. If fifty people were surveyed to assess their opinions about state supported preschools for all children up to age five, what would you expect in terms of the surveys' margin of error?

6. For each of the scenarios below, identify the sampling blunder, speculate about the influence of the bias, and then make a recommendation for removing the biasing influence:

   a. A researcher wanted to know how people in the local community felt about the use of physical punishment in the public schools. He spent the afternoon at Wal-Mart and randomly approached one-hundred shoppers to ask their opinion (all agreed to cooperate). The random selection was accomplished with the use of a random number table (the numbers determined which shopper to target, e.g., the sixteenth to exit, then the thirtieth to exit, then the ninth to exit, etc.).

   b. A researcher wanted to know how students at the University felt about mandatory fees from all students to support a child care center for students with children. The researcher set up a table near the dormitory where many different types of students come and go. Those who stopped at the table and seemed friendly were asked to complete the questionnaire.

   c. In order to study differences in occupational aspirations of Catholic high school students and public high school students, a researcher randomly sampled (using school rosters with a random number table) 200 students from the largest Catholic high school and the largest public high school.

   d. In order to learn more about teachers' feelings about their personal safety while at school, a questionnaire was printed in a nationwide subscription journal of interest to many teachers. Teachers were asked to complete the questionnaire and mail it (postage paid) to the journal headquarters for tabulation.

   e. In order to study the factors that lead teachers in general to quit the profession, a group of teachers threatening to quit was extensively interviewed. The researcher obtained the group after placing an announcement about the study on the teachers' bulletin board at a large elementary school.

MULTIPLE CHOICE QUESTIONS

1. Which of the following sets of scores has the *largest* standard deviation? (Hint: A calculator is not needed.)
   a. 3, 5, 6, 5, 7
   b. 21, 20, 22, 19, 20
   c. 101, 100, 103, 102, 102
   d. 2, 6, 9, 15, 25
   e. 90, 89, 91, 92, 88

2. If the average height of adult men were 5 foot 10 inches, what would be a *reasonable* standard deviation?
   a. 1 inch
   b. 3 inches
   c. 8 inches
   d. 12 inches

e. 15 inches

3. What is the *total* required sample size for a two-group study with a presumed *medium* effect size (with other influences set to their standard values)?

    a. about 50
    b. about 60
    c. about 125
    d. about 400
    e. about 1200

4. If a researcher finds that a two-group difference was not statistically significant but the sample size was inadequate, the interpretation is therefore:

    a. ambiguous
    b. proven
    c. powerful
    d. disproven
    e. sufficient

5. What is the most common per-group "rule of thumb" as far as sample size is concerned?

    a. 10
    b. 30
    c. 100
    d. 400
    e. 1200

6. Required sample sizes for surveys are linked to the concept of precision or tolerance, but more commonly referred to as:

    a. alpha
    b. effect size
    c. standard deviations
    d. margin of error
    e. random validity

7. What are the two central ideas behind the concept of random selection?

    a. tails and power
    b. effect size and alpha
    c. equal and independent
    d. delta and significance
    e. bells and percentiles

8. Random selection is properly accomplished with which of the following?

    a. coin flips
    b. hats with numbers (or dice)
    c. capsules and fishbowls
    d. spreadsheets
    e. table of random numbers

9. The group that researchers hope to make generalized statements about is called the:

    a. cluster
    b. sample
    c. population
    d. strata
    e. subsample

10. The term that refers to generalization is _____; two types are _____, referring to people; and _____, referring to settings.
    a. internal validity; precision; tolerance
    b. instrument validity; construct; content
    c. power; cluster; strata
    d. significance; alpha; beta
    e. external validity; population; ecological

Answers: 1) d   2) b   3) c   4) a   5) b   6) d   7) c   8) e   9) c   10) e

THE RELIABILITY AND VALIDITY OF MEASURES

OVERVIEW

This chapter addresses one of the most important issues faced by educational researchers: the worth of measured outcomes. Just as the strength of a chain is measured by its weakest link, the value of a research study is often compromised by a weak step in the research process. Often the one weak step is in the measurement proccss. Meaningful research questions with strong sampling designs can be rendered pointless if the researchers' measures are not sound. If the researcher is not measuring what is supposed to be measured, how can the results be meaningfully interpreted? It turns out that measurement soundness is reflected in two qualities: reliability and validity. This chapter looks at the all-important concerns surrounding the measurement of hypothesized effects in educational research, or the "B" in the expression *If A, then B.*

INTRODUCTION TO RELIABILITY AND VALIDITY

Recall from Chapter 2 that a researcher's outcome measure is usually referred to as the *dependent variable*. High priority is placed on the dependent variable satisfying at least two criteria: reliability and validity. *Reliability* refers to the consistency of the outcome measure; *validity* refers to the accuracy of inferences that are made based on the outcome measure. An example of a reliable (consistent) measure is one that yields the same (or similar) score if a person is tested twice. An example of a valid measure is one in which a prediction made from a score is true, as in the case of the (hypothetical) ABC Test of School Attitude if it can be said that Samuel actually dropped out of high school in accordance with a prediction made on the basis of his ninth grade test score. Dependent variables should be reliable and valid no matter how they were obtained and in what form they were used (ratings, observations, surveys, portfolios, interviews, formal testing, etc.). This is important for an obvious reason: If the researcher is not measuring what he or she thinks is being measured, then the research question cannot be answered. (Some other research question may be answered, but how would the researcher even know what the question was?) For example, a researcher may think that spelling ability is being measured, when in fact it is really hearing ability. Or maybe the researcher thinks that school ability (intelligence) is being measured when in fact it is pure motivation to do well in school. Research is meaningless to the extent that the dependent measure fails to measure what it is supposed to measure.

The concepts of reliability and validity are broadly applicable, and there are no measures in educational research that are exempt from meeting the standards imposed by these concepts. This is true despite the huge variation in dependent variables used by educational researchers. Chapter 4 described some the of the myriad of measures used in educational research, all of which should measure up to be useful.

The important concepts of reliability and validity are rather technical, and they are best understood in reference to two statistics: *variance* and *correlation*. We will briefly explain these in the sections that follow, then we will see how they help explain the concepts of reliability and validity.

Variance

In Chapter 6 we saw how the standard deviation was computed from a set of scores, and how it was interpreted by reference to the normal distribution. The *variance* is the *square of the standard deviation*. (Since the variance is calculated first, it is more precise to say that the standard deviation is the square root of the variance.) If the standard deviation of a set of scores is, for example, 3, the variance becomes 9. The variance is not interpreted by reference to the normal curve; in fact, it is not interpreted against any backdrop. Simply, one can say that if a set of scores has a variance of 45, and another set has a variance of 66, then the latter set of scores is more variable (scattered or dispersed) around the mean. In a general way, educational researchers study the variance in measures, like achievement test scores. What contributes to this variance? How can this variance be explained? If the variance of a set of reading achievement scores were 450, researchers could begin to *partition* this value by, for example, attributing eighty units of the 450 units of variance to, maybe the completeness of homework reading assignments, fifty units might be attributed to the method of grouping used during reading instruction, thirty units attributed to the level of parental involvement, fifty units to socioeconomic status, ten units to birth order... You get the idea. Needless to say, the study of variance and its partitioning (explanation) is a primary focus of educational researchers.

Correlation[1]

In an attempt to explain the variance uncovered in a research study, researchers frequently determine what *other* variables are related to scores obtained in a study. We can learn a great deal about the meaning of test scores by determining whether they are related to other variables. The primary method for examining relationships between two or more variables (hence explaining variance) is via a statistical maneuver called the *correlation coefficient,* first mentioned in Chapter 5. This technique is best explained by its visual representation, the *scattergram.*

By way of illustration, let us consider one class, Ms. Robinson's, and see whether students' reading scores are related to, or correlated with, their scores on a math test as shown in Table 7.1. Constructing a scattergram of these scores involves finding the intersection of each student's two scores from two axes, or lines, drawn at right angles (each axis represents a test). Let's see how this is done. One of the students in Ms. Robinson's class, Stan, scored 91 on the reading test and 14 on the math test. Figure 7.1 shows his point as the intersection of his reading score (along the horizontal

---

[1]The material on pp. 148–151, Table 7.1 and Figure 7.1 were adapted from *Educational Psychology in the Classroom* by H. C. Lindgren and W. N. Suter. Copyright © 1985 Brooks/Cole Publishing Company, Pacific Grove, CA, a division of International Thompson Publishing Inc. By permission of the publisher.

TABLE 7.1 Ms. Robinson's Reading Test Scores Paired with Math Test Scores

Student	Reading Score	Math Score
Daniel	70	6
Juan	73	5
Marsha	70	5
Bill	73	9
Rujal	89	15
Karyn	61	3
Steve	76	8
Bobbie	73	7
Stan	91	14
Stella	73	6
Rita	69	7
Marco	61	3
William	70	7
Thom	73	6
Georgette	94	12
Nancy	76	8
Nambodiri	90	10
Kathy	89	12
Maggie	78	6
John	78	5
Sam	59	3
Peter	54	5
Gretchen	78	7
Linda	69	7
Susan	84	9

axis) and his math score (along the vertical axis) using dashed lines. Each of Ms. Robinson' students has been similarly represented on the scattergram shown in Figure 7.1. We have indicated by dashed lines the two axes for Stan's scores; you will have to imagine the others. These dashed lines do not appear on scattergrams; we used them only to illustrate the process.

Note that the plot of intersection points in Figure 7.1 shows that high reading scores are associated with high math scores, and low reading scores are associated with low math scores. Such correlations are said to be *positive*, since high scores tend to occur together and low scores tend to occur together. When this happens, the scores distribute themselves along an imaginary line running from the lower left to the upper right. A *negative* correlation, by contrast, occurs when high scores on one variable are associated with low scores on the other variable. The plot of points in that case would extend from the upper left to the lower right, as shown in Figure 7.2. When

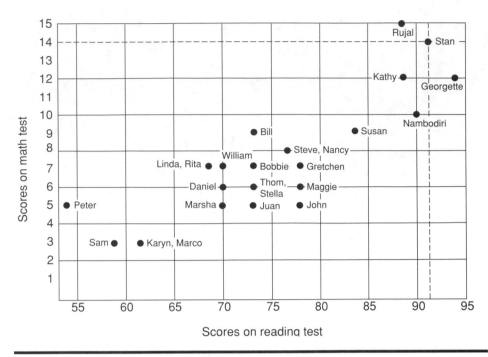

FIGURE 7.1 Scattergram of reading and math scores for students in Ms. Robinson's class. Stan's scores are plotted using dashed lines, but the whole plot reveals a positive relationship.

there is no relationship between variables or test scores, then there is no systematic tendency for high scores on one variable to be associated with high *or* low on the other variable. If Ms. Robinson's reading and math scores were *unrelated*, then high scores on the reading test would be associated equally often with high, moderate, or low

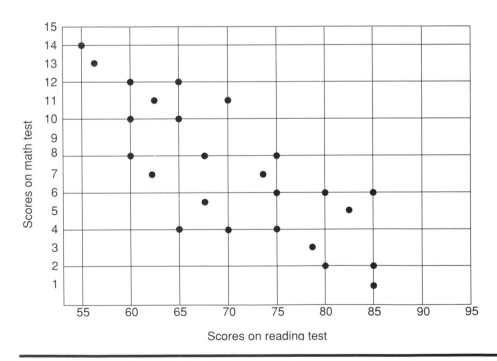

FIGURE 7.2 Scattergram for reading and math scores with names omitted, showing a negative relationship.

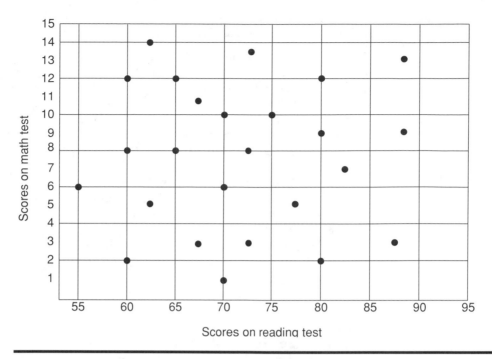

FIGURE 7.3   Scattergram for reading and math scores with names omitted, showing no relationship.

scores on the math test. This lack of relationship would appear on a scattergram as a round cloudburst, or "shotgun" blast of points as illustrated in Figure 7.3.

The exact relationship shown visually on a scattergram can be determined by a *correlation coefficient,* which quantifies the extent to which the variables are related. The correlation coefficient, symbolized as *r,* is a single value, or index, that ranges between -1.00 and +1.00 and describes both the *direction* (negative or positive) and *strength* of the relationship. The higher the *r* (closer to 1, either positive or negative), the greater is the strength or magnitude of the relationship. Strong relationships on a scattergram will show up as points that appear to fall along a straight line, as in Figure 7.1; weak or nonexistent relationships appear as a "blob" of points with little or no discernable straight-line pattern, as in Figure 7.3.

Variables which are not related at all are summarized with an *r* of zero. Consider the last digit of your phone number and the last digit of your social security number. It is inconceivable that these are related in any way, hence a scattergram would be a round blob of points, as in Figure 7.3, and the correlation coefficient *r* would equal zero. (You might try constructing a scattergram with both axes running from zero to nine in your class to confirm this *r* of zero). In sum, positive correlations can be interpreted as The higher on test A, the higher on test B; negative correlations can be interpreted as The higher on test A, the lower on test B; and zero correlations can be interpreted as The higher on test A, the higher *or* lower on test B.

Because the test scores in Figure 7.1 tend to be positively correlated, it is possible to predict with greater or lesser accuracy how well a student did on one test if you know how well he or she did on the other test. The accuracy of this prediction depends on how strongly the variables are correlated. Lower correlations, as we have seen, appear as plots with much scatter, hence lower predictability. Higher correlations, with little scatter on a plot, allow much more reliable predictions. With these ideas of variance and correlation in mind, we can now sharpen our focus on one of the most basic qualities of a good measure, its reliability.

RELIABILITY EXPLAINED (IN THEORY)

The theory behind reliability is abstract and, frankly, difficult to understand at first glance. Your understanding will be aided, however, with a fictional but concrete example. Let's focus on this example first, then we'll describe elements of the theory by reference to the example. Consider the scores shown in Table 7.2 from a sixteen-item Spelling Test. Assume that sixteen words were randomly chosen from a huge pool of many thousands of such words, and this particular selection of words is called "Spelling Test Form A." The number of correct words spelled appear under the heading "Obtained Score."

Next, as an introduction to reliability welcome to Fantasy Land, where we know students' *true scores*, or the scores they would obtain if there were no measurement error. (True scores are sometimes referred to as *universe scores*.) You can think of true scores, in the case of spelling, as the score you would get if you were tested using the huge pool of thousands of words which define the universe of all possible words (hence, universe score). For example, if the student can actually spell correctly 7,500 of the 10,000 words in the pool, the true score is seventy-five percent. You would also expect a score of twelve on each test of sixteen words (seventy-five percent of sixteen is twelve). You can also think of true scores as the average of thousands and thousands of obtained scores on many, many different forms of the sixteen-item spelling test constructed by sampling from the huge pool of words (positive and negative measurement error balances over the long run). Of course, you would never expect anyone to actually take thousands of sixteen-item spelling tests, but you can at least *imagine* doing this for the purpose of understanding reliability. If they did, the average score would be 12 (but some test scores would be higher and some lower).

Table 7.3 shows the true scores and errors for the same students. The errors were calculated by simply subtracting the true score from the obtained score on Form A. I've also included make-believe scores on a retest using a parallel form (Form B) of the Spelling Test. (Form B was simply the result of another random sampling of sixteen words from the huge pool.) You will also find what are called *split-half scores* on the first test (Form A). These split-half scores are easy to compute. Simply imagine scoring the even-numbered items on form A and the odd-numbered items on Form A. Finally, I've computed the means and standard deviations for true scores, errors, and Form B Retest Scores.

TABLE 7.2   Correct Words in Spelling Test Form A

Student	Obtained Score	
Merry	8	
Paula	7	
Craig	9	
Keith	8	mean Form A = 10.30
Bryan	7	variance Form A = 7.21
David	13	
Roger	12	
Kathy	12	
Hazel	12	
Eddie	15	

The theory behind reliability presumes that errors are random and that they balance out. What is the mean for the error scores? It is zero as expected, due to a wash-out. Test theory also presumes true scores, obtained Form A scores, and retest Form B scores have the same mean. You can see that in fact they do.

Most importantly, test theory defines *reliability* as the *ratio of true score variance over obtained score variance*. Think of reliability as the proportion of obtained score variance that is attributed to true score variance. What, then, is the reliability of obtained Form A scores? It is 4.21/7.21, or .58. You can also think about reliability in terms of a percentage (although it is reported as a proportion): fifty-eight percent of the variance in obtained scores is attributed to true scores. Think of variance as simply score differences across people—the 8 versus 13, 9 versus 12, 7 versus 9, etc. Reliability tells us that fifty-eight percent of those differences are due to true differences in the trait being measured. The other forty-two percent is attributed to errors such as accidental mistakes, inattention, carelessness, bad luck (in the sense of getting stuck with difficult words), poor guessing, and a myriad of other influences (including all the counterparts, such as good luck, etc.).

The above definition also suggests that *reliability* is the *square of the correlation between obtained scores and true scores*. Like all reliability coefficients, it is interpreted as the proportion (or percentage) of explained variance. How much variance in obtained scores (Form A) can be explained by true scores? A simple correlation between obtained scores (Form A) and true scores yields a coefficient of .76. Squaring this value (.76 squared) results in .58, which is, as expected, the same value as the ratio of true score variance (4.21) divided by obtained score variance (7.21), as described above. However you look at it, reliability is informative because it tells us what fraction of the pie is linked to the "true stuff," so to speak. Researchers like their measures to contain at least eighty percent of the "truth."

TABLE 7.3   Means and Standard Deviations for Form B Retest Scores

Student	Obtained Score Form A	True Score	Error	Retest Obtained Score Form B	Form A Split Half	
					Odd	Even
Merry	8	7	+1	9	3	5
Paula	7	8	-1	10	3	4
Craig	9	9	0	10	3	6
Keith	8	10	-2	8	4	4
Bryan	7	10	-3	7	4	3
David	13	10	+3	10	5	8
Roger	12	10	+2	12	6	6
Kathy	12	12	0	14	7	5
Hazel	12	13	-1	13	7	5
Eddie	15	14	+1	10	7	8
mean =	10.30	10.30	0	10.30		
variance =	7.21	4.21	3.00	4.21		

RELIABILITY EXPLAINED (IN PRACTICE)

Test–Retest Reliability

What good is this, you may ask, since we never know true scores in the first place? This is Fantasy Land. What about the real world? Test theory has shown that the *correlation between obtained Form A scores and retest Form B scores equals the reliability.* So we don't need true scores after all! A simple correlation between obtained Form A scores and retest Form B scores is in fact .58. This type of reliability is known as the *coefficient of stability and equivalence. Coefficient* refers to the value of the correlation, *stability* refers to the test/retest procedure, and *equivalence* refers to the parallel forms that were used. If a reliability procedure had used the same test as a retest after an interval of time (Form A given twice, the second time after, say, two months), the resultant reliability value would be known as the *coefficient of stability.* If a reliability study had used a different but parallel test in an immediate retest procedure, the resultant reliability value would be known as a *coefficient of equivalence.*

Internal Consistency Reliability: Split-Half, KR, and Alpha

What happens, you may wonder, if a retest with the same or parallel form is not possible? There is a solution. It is called *split-half reliability,* a subtype of reliability called *internal consistency* reliability. It involves splitting a single test into two equivalent (parallel) halves. An early form of this type of reliability split a test into halves by scoring all even-numbered items and scoring all odd-numbered items. You can think of it as a type of retest using two tests (each only half as long) given without any time interval between testings. These two (half) test scores are then correlated in the usual way. This type of reliability involves a statistical adjustment called *Spearman-Brown (SB)* to compensate for the shortened length of the two half-tests. The formula is:

$$\text{SB adjusted reliability} = \frac{2 \text{ times odd/even correlation}}{\text{odd/even correlation} + 1}$$

The simple correlation between odd/even is .41, applying the SB formula [2(.41)/ .41 +1] yields the familiar coefficient of .58, as expected.

More modern versions of this odd/even split take into consideration all possible ways to split a test into two halves, including one random half with the other random half. (What is so special about odd versus even? Nothing.) There are, of course, thousands of ways to split a reasonably long test into two halves, and formulas have been developed which quickly compute the average of all possible split-half reliabilities. One common formula is KR20, which was named after its developers, G. F. Kuder and M. W. Richardson, and formula #20 in their article which described this type of reliability. KR20 can be estimated with a simpler formula, KR21, which assumes test items have equal difficulty levels (the KR21 estimate is slightly lower than the KR20 value). The simpler KR21 formula is:

$$\text{KR21} = \frac{k}{k-1}\sqrt{1 - \frac{\text{mean}(k - \text{mean})}{k(\text{variance})}}$$

where k refers to the number of items on the test

KR20 and KR21 are limited to the extent that test items can be scored on a right or wrong (1 or 0) scale. Some measurement scales have other values (e.g., a 1–7 agree/ disagree attitude scale, a 1, 2, 3 never, sometimes, always scale, etc.). Another reliability formula has been developed for this purpose called Cronbach's alpha, after its developer, L. J. Cronbach. Alpha, as it turns out, is a general, all purpose formula because, if applied to a right/wrong scale, it is equivalent to KR20. Hence, alpha can be applied to *all* types of scales (including right/wrong), and appears to be the most widely used form for testing internal consistency reliability. This is because many measuring instruments depart from a simple right/wrong scoring system.

All internal consistency reliability coefficients can be interpreted as the expected correlation between one test and a hypothetical, parallel form administered without any time interval. As such, these forms of reliability can also be interpreted in terms of the percentage of obtained variance that is true variance. In this particular case, we can say that fifty-eight percent of the differences (or variance) in scores can be traced to true (or "real") differences in the ability being measured; the other forty-two percent can be attributed to unwanted random error.

Inter-Rater Reliability

Researchers often use raters to collect information which serves as the dependent variable. Examples here include observers' rating of second graders' hyperactivity, teachers' effectiveness, tenth graders' creativity, eighth graders' writing ability, seventh graders' self-esteem, or a school's climate. *Inter-rater reliability* can be applied to these situations in order to determine the consistency of observations. Lack of inter-rater reliability would be evident if, in the scoring of students' essays, one rater awarded a rating of 7 (on a 1–7 scale) to one student but another rater awarded a 2. When raters disagree, the researcher cannot be certain about the "truth." This type of inconsistency suggests error, for if there exists a "truth" about the scored essay (let's say it is a true 7), then both raters cannot be correct.

Inter-rater reliability can be determined by the familiar correlation maneuver. In the case of two raters, a scattergram of both of their ratings for several essays would provide a visual display of their consistency. Examine the two plots in Figures 7.4 and 7.5.

As revealed by the wide scatter, it is clear from Figure 7.4 that little or no consistency exists between raters whereas, Figure 7.5 shows general consistency as evi-

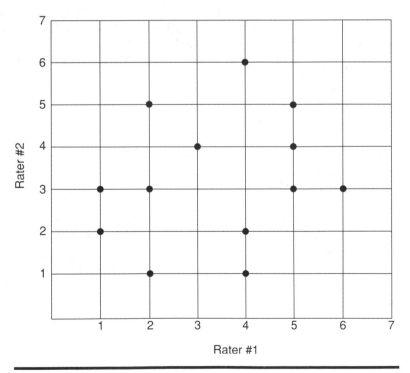

FIGURE 7.4 A scattergram showing two raters' evaluations of thirteen essays reveals low inter-rater reliability (.22).

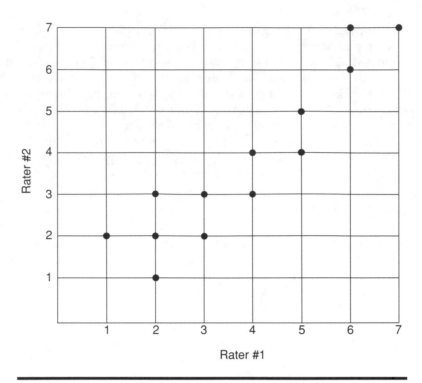

FIGURE 7.5 A scattergram showing two raters' evaluations of thirteen essays reveals high inter-rater reliability (.92).

denced by the lack of scatter. High inter-rater reliability is usually obtainable when raters are sufficiently trained with practice and feedback and can agree on what they are being asked to rate. For example, raters would not be expected to visit schools and simply rate the overall "climate." They would be asked to evaluate specific dimensions, such as students' behavior, administrators' friendliness, teachers' burnout, or whatever other factors are agreed upon as contributors to school climate.

There are other formulas that can be used to determine the reliability of more than just two raters (not surprising, they are correlation maneuvers called *correlation ratios*). Also, inter-rater reliability coefficients are sensitive to consistency in terms of relative agreement; they do not determine absolute agreement. For example, Rater A may rate three essays using ratings of 2, 3, 4; Rater B may rate the same essays 5, 6, 7. Rater B is simply more lenient and believes all of the essays deserve higher ratings than those awarded by Rater A. There is perfect relative agreement, however, since the three essays can be rank ordered in perfect agreement. This is a case of perfect reliability, but zero agreement. An *agreement index* can be calculated by dividing the total number of agreement by the total number of agreements *plus* disagreements.

We have seen that reliability can be explained in terms of true score variance. Reliability can also be described in terms of *consistency, dependability,* and *reproducibility.* This consistency can be thought of as consistency over four general sources: **time, forms, items,** and **raters.** Consistency over time is often referred to as *stability* (or *test–retest*); consistency in forms as *equivalence* (or *parallel form*); consistency in items as *internal consistency*; and among raters as *inter-rater reliability* (or *relative agreement*). These different types of reliability are sensitive to different sources of error (inconsistency), and there is no reason to expect their equivalence. Because of this, it is not correct to assume that, for example, internal consistency (errors due to item variation) would be the same as stability (error due to time factors). (In our demonstration example from Fantasy Land using true scores, the data were rigged to show the equivalence of retest and internal consistency. This was for the purpose of showing how different types of reliability are conceptually similar in the sense that they are all sensitive to errors, but one would not expect them to be equivalent in practice.) The different types of reliability are summarized in Table 7.4.

Reliability of Scores, Not Tests

Perhaps the most misunderstood fact about reliability is that it describes a facet of a *set of scores* produced by a testing instrument and not the instrument itself. Because of this, it is not technically correct to say that such-and-such instrument has a reliability of .85 (or whatever). By contrast, you should say that the *set of scores* from a particular sample in a specific situation can be described with a reliability of .85. It must be emphasized that the reliability of scores from a test is influenced greatly by the composition of the sample taking the test. When there is larger variance in scores (greater range of talent, greater spread in ability, etc.) reliability tends to be *higher.* By contrast, when the group heterogeneity is low, reliability tends to *decrease.* This is one reason why a test may produce scores with a reliability of .90 in one study and scores with a reliability of .50 in another. It is the amount of variability in a group, not the size of the group per se, that affects reliability. (Size of the sample affects reliability only to the extent that it affects its variability.)

The introduction of *un*reliability (score *in*consistency) in a set of data lowers the sensitivity or power of a statistical test used to analyze the data. This lack of sensitivity or power in a statistical test makes it more difficult to find relationships, when in fact relationships do exist in the population represented by the sample. In other words, unreliability tends to increase the probability that the conclusion will show that a relationship does *not* exist in the population when, in reality, it does. All sources of error in measurement tend to contribute to this "missed sighting."

In published research, one typically finds a statement describing the reliability of an instrument being used to answer the research question. (More technically, it is the reliability of scores produced by that instrument.) Unfortunately, this statement usually refers to the reliability of the instrument as used in another study. This is unfortunate because reliability is influenced by many factors, and the reliability of scores in a research study may be very different from what someone else has reported using a different sample. Therefore, in a published research report, reliability coefficients should always be reported describing the data collected from the instrument as used *in the study.* Because one researcher's reliable data from a test may not generalize at all to your data from the same test, the computation of reliability in a published study should be routine. This is important because if it were low (for example, below .60), a fair test of the hypothesis would not be possible. How would you know whether a finding of "no difference" was because no relationship exists in the population, or whether it *does* exist but was overlooked due to too much unreliability (error) in the sampled data? You wouldn't know for sure, of course, but information about the

TABLE 7.4 Different Types of Reliability Using the Hypothetical ABC Test of Spelling

Reliability Type	Errors Over	Question
Stability (test-retest)	Time	Are scores similar at both times?
Equivalence (parallel form)	Forms	Are scores similar on both forms?
Internal Consistency (e.g., alpha)	Items	Are responses similar across items?
Observer (inter-rater)	Raters	Are raters in relative agreement?

reliability of the measures will help you make a more informed conclusion. Different conclusions will be made if no relationships are uncovered with reliable versus unreliable data.

The reliability of measures is threatened, as we have seen, by the introduction of countless sources of error. There is one variable, however, that is known to *increase* the reliability of measurements. That variable is test length. All other factors held constant, it can be shown that reliability increases as test length increases (assuming that the test is not so long that respondents become careless from fatigue). This should make some intuitive sense, for a very short (say, two-item) test of spelling ability might yield a score of 2 out of 2 correct from a relatively poor speller—thanks to error due to lucky guesses. Lucky error probably would not explain a good score on a longer test (30 out of 30 correct); the truth would more likely come out, maybe as a score of 5 out of 30. In fact, test developers don't worry much about lucky guesses, even on relatively short tests. The probability of scoring one hundred percent by correctly guessing only five multiple-choice questions, each with only four choices, is very slim indeed—1 out of 1,024!

Standard Error of Measurement

The reliability coefficient is closely associated with another useful measurement statistic called the *standard error of measurement,* often abbreviated SEM. Whereas the reliability coefficient refers to a *set* of measures, the SEM is most useful for interpreting an *individual's* score. Given one person's obtained score, we can use the SEM to estimate how far away their true score probably lies. It turns out that about sixty-eight percent of the test-takers on a given test would have true scores that are within 1 SEM of their obtained scores; ninety-five percent would have true scores that are within 2 SEMs of their obtained scores. Only about five percent would have true scores that differed by more than 2 SEMs from their obtained scores. In other words, if you double the SEM, add and subtract that value from the obtained score, you have a person's interval that probably includes their true score. This would be true for ninety-five out of one hundred test takers with such intervals; whether it is true for one particular person is not known. We can only say that the interval probably does span the true score for a specific person, since it does for ninety-five percent of the people. Here is another example. If you score 500 on the GRE Verbal section, and the SEM is 30, then we can say that your true score probably falls (with a .95 certainty) between 440 and 560. (Taking that test thousands of times would probably earn you an average between 440 and 560.) The SEM can also be thought of as the standard deviation of one person's obtained scores around their true score.

The SEM has an easy calculation, if the reliability coefficient is known. The formula is:

$$SEM = SD\sqrt{1 - \text{reliability}}$$

where SD refers to the standard deviation of a set of scores. Let's apply this formula to a set of intelligence test scores. Assume the standard deviation was about 15 and the reliability was about .89, we then have SEM = 15 $\sqrt{1 - .89}$ = 5.00 (rounded). If Mary scored 115 on an IQ test, her true score would probably fall (chances are 95 out of 100) in the interval 105–125. The SEM also has a use in classroom tests as well. For example, recent test scores for a course I teach had a reliability of .85 with a standard deviation of about 8, hence a SEM of about 3. The lower-bound cutoff for an A was 90, but I lowered it by 3 points (the value of the SEM) to account for unreliability in the form of errors of measurement. A classroom test with a lower reliability, like .60, might warrant an adjusted cutoff 2 SEMs below the original one to account for substantial error of measurement.

VALIDITY

Validity is considered the most important quality of a measured dependent variable. This is because validity is concerned with whether the instrument used actually measures what it is supposed to measure. The concern is as basic as "Do those ratings of hyperactivity really reflect hyperactivity and nothing else?", or "Do those scores from the self-esteem instrument actually reflect self-esteem and nothing else?", or "Does this test of scholastic aptitude actually predict school achievement?", or "Does this test of science knowledge accurately measure the extent to which the course objectives were met?"

Validity is the primary concern of all researchers who gather educational data. Reliability plays second fiddle to validity because reliability is of little concern if the measure is not a valid one. Who would care about reliability (consistency) if validity is lacking? There is no value in consistently measuring something that is off-target, or that you do not want. It is true that reliability is a sufficient condition for validity in the sense that reliability must be present for validity to exist. How could an instrument measure what it is supposed to measure if it is full of errors? Reliability, though, does not guarantee validity. This is because a measure may be reliable, but still not measure what it should. It might reliably measure something else.

It is important to keep in mind that reliability tells us how well an instrument is measuring *whatever it is measuring*. If it is measuring whatever it is measuring with little error, then we know that it is reliable. Reliability does not tell us *what* is being measured, only how well it is measuring. The issue of *what* is being measured is the concern of *validity.*

An image might help here, as shown in Figure 7.6. Think about throwing darts at a target. Reliable tosses strike consistently in one place, but may or may not be near the bull's eye. Hitting consistently in the upper right would illustrate reliability without validity—not too impressive. Hits in the bull's eye, where they are supposed to be, would illustrate validity. Like darts which consistently hit in the center, researchers strive for reliable *and* valid scores with their instruments.

Researchers have found it is useful to approach the issue of validity from three angles, each angle being relevant for the specific purpose the instrument is intended to serve. These three types of validity are: *content, predictive,* and *construct.* (In fact, there are several other types of validity, but these "big three" appear to satisfy the concerns of most researchers.) Each of these three will be described next. It is important to keep in mind the specific purpose for which a test was designed and constructed, or at least

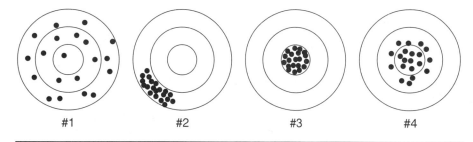

FIGURE 7.6   Reliability and validity applied to dart throwing. Darts thrown in the bull's eye are valid—that's where they are supposed to be. Darts thrown in a consistent area—anywhere on the target—are reliable. Note that throws can be reliably off-target. #1 reveals low reliability and low validity, #2 reveals high reliability but low validity, #3 reveals high reliability and high validity, and #4 reveals fair reliability and fair validity. (After Wallen & Fraenkel, 1991, p. 96).

the specific purpose for which the test is put. It makes little sense to discuss a test's validity in a broad sense. *It is far more meaningful to discuss a test's validity for a specific purpose.*

Content Validity

Content validity is of greatest concern for researchers who study achievement. (It is also of prime importance for classroom teachers who construct classroom achievement tests.) As an example, consider the Stanford Achievement Test Series. It was designed to provide "information upon which decisions for improving curriculum and instruction can be made" (Stanford Achievement Test Series, 1989, p. 9). A test with such a purpose must assess the extent to which educational objectives are being met, that is, whether students are learning what is being taught (assuming what is taught matches the instructional objectives). It would be especially informative to determine which teaching methods and techniques, for example, are associated with unusually high achievement.

To meet this end, the test constructors of the Stanford Achievement Test first reviewed states' and districts' guidelines and curricula as well as examined the widely used textbooks at all levels. The test objectives were then formulated from a large pool of concepts and skills which were universally taught. At each step in the test construction, curriculum specialist and content area experts reviewed what are called "blueprints" for determining the "breadth" and "depth" of tested objectives. Ultimately, the content validity of the Stanford Achievement Test was strengthened by assuring it contained a representative and balanced coverage of what is termed the "national consensus curriculum" (1989, p. 9). Less careful test construction would have jeopardized the test's content validity by including mismatches between instructional objectives and test content. The content validity of tests is important because without it, one would not know whether low achievement test scores were the result of learning deficits or learning/testing mismatches. Assessment of content validity is frequently made by expert judgments with the aid of descriptive statistics, as opposed to complex statistical manipulations. As a student, you've probably experienced the feeling of test invalidity when you encountered a classroom test item that was not linked to any instructional material. That's not fair!

Predictive Validity

Very often educational and psychological tests are constructed with the intention of predicting a future outcome. The Scholastic Assessment Test (previously Scholastic Ability Test) was constructed with this purpose in mind. Could high school students' success or failure in their first year of college be predicted on the basis of test scores? If so, then the SAT would have strengthened its validity for predicting academic success. (The SAT was developed for other purposes as well, including the tracking of ability on a national basis over time, since 1941.) Because the SAT was concerned with predicting college success, as opposed to assessing high school achievement, it was not a concern to match test items with high school curricula. The primary concern was assessing how well students could reason, both verbally and mathematically. The test content samples verbal reasoning skills in many ways, but most commonly through reading comprehension. The ability to answer questions after reading a passage is enhanced not so much by a knowledge base reflecting the high school curriculum, but by an ability to comprehend written information and use verbal reasoning skills. One would gather information about the predictive validity of such tests by showing that scores are, in fact, linked to future measures of college success (e.g., grades).

It is easy to imagine many contexts in which educators could use such "crystal balls." Predicting an event like dropping out of high school by use of measures collected in junior high school is one example. This information could be used by targeting high risk students and intervening with appropriate methods shown to decrease the chances of dropping out. Forecasting in this way is valuable because once the dropping out process has begun it is often too late to stop.

Predicting which one of several methods of instruction is linked to the greatest probability of success is another application of predictive validity. For example, a student's preferred learning style could be measured on a scale of 1–10 reflecting a level of structure (lower scores reflect a preference for less structure and higher scores a preference for more structure). If it can be shown that scores on the learning style test do in fact predict which method of teaching results in the greatest success, then the scores could be used for placement recommendations. The test, therefore, would have predictive validity for that specific purpose.

Construct Validity

Validation as a Process.   As you might expect, the construct validity of measures is appropriate whenever the instrument is supposed to measure a construct. Recall from Chapter 2 that a *construct* is a label for an abstract trait or ability that is only presumed to exist. Take intelligence, undoubtedly the single-most influential, and enduring construct in education. Behind every construct exists a theory to explain it (recall that constructs don't exist in a vacuum). The theory, as we have seen, produces testable hypotheses. If the hypotheses are supported using the instrument designed to measure the construct, then it can be said that the *construct validity* of the measure is supported, at least partially. Notice that a bundle of three outcomes results from a favorable test of a theory: (1) the research hypothesis is supported, (2) the theory is made more credible, and (3) the construct validity of the measure is supported. Establishing the construct validity of a measure, then, is rather indirect and somewhat convoluted. Thus, construct validity cannot be demonstrated in a one-shot study. It is a slow process and parallels the same tedious path that leads to the eventual acceptance of a theory.

Construct validation can also be easily sidetracked. This is because a research hypothesis may not be supported (maybe the theory that spun the hypothesis was wrong) even though the construct validity of the measure was intact. The construct validity of a measure is enhanced if the research hypothesis is supported, but a null research finding sheds no light on the construct validity of the measure. A null finding is ambiguous, because there are many reasons for a finding of no difference, aside from a lack of construct validity with the measure. Some examples of these include: inadequate sample size, poor controls, biases, and, of course, a flawed theory. Construct validation is a type of "piggy back" to the process of supporting a research hypothesis and testing a theory.

How, you might wonder, are null research findings ever useful if they could always stem from measures which might lack construct validity? The truth is that construct validation is a *process*. Over time (a long time, usually), the construct validation of an instrument is said to be "established" (at least tentatively). The Weschler and Stanford-Binet intelligence scales, for example, are reasonably well accepted as construct valid measures of traditional intelligence (verbal, spatial, and numerical reasoning). (These tests were never intended to assess "street smarts," "people smarts," or introspective, athletic, or musical intelligence). When these construct validated measures are used to test theories about intelligence and the research hypotheses are not supported, then one can assuredly conclude that the theory which generated the research hypotheses is flawed and should be rejected. (This still assumes adequate sample size, proper controls, and the like.) Needless to say, it is highly desirable to use instruments with at least some level of established construct validity. This position, in its extreme, is dangerous, though, because it leads to scientific "ruts" and an unwillingness to explore new constructs by using measures which obviously lack established validity.

Example: Self-Esteem. Let's explore another important construct, *self-esteem,* to see how measures of this construct might be validated. At present, there appears to be no measure of self-esteem with established, long-lived validity (no "golden standard"). Researchers working in the area of self-esteem need a theory for guidance, and selection of a theory will further guide the choice (or construction) of an instrument used to measure self-esteem. The choice may center on, for example, the *Coopersmith Self-Esteem Inventory* (SEI, Coopersmith, 1967), specifically Version A with fifty true/false questions. If this instrument has construct validity, then it should be sensitive to the generally agreed-upon developmental changes in self-esteem. Berger (1991) reported, "In general, self-esteem, which is usually quite high in early childhood, decreases in middle childhood, reaching a low at about age 12 before it gradually rises again" (p. 396). *The Coopersmith Self-Esteem Inventory* when administered to children across this age span should show these peaks and valleys in scores if it is indeed measuring the trait (self-esteem) that it presumes to measure. If the scores show this pattern, then one can conclude that the *Coopersmith Self-Esteem Inventory* has one more notch recorded in support of its construct validity.

Another approach to the inch-by-inch construct validation of the *Coopersmith Self-Esteem Inventory* would include matching the scores of the Coopersmith with other instruments believed to measure the same construct. The rationale here is simple: two measures of the same thing should converge, in the sense that they are in agreement when used to measure the self-esteem of a group of participants. If the two tests reveal discrepant findings then, once again, the results are ambiguous. One (but which one?) or both of the instruments do not measure what they intend to measure, since if they did the scores would have to be similar.

You may have guessed that there are countless ways to amass evidence in favor of construct validity. One final example will illustrate the range of approaches. Self-esteem, as a theory would suggest, not only predicts that the self-esteem measure be related to other variables it should be related to, but also that it *not* be related to variables it should *not* be related to. For example, self-esteem in theory should not be related to, say, social desirability (the tendency to portray oneself in a favorable light, even at the expense of honesty). If these two constructs are related, it suggests that the measure of self-esteem might be contaminated, to some degree, by this other personality trait. Such contamination would, of course, threaten the validity of the self-esteem test because it is supposed to measure self-esteem, not social desirability. It could also be argued that self-esteem should not be related to, say, preferred learning styles, but should be related to scholastic achievement (at least according to the theory that guided the development of the self-esteem instrument). Collecting data by ad-

TABLE 7.5   Summary of Differences between Content, Predictive, and Construct Validity

Test:

ABC Test of Vocabulary

Content:	Does it measure the achievement of vocabulary knowledge as reflected in the instructional objectives?
Predictive:	Do test scores predict who will not do well in English next year?
Construct:	Does this test measure what we call verbal intelligence?

XYZ Test of Creativity

Content:	Does the test measure the flexible thinking that was taught in Lesson 1?
Predictive:	Do test scores predict who will earn patents?
Construct:	Does this test measure the trait of creativity?

ministering the self-esteem, learning style, and achievement tests would provide information to evaluate the construct validity of the self-esteem inventory. Table 7.5 summarizes the major differences between content, predictive, and construct validity.

CHAPTER SUMMARY

Educational researchers use a wide variety of instruments in the conduct of their research, but whatever their form, the measures must satisfy two criteria to be useful: reliability and validity. *Reliability* is an index that is sensitive to errors of measurement (the difference between obtained scores and true scores) and is best understood as consistency. Different types of reliability can be computed, each one sensitive to different types of consistency. These include test–retest reliability (consistency over time), parallel form reliability (consistency between two forms of the same test), internal consistency reliability (consistency among items), and inter-rater reliability (consistency among raters). A reliability coefficient does not reveal what the instrument actually measures; only how well (how much error) it measures. *Validity*, by contrast, is the standard that reflects the meaningfulness of the scores, or what is actually being measured. Valid instruments, then, measure what they are supposed to measure. An instrument yields valid scores to the extent that the inferences made on the basis of test scores are accurate. Three types of validity can be assessed: *content* (the match between items on a test and the domain of all admissible items), *predictive* (the match between predictions based on test scores and the actual outcome that the test is trying to predict), and *construct* (the match between test scores and the trait that the test is measuring according to the theory behind the trait).

　　　Let's see how these important concepts of reliability and validity are applied in a published research report.

GUIDED TOUR

Let's turn our attention now to a guided tour of published educational research. This will help solidify important terms and concepts described in this chapter.

Cultural Literacy:
A Concurrent Validation

Joseph F. Pentony

University of St. Thomas

Houston, Texas

E. D. Hirsch's (1987) book *Cultural Literacy* has raised

much interest and controversy over the construct of

The author gratefully acknowledges the assistance of E. D. Hirsch, Brenda Loyd, David Osberg and the members of the University of St. Thomas English Department.

cultural literacy. It is the purpose of this investigation to evaluate the reliability and the validity of the Cultural Literacy Test. The test was administered to 150 college students. A split-half reliability coefficient of .93 was obtained. The test scores yielded a correlation of .59 with the Verbal SAT and .31 with grades in freshman English. No statistically significant correlation was obtained between scores and GPA. The Cultural Literacy Test did differentiate between the ability levels of freshman English. It was concluded that the reliability and validity of the construct and test of cultural literacy is supported.

Cultural Literacy, a book by E. D. Hirsch, has generated enormous interest since its publication in 1987. Its major thesis is that poor readers do not know much about our cultural background and are therefore put at a serious disadvantage in reading comprehension. Hirsch conducted studies comparing the reading comprehension of community college students with that of university students and found surprising results. Community college students did as well as university students on topics not requiring cultural knowledge (friendship) but more poorly on topics requiring this knowledge (e.g., Ulysses S. Grant and Robert E. Lee). Community college students did as well as university students on tests of memory and vocabulary, and on the mechanics of eye movements, but on tests of cultural literacy community college students did more poorly (see Hirsch, 1987, p. 41–47). This gap in reading comprehension is particularly disabling to the children of the lower and possibly the lower-middle socioeconomic classes (Hirsch, 1987, p. 142). Hirsch vigorously denied the criticism that he wanted to invent a list of cultural literacy information but claimed that a list already exists and that he had merely made it explicit (Hirsch, 1987, p. 143–145). The list is used much to the disadvantage of the lower socioeconomic classes because middle class children learn this implicit list at home and the lower classes do not. He has subsequently developed a dictionary of cultural literacy for adults (Hirsch, Kett, and Trefil, 1988) and even for children (Hirsch, 1989) and noted that only a relatively small amount of information stands between the literate and the illiterate. This dictionary consists of 5000 items and may serve as 5000 nodes within the context of network theory in cognitive psychology in which Hirsch embeds his construct of cultural literacy.

Hirsch (1988) has developed a 115-item test to measure his construct of cultural literacy, and has reported a correlation of .82 between the Verbal SAT and the Cultural Literacy Test with 11th and 12th graders in a randomly selected Virginia sample. The test manual reports national norms for 11th and 12th graders (Hirsch, 1990). There appear to be no studies assessing the Cultural Literacy Test against criteria other than another test. Kosmoski (1989) found a significant positive correlation between her Cultural Literacy Assessment Test and academic achievement with fifth graders. Anastasi (1988) has stressed that there "is an increasing need for the use of tests in educational evaluation for *many* (italics is the author's) purposes" (p. 416). [1] The purpose of the present research is to assess the reliability and validity of this test against different criteria (e.g., Verbal SAT, GPA, and grade earned in freshman English). If the test is shown to be valid, then Hirsch's construct may be supported. That is, it is expected a test of cultural literacy correlates particularly with such measures as Verbal SAT, GPA, and grade in freshman English. However, it should not correlate too highly with other tests (Anastasi, 1988) because it would not give any additional information. From this perspective Hirsch's correlation of .82 with Verbal SAT is a potential

[1] *The only way to learn about a test's reliability and validity is by conducting empirical studies. Such studies are designed to show how much error is contained within the measure (its reliability) and whether or not the test scores are related to other critical variables that it should be related to (its validity). As we have seen, many educational tests are designed to measure constructs, in this case, the construct of cultural literacy. It is the theory behind the construct that dictates which variables should be related (or unrelated) to the test scores and how strong the relationships should be. This is what Pentony is describing in this section. We learn about a test's validity only by examining its relationship with other measures; this is a slow, plodding activity.*

problem—if the relation is this high, maybe Hirsch is just measuring verbal aptitude in a different way.

Specifically it was hypothesized that the students in the Honors English class would be superior to the students in the Regular sections who would be superior to those in the Remedial sections on the cultural literacy measure. It was also predicted that the Cultural Literacy Test would correlate significantly with English course grades, grade point average, and Verbal SAT scores.

Method

Sample

A total of 171 students were registered in first-semester freshman English at the University of St. Thomas, Houston, Texas. The 150 subjects studied comprised 88% of all fulltime first semester freshmen. Sixty-eight percent of the students at this university are Anglo, 13% Hispanic-American, 5% black, and 7% are from foreign countries.

Test Administration

Subjects were administered Hirsch's (1988) Cultural Literacy Test in their regular classroom. Directions were modified in order to interface with a NCS answer sheet as this procedure would allow an item analysis to be performed. The test takes approximately 50 minutes.

Statistical Analyses

A correlation matrix of six variables was generated and included the total score, odd and even items in order to calculate an estimate of reliability and the three criterion variables: (a) grade earned in the freshman English course, (b) grade point average, and (c) Verbal SAT. The freshman English grade was composed of the following weights: (a) 40% written papers, (b) 25% tests, (c) 25% final exam, and (d) 10% class participation and other. All correlations were Pearson product-moment coefficients. The 150 subjects were assigned to one of three sections based on their scores on the SAT Verbal: (a) Remedial (SAT verbal score of 400 and below), (b) Regular, and (c) Honors English (SAT verbal score of 540 and up). A one-way analysis of variance (ANOVA) was performed between type of section with scores on the Cultural Literacy Test serving as the dependent variable. Finally, a stepwise regression analysis was performed with SAT, grade in English, and GPA employed as the mediators and Cultural Literacy scores as the criterion.

Results

It can be seen from Table 1 that the total scale score for the Cultural Literacy test correlated significantly with grade in the English course ($r = .31$) and with Verbal SAT ($r = .59$). Total score did not correlate significantly with overall GPA ($r = .06$). Verbal SAT predicted grade in freshman English ($r = .32$) about the same as did the Cultural Literacy Test; but the Verbal SAT predicted GPA better than the Cultural Literacy Test ($r = .27$). The ANOVA results indicated that the Honors section ($n = 15$; $M = 93.0$. $SD = 8.6$) was superior to the Regular section ($n = 118$; $M = 76.7$; $SD = 14.8$) which was in turn higher than the Remedial section ($n = 17$; $M = 64.1$; $SD = 13.5$) ($p < .001$). The obtained odd-even reliability coefficient was $r = .88$; with the Spearman-Brown adjustment, it reached $r = .93$. [3]

TABLE 1   [2] The Relationship of the Cultural Literacy Test Verbal SAT, GPA, and Grade in Freshman English (Decimal Points Omitted)

	Cultural Literacy	SAT	GPA
SAT	59		
GPA	06	27	
ENGL	31	32	66

Note. $r = .159$, $p = .05$; $r = .206$, $p = .01$.

[2] *Here is a summary of the correlations of the Cultural Literacy Test scores with other measures. Remember, it is the pattern of relationships (some strong, some weak) which are interpreted by the researcher as support (or lack of) for the validity of the test for the specific purpose for which the test was put. Note that these relationships are relevant to the construct validity of the test. (See #4 on the following page.)*

[3] *Here is a description of the reliability of the test scores. Remember that there are several different types of reliability, each type being sensitive to different types of error. Also, remember, there is no such thing as the reliability of a test. It is the set of scores produced by the test that can be described in terms of reliability. In this case, a type of internal consistency reliability is reported, the split-half coefficient. (It is a special case of the more general alpha coefficient.) Its value of .93 is very high, suggesting that there is little measurement error in the scores. This small amount of error shows up as consistency across scores, in the sense that the differences across people appear to reflect true underlying differences in the trait being measured. Another way to think about this is that the high split-half reliability tells us that the differences among students are "real." Please recall, though, that reliability does not tells us what the test measures. It only tells us how well the test measures whatever it measures.*

A stepwise regression was performed with SAT, grade in freshman English, and GPA used as predictor variables. The beta coefficients were .56 for SAT and .17 for grade in freshman English. The R squared between the Cultural Literacy Test and SAT was .39 and rose to .42 when freshman English grade was included. GPA did not reach the predetermined cut-off score ($p = .05$ or less) to be included in the equation.

For the total sample, the mean for the SAT was 458.9 ($SD = 95.7$); for GPA, 2.62 ($SD = .87$); and for grade in freshman English, 2.85 ($SD = .87$) (i.e., a C+). As the Verbal SAT correlated significantly with GPA and grade in freshman English, the validity of the two criteria measures employed is considered to be supported.

Discussion

It appears that the Cultural Literacy Test is very reliable with a high split-half reliability estimate of .93. It can be seen that three of the four hypotheses were confirmed; that is, there were significant positive relationships between the Cultural Literacy Test and the Verbal SAT, level of English section, and grade in freshman English. However, the prediction relating to overall GPA was not borne out. Possibly, GPA is not easily predicted at the University of St. Thomas as its correlation with Verbal SAT ($r = .27$) is lower than usually reported in the literature (Anastasi, 1988). **[4]** Thus, there appears to be moderate support for the validity of the Cultural Literacy Test and for the general construct of cultural literacy. Of course, to establish the construct validity of cultural literacy, more than one study is needed. It is interesting to note that the Cultural Literacy Test correlated with grade in freshman English but not with overall GPA. This result is not unexpected as Hirsch (1987) noted that reading and writing are closely interrelated, and a major part of the grade in freshman English involves writing skills. The present author be-

[4] *Here is a "judgment call," as there is no one single "index of validity" (as is more common with reliability). The overall interpretation is "moderate" support for the validity of the Cultural Literacy Test. Others, however, may examine the same data and set of relationships, yet offer a different interpretation. This is not uncommon, and the problem of contrary interpretations of the same data applies to educational research in general.*

lieves that the correlation of .59 with the Verbal SAT shows more discriminant validity than that of .82 reported by Hirsch, because a high correlation indicates that the two tests are measuring the same thing. For this sample, the Cultural Literacy Test predicts grade in freshman English as well as the Verbal SAT does. Hirsch would probably claim that the Cultural Literacy Test is more explicit and therefore fairer than the Verbal SAT. Overall, Hirsch's construct of cultural literacy is moderately supported. The construct of cultural literacy, as separate from general verbal intelligence, is a useful one because it is more specifically remedial. For example, the test could target specific weaknesses for specific classes or individuals.

Messick (1989) has addressed the issue of population generalizability; i.e., validity across different populations. As the sample sizes for Honors and Remedial sections were quite small it is not possible to address this issue in the present study. Future research using other samples, particularly community college students, is needed; Hirsch (1987) argued that the lack of cultural literacy is particularly disabling in this setting. Two studies now support the reliability and validity of the Cultural Literacy Test, so its validity for practical use appears promising but is not yet convincing.

References

Anastasi, A. (1988). *Psychological testing* (6th ed.). New York: Macmillan.

Hirsch, E. D. (1987). *Cultural literacy.* Boston: Houghton-Mifflin.

Hirsch, E. D. (1988). *Cultural literacy: Standardization edition.* Chicago: Riverside.

Hirsch, E. D. (1989). *A first dictionary of cultural literacy: What our children need to know.* Boston: Houghton-Mifflin.

Hirsch, E. D. (1990). *Cultural literacy test: Manual for administration and interpretation.* Chicago: Riverside.

Hirsch, E. D., Kett, J. F., and Trefil, J. (1988). *The dictionary of cultural literacy: What every American needs to know.* Boston: Houghton-Mifflin.

Kosmoski, G. J. (1989). Relationship between cultural literacy and academic achievement. *Dissertation Abstracts International, 50,* 2771-A. (University Microfilms Order No. DA9003918).

Messick, S. (1989). Validity. In Linn, R. L. (Ed.), *Educational measurement.* New York, Macmillan.

APPLICATION EXERCISES

1. For each of the scenarios below, determine whether the researcher is assessing reliability or validity. If reliability, then determine whether it is an instance of test–retest, internal consistency, or inter-rater reliability. If validity, then determine whether it is an instance of content, predictive, or construct validity.

   a. A researcher administered the new Test of Teaching Potential to graduating education majors and then correlated the test scores with principals' ratings of teaching effectiveness after one year on the job to see whether the test scores were related to job performance.

   b. A researcher correlated two observers' evaluations of teachers' effectiveness as revealed on the new Teacher Observation Form to see if the observers' evaluations were similar.

   c. A researcher developed a test of the trait optimism and then compared students who were judged to be "happy" versus "not happy" to see if they had different levels of optimism as expected if the Happiness Theory were credible.

   d. A researcher created an achievement test of geographic knowledge and compared the test items with a representative sampling of the knowledge-level objectives from widely used textbooks related to geography.

   e. A researcher tested a sample of students using the Occupational Interest Test. The test was administered again six months later to see if interests were fleeting.

   f. A researcher administered the new Test of Stress to teachers and then computed alpha to see how well the items "hung together."

2. Suppose you developed an instrument to measure charisma because you believe this is an important quality in teachers. What would you assess first, reliability or validity, and why? What type of reliability is most relevant? Why? What type of validity is most relevant? Why?

3. Now answer the questions posed in #2 above as they are related to an instrument designed to measure teachers' likelihood of changing careers. Repeat with an instrument designed to measure students' knowledge of the Constitution.

MULTIPLE CHOICE QUESTIONS

1. Reliability is concerned primarily with score:
   a. meaningfulness
   b. usefulness

    c. consistency

    d. practicality

    e. efficiency

2. Validity is concerned primarily with score:

    a. reliability

    b. dependability

    c. precision

    d. meaningfulness

    e. efficiency

3. Scattergrams which reveal very little scatter along an imaginary straight line projecting from the lower left to upper right would suggest which of the following correlations?

    a. negative and high

    b. negative and low

    c. zero

    d. positive and high

    e. positive and low

4. If the reliability coefficient for a set of scores is .90, then we know that:

    a. 90% of the variance is valid; 10% is reliable

    b. 90% of the variance is true; 10% is error

    c. 90% of the variance is obtained; 10% is unknown

    d. 81% of the variance is true; 19% is error

    e. 81% of the variance is unreliable; 19% is reliable

5. Which of the following pairings of type of reliability with type of error is *incorrect*?

    a. stability: time

    b. equivalence: forms

    c. internal consistency: constructs

    d. observer: raters

6. Split-half, KR, and alpha are all types of reliability classified under:

    a. stability

    b. equivalence

    c. internal consistency

    d. observer

7. Which of the following would be most informative to estimate the amount of error in an individual's score?

    a. alpha

    b. KR20

    c. SEM

    d. r

    e. variance

8. Classroom teachers who develop tests are most directly concerned with _____ validity; researchers who test theories to explain traits are more directly concerned with _____ validity.

    a. content; construct

    b. predictive; content

    c. construct; content

    d. content; predictive

    e. predictive; construct

9. Which of the following is true?
    a. Reliable scores are nearly always valid.
    b. Reliability is concerned with what a test measures
    c. The SEM measures a test's validity
    d. A reliable test measures well whatever measures
    e. Construct validity is not theoretical; it is *practical*

10. It is most meaningful to think about test validity:
    a. across parallel forms
    b. for a specific purpose
    c. as a subtype of reliability
    d. in terms of measurement error
    e. across time, forms, items, and raters

Answers: 1) c   2) d   3) d   4) b   5) c   6) c   7) c   8) a   9) d   10) b

Chapter *8*

RESEARCH BIAS AND CONTROL

OVERVIEW

We have seen how educational researchers attempt to understand constructs and complex phenomena by uncovering relationships that may help expose them. Frequently, researchers find that their viewing of these relationships is blocked by unwanted sources of contamination, like smudges on eyeglasses. These blockades are often referred to as *biasing effects*, such as the experimenter expectancy effect, the Hawthorne effect, and the John Henry effect. This chapter is concerned with understanding these biases and learning how researchers attempt to combat their contaminating influences.

EXPERIMENTER EXPECTANCY AND BLINDING

Perhaps the granddaddy of all troubling effects in educational research is the *expectancy effect*, or the tendency of researchers to bring about the very finding they are expecting. This effect is sometimes referred to as the *self-fulfilling prophecy* effect or the *Pygmalion* effect, after a Greek mythological sculptor whose statue of a beautiful woman came to life in fulfillment of the love-sick sculptor's hopes. This is a serious problem because in the absence of expectation the same finding may not occur. Consider once again a researcher who, contrary to previous examples, believes that students learn to spell words faster and easier if they practice on a computer as opposed to writing the words by hand. To test this notion, assume eighty children were randomly assigned to two groups. One group spent five study trials learning forty new words on the computer, while the other group spent five study trials learning the same words through handwriting. Next, the researcher (who is now convinced that computers are superior to handwriting), asks each child (individually) to spell each word aloud as a test of their learning. The researcher then simply scores each spoken spelling as correct or incorrect and compares the overall performance of both groups.

The biasing influence of the researcher's beliefs could bring about the expected result in many ways. Consider, for example, Aimee, known by the researcher to be in the computer group. As she spells "house," she stumbles with the letter "u" and in fact begins to say "w." Aimee immediately notices a clear but subtle change in the researcher's facial expression, as if to signal disappointment or disapproval. Aimee stops her spelling, thinks about it for a second, then backs up to replace the beginnings of a "w" with a "u." The researcher's face, particularly the eyebrows, returns to its original "Yes, that's right!" expression. This example, admittedly dramatic, illustrates how just one factor, nonverbal communication, might contribute to the strength of the expectancy effect.

The expectancy effect may be explained in many other ways too. Consider Aimee again, who is less than perfect in her pronunciation. As she spells "turtle," she muddles the last three letters. Although she actually says "t-u-r-*d*-l-e," the researcher misinterprets the "d" for a "t" and consequently scores the spelling as correct. A compounding problem could likewise occur in the handwriting group, where worse spelling performance is expected. The researcher, especially tuned to hear errors where they are expected, may in fact interpret a garbled "t" as an incorrect "d."

It is important to recognize that scientific researchers, because they are human, are subject to the same kinds of hopes and wishes that teachers, doctors, parents, and gamblers are subject to. Fortunately, the research process has a built-in control for this type of bias. The control is known as *blinding,* and is used whenever and wherever it is possible by careful researchers. (Recall the story about Clever Hans in Chapter 1.) Blinding involves keeping data collectors "in the dark" with regard to information such as into which group a particular subject is assigned (e.g., treatment or control). This is usually accomplished by the use of independent observers who are trained for the specific purpose of collecting data but otherwise have no other knowledge of subjects' grouping, or even what the research question is. Blind observers are less likely to be influenced by factors such as expectations or hopes if they have little or no awareness of information known to affect perceptions or judgments.

Blinding is used at all stages of the research process if feasible. Consider a make-believe study designed to test the influence of a new drug, let's call it Normid, designed to overcome restlessness and inattention associated with hyperactivity. Furthermore, let us suppose that three different methods of administration were tested: pill, injection, and patch (slow release over time with a bandaid-like application). A control (placebo) group would also be used in order to assess the overall effectiveness of the drug. To this end, let's assume that one hundred hyperactive students were randomly assigned to one of four groups: Control, Pill, Injection, and Patch. The school nurse, responsible for the drug's administration, must be kept blind in order to avoid influencing students' behavior with subtle or nonverbal communications during the administration. The nurse would therefore have to give *all* students (even the controls) a pill, an injection, and a patch. Students in the control group would receive a saline solution injection, a baking soda pill, and a dry or empty patch. Of course, all pills, injections, and patches would be coded somehow in order to be certain all students were receiving their randomly assigned condition. (Notice also that the students themselves would be blind to their conditions using this technique, hence controlling for another bias called the *guinea pig effect* described later.) When students' behavior is observed (e.g., fidgeting), it would be important to make certain that the observers were blind to conditions as well. This is because ambiguous perceptions and resulting questions such as, "Was that a fidget?" could be interpreted in accordance with knowledge of group membership as "Yes, that probably is a fidget since he's in the control group," or "No, he's in the group that receives injections—presumably the most effective treatment."

Marketing researchers, like educational researchers, are well aware of problems stemming from failure to blind. Consider tasting three different types of chocolates, for example. Possibly the color of chocolate may influence the taste ratings, yet the marketers are interested in taste, not visual appearance. In this case, the tasters would quite literally be blinded (with a blindfold) so that their ratings would reflect taste, uncontaminated by the chocolate's visual appearance.

Teachers who grade essays will probably have little trouble understanding the value of blinding. Knowing that a student is especially able, for example, may lead to quicker reading, less scrutiny, and a faster positive judgment of the essay. Any ambiguity could reasonably be misinterpreted in the student's favor. And, unfortunately, the reading and evaluation of a weaker student's essay might be a search for confirming evidence.

For educational researchers, it is wise to use blinding as a control technique at every opportunity. This is true even in situations where bias seems unlikely. The fact is that researchers do not know all of the circumstances that foster expectancy bias nor all the mechanisms through which it operates. Because of this, again, it is wise to use blinding as a scientific control whenever it is practical. This includes blinding the subjects themselves, as well as using blind raters, observers, data collectors, scorers, and the like.

HAWTHORNE EFFECT, JOHN HENRY EFFECT, AND PLACEBOS

The *Hawthorne effect*, recall from Chapter 1, has enjoyed a long but controversial history (Adair, Sharpe, & Huynh, 1989; Franke & Kaul, 1978; Rice 1982). This effect, discovered in the 1920s at the Hawthorne Western Electric Plant near Chicago (Roethlisberger & Dickson, 1939), refers to research participants' behavior changing merely as a result of their awareness of being in a research situation. Participants' behavior could change, for example, simply by knowing the research hypothesis or by receiving special attention in a treatment group. This Hawthorne effect—also known as the *guinea pig effect, novelty effect,* or even the *gee whiz effect*—must be controlled or the researcher will not know whether a change in behavior is the result of a genuine treatment effect or the workings of the Hawthorne effect.

How might the Hawthorne effect work? Imagine yourself in an educational research study, one that investigates the effect of using computers in an innovative way to study science. Your classroom is loaded with new computers; many people are peeking in to see all of the equipment, new faces (computing technicians) are present, and a local news crew arrives to produce a story about technology in the classroom. Teachers are a bit bewildered, but are surely excited. All of the attention given to your classroom is convincing that your class is truly "special." This, naturally, keeps you attentive and you are eager to begin your introduction to cyberspace.

At the end of the two-week unit, your achievement level is compared with a comparable class that was taught the same material through a traditional "talk-and-chalk" method. The results reveal that your computer-oriented class outscored the traditional class by a wide margin. What could explain this finding? Was it the use of computers? Or was it all of the attention that surrounded the computers? Would the traditional class score similarly if it were also in the spotlight? Would the computer class's performance drop once all the hoopla ended (the *honeymoon-is-over-effect*)? The difficulty in answering these questions highlights the problems related to the Hawthorne effect. Often, it is hard to untangle the influence of a treatment effect (e.g., a new method of teaching) from the special attention or novelty associated with its implementation.

Medical research, in the case of drug trials, controls such influences by using a *placebo* group, or a control group treated identically to an experimental group but whose capsules contain only baking soda. Educational researchers have a greater challenge, for their treatments are usually not drugs in capsule form, but complicated methods of delivering instruction. The concept of a *placebo* in educational research still exists, however, and it usually takes the form of a second treatment group, one that provides novelty, attention, and related factors but lacks the critical essence of the first treatment group. In the classroom computer scenario, for example, possibly the traditional "talk-and-chalk" classroom might receive computers in their classroom (along with the media hoopla), but they would not begin using them until after the two-week unit test. Admittedly, the use of placebos in educational research involves creative challenges.

A related bias in educational research is known as the *John Henry effect*, in which the control group outperforms itself by trying to perform as well as the experimental group. The enhanced performance of a control group may be in response to a perceived threat, or even a response to feeling "left out." John Henry, as the legend goes, was a railroad worker who drove spikes in rails using only his sheer strength and a sledge hammer. Feeling his job was threatened by a new spike-driver machine, he mustered all his strength and speed to show that he was just as good and fast as the automated machine. In the classroom computer situation described above, it may be possible that teachers in the "talk-and-chalk" control group feel similarly threatened by computers, hence they try their very best to raise achievement scores to the same level as the computer classroom. Or maybe students in the traditional class, fearing technology or feeling intimidated, put forth extra effort to achieve beyond their usual level. It is in this sense that a control group "outperforms" itself. The John Henry effect, in this case, would mask the enhanced performance of the treatment group.

CAMPBELL AND STANLEY THREATS AND CONTROL GROUPS

In one of the most influential papers ever published in educational research, Donald Campbell and Julian Stanley (1963) described a handful of commonly appearing sources of bias, or *threats*, as they called them, in the conduct of educational research. They were called "threats" because they endangered the *internal validity* of the study. This term, also coined by Campbell and Stanley (1963), refers to how effectively a research design controls for contaminating influences. Recall from Chapter 2 that researchers are always on guard against alternative hypotheses—those explanations of the results other than the research hypothesis. Internal validity is present, then, if no alternative hypotheses exist. If the research design incorporates tight controls, then the research is internally valid, alternative hypotheses are absent, and the researcher can be confident that the results are due to the treatment's influence. When internal validity is lacking, sources of influence other than the treatment could explain the results. These other contaminating and biasing sources, or threats, must be controlled if the research results are to be meaningful.

Here is an example of research that lacks internal validity. In a test of learning while asleep, subjects were given a pretest of their knowledge of high energy physics. Then they slept in a laboratory for five nights. While asleep, the researcher played audio recordings of five lectures on high energy physics. A posttest after the fifth day revealed the knowledge scores had increased. The researcher concluded that the learning-while-asleep treatment was indeed effective. Do you think that the effects were in fact due to the treatment and nothing else? Hardly, and because there are many reasons for the results—other explanations—we would say that the study lacked internal validity. (Subjects may have learned more about the topic during their waking hours, they may not have been asleep during the lectures, the posttest may have been easier than the pretest, etc.). In sum, internally valid studies are well controlled, consequently one can be reasonably certain that the results are due to the treatment—and nothing else.

Campbell and Stanley (1963) also described many research designs that controlled for the threats' influence, hence strengthening the internal validity of a study. Many of these designs incorporated the use of control groups. In the next section, we will describe these common but threatening sources of influence and explain how their potentially contaminating effects can be neutralized.

Extraneous Events

Extraneous events (originally termed "history" and "maturation") refer to outside influences that occur between a pretest and a posttest in addition to the treatment. Let us presume that the treatment is a ten-week workshop designed to increase the SAT scores of graduating seniors. In order to test the effectiveness of this treatment, one hundred seniors took the SAT, enrolled in the workshop, then retook the SAT upon completion of the workshop. And, sure enough, scores increased from 1150 to 1350. Although the workshop designers would like to conclude that their training was responsible for the increase, they could not easily do so because of other possible events that occurred along with the treatment which might have increased the scores. For example, some students may have purchased a self-study guide describing how to take aptitude tests; others may have seen an article in the newspaper describing how some students can correctly choose the answer on a reading comprehension passage without reading the passage; still others may have already received rejection notices from colleges they applied to and as a result, simply tried harder on the SAT retake after the sobering rejections. Furthermore, others may have learned some test-taking skills from their math instructor who prepares students to take his difficult tests; still others may have seen a popular program on television concerned with the value of exercise on mental acuity, and, as a consequence, started regular exercise during the workshop (assuming exercise does influence mental prowess).

Some of these influences stem from changes within the research participants themselves simply as a function of the passage of time. For example, many test-takers could have been under the weather during the pretesting (it may have been administered during the height of the flu season, or the worst week of pollen counts) but were generally healthier during the posttest, hence scoring higher. It could also be argued that subjects themselves had higher abilities at the posttest since ten weeks of instruction had elapsed since the pretest. They may have had larger vocabularies, greater knowledge of math and geometry, greater "cultural literacy" which could enhance their reading comprehension, or more knowledge of Latin which could help them with word meanings, and so forth.

Consider another example. One hundred people with lower back pain undergo acupuncture for ten weeks and find that their pain was greatly reduced. (Do you remember this from Chapter 1?) We know that time is a great healer, and these back pain sufferers may have been cured without any treatment. (Remember that backache you had that disappeared after a few weeks without any treatment?) Researchers must consider other events that co-occur with the mere passage of time, including all of the changes within the subjects themselves (even short term, such as fatigue) in addition to the changes on the "outside."

Instrumentation

Instrumentation is another class of threatening influences, all of which refer to bias stemming from the process of measurement in the research setting. The threat of instrumentation refers to how taking one test can influence one's performance on a second test [what Campbell and Stanley (1963) referred to as *testing*] as well as influences related to the change in the measuring process itself. Using the pretest–posttest SAT training example described above, it is quite possible that an increase on the posttest (second test) could be related to the experience of taking the pretest (first test). How could this happen? The concept is simple: you improve with practice. (Have you ever hung wallpaper? Didn't the second room turn out better than the first room?) Simply becoming familiar with the test format or knowing what to expect may lead to a posttest advantage. For example, in the reading comprehension section of the SAT, you know because of your experience with the pretest that the posttest is a race against the clock, with no time to reflect. You may have also learned that geometry was fully represented on the SAT, so you review your geometry textbook before the second testing. You might also be more relaxed the second time around, knowing what's ahead. You may have also learned to eat a better breakfast the second time around!

Instrumentation is a problem because it would be hard to disentangle the workshop effect from the testing effect.

Another instrumentation threat is known as *pretest sensitization.* Sometimes the experience of taking a pretest creates an effect by itself, one that might magnify (or wash out) the treatment effect. For example, consider a workshop in human sexuality for high school students. To assess students' knowledge before the workshop, they are given a pretest. After the workshop, they are given a posttest to evaluate learning gain. The pretest might be loaded with interesting true/false questions such as: "Women can get pregnant before their first period," or "Women have only a forty-eight hour interval per month when they can get pregnant." In this case, the pretest itself might stimulate sufficient interest among students to the point where they search out answers before the workshop even begins! It would be difficult to disentangle the amount learned in response to the pretest from the amount learned as a result of the instruction within the workshop.

Or consider a weight-loss study in which all subjects are first weighed, then given hypnotic therapy for ten weeks, followed by a final weighing. Quite possibly some subjects have avoided the scales for months, not wanting to face the reality that they have never been heavier. That simple shocking truth—over 200 pounds—itself may be sufficient motivation to lose weight. If subjects did lose weight after ten weeks of hypnosis, how would you know whether it was due to the hypnosis effect or the shocking reality of the initial weighing?

Instrumentation also refers to changes in the measuring instrument itself between testings. We are aware, for example, that bathroom scales might become inaccurate over time due to corrosion in the components or weak batteries. The same process can occur with educational measures, including human observers who change over time, for example, by becoming careless or more lenient. Consider other illustrations of instrument changes. Periodic recalibration of SAT scores (as was done recently), whereby scores are raised by a specific number of points, may be interpreted as a treatment effect when in fact all scores were simply increased for statistical reasons. Subjects' interpretation of items on a questionnaire could change over time too. One true/false item from a widely used personality inventory—I like gay parties—would probably be interpreted differently today than it was in the 1930s when the test was constructed.

Mortality

Yet another class of threatening biases is *mortality.* Often referred to as *attrition* or *loss of subjects*, this problem occurs when research participants drop out of a study. The occasional and haphazard dropping out of a few subjects due to personal reasons such as sickness, relocation, etc., does not present a serious bias. The more serious problem is the systematic loss of subjects who drop out because of a common reaction to the treatment. In the SAT workshop example, mortality would be a problem if the lowest scoring twenty percent of the sample decided not to continue with the treatment (workshop) for whatever reasons (fear of failure, embarrassment, assault of self-esteem, feelings of hopelessness, etc.). You can readily see that this would be a problem because, on average, the posttest SATs would be higher than the pretest SATs since the lowest scoring subjects could not contribute to (by lowering) the posttest scores. This would be true even if the workshop had absolutely no effect whatsoever on the raising of SAT scores; the scores would only *appear* to be higher. Similar problems occur in other studies as well, including diets that may appear to be successful in reducing weight only because those who were not successful (heavier) dropped out. The success rate of a smoking cessation study could also be artificially high because of those failures who simply were not present to be tabulated. Campbell and Stanley

(1963, p. 12–13) present a humorous example of sexism in their writing from a previous era when they describe mortality (humorous now, serious then). They stated that a study may show that senior women students tend to be less beautiful than first-year women students. Why? Not because the harsh four years of stress and study is de-beautifying, but because beautiful girls drop out of college when they get married, leaving the less beautiful ones behind. (Seriously!) The implication here is that girls only go to college to find husbands and, if that's not bad enough, only the prettiest ones are successful!

Regression

Another source of bias is called *regression*. This is a tricky statistical threat which manifests itself whenever extreme scorers (high or low) are retested. Their retest scores tend to be closer to the mean (less extreme) in the absence of any other influence. The shift closer to the mean is relatively small, but it is reliable. (This effect is explained, in part, by large measurement errors, such as very poor luck in guessing, which contributed to the low scores on the first test but which are less likely to occur again on the second test.) The only problem arises when a group is selected *because* of their extreme scores (say, a group of low scoring students on the SAT), then given a treatment (workshop to boost scores) followed by a retest. How much of the increase in scores is due to the workshop effect (if any) and how much is due to the phenomenon of regression? (Remember, the scores naturally move closer to the mean—increase in this case.) That question is difficult to answer without the use of a control group (described later in this chapter). The concept of regression can be seen in other fields as well, including genetics—if it can be shown that very short parents are likely to have short children, but not as short as the parents. In this sense, the children's height has moved closer to the mean.

Selection

There is one more biasing threat worth describing, that being *selection*. This problem occurs whenever experimental and control groups are selected in a manner which does not reasonably assure their equivalency (the "apples and oranges" problem). If the experimental and control groups are not comparable to begin with, how could you know whether a difference observed after a treatment was, in fact, due to the treatment and not the pretreatment difference? The problem is that you wouldn't know. The problem usually appears when, for example, one school is chosen for participation as the experimental school while another school is chosen as a control. Although the control might be chosen because of its apparent comparability with the experimental school, the comparability may be only superficial. There is no better way to create comparable groups than random assignment, as we shall see in the next section.

RANDOMIZED CONTROL GROUPS

Neutralizing Threats

Fortunately, these sources of bias in research—extraneous events, instrumentation, mortality, regression, and selection—can be controlled (their threat neutralized) through the use of a *randomized control group*. Using the SAT workshop as an example, a randomized control group would be formed by choosing *randomly*—via a random number table—half of the subjects for use as a control group. This group would complete the SAT pretest but, unlike the experimental group, would not be exposed to the workshop designed to boost SAT scores. The control group, however, would be posttested in the same manner as the experimental group. Because of the random process at work, it can be assumed that both groups are essentially equivalent in terms of factors that may affect SAT scores (test-taking skills, aptitude, interests, motivation, attitudes, etc.). Think about the threat of extraneous events described earlier. It should be apparent that those sources of bias should affect both groups equally—use of self-study guides, college denials, exercise habits, pollen, changes in vocabulary, cultural literacy, and so on. Notice that it is not possible to eliminate the influence of self-study, exercise, pollen and all the others; it is only possible to arrange that this influence, whatever it may be, is exerted *equally* across the two groups. The logic is straightforward: Arrange for only one influence (the independent variable) to be different between the control and experimental groups—the workshop in this case—while all other influences are held constant across both groups. Any difference observed in the outcome (SAT scores in this case) could only be attributed to the one factor that was allowed to vary.

The value of a randomized control group also applies to the problems associated with instrumentation. Remember the practice effect resulting from an SAT retake? And the influence linked to expectations? Or the geometry review? Or the better breakfast? Or the change in scoring? The control group effectively neutralizes these threats, again not by eliminating the influence altogether, but by equalizing it across the two groups.

The same logic applies to regression bias. Because one would expect that the two randomized groups would contain roughly the same number of extreme scorers, the threat is essentially neutralized. Its influence in the experimental group would be offset by an equal influence in the control group. And, as we have seen, we are not concerned about an influence that affects both groups similarly. Above all else, we want to avoid situations where one group gets influenced more by biasing factors.

The mortality bias is somewhat more problematic. The influence of subjects dropping out of the workshop haphazardly (due to the flu, relocation, etc.) is not a problem since this influence would also affect similarly the control group. The darker side of mortality exerts itself if there is something about the treatment itself that leads to a less haphazard dropping out. For example, if the workshop involves practice tests which threaten the self-confidence of low scorers, then they might be likely to quit sometime during the ten-week treatment, artificially raising the overall average of the workshop group. The control group's low scorers would not feel the same threat, hence would be less likely to quit. Mortality bias of this *non*haphazard type, then, has no simple solution. This is why researchers try their very best, within ethical boundaries, to discourage dropping out.

Finally, bias due to selection is easily controlled if you can randomly assign subjects to form experimental and control groups. If this is not possible (as is often the case), then the selection bias is always present. Selection bias is especially troublesome because the control group (if not formed randomly) may be different from the experimental group in many ways. The alternative to random assignment is *matching*, whereby control subjects are chosen because of their similarity to the experimental subjects. In educational research, the matching variables are usually age, sex, and socioeconomic status. Although this technique can neutralize the influence of those variables, there is no control for the influence of other, unmatched variables, some of which may be dramatic in their influence but hidden from view. In short, matching is never a good substitute for random assignment.

Thus far, we have seen how a treatment group is subjected to many influences other than the treatment itself, including all of the sources linked to extraneous events, instrumentation, mortality, regression, and selection. The treatment group is, in actuality, the treatment plus extraneous events plus instrumentation plus mortality plus regression plus selection. By contrast the control group is merely extraneous events plus instrumentation plus mortality plus regression plus selection. The statistical analysis, therefore, can extract the influences of these biases from the treatment group after examining their strength in the control group. What is left, then, is the relatively pure influence of the treatment itself.

The Random Process

Let me emphasize the value of a *randomly* formed control group. Imagine a group of one hundred students formed into two random groups. Choose a variable, any variable. What about the amount of protein in grams consumed at breakfast? If this could be measured accurately, one would find that the average protein for both groups is about the same, hence controlled. Consider another variable: the number of hours of sleep during the previous night. If one group slept an average of seven hours and sixteen minutes, then the other group probably slept about seven hours and sixteen minutes as well. Choose another variable, and the outcome will be the same. Because the two groups are about the same on these extraneous variables, it can be said that their influence is controlled.

Random assignment also has a hidden strength. (Do you remember Factor Q, first mentioned in Chapter 5?) Be futuristic for a moment and consider Factor Q, not discovered until the year 2020 but believed to dramatically affect memory. That does not pose a problem in today's research, as long as groups are formed randomly. Factor Q, like the protein in breakfasts, will be about the same, hence controlled, across the two groups. In this sense, random assignment controls for all known *and* unknown sources of extraneous bias related to the research participants themselves. That is why it is so important.

Many of the threats to internal validity are controlled quite well by the particular research design and the random processes utilized by a researcher. In fact, that is the purpose of the architectural plan (design) of the study—to make sure the findings cannot be explained away by some unwanted, extraneous influence. We will examine research designs in the next two chapters and see how their features attempt to increase internal validity.

It is important not to confuse *internal* versus *external* validity. External validity was introduced in Chapter 6 in the discussion of sampling and refers to *generalization*, or how well the findings apply to the people and settings beyond the borders of the sample. In this chapter, we have seen that internal validity refers to the control of unwanted sources of influence, such as the Campbell and Stanley (1963) threats and other effects (e.g., experimenter expectancy) described earlier in this chapter. A sharp distinction should be drawn between them since they refer to very different concerns of researchers. In a sense, internal validity has the highest priority, for if the results are rendered uninterpretable because of contaminating threats and rival explanations, then the generalization of findings becomes irrelevant. If the results are meaningless, no one would care about their applicability.

ORDER EFFECTS AND COUNTERBALANCING

Let's consider one more bias in educational research, *order effects*. This is a problem when participants receive several tests, treatments, tasks, etc. and the particular order of their administration affects responses. For example, if you were to complete five tests of cognitive ability, each one lasting one hour, it is reasonable to expect that the last test would be negatively affected by fatigue due to the effort and attention required by the first four. The first one, however, might be negatively affected by your slow mental warmup or anxiety, to mention a few factors. Your performance might even be affected by *carryover*, or the influence of one test on the other. Possibly, some strategy that you used (and perfected) in the third test could be used successfully during the fourth test. Or maybe some nagging question in the first test affected negatively your performance on the second test. (The same concept can be applied to eating: Does dark chocolate taste as good if it is preceded by milk chocolate? Would you enjoy chocolate more for an appetizer or for dessert?)

Order effects and carryover effects could influence all types of measures, including attitudes, interests, and opinions, to name just a few. Your opinion about abortion, for example, might change somewhat depending on whether or not you were just measured on religious commitments. Order effects can also affect your responses to different treatments, too. For example, imagine being asked right now to remember a list of twenty words without any specific instruction on how to do so (a control condition). Next, imagine learning a new list of twenty words with the specific instructions to form bizarre images to each word. What do you suppose would happen if you were given the imagery instructions first, followed by the control instructions? Would it be possible *not* to form images in the control condition? Or, consider the spelling of the word *sacrilegious*. If you were asked to spell *religious* first, do you think you would be less likely to spell *sacrilegious* correctly? (Note the transposed *i* and *e*.)

Fortunately, there is a relatively simple way for researchers to neutralize this bias (once again, not eliminate it, just control it). This is done using a technique called *counterbalancing*, whereby subjects receive a different order of tests, treatments, booklets, words, etc. This is often accomplished by a random technique, in which each subject receives a different random order of words, tasks, drawings to rate, or whatever is being administered. This scatters the influence of order and carryover so that, on average, each word, task, drawing, etc., is affected positively and negatively in roughly the same amounts. (The greater the number of subjects, the better controlled are the effects.) Other types and applications of counterbalancing with quasi-experiments are described in Chapter 9.

CHAPTER SUMMARY

All researchers must contend with troubling sources of bias and contamination in the conduct of their research. The *expectancy effect*, or the tendency to perceive and even bring about the findings that are hypothesized, is controlled by *blinding*, or being kept "in the dark" with regard to biasing information such as whether a subject is in the experimental or control group. Other effects such as the *Hawthorne effect*, or the tendency of subjects to be influenced by their knowledge that they are being studied, may be neutralized to some extent with control (or placebo) groups. There are numerous threats to the internal validity of a study (including extraneous events, instrumentation, mortality, regression, and selection) which contribute to misinterpreting a biasing effect as a treatment effect. Many of the threats can be well controlled with a randomized control group. Other contamination such as *order effects* (the influence attributed to, for example, a treatment being first or last) can be controlled by alternating orders via counterbalancing.

Now let's examine how some of the control procedures described in this chapter have been applied in a published research report.

GUIDED TOUR

Let's turn our attention now to a guided tour of published educational research. This will help solidify important terms and concepts described in this chapter.

Modified Reciprocal Teaching in a Regular Classroom

C. Dean Miller

Colorado State University

Larry F. Miller

Poudre R-1 School District

Fort Collins, Colorado

Lee A. Rosen

Colorado State University

Abstract

This study was designed to increase reading comprehension and academic achievement of students through the use of a modified reciprocal teaching program. Modified reciprocal teaching involved small groups of students working together to read and comprehend a portion of text. The students took turns "teaching" these groups by assisting the rest of the group in selecting key words and phrases, summarizing, questioning, clarifying, and predicting. Students were randomly assigned to one of three seventh-grade regular education social studies classes. One class used modified reciprocal teaching twice a week for 8 weeks. The other two classes received a traditional instructional program. All classes were taught by the same teacher. Significant differences included higher scores on comprehension tests and writing samples, improvement in second-quarter social studies grades, and better conduct records for students who participated in modified reciprocal teaching. Several explanations for the superior performance of the modified reciprocal teaching group are hypothesized.

Fostering and enhancing reading comprehension continues to be of interest and concern to many educators. Palincsar and Brown (1984) recently reported two innovative studies that were designed to facilitate and enhance comprehension-fostering and comprehension-monitoring skills of low-achieving seventh graders. The two studies were formulated and based on several functions they believed were common to strategies that could be used for instruction of comprehension skills. They selected four activities that embodied these functions: (a) summarizing, (b) questioning, (c) clarifying, and (d) predicting. Palincsar and Brown believed that these four activities would serve a dual function of enhancing comprehension as well as providing opportunities to monitor whether or not comprehension was occurring. Palincsar and Brown's two studies involved a total of 27 students. The results were impressive. For both regular and special education children sizable gains were found on tests of comprehension and the gains were maintained over time. In addition, the comprehension-fostering and comprehension-monitoring skills generalized to other classroom comprehension tests.

Palincsar and Brown called their approach "reciprocal teaching." Reciprocal teaching involved a teacher and student(s) taking turns leading a dialogue based on sections of a text. The teacher modeled and demonstrated the four activities the students were to use when they read—summarizing, questioning, clarifying, and predicting. Students were encouraged to participate at whatever level they could. The teacher provided guidance, feedback, and encouragement at the appropriate level for each student.

At this time, there were no other studies examining the effects of reciprocal teaching. Thus, the present study sought to expand our knowledge base in this important area. Reciprocal teaching was modified for the present study based on the premise that regular education students—and not just the low-achieving students previously studied—could benefit from an approach to learning that focused on the four activities identified by Palincsar and Brown: summarizing, questioning, clarifying, and predicting. Brown, Campione, and Day (1981) reported that summarizing can facilitate learning by helping readers clarify the meaning and significance of discourse. In addition, identification of the key words and phrases contained in the material to be learned was added as a component (Winograd, 1984). Support for this comes from theory and research that suggest that comprehension involves the construction of knowledge rather than the storage of knowledge (Brown & Smiley, 1978; Glaser, 1979). For example, Eylon and Reif (1984) stress the importance of knowledge organization, particularly a hierarchical organization of knowledge that the learner must actively construct. A hierarchical organization must include knowledge at each level such as a main idea (high level) supported by more specific knowledge at a lower level in the hierarchy, Thus, summarizing or constructing the main idea based on the key words or phrases can be used to help the student comprehend the information (Harris & Sipay, 1980; Pearson & Johnson, 1978).

Method

Subjects

A seventh-grade social studies teacher allowed the study to be conducted with her three social studies classes. Students were randomly assigned to the three classes, and the three classes were randomly assigned to one of three conditions: modified reciprocal teaching (MRT) ($n = 26$); control group I ($n = 20$); and control group II ($n = 18$). **[1]** All three classes covered the same academic material and completed the same projects and classroom tests, which were graded and recorded by the same classroom teacher. **[2]** The three groups did not differ significantly on the vocabulary score on the Metropolitan Achievement Test, $F(2, 63) = .95$, $p > .05$, which was administered 3 weeks before the study began.

Group Leaders

Five persons served as group leaders. Three were graduate students in school psychology, one was an undergraduate psychology major, and one had received a bachelor's degree in psychology. Four worked as group leaders with the fifth person acting as an alternate. An alternate was used on two occasions.

Each group leader and the alternate received approximately 4 hours of training that included rehearsing and practicing reciprocal teaching. The training included viewing a videotape of a reciprocal teaching session. The tape was provided by Palincsar, author of the original reciprocal teaching research (Palincsar & Brown, 1984). In addition, some of the training materials from the original studies were used in training the group leaders.

Procedure

Modified reciprocal teaching. MRT was conducted 1 hour on Tuesdays and Thursdays for 8 weeks. The class of 26 students was divided into two groups of 6 students each and two groups of 7 students each. **[3]** Students were randomly assigned to the four groups. All the students participated in MRT, not just the low achievers. Leaders were randomly assigned to the groups. The group leaders introduced MRT to their groups by explain-

[1] *Here we see the researcher's most powerful control procedure: random assignment to groups. We know that researchers use random assignment whenever and wherever they have the opportunity, and for good reason. No other method arranges for comparable groups, hence control, so effectively. The control is achieved not by eliminating extraneous influences related to the learners (attitudes, interests, abilities, prior knowledge, hearing, etc.), but by scattering their influence haphazardly over all conditions or groups.*

[2] *Here we see the word* same *used three times in one sentence. The concept of* sameness *(or more technically* constancy*) is another important technique for controlling extraneous influences. Holding the influence of extraneous variables constant across the three conditions neutralizes the potential contamination due to academic materials, projects, and the grading of tests. Obviously, you would want to avoid a situation where the Modified Reciprocal Teaching (MRT) group covered more interesting material (with better designed projects) while the two control groups attempted to learn harder, duller material. Any differences in the dependent measures could then be attributed to teaching differences (the independent variable, which is what the researchers wanted) or to other unwanted influences such as the type of academic materials. Exposing all learners to the same influences in this way successfully holds unwanted influences in check.*

[3] *Here we see the powerful control technique of randomization used twice, in the assignment of students to learning groups within the MRT condition and in the assignment of leaders to groups. Again, researchers try to avoid arbitrariness via randomness, fearing that a subtle contaminating bias could distort the results.*

ing the purpose and the activities that they would be using when each person took her or his turn being the "teacher." The study activities included (a) questioning, (b) clarifying, (c) summarizing, (d), predicting, and (e) identifying the key words and phrases. The group leaders began the first few sessions by being the "teacher," which enabled the leaders to model the behaviors they wanted the students to imitate. Following all MRT teaching sessions the students completed a 10-item comprehension test and produced a writing sample.

Control group I. This social studies class did not receive MRT but did complete the 10-item comprehension tests and the writing samples. **[4]**

Control group II. The students in this social studies class did not receive MRT and they did not take the comprehension tests or do the 3-minute writing samples. These students completed only pre- and postmeasures. This group was included to act as a control/comparison group for the frequent testing conducted in both the MRT group and control group I.

Measures

Data were collected on the following measures for 11 of 16 sessions. Interruptions such as pep assemblies, vacations, and class projects prevented collection of data at every session.

Comprehension test. A 10-question multiple-choice test was prepared for each session of MRT. The test was administered to the MRT group and control group I during the last 10 minutes of each class period. **[5]** The teacher had no knowledge of what the tests contained until after they had been completed by the students. Two types of questions were used for the comprehension test: (a) text-explicit questions, which meant the answer was explicitly mentioned in the text (e.g., In what year did Columbus discover America?), and (b) text-implicit questions, which meant the answer had to be inferred across adjacent segments of the text (e.g., What was the

[4] *Control groups (yes, more than one!) are often necessary to neutralize the contaminating influences stemming from the "Campbell and Stanley" threats described in this chapter (in this case, instrumentation in the form of testing, and extraneous events). Let's examine this a bit more closely. The researchers used three groups summarized below:*

> *Experimental Group: MRT + tests + pre/post measures*
>
> *Control Group I: No MRT + tests + pre/post measures*
>
> *Control Group II: No MRT + no tests + pre/post measures*

Focus on the first two groups (Experimental versus Control Group I).

- *This comparison assesses the MRT effect (if any) while controlling for tests (this is because both groups are exposed to the same influence—tests). This comparison is important because it provides the pure MRT effect without a confounding influence of tests. If Control Group I had no MRT and no tests (and performed lower than the Experimental Group), the difference could be attributed to either the MRT effect, the testing effect, or both. The findings would be ambiguous. They, of course, want to attribute the difference to MRT, not to the tests. Next, focus on the two control groups only. This comparison assesses the pure testing effect. (Neither group had MRT, so the MRT effect was not relevant in this comparison). In this way, the three groups in concert provide good information about both the MRT effect and the testing effect, each uncontaminated by the other's influence.*

  Note that there is no good control for the Hawthorne effect (the guinea pig effect). This would require a third control group, one receiving some type of "special" teaching, but one that is not expected to affect reading comprehension. This group's performance could then be used to separate the MRT effect from the "gee whiz" effect associated with being treated in a special way.

[5] *Here we see a control for the potential biasing influence of the teacher. Had she known what the test items were, then she may have consciously or unconsciously tipped the scales in favor of the Experimental Group (since they were expected to do better in their reading comprehension). Quite possibly, the teacher may have emphasized test content more in the presence of the MRT students. In this sense, however, the teacher was blind to the content of the tests.*

primary purpose of Columbus' voyage?). All of the questions were either written or selected by two of the authors.

Writing sample. A 3-minute writing sample was completed in both groups. A story starter (e.g., Last weekend, I...) was written on the board and students began writing when instructed to do so. The writing sample was scored by counting the number of words written. Numbers, dates, and addresses were not counted.

Other measures. Grades were collected for all students at the end of both the first and second quarters of the school year. Data were also collected regarding each student's conduct. Conduct consisted of absences (excused and unexcused), tardies (excused and unexcused), and suspensions (in school and out of school). **[6]** This information was obtained directly from the attendance officer and not from the students.

Results and Discussion

The comprehension test scores of the MRT group and control group I were significantly different, $F(1, 44) = 15.38, p < .001$. Students receiving MRT did significantly better than students who were taught in a traditional manner. The overall means on the comprehension tests were 6.40 ($SD = 1.61$) and 5.16 ($SD = 2.22$) for the MRT group and control group I, respectively.

In addition, students in the MRT group wrote an average of 13 more words per 3-minute writing sample than the students in control group I. The overall means were 61.58 ($SD = 17.84$) words per 3 minutes for the MRT group and 48.59 ($SD = 17.95$) for control group I. The difference between the two groups was significant, $F(1, 44) = 14.32, p < .001$.

Grades for the first quarter were not significantly different among the three groups. However, using analysis of covariance, with the first-quarter grades as covariate, second-quarter grades were significantly different, $F(2, 59) = 3.84, p < .05$. The

[6] *Do you see any bias or contamination (distortion) associated with asking the students themselves about the frequency of such undesirable behaviors as tardies and suspensions? Clearly yes. They may have truly forgotten about tardies, or even exaggerated them for whatever motivation. Or they may have denied the true frequency of suspensions, wanting to appear better behaved. Clearly, a more objective method was decided upon, and for good reason. Note: Although this chapter is not directly concerned with operational definitions, do you have a reaction to how they defined writing skill? (See the "Writing sample" section under "Measures.")*

means for the second-quarter grades, with 4.0 equalling an A, were as follows: control group I, $M = 2.17$ ($SD = 1.07$); control group II, $M = 2.28$ ($SD = 1.36$); and MRT group, $M = 2.80$ ($SD = 1.21$). Tukey post hoc analyses indicated that the MRT group had significantly better grades than control group I ($p < .05$). No other differences were significant.

Information regarding students' conduct was also analyzed. There was a significant difference among the three groups in the total number of conduct incidents, x^2 (2, $N = 64$) $= 32.35$, $p < .001$. Control group I had a total of 132 incidents reported, followed by control group II with 83 incidents, and the MRT group with 61.

All of the significant differences among the three groups resulted from the MRT group's superior performance. The MRT group had an overall superior performance on the comprehension tests and writing samples. Grades were considerably higher during the second quarter for students in the MRT group relative to the students in the control groups. In addition, conduct was better for students in the MRT group than for students in the two control groups. These outcomes strongly favor the use of modified reciprocal teaching in a regular classroom.

Several hypotheses explain the superior performance or students who participated in modified reciprocal teaching. First, reading was goal directed, the goals being to select key words or phrases, summarize the main idea, and formulate questions to test the other students' understanding of what had been read. Second, students were actively involved in reading to either ask the questions when they were the "teacher," and answer the questions asked by the "teacher." Taking turns being the teacher appeared to be very motivating for many of the students. Student involvement in summarizing, identifying key words and phrases, asking questions, and answering questions required more encoding effort than is required in passive reading and outlining. Third, paraphrasing was evident in students' statements about the main ideas. Perhaps paraphrasing enabled the students to encode the information in a way that had more meaning for them than they could obtain through passive reading or rote memorization. Fourth, modified reciprocal teaching provided opportunities for clarifying misunderstandings as well as defining words or concepts that were not understood by everyone in the group. Fifth, simply participating in a small group focused on the facilitation of learning may have impacted the students' performance. In addition, the students were also affected at least somewhat by the approach being fun, the challenge of being the "teacher," being given a chance to participate actively in discussion, and the variety and change in daily routine. Further research will have to be conducted before the individual contribution of the various factors involved in modified reciprocal teaching can be analyzed.

It should be noted that the application of reciprocal teaching in this study was slightly different than that used in the original studies reported by Palincsar and Brown (1984). The present research was conducted with an entire regular classroom as opposed to pulling out low-achieving students, reciprocal teaching was modified to include identification of key words and phrases, and reciprocal teaching was conducted only 2 days a week as opposed to intensive daily intervention. Even with these differences, however, the benefits and improved performance were substantial.

In conclusion, the data consistently favored the students in the modified reciprocal teaching class, and a majority of the students indicated they enjoyed MRT and would like to have it continued. In fact, we believe the strongest evidence and support for MRT was in the improved grades of students in the MRT class. Thus, we would not hesitate to recommend modified reciprocal teaching as a promising approach to increase student interest, involvement, and achievement in regular education classrooms.

Acknowledgment

We gratefully acknowledge the assistance of Sherry Ritch, principal; Rich Kruetzer, dean of students; Lori Gutierrez, social studies teacher, Lisa Gabardi-Bianchi, Dan Doyle, Doug Strachan, Lisa Strassburger, and Greg Thwaites, group leaders; as well as students of the Poudre R-1 Schools for their help with this research.

Requests for reprints should be sent to C. Dean Miller, or Lee A. Rosen, Department of Psychology. Colorado State University, Fort Collins, CO 80523.

References

Brown, A. L.. Campione, J. C., & Day, J. D. (1981). Learning to learn: On training students to learn from texts. *Educational Researcher, 10,* 14–21.

Brown. A. L., & Smiley, S. S. (1978). The development of strategies for studying texts. *Child Development, 49,* 1076–1088.

Eylon, B-S., & Reif, F. (1984). Effects of knowledge organization on task performance. *Cognition and Instruction, 1*(1).

Glaser, R. (1979). Trends and research questions in psychological research on learning and schooling. *Educational Researcher, 8,* 6–13.

Harris, A., & Sipay, E. (1980). *How to increase reading ability.* New York: Longman.

Palincsar, A. S., & Brown, A. L. (1994). Reciprocal teaching of comprehension-monitoring activities. *Cognition and Instruction, 1*(2), 117–175.

Pearson, P. D., & Johnson, D. D. (1978). *Teaching reading comprehension.* New York: Holt, Rinehart & Winston.

Winograd, P. N. (1984). Strategic difficulties in summarizing texts. *Reading Research Quarterly, 19,* 404–425.

APPLICATION EXERCISES

1. For each of the scenarios below, determine whether the researcher inadvertently allowed the influence of the expectancy effect or the Hawthorne effect (or both). Then decide how the researcher should change the procedural methodology so that the influence is controlled.

   a. A researcher tested the idea that students' interest and achievement in world geography could be enhanced by Internet dialog with other students across the globe. A special room in the school was set aside for Internet students; also, specially trained consultants were hired for this research to help students individually make links with foreign peers. The invited consultants were also evaluating their own software (one that automatically translates one language to another), and each of the participating students were interviewed (and tape-recorded) to determine their reactions to the experience. The school's principal was eager for others to see this new educational opportunity and invited other educational administrators to visit the "Internet room" during the international exchanges. After twenty Internet-based geography lessons, students were given an interest questionnaire and an achievement test covering the objectives in the lessons. The researcher arranged for a control group of similar students who received instruction on the same material but in a traditional format. The questionnaires and exams were administered and scored by an impartial "outsider" who had no knowledge about the nature of the research.

   b. A researcher was convinced that students could learn complex material much better if they were provided with a good analogy before being exposed to instruction. The topic he chose to present was genetics; half of the students were given an analogy related to card-playing, the other half was not. He gave the fifteen-minute lecture himself to small groups of about six students. The following day, he asked all students to write a short essay explaining how genetics determine human characteristics. The researcher sorted them into two piles (the analogy group and the control group). Next he scored each essay using a global ten-point rating scale to measure their general understanding of genetics.

2. Consider each of the scenarios below and decide which of the following threats to internal validity are most apparent: extraneous events, instrumentation, mortality, regression, and selection.

   a. A researcher surveyed high school students to learn more about their practice of smoking cigarettes. The first part of the questionnaire tested their knowledge of the effects of smoking from a medical and physiological perspective. The second part assessed their attitudes toward smoking, and the third part queried their frequency of smoking. Then a group of volunteer smokers participated in a five-week course after school which was designed to provide knowledge, change attitudes, and (hopefully) reduce smoking. Those students who completed the entire course (about half of the original number) were post-tested using the same survey. The findings revealed greater knowledge, more negative attitudes, and fewer smokers as a function of the course. The researchers concluded that the program was successful. The timing was opportune, since many students were completing a driver training course and learning that discounts are provided for nonsmokers by most insurance companies.

   b. A group of second graders scoring at the bottom ten percent on a reading test were targeted for intensive daily instruction for two weeks. They were retested after the remediation using the same instrument (but with clearer instructions) and scored significantly higher. A comparison group identified at another school as needing—but not yet receiving—remediation was also tested using the same instrument. They scored lower than the remediated group. This finding, coupled with the group's significant gain, led the researcher to conclude that the intensive instruction was effective.

3. For each of the scenarios presented in #2 on the preceding page, describe how the inclusion of a control group would affect the influence of the threats which were identified.

4. A researcher for a textbook publishing company evaluated five short stories—call them A, B, C, D, and E—by asking sixth graders to rate how enjoyable each story was after its reading. All students read the stories in the order presented above and completed their assessments by rating their enjoyment after each story. What problem is illustrated here, and how would you go about controlling its influence?

MULTIPLE CHOICE QUESTIONS

1. The Pygmalion effect in research is concerned most directly with:
   a. randomization
   b. order effects
   c. expectations
   d. matching
   e. regression

2. The Hawthorne effect is also known as the _____ effect.
   a. Pygmalion
   b. regression
   c. four-wheel-drive
   d. placebo
   e. novelty

3. If the John Henry effect were exerting an influence, one would expect:
   a. poor performance in the control group
   b. better performance in the control group
   c. poor performance in the treatment group
   d. better performance in the treatment group
   e. equal performance in the control and treatment groups

4. The control of expectancy influences is usually accomplished by:
   a. blinding
   b. randomization
   c. counterbalancing
   d. matching
   e. none of the above

5. Often there are influences between a pretest and a posttest other than the treatment itself due to the mere passage of time or "outside" influences, a threat more commonly called:
   a. mortality
   b. regression
   c. instrumentation
   d. selection
   e. extraneous events

6. The fact that measuring scales change over time or that people learn from test-taking is a threat known as:
   a. mortality
   b. blinding

   c. instrumentation
   d. expectancy
   e. regression

7. Selection is a threat arising from failure to:
   a. use random assignment
   b. counterbalance across conditions
   c. blind subject and experimenters
   d. use control groups
   e. check reliability

8. When a researcher can be confident that results can be attributed to a treatment's influence and nothing else, it is said that the study is:
   a. externally valid
   b. empirically valid
   c. alternatively valid
   d. intrinsically valid
   e. internally valid

9. Counterbalancing is a technique that controls for:
   a. lack of random assignment
   b. failure to blind
   c. order and carryover effects
   d. guinea pig influences
   e. experimenter expectancy

10. The most powerful control technique, given the sheer number of influences potentially controlled, is:
   a. blinding
   b. random assignment
   c. counterbalancing
   d. matching
   e. use of placebo groups

Answers: 1) c   2) e   3) b   4) a   5) e   6) c   7) a   8) e   9) c   10) b

Chapter 9

COMMON EXPERIMENTAL RESEARCH DESIGNS

OVERVIEW

You would probably not begin a driving vacation without a road map. A coach would probably not begin first down without a strategy. A landscaper would probably not begin moving dirt without a plan. A contractor would probably not begin construction without a blueprint. A sculptor would probably not begin a carving without an image in mind. And an electrician would probably not begin a repair without a wiring diagram. Likewise, a researcher would probably not initiate data collection for a research study without the guidance of a research design. This chapter describes the valuable function that experimental research designs provide in the conduct of educational research.

RESEARCH DESIGNS

There are hundreds of potentially useful research designs, and the choice of one specific research design is guided by many factors. Perhaps the most influential factor is the type of research study undertaken, as described in Chapter 5. Some types of research, for example experimental and quasi-experimental research, offer a vast array of designs. Other types, for example, causal comparative research, offer a limited selection. And some types of research, such as correlational research, offer a small number of basic designs, but a large variety of data analysis techniques. These techniques may be simple, as in a scattergram of raw data, or extraordinarily complex, as in a structural equation modeling which attempts to discover "hidden" variables via correlations and to test the causal connections between them.

Because of their vast array, the topic of research design can become overwhelming quickly. Therefore, we will restrict our discussion to those research designs which are used commonly by educational researchers. They represent a sampling across different types and complexities of educational research and data analysis. This chapter is concerned with common *experimental* research designs, that is, designs that involve some type of intervention or treatment. For the purpose of organization, these designs will be described under the following types: *true experimental, quasi-experimental,* and *single-subject*. The following chapter will describe common non-experimental research designs (correlational, causal comparative, and descriptive). They are non-experimental since they do not incorporate any treatment intervention.

TRUE EXPERIMENTAL DESIGNS

True experimental research designs have two essential features: (1) *manipulation* of the independent variable, and (2) *random assignment* to groups. You will recall from Chapters 2 and 5 that a true independent variable involves manipulation coupled with random assignment. A true experimental design, therefore, is one that incorporates a true independent variable. You will also recall from Chapters 2 and 5 that a manipulation refers to the creation of group conditions by the researcher. In its most basic form a manipulation would include a treatment group and a control group. The presence of a control group itself is not essential for a true experiment, although it is commonly used to rule out threats to internal validity as described in Chapter 8. A true experiment might utilize just two different types of researcher-induced treatments without a pure control comparison. Four examples of true experimental research designs include the following:

- Randomized posttest control group design
- Randomized pretest–posttest control group design
- Randomized matched control group design
- Randomized factorial design

Randomized Posttest Control Group Design

The basic building block of experimental designs is the *randomized posttest control group design*, as shown below:

$$R \quad T \quad \text{Post}$$
$$R \quad C \quad \text{Post}$$

with R referring to random assignment, T referring to a treatment or experimental intervention, C referring to a control or comparison group, and *Post* to a posttest.

The essential conditions are the use of a treatment group that receives a specific intervention, a posttest to measure (assess) the influence of the treatment effect (if any), a control group to rule out threatening sources of contamination, and random assignment for the control and treatment groups. This design is one of the simplest, yet strongest, techniques in the educational researcher's arsenal, at least from the perspective of controlling biasing influences.

Let's consider an example very similar to the one described in the last chapter. Suppose a researcher wanted to determine if high school students' scores on the Scholastic Assessment Test (SAT) could be increased significantly by six hours training in the use of a novel method for test preparation one week prior to the exam. To this end, 1000 students in the Chicago area who had registered to take the SAT were contacted to obtain permission and approval for participation in the study. Five hundred students were randomly assigned to the treatment group, which would receive six hours of test-taking tips and strategies in one of many small groups on the Saturday prior to the exam. Each session was led by a teacher/leader who trained students to be "testwise" and offered many opportunities for practice. The remaining 500 students were retained as a control group, and were simply contacted for permission to use their SAT scores as part of a research project. No attempt was made to eliminate those control group students who had attended other workshops on test-taking skills or who had studied on their own. The control group, therefore, represented a subsample of the population who had received a "control" mixture of other types of training or no training at all. As a result, this design really tested whether the novel test preparation program resulted in higher scores compared to the hodgepodge of methods students typically use in the absence of an opportunity to prepare with the new method. Let's assume that all control and treatment students who were contacted agreed to participate. Here are the results: control group mean = 480 and treatment group mean = 590.

Because this research design is strong for ferreting out cause-and-effect relationship, one could be reasonably comfortable in concluding that the new test preparation program was the cause of the enhanced performance. This is because there exists a control group to assess the effects of extraneous influences. To understand this, just imagine what would happen if the treatment group were actually a second control group and never received the test preparation training. If both control groups' scores were then compared, one would expect to find nearly identical means—after all, one would be comparing two randomly-assigned control groups. This is not to say that there are no extraneous influences in this study, like flu outbreaks, uncomfortable testing environments, emotionally-charged news events, advice from friends on taking the SAT, and so forth. The important point is that *all of these influences and biases would affect both groups equally.* How could the news, weather, or flu viruses affect only one group? These influences are not selective, of course, and all research subjects are equally affected. In this sense, we can say that the control and treatment groups' scores reflect weather, news, viruses, and the like, but the treatment group also has the specific influence attributed to the training in test-taking skills. Using this rationale, we can safely conclude that the 110 point difference reflects the unique influence of the treatment program itself.

Here is another example of the randomized control group design. Let's assume that a researcher wanted to test the effectiveness of an educational intervention designed to reduce the number of high school students who smoke. Assume that 1000 ninth graders were selected to participate, and 500 were randomly assigned to the treatment group consisting of information about the hazards of smoking, including guest speakers with terminal lung cancer. The remaining 500 students were assigned to the control group and were not targeted in any special way. The posttest measure was collected near the end of high school and was simply a count of the number of students in each group who smoked regularly. Here are the dramatic results: treatment group = six percent smokers; control group = twenty percent smokers. These hypothetical results favor the intervention, and there are no obvious alternative explanations for the findings. Even if there were powerful extraneous influences—like the continual release of new studies showing the health consequences of smoking, or the implementation of substantially lower car insurance rates for nonsmokers, or the smoking-related death of a teen idol—the findings would still provide a strong causal link between the educational intervention and the reduced smoking rate. This is because the extraneous influences affected both groups equally. It is the presence of a control group which allows the researcher to "subtract out" extraneous influences to arrive at a purer measure of the treatment's effect. If there were no control group, then we would not know whether the low six percent smoking rate in the treatment group was due to the intervention itself, or to the smoking-related death of a teen idol, or to a combination of both or any one of the hundreds of other plausible explanations related to extraneous influences.

Contrast With Pre-experimental Designs. In order to emphasize the strength of true experimental designs such as the randomized posttest control group design described above, consider two "pre-experimental" designs, or weak designs that do not have the essential characteristics of a true experiment: manipulation and random assignment to groups. An example of a weak pre-experimental design is the *one group pretest–posttest design,* as shown below:

Pre *T* Post

As suggested by its name, this design involves merely pretesting a selected group of participants, administering a treatment, then posttesting the group to determine whether a shift in scores occurred from pretest to posttest. Notice that this design has virtually no control for biasing influences in the form of threats to internal validity, such as those described in Chapter 8 (extraneous events, etc.). Consider one example of this design. Suppose a researcher wanted to test the effects of exercise on the ability to recall a list of words. A group of thirty students were shown forty common words on a screen. Following this, they were asked to write down all of the words they could remember in a three-minute period. Next, the students walked briskly around campus for forty-five minutes. They were then shown another list of forty common words followed by another three-minute period to write down all words they could remember. Here are the results: pretest average = eleven words, posttest average = sixteen words. Does exercise increase our memory span? It may appear that way, but because this weak design does not control for extraneous influences, no such conclusion is possible. Isn't it plausible that students learned how to recall more words just from the pretest experience? They may have realized during the pretest that there is a better strategy for recall, and then applied this strategy during the posttest. If there were a control group of students who did not exercise but were pretested and posttested, then this group probably would have scored higher because of the pretest effect, and its influence would have been subtracted from the exercise group to assess the pure influence of exercise. The control group in this situation would, of course, control for more than just the pretest effect. It would control for the extraneous influences due to word difficulty, time of day, and literally thousands of other influences.

Let's consider one more weak pre-experimental design to highlight the value of strong designs such as the randomized posttest control group design. The second weak design is often referred to as the *static-group comparison design*, and is shown below:

$$T \quad \text{Post}$$

$$C \quad \text{Post}$$

Notice the deliberate absence of the symbol *R*, which you will recall refers to random assignment. This is why the design is referred to as *static*, meaning inactive, passive, or intact. There is no active movement of subjects into groups, as the random assignment procedure would require. Typically, with this design one group is located (already intact) and given some type of treatment, while another, *similar* group is located to function as an intact comparison. For example, suppose a school implements a new system of blocked scheduling, whereby students are exposed to fewer classes each day (alternating days), but longer sessions in each class (two hours). Across town there may be a similar school which retains its traditional scheduling, and because of its comparability, functions as a type of control. After three years, the standardized achievement test scores of each school are compared and clearly show higher overall achievement at the blocked school. Is this evidence to support blocked scheduling? Yes, but the conclusion should be tempered somewhat in light of the fact that it is not as strong as a randomized control group design. The two schools may have *looked* comparable, but because they were not formed with random assignment, group comparability could be illusory. Maybe the blocked scheduling school would have scored higher even if they had retained their traditional scheduling due, in part, to the influence of an uncontrolled extraneous variable.

These weak pre-experimental designs can be greatly improved by the technique of *matching*, and as such would be called *quasi-experimental* designs, as explained later in this chapter. Matching would be accomplished by selecting two schools that are initially alike on important factors, like ability, motivation, and socioeconomic status prior to implementing blocked scheduling. It could then be said that the two schools were matched on ability, motivation, and socioeconomic status. Careful matching may approximate randomness in some situations, and in real life, this may be as close to ideal as possible. You are probably wondering how students could ever be randomly assigned to a school. In truth, they rarely are, but the random process could still exert its control via another level of random assignment. Entire *schools*, maybe hundreds, could be randomly assigned to a blocked schedule or a traditional format. This, of course, is a much more complex experiment.

Randomized Pretest–Posttest Control Group Design

This strong design is represented below:

$$R \quad Pre \quad T \quad Post$$
$$R \quad Pre \quad C \quad Post$$

where *Pre* refers to a pretest.

The design differs from the randomized posttest control group design only in that all participants are pretested before the treatment is implemented. The use of a pretest allows for the assessment of change (gain) and functions as a type of personal baseline. In this sense, each subject serves as his or her own control, and the treatment effects can be evaluated in terms of a shift from the starting point. The control group, of course, allows the researcher to control for extraneous influences such as the effect of a pretest on the performance on a posttest, a change due to the mere passage of time, and many other influences which could mistakenly be attributed to the treatment.

Let's consider an application of this reliable design. Assume a researcher wanted to evaluate the effectiveness of a treatment designed to reduce the amount of television watched by eighth graders. The treatment involved a series of interesting activities at home over a three-month period created specifically to compete with television watching after school, in the evenings, and on weekends. After random assignment to groups, one hundred eighth graders in each group agreed to log their television viewing (as accurately as possible) every day (the Pretest Phase). Each subject's television watching could therefore be summarized by the average number of hours watched during the Pretest Phase (after random assignment but before the treatment was initiated). Then the activities began for the treatment group only (Treatment Phase), lasting one month. Neither group logged their television viewing during this phase. Finally, after the treatment ended, both groups logged their television watching for one month during the Posttest Phase, the end of which marked the completion of the study. Table 9.1 displays the results, expressed in average hours during the Pretest and Posttest Phases.

Notice that the pretest for the treatment group is somewhat lower than the control group. This fact is considered in the analysis of the posttest scores, since a portion of the 42 versus 86 gap in the posttest scores is due to the treatment group's somewhat lower initial baseline. These designs are usually analyzed statistically with a technique called *analysis of covariance*, which adjusts posttest scores on the basis of differences in

TABLE 9.1 Results of Pretest and Posttest Phases

	Phase	
Group	**Pretest**	**Posttest**
Treatment	89	42
Control	94	86

pretest scores. Also notice that posttest hours in the control group were somewhat lower than the pretest hours. The fact that television viewing declined in the control group is also considered in the analysis, that is, a portion of the rather dramatic decline in the treatment group (89 to 42) is in part explained by the control group's decline (albeit small). The control group serves an especially valuable function in this study, because without it, we would not know how to interpret the decline in the treatment group. Maybe the pretest phase was completed in April and the posttest phase completed in June; television watching might naturally drop in June because of better weather, frequent reruns, and the like. Or possibly a new water park opened in June, and the students spent less time watching television because they were frequently visiting the park. Because of the control group, the results provide compelling evidence that the treatment itself was responsible for the decline. If the control group had also declined as dramatically, the researcher would have to attribute the treatment group's decline to some factor other than the treatment, like weather, programming, family vacations, a novel community program designed to encourage students to read more, on any number of competing explanations.

Randomized Matched Control Group Design

This especially strong design is presented below:

$$M \quad R \quad T \quad \text{Post}$$
$$M \quad R \quad C \quad \text{Post}$$

where *M* refers to matched.

It is similar to the randomized posttest control group design, but is distinguished by the use of matching prior to random assignment. A researcher may choose this design if the sample size is too small (perhaps less than forty per group) to reasonably assure group comparability after random assignment. Subjects are first rank ordered on a variable closely related to the posttest. Then one of the two highest—forming a matched pair—is randomly assigned to *T* or *C*, with the remaining one being assigned to the other. The next highest matched pair is similarly assigned, and this continues until the lowest two matched subjects are assigned randomly. After assignment is complete, the two case-by-case matched groups formed with this technique are nearly identical on the matched variable, and probably comparable on other variables as well. Less is left to chance when using matching prior to random assignment. The choice of the matching variable is crucial, for nothing is gained if it is not related to the posttest. For this reason, the matching variable is often a pretest version of the posttest measure. (A pretest is usually more highly correlated with a posttest than most other measures.)

Here is an example. A researcher planned to test whether a new method for teaching reading called *Read Now!* was more effective than one currently in use. To this end, sixty first graders' reading skills were assessed with a pretest, then rank ordered from most advanced to least advanced. Pairs were formed by coupling the two highest, next two highest, etc. until the two lowest were coupled as a pair. One member of each pair was randomly assigned to *Read Now!* while the other was retained as a control. The two groups, now nearly identical (on average) in their pre-treatment reading ability, were exposed to the treatment or control instruction for twelve weeks followed by a posttest measure of reading achievement. Any posttest difference could hardly be attributed to pre-treatment reading differences since they were the same on average. If other extraneous influences (e.g., teachers' skill) are controlled, then the researcher is entitled to conclude that the manipulation (the true independent variable of teaching method) probably caused the difference in the outcome.

Randomized Factorial Designs: Interactions and Main Effects

The term *factorial* in research refers to designs that combine two or more independent variables in a single experiment in order to determine their joint effect, in addition to the overall effect of each variable singly. The joint effect of two variables is referred to as an *interaction*, an important, but difficult, concept. You may be familiar with the concept of interaction already, possibly in the form of warnings about drug interactions. This occurs if two drugs—each one separately having a small effect—when combined have an amplified effect. For example, some medication may make you a little sleepy, so might a glass of wine. The combination of medication and wine may, however, knock you out until you awake in an emergency room. In a sense, an interaction occurs when the total effect is more than the sum of its parts. Interaction can also work in the opposite way—each of two drugs may have a small effect, but when taken together have no overall effect. Here the total is less than the sum of its parts.

Another example of interaction may be found in weight loss. If you diet (but don't exercise), you may lose a few pounds, say three. And if you exercise (but don't diet), you may lose a few pounds, say four. But dieting and exercise together may result in a loss of fifteen pounds! If diet and exercise did *not* interact, you would expect a weight loss of seven pounds (three for diet, four for exercise). Let's examine this idea more closely, in the context of a factorial design in educational research.

A researcher wanted to know whether fifth graders learn to spell better by practicing on a computer or by using handwriting (yes, once again). She also wanted to compare these two learning strategies on relatively easy versus hard words. She had reason to believe that handwriting might be better for easy words but the use of a computer might be better for harder words. This design, therefore, called for four groups: easy words/computer, hard words/computer, easy words/handwriting, hard words/handwriting. This type of factorial design is usually called a 2 × 2 factorial, the numbers referring to the categories of each factor (variable). Multiplying, as suggested by the "×" sign, produces the number of groups required in the design. If the researcher wanted to test for differences across three methods, a 3 × 2 factorial, or six groups, would be required. Also, since there are two factors combined within the same study, this design is referred to as a *two-way factorial*. To test the idea that the best method of spelling practice (computer versus handwriting) is determined by the difficulty of words, 200 students were randomly assigned to one of the four groups, and they received five practice trials (using the computer versus using handwriting) in an attempt to spell thirty new words which were relatively easy (e.g., harp) or relatively difficult (e.g., fight). On the final test, each student was asked to spell aloud each practiced word. The results are in Table 9.2, which shows the number of correct words out of thirty for each group.

As expected, the easy words were learned better than the harder words in all groups. We know this because, on average, students spelled 23 easy words correctly but only 13 hard words correctly. These values were obtained by merely computing

TABLE 9.2 Number of Correct Words out of Thirty for Each Group

	Method	
Word Type	**Computer**	**Handwriting**
Easy	20	26
Hard	16	10

the average of the easy words overall (20 + 26/2 = 23) and comparing this to the average of the hard words overall (16 + 10/2 = 13). "Overall," in this sense, refers to the average across all categories of the other variable (the categories of *Computer* and *Handwriting* under the variable *Method*). This overall effect of Word Type is referred to as a *main effect* of Word Type, and in this case, because the overall averages are different, we would say that there *is* a main effect for word type.

Furthermore, the number of words learned with a computer did not differ from the number of words learned with handwriting. Using the computer resulted in an overall average of 18 (20 + 16/2 = 18); using handwriting overall also resulted in an average of 18 (26 + 20/2 = 18). The term *overall*, once again, refers to the average across all categories of the other variable (the categories of *Easy* and *Hard* under the variable *Word Type*). This overall comparison between Methods is referred to as the *main effect* of Method, and in this case, because the overall averages are the same, we would say that there is *no* main effect for Method.

Here comes the interesting part, the interaction or joint effect of Word Type and Method. Examining the data above reveals that the answer to the question "Which method is better: computer versus handwriting?" is "It depends." This is the essence of an interaction between variables—the effect of Method on spelling scores depends on whether the words are easy or hard. If the words are easy, then handwriting is superior, but if the words are hard, then the computer is superior. This complex, interactive relationship is best depicted in a graph, as shown in Figure 9.1. Interactions between variables always appear with nonparallel lines when graphed. The nonparallelism is simply another way to illustrate a finding qualified by "It depends."

Let's change the results of our spelling experiment somewhat in order to reveal what a *non*interactive result would look like. The altered findings are shown in Table 9.3.

Notice that there exists a main effect for Word Type: an overall average of 23 for Easy words versus an overall average of 19 for Hard words. Further, there also exists a main effect for Method: an overall average of 18 for Computer versus 24 for Handwriting. The answer to the question "Which method is better: Computing versus Handwriting?" no longer is "It depends." The answer is handwriting, for both easy and hard words. The handwriting condition, when compared to the computer condition, resulted in a six-point boost (20 versus 26) for easy words, and a six-point boost (16 versus 22) for hard words. Because of this outcome, we would say that there is *no* interaction between Method and Word Type. This lack of interaction is depicted in Figure 9.2, where the parallelism in the graph is obvious.

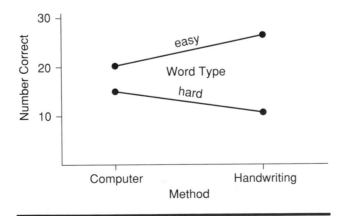

FIGURE 9.1   Graph of correctly spelled words as a function of method and word type. Note the interaction revealed by nonparallel lines.

TABLE 9.3 *Non*interactive Results of the Spelling Test Comparing Computer-Aided and Handwriting Learning Methods

Word Type	Method	
	Computer	Handwriting
Easy	20	26
Hard	16	22

Factorial designs are very common in the practice of educational research for the simple reason that interactions are very common in the classroom (and in life outside the classroom). For example, some students, depending on learning style, may thrive in a competitive atmosphere, others in a cooperative atmosphere. Which atmosphere is best? It depends on learning style and probably many other variables.

Let's revisit the example of interaction in the context of warnings about drug interactions described earlier in this section, this time with numerical values. In these cases, the effect of a drug depends on what other drugs (or food) are taken. Recall that some drugs may have amplified effects, in the sense that taken in combination yield an effect stronger than each one taken separately. The alcohol and sleeping pill interaction is one of the best known. Let's say on a 1–10 scale where 1 is wide awake and 10 is asleep, one drink with alcohol makes you sleepy to the tune of +3 (it increases your sleepiness three units regardless of where you are on the scale prior to the drink, from 2 to 5 or 6 to 9, for example. Let's also say that the sleeping pill makes you sleepy to the tune of +2. Taking *both* alcohol and the sleeping pill would make you sleepy in a *compounded,* or interactive way—perhaps +7. If they did *not* interact, taking both would affect your sleepiness by +5 (+3 for alcohol, +2 for the sleeping pill). This interaction is revealed by the *non*additive influence of +3 and +2 to equal +7 (not +5). For this reason, some researchers often refer to interactive effects as *nonadditive,* and noninteractive effects as *additive.*

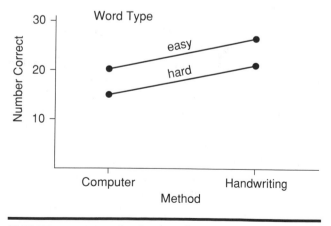

FIGURE 9.2 Graph of correctly spelled words as a function of method and word type. Note the lack of interaction revealed by parallel lines.

QUASI-EXPERIMENTAL DESIGNS

Recall from Chapter 2 that a distinction was made between two types of independent variables: true and quasi. (Also recall that the term *quasi* means "somewhat.") True independent variables allow random assignment to their conditions; quasi independent variables lack random assignment. In the same way, quasi-experimental research designs are experiments, to some degree. What they lack is the critical element of random assignment to groups. Quasi-experiments, then, are designs which use quasi (not true) independent variables. There still exists a treatment in quasi-experimental designs, in the sense that the researcher introduces a treatment or experimental program (called an intervention, from *intervene*). But control over extraneous variables may be threatened, at least to some degree, with these designs since groups have not been formed using the power of random assignment. Let's examine several common applications of this concept.

Matched Comparison Group Design

This design involves one group which receives a treatment and another group, usually chosen because of its similarity with the treatment group, functions as a baseline comparison group. The two groups, however, are intact (they already existed before the intervention) and so are probably not comparable. (And most surely not comparable in the strict sense that random assignment would provide.) This design is shown below:

$$M \quad T \quad \text{Posttest}$$
$$M \quad C \quad \text{Posttest}$$

This type of quasi-experimental design is used often, and its strength rests on how well the extraneous influences have been controlled through matching. For practical and ethical reasons, students (because they are not like mice in a laboratory) simply cannot be assigned to random groups. The next best thing to random assignment is matching, but once again, matching is less desirable than the true random process as a control procedure. But don't get the idea that random assignment is a magic potion; well-conceived matching designs can approximate the level of control provided by random assignment.

Matching involves the selection of a comparison group (or an individual subject) that is similar to the treatment group on one or more important variables that have a bearing on performance (the matched variables). For example, let us suppose that a new program—Operation Stop Dropout—designed to reduce the dropout rate was implemented at North Hills High School, a large inner city school plagued by a forty percent drop out rate. The program involved the use of small group discussions and guest speakers. In order to evaluate its effectiveness, a comparison school was selected because of its similarity to North Hills—a current dropout rate of forty percent, a minority enrollment of about eighty-five percent, and standardized achievement test scores in the bottom twenty-five percent. One could argue that even in the absence of a comparison group, if a dropout rate decreased from forty percent to fifteen percent, then it would be obvious that the program was effective. But wait, a television spot (unrelated to the Operation Stop Dropout) that encouraged students to stay in school aired frequently during the same year that the new program was implemented. And Volkswagen announced it would begin construction of a new assembly plant to reintroduce the famous Beetle and beloved bus just thirty miles away from the high school. It would need at least 1500 high school graduates for top paying factory jobs. Furthermore, the U.S. Army started another promotional blitz to attract capable high school graduates for specialized training. Now, what do you think about the dropout rate reduction from forty percent to fifteen percent? Is it due to Operation

Stop Dropout? Or is it due to the other coincidental influences just described? Or a combination? Without a carefully matched comparison group, one could not reasonably attribute any improvement in the dropout rate to the new program itself. The matched comparison group, in other words, shows us what probably would have happened to the treatment group had the treatment not been implemented. It is an attempt to control for the other plausible explanations, such as the threats to internal validity described in Chapter 8. Ideally, from a research point of view, one would like to find that North Hills' dropout rate declined after the treatment, while the comparison school's dropout rate remained steady.

The decision concerning which variables should be matched between the treatment and comparison group should center on those variables which are most closely related to the measured outcome (dependent variable), in this case the dropout rate. This would suggest that current dropout rate, minority enrollment, and standardized achievement test scores are all related in a substantial way to future dropout rates. In fact, undoubtedly the three most common matching variables in educational research are age, sex, and SES (socioeconomic status) for the simple reason that they are related to many educational outcomes. Matching on irrelevant variables, such as astrological sign or color of the school desks, would have essentially no effect on the control or interpretability of the research results.

Time Series Quasi-Experiments

Sometimes a comparison group is simply not feasible for a variety of reasons (cost, ethics, practicality, etc.) So a design known as a *time-series quasi-experiment* derives its control from observations over time instead of the comparison of one group against another. A time-series design is shown below:

Pre Pre Pre Pre Pre T Post Post Post Post Post

In this design, the object is to link a break in the trend revealed over time to the introduction of the treatment which occurred at the same time as the break in the trend. For example, let's say that a large urban school district has observed that a small but worrisome number of teachers resign after their first year. Records have been kept on the number of these resignations for the past ten years, and they reveal a consistent baseline: 11, 12, 10, 10, 12, 9, 10, 11, 11, 12. Now assume that the district implements a program for all new teachers which features a hotline to call with problems, a pairing with an experienced teacher, and monthly therapy sessions to discuss anxieties, doubts, and other undesirable emotions. To evaluate the effectiveness of this program after five years, the pre-program trend is compared to the following post-program trend: 4, 5, 2, 3, 4. Further analysis reveals that such a drop in the attrition rate could hardly be explained by chance. In other words, the drop is probably "real," but one must be cautious in attributing the decline to the program itself, for there may have been other new influences (large pay increase, reduction in class size, six new schools) that could explain the result. In the absence of other explanations, the break in the trend over time corresponding to the onset of the program is fairly convincing evidence that the program itself was the causal mechanism. Some of the difficulties associated with time series interpretations are revealed in Figure 9.3.

Counterbalanced Quasi-Experiments

Some educational research questions may be answered by comparing the same participants' responses across *all* categories of an independent variable. In this type of design, all participants receive each of the treatment and control conditions; in a sense, each subject acts as his or her own control. Here is an example. A researcher posed the

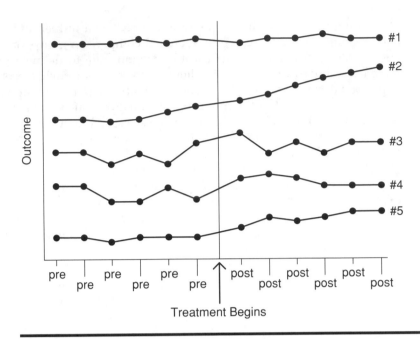

FIGURE 9.3 Possible outcomes in a time series quasi- experiment. Evidence that the treatment caused a shift over time is strongest with outcome #5. #1 appears flat, #2 reveals an upward trend *before* the treatment, #3 is "jerky" both pre and post, and #4 has an upward "blip" that is temporary. In #5 only are all of the post outcomes higher than the pre outcomes. [After Wallen & Fraenkel, 1991, p. 204.]

following question: What type of background noise, if any, results in the greatest reading comprehension—silence, dull hum of a motor, or nature sounds (ocean, river, birds, etc.)? To answer this question, one hundred students read a 500-word excerpt from a book on one of three relatively obscure topics: the history of Siberia, the history of Greenland, and the history of Korea. All three paragraphs were judged to be equally interesting and equally difficult.

All subjects read excerpts in all three background noise conditions. The researcher, though, was careful to avoid confounding noise condition with excerpt and with order. To accomplish this, each noise condition was determined randomly to be first, second, or third for each subject. Also, for each subject, a random excerpt was selected for each noise condition, creating a type of double random selection. For example, the first participant, Bob, received the following randomized order of noise conditions: motor noise, nature sounds, silence. Specifically, the in the motor noise condition, he read about Siberia; in the nature sounds condition, Korea; in the silence condition, Greenland. Then the second participant, Susan, received the following randomly determined noises and topics: nature sounds while reading about Greenland, silence while reading about Korea, and motor noises while reading about Siberia. This design is said to be *counterbalanced*, a term you will recall from Chapter 8 where the concept of control was discussed. It was counterbalanced in the sense that any advantage motor noise might have had in being first (for Bob) is offset by it being second for, say, Tim, and third for Susan. Similarly, any advantage that might exist for Siberia being first and being paired with motor noise, as with Bob, is offset by its being second or third for other participants and being paired with silence and nature sounds.

This type of randomized counterbalancing establishes control by having each noise condition, on average, occur first, second, or third and having each noise condition preceded and followed by the other two conditions, on average, an equal number of times. The same principle holds for the three different excerpts. Over many participants, the random process equalizes order effects (the advantage of being first or the disadvantage of being last) and carryover effects (the advantage Greenland might have by following Siberia or the disadvantage Korea might have by following Siberia). You can probably understand these order and carryover effects by imagining being in a market research study providing taste ratings after sampling chocolate Brands A, B and C in that order. Brand C chocolate might suffer from being last if overstimulated taste buds begin to tire out (an order effect) and by contamination from the two preceding (a carryover effect).

Randomized counterbalancing is just one type of counterbalancing, although it is considered by many to be the best because of the random processes at work. A potential drawback of randomized counterbalancing is the practical difficulty of determining and administering a random order of conditions for each subject. Let's consider one type of *systematic counterbalancing*, called a *Latin Square*. Only four different orders are required in this highly efficient design. Imagine four conditions—call them A, B, C, and D for simplicity (they might be four different background noises, in keeping with our present example). A Latin Square would involve only four different orders, as shown below:

Order 1:	A	B	D	C
Order 2:	B	C	A	D
Order 3:	C	D	B	A
Order 4:	D	A	C	B

Notice that each condition (A, B, C, D) occurs in each possible ordinal position (first, second, third, and fourth). Also notice the control for carryover. A B in Order 1 is counterbalanced by B A in Order 3, B C in Order 2 is counterbalanced by C B in Order 4, D C in Order 1 is counterbalanced by C D in Order 3, etc. This is an unusual design indeed, for it seems to control for so much with only four counterbalanced orders.

Research designs that arrange for all subjects to experience all treatment conditions are often referred to as *repeated measures* designs or *within subjects* designs; "repeated measures" in the sense that subjects are measured repeatedly (once in each condition) and "within subjects" in the sense that comparisons are made within the same subject (across all conditions) instead of between subjects as you would in a study where each group consisted of different subjects. Such designs may also be called counterbalanced designs, after the control technique described above. These counterbalanced designs are considered very sensitive, in the sense that they are more apt to show a treatment effect (if one exists) than designs that use groups of different subjects. The drawback is that in many situations counterbalanced designs are inappropriate because order and carryover effects render meaningless results. For example, if you wanted to know which of two methods for teaching psychology—lecture versus self-paced programmed instruction—were best, it would make no sense for subjects who first learned about psychology in the lecture condition to then be exposed to the same content in the self-paced programmed instruction. They have already learned the material. In this case, only two randomly assigned, separate groups could be compared. These designs, in contrast to within-subjects designs, are appropriately called *between-subjects* designs.

SINGLE-SUBJECT DESIGNS

As suggested by its title, these designs involve studying the effect of a treatment on a single subject (or a single group, such as one entire classroom). These designs are considered "experimental" since they involve the introduction of a treatment of some sort, and they accomplish their control through the use of comparisons between baseline observations and treatment observations. These designs, then, involve observing behavior over a period of time as a function of baseline and treatment conditions.

Baseline performance in the absence of treatment, usually labelled *A*, is compared with treatment performance, usually labelled *B*. These designs, in fact, are typically referred to as *ABAB, BAAB, ABA* or some other configuration showing how the baseline and treatment conditions are alternated. Some of these designs, despite their basic simplicity, can be very sophisticated indeed. First, let's consider an example of a basic design.

ABAB Design

In order to determine whether sugar resulted in hyperactive behavior in a seven-year-old boy, a researcher observed the behavior of the student for two hours in the morning after he ate his usual high-sugar cereal. The observer recorded the frequency of hyperactive behaviors daily for two weeks. These results are shown in Figure 9.4, for weeks 1 and 2.

This phase of the design establishes the baseline, or A, the behavior in the absence of a treatment effect. Next, the researcher begins observation after greatly restricting the amount of sugar in the same cereal. The observation is continued for two weeks and the results are shown in Figure 9.4, under Weeks 3 and 4.

The treatment phase, or B, revealed a clear decrease in the frequency of hyperactivity. Thinking that the decrease might be due to other factors, the researcher reinstituted the high-sugar cereal (the A, or baseline phase) and observed the resultant behavior as shown in Figure 9.4, under Weeks 5 and 6. As expected, the hyperactive behavior increased with the re-introduction of sugar. Finally, as a double check, the researcher withdrew the sugar (B, or treatment) and observed behavior once more for two weeks as shown in "Weeks 7 and 8" in Figure 9.4.

These findings are rather compelling, especially when all phases are shown together as revealed in Figure 9.3. The visual impact leaves little doubt that hyperactivity is linked to high sugar. Of course, you could not rule out coincidence with one hundred percent certainty. Possibly, some other influence in the classroom occurred at the same time as sugar withdrawal; as a result, the data, although appearing persuasive, would in fact be misleading.

Multiple-Baseline Design

Another, more complex, single-subject design, called the *multiple-baseline design*, is probably stronger for ruling out extraneous influences. It may be thought of as a

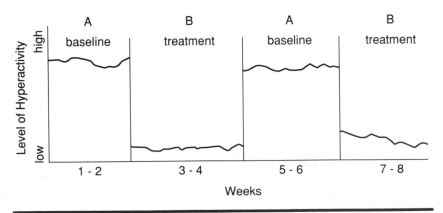

FIGURE 9.4   Fictional results of an ABAB single-subject design where treatment is alternated with baseline (control) to see its effect on hyperactivity.

BBBB, BAAA, BBAA, BBBA, BBBB design. Here is how that design might be employed in a sugar–hyperactivity study. The single-subject, in this case, is actually a single group. Imagine four students in the same class, Albert, Bob, Carl, and David, all of whom are perceived by their teacher as hyperactive. All four students would be observed for a period of time, say two weeks, to establish their baseline level of hyperactivity. Then one student, Albert, would be withdrawn from sugary cereal while the others would continue with baseline observations. Next, after two weeks, another student (Bob) would be withdrawn from sugary cereal (the treatment) and observed over two weeks. (Albert would continue under the treatment as well.) The other two would still be observed under the baseline condition. At the next step, Carl would be withdrawn from sugar to join the first two who had been withdrawn. Finally, David would be observed in the treatment phase for two weeks. One possible outcome of this design is shown in Figure 9.5 in phases.

You can see the obvious staircase pattern in the data. This design is very effective for ruling out co-occurring influence in the environment (classroom) since you would expect in Phase II the hyperactivity of Bob, Carl, and David to also decrease if some influence in the classroom, but not sugary cereal, were responsible for the decline. The same control is also built into Phases III and IV. The phases of a multiple-baseline design, therefore, have built-in controls and multiple treatment observations, making this design especially strong for revealing cause-and-effect relationships.

CHAPTER SUMMARY

Experimental research is characterized by an intervention of some sort (as opposed to comparisons between groups which already differ). A wide variety of experimental research designs exist, including true, quasi-, and single-subject. True experimental designs incorporate a manipulation with random assignment to groups (e.g., the random-

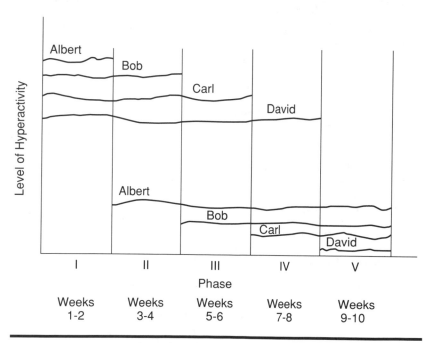

FIGURE 9.5 Fictional results of a multiple-treatment design. Treatment effects are observed concurrently with controls. The staircase pattern shows convincing evidence for treatment effects while controlling extraneous influences.

ized posttest control group design). The strength of this design is highlighted by its contrast to "pre-experimental" designs having very little control over threatening influences. True experimental factorial designs are especially useful, for they yield information about main (overall) effects as well as interactive (nonadditive, compounding) effects. Quasi-experimental designs incorporate treatments or interventions, but lack the key element of random assignment to groups. This characteristic seriously compromises control in these designs. Alternatives to random assignment, such as matching, yield quasi-experimental designs such as the matched comparison group design. Single-subject research designs also involve an intervention, and they often achieve their control by alternating baseline and treatment observations over time.

Now let's turn our attention to a guided tour of an experimental design as it was applied in a published research report.

GUIDED TOUR

Let's turn our attention now to a guided tour of published educational research. This will help solidify important terms and concepts described in this chapter.

Brief Reports

INTERSPERSED POSTPASSAGE QUESTIONS AND READING COMPREHENSION ACHIEVEMENT

Michael Lee Seretny

Neuropsychology Lab

Ball State University

Raymond S. Dean

Ball State University and

Indian University School of Medicine

In this study, we examined the effect of interspersed postpassage questions on comprehension for second-grade children. Readers of three levels of reading achievement were either instructed in the use of questions or taught reading in a regular fashion. Results from the reading comprehension subtest of the Science

Correspondence concerning this article should be addressed to Michael L. Seretny, Ball State University, Neuropsychology Lab, TC 517, Muncie, Indiana 47306.

Research Associates Achievement Test Battery showed that although questioning instruction had little effect on the above average readers, both normal and below average readers made significant gains in comprehension when instructed in the use of postpassage questions. The results are described in terms of strategy development.

An important variable for learning from prose appears to be the degree to which readers process textual material. Numerous mathemagenic devices have been shown to increase learners' immediate and delayed recall. The use of inserted questions is one method that seems to be an effective aid in children's learning textual material. Moreover, postpassage questions have been shown to facilitate test performance more than prequestions (e.g., Frase, 1970). Questions that appear after the passage may promote both specific discrimination and the acquisition of nonreferent (incidental) material (Frase, 1970). Review of the literature in this area, however, reveals conflicting results. For example, Fincke (1968) and Landry (1967) found that placing questions before a reading passage did not consistently facilitate increased comprehension as compared to no-question groups.

Clearly, the bulk of the research in this area has used adult samples. Swenson and Kulhavy (1974), in an attempt to extend findings with adults to school-age children, found that interspersed postquestions strongly facilitated comprehension for relevant material.

In the present investigation, we were interested in the transfer of inserted question strategies with children. Specifically, we examined the value of asking interspersed questions gleaned from the teachers' edition of a basal reader. In light of the past research showing a direct instructive influence for such questions, our focus was on the extent to which this approach could be applied with basal readers. Indeed, although the literature reports positive findings, these results were established with contrived textual materials in artificial settings.

Method

Subjects

The subjects for this study were drawn from all the students entering second grade at an elementary school in Indianapolis, Indiana. Fifty-four students (32 boys and 22 girls), all seen as normal readers by the school, 93% of the second-grade class, were randomly assigned to one of two second-grade classrooms. The mean age of the second graders was 7.28 years.

Design and Procedure

Two factors, entering reading level (top vs. middle vs. lower third) and use of interspersed postquestions (control vs. adjunct questions) were combined factorially to form six experimental groups. [1] The dependent variable was the children's score on the comprehension subtest of the Science Research Associates Achievement Test Battery (Level B/Form 1).

Subjects were assigned to one of three reading ability groups on the basis of their scores on the Houghton Mifflin Reading Placement Test. From within each of these three groups, subjects were randomly assigned to either a treatment instruction group or a control instruction group. [2] The students and two second-grade teachers were given the first 2 weeks of classes to get acquainted. A researcher met with the two classroom teachers to discuss the experiment and to provide the instruction in using interspersed questions.

Both the experimental and control groups received instruction from each of the two teachers assigned to the second grade. The teacher that was randomly assigned to begin instruction with the treatment group provided reading instruc-

[1] *We see here that these researchers used an experimental factorial design in this study. They used two factors, one with three categories (reading levels: top, middle, lower) and one with two categories (interspersed postpassage questions: control versus adjunct questions). Their design is therefore described as a 3 × 2 factorial, yielding six different groups.*

[2] *One of their factors is a true independent (manipulated) variable (interspersed postpassage questions), and as such, enables the random assignment of subjects to the two groups. (The other variable is an attribute variable, since its groups are formed on the basis of some preexisting attribute.) Because of this manipulated independent variable, this is considered a true experimental design. And, as we have seen, because two factors have been combined, this is also considered a two-way factorial design. Furthermore, because of the use of a control group and posttest (coupled with the random assignment to control versus adjunct groups), this design is more completely labelled a two-way factorial randomized posttest control group true experimental design (Whew!).*

tion using interspersed postquestions for the first 4 weeks of the study. Then that same teacher provided instruction to the control group, without the use of interspersed postquestions, for the final 4 weeks of the instructional period or the study.[3] In this manner, both groups were instructed with identical basal texts, under their respective interspersed questioning condition by both of the second-grade teachers to control for teaching style and students' preference for a given teacher.

[3] *Do you recognize the control procedures used to hold constant the influence of extraneous variables?*

Both groups covered one story per week in the second-grade Houghton Mifflin Reading Series. The control instruction groups received the identical basal selection in small-group instruction without the interspersed questions. In essence, the treatment condition involved the teaching of the comprehension strategy by implementing interspersed questions during the oral reading of a basal selection. As the children orally read each selection, the teacher stopped after each page and orally asked and discussed the interspersed questions. In this manner, students were taught to make hypothetical judgments based on prompts from the interspersed questions.

Results and Discussion

Each subject's responses to the Science Research Associates comprehension subtest were scored for total number correct. Analysis of these data revealed a significant main effect for treatments, $F(1, 48) = 23.77$, $p < .001$, $MS_e = 3.29$, with the adjunct-question group exceeding the performance of the no-question group. The main effect for reading level was also significant, $F(2, 48) = 76.49$, $p < .001$. These results were qualified by the two-way interaction of treatment and reading level, $F(2, 48) = 5.47$, $p < .007$. The six means are given in Table 1. Contrasts of the six means showed that instruction had little effect for the above average readers, compared with other learners ($p > .05$).

This finding must be interpreted, however, in light of the above average readers' extremely high scores on the dependent measure. Indeed, both average and below average readers profited significantly ($p < .05$) from instruction with interspersed questions. **[4]**

The present results replicate the Swenson and Kulhavy (1974) study in terms of the comprehension and retention effects of postpassage questions with children. The present experiment was unique, however, in that the transfer of the question strategy was shown to facilitate performance on new text materials. Obviously, this approach has implications for instructional practices with basal reading in the primary grades. Although the interaction of postpassage question instruction and reading ability levels showed a greater effect for average and below average readers, this finding can be attributed to above average readers' showing almost total mastery on the dependent measure. With the instruction of the below average reader being critical in the implementation of any instructional procedure, however, the present findings are important. This is true because it seems that interspersed questions facilitate their comprehension and retention of textual materials above a typi-

[4] *Here we see how factorial designs are "partitioned" into their separate sources. The main effect for treatments (independent variable) suggests that the treatment (adjunct question) group overall outperformed the control (no-question group) overall. It is important to recognize which means are being compared in this analysis. The overall treatment mean is 20.96 [(23.22 + 21.78 + 17.89)/3]. And the overall control mean is 18.55 [(22.78 + 19.44 + 13.44)/3]. Overall here means "over all levels of the other factor," reading level.*

The main effect for reading level also suggests that there are overall differences across the three reading groups. The means being compared here are: 23.00 [(23.22 + 22.78)/2] versus 20.61 [(21.78 + 19.44] versus 15.67 [(17.89 + 13.44)/2]. The overall concept here again refers to over all levels of the other factor, the instruction group as shown in Table 1 (Treatment and Control).

Finally, notice the interaction reported in the results. Recall from this chapter that the presence of an interaction tells us that the influence of the interspersed postpassage questions depends on the specific level of the reading group. Evidently, the treatment has a greater effect (compared to the control) for one category of reader than it does for another. Examine Table 1 of the Seretny and Dean article and and you can see that the influence of the treatment is very small (23.22 versus 22.78, or less than ½ point) for above average readers, but rather large (17.89 versus 13.44, or almost 4½ points) for below average readers. Clearly, one type of reader is affected differently by the treatment than another type, or simply, the treatment effect depends on reading group. Recall that the essence of interactive influence is the concept of "it depends."

TABLE 1   Means and Standard Deviations on SRA Criterion Measure by Treatment an Control Groups

Instruction group	Reading group		
	Above average	Average	Below average
Treatment			
M	23.22	21.78	17.89
SD	1.09	1.30	2.42
Control			
M	22.78	19.44	13.44
SD	1.09	1.51	2.74

Note. SRA = Science Research Associates.

cal instructional approach. Clearly, the present results suggest the utility of teaching the mathemagenic strategy of interspersed postpassage questions as part of the reading instruction. This point of view is consistent with Jenkins and Pany's (1981) suggestion of the importance of teacher questioning on the development of children's comprehension.

In sum, the present investigation suggests that an internal strategy or heuristic may enable the young reader to develop a strategy useful in processing and retaining basal textual material. As demonstrated here, this approach may begin to assist students in internalizing a strategy that will offer them the skills necessary to function more independently.

References

Fincke, W. (1968). The effects of asking questions to develop purpose for reading on the attainment of higher comprehension levels in a population of third graders. *Dissertation Abstracts International, 29,* 1778.

Frase, L. T. (1970). Boundary conditions for mathemagenic behaviors. *Review of Educational Research, 40,* 337–347.

Jenkins, J. R., & Pany, D. (1981). Instructional variables in reading comprehension. In J. Guthrie (Ed.), *Comprehension and teaching research reviews.* Newark, DE: International Reading Association.

Landry, D. L. (1967). The effect of organization aids on reading comprehension. *Dissertation Abstracts International, 27,* 3229.

Swenson, I., & Kulhavy, R. W. (1974). Adjunct questions and comprehension of prose by children. *Journal of Educational Psychology, 66,* 212–215.

Received February 6, 1985
Revision received December 18, 1985

APPLICATION EXERCISES

1. For each of the scenarios below, determine whether the researcher is conducting an experimental study or a non-experimental study. If *experimental*, decide whether it is a *true* experiment or a *quasi*-experiment. If it is a *quasi-experiment*, describe both the limitations of the design and the changes required to qualify as a true experiment.

   a. A researcher randomly assigned 120 students to four treatment groups in an effort to learn more about how different types of studying (the treatment) influence achievement.

   b. A researcher randomly selected one hundred teachers from a large school district and divided them into two groups: those with a master's degree and those without. He then assessed their levels of multicultural awareness to see if these were related to their educational attainment.

   c. A researcher formed two groups of parents: those who demonstrated a parenting style that included a strong emphasis on developing autonomy, a weak emphasis on developing autonomy, and no emphasis on developing autonomy. Then he measured the children's self-esteem and achievement motivation to see if they were linked to the different parenting styles.

   d. A researcher recruited 200 volunteer college students who were self-reported to be test-anxious. A random half was instructed on the use of meditation prior to exams; the other half was not (they merely served as a control and were provided with meditation training after the study was over). Students' anxiety levels were assessed after the training just prior to final exams.

   e. Identical twins were observed in a study of the influence of college on people's overall satisfaction with life. Fifty twins were located who satisfied this requirement: one twin graduated from a four-year college, and the other twin never attended college. The researcher then compared the two groups on a measure of their overall happiness.

   f. A researcher studied the number of math and science teachers who graduated from state-supported colleges and universities. In an attempt to increase this rate, a special program was implemented that provided partial tuition payment for teachers in training for math and science positions. The researcher compared the trend before and after the implementation to determine whether the program accomplished its goal.

   g. A researcher studied how students' sleepiness after lunch is affected by varying types of illumination in a study hall (fluorescent, incandescent, and halogen). All students were observed under each condition in a counterbalanced design.

   h. A researcher investigated how students' attitudes and achievement are effected by pop quizzes. Three randomized groups were formed: pop quiz twice a week, pop quiz once every two weeks, and no pop quizzes.

   i. A researcher studied the influence of class size on reading achievement by arranging for all second graders in a district to be in classes no larger than fifteen. He compared the end-of-year reading achievement in the size fifteen classes with similar classes in another district, all with sizes between twenty and twenty-five.

2. Interactions are common in everyday life, in the sense that the influence of one factor on your behavior depends on the level of a second factor. How the weather affects you, for example, might depend on how much sleep you've had. Or the influence of coffee as a "perk-me-up" may depend on when you ate your last meal. Provide an original example of the interacting influence of two variables on your behavior, being very careful to include the concept of "it depends."

3. Assume a researcher used a 2 × 2 factorial design to study how diet and exercise affect weight loss. Here are the results, expressed in pounds lost after six months,

for the four treatment combinations: both diet and exercise: 10; neither diet nor exercise: 0; diet but no exercise: 2; no diet but exercise: 1.

a. Form a table showing the means for each "cell."
b. Graph the results.
c. Evaluate each main effect and the interaction effect using the guidelines described in the chapter.
d. Repeat a–c above, substituting the following cell means, respectively: 10, 0, 0, 10.

MULTIPLE CHOICE QUESTIONS

1. What are the two essential features of *true* experimental designs?
   a. dependent and attribute variables
   b. blinding and counterbalancing
   c. manipulation and random assignment
   d. theory and matching
   e. pretest and posttest

2. When the symbol *R* is used to describe a design, we know that the design includes:
   a. random selection
   b. random assignment
   c. response measures
   d. retrospective reports
   e. randomized counterbalancing

3. The "Pre T Post" design is an example of which of the following designs?
   a. true experimental
   b. quasi-experimental
   c. single subject
   d. pre-experimental
   e. post experimental

4. What feature of the randomized pretest posttest control group design controls for extraneous influences such as the effect of a pretest on a posttest and a change due to the mere passage of time?
   a. C
   b. T
   c. Pre
   d. Post
   e. R

5. Assume a researcher factorially combined male versus female and treatment versus control. Here are the results: male treatment = 7; male control = 1; female treatment = 5; female control = 3. Which of the following summarizes these findings?

Main Effects

	Treatment?	Sex?	Interaction?
a.	no	yes	no
b.	yes	yes	yes
c.	no	no	yes
d.	yes	yes	no
e.	yes	no	yes

6. Which of the following best captures the essence of interaction?

    a. nonadditivity and nonparallelism
    b. additivity and nonparallelism
    c. nonadditivity and parallelism
    d. additivity and parallelism

7. What critical feature is lacking in quasi-experimental designs?

    a. matching
    b. pretest
    c. random assignment
    d. treatment
    e. counterbalancing

8. A Latin Square is a type of:

    a. counterbalancing
    b. randomization
    c. matching
    d. time series
    e. pretest

9. A baseline, treatment, baseline single-subject design would be represented as:

    a. BAB
    b. ABA
    c. pre pre treatment
    d. A B D C
    e. M C T

10. Which of the following types of designs would be strongest for establishing cause and effect?

    a. static-group comparison
    b. time series
    c. matched comparison group
    d. randomized posttest control group
    e. one group pretest posttest

Answers: 1) c   2) b   3) d   4) a   5) e   6) a   7) c   8) a   9) b   10) d

Chapter 10

COMMON NON-EXPERIMENTAL RESEARCH DESIGNS

OVERVIEW

In the preceding chapter we described a sampling of the many experimental designs used in educational research. This chapter continues a sampling of research designs, but the focus is now on *non*-experimental designs, those designs that lack an intervention (treatment) component. This difference is crucial since non-experimental research designs do not lend themselves well to interpretations about cause and effect, of interest to so many scientific researchers. We'll examine three broad classes of non-experimental research designs: causal comparative, correlational, and descriptive.

THE CAUSAL COMPARATIVE DESIGN

Recall from Chapter 5 that educational researchers must frequently study phenomena as they naturally occur, without intervention of any sort. This is because it may not be practical, ethical, or feasible to arrange for the occurrence of a factor believed to cause some effect. The influence of divorce, for example, on the educational achievement and motivation of young students cannot be studied in any other way. (Can you imagine randomly assigning married couples to a divorce group? Or high school students to a dropout group?) As we saw in Chapter 5, researchers who study group differences that already exist refer to their designs in general as *causal comparative*. They are so named because the researcher is comparing different groups in an effort to explain the *causes* (or effects) of such differences. Examples of independent or attribute variables that are nearly always studied using causal comparative designs are differences in sex, ability, personality, socioeconomic status, preschool experiences, parenting styles, family structures, classrooms (such as single-sex versus coed), and, in general, schools or teachers. There are hundreds more, all considered important but all not readily amenable to experimental manipulations.

Ex-Post-Facto Designs

Forming Groups. The basic causal comparative design is sometimes referred to as an *ex-post-facto design*. As implied by its title (*ex post facto* means "retroactive, or prior to"), this design involves a comparison between groups whose differences are pre-existing, or prior to the researcher's observations. For example, a researcher might classify students into groups according to how much television they watch (a pre-existing condition) and then compare their academic achievement (GPA) to learn whether television watching is related to achievement in school. Or consider the example of a researcher classifying high school students according to gender (a pre-existing condition) to see whether they differ in terms of strength of career aspirations. Or consider the researcher who classifies high school girls by their school type (all girl versus coed) to see whether there are differences in academic aptitude (SAT scores).

Notice that the designs described above focus on a presumed *cause* (television, gender, coed schools) of some effect (achievement, aspiration, aptitude, respectively). The grouping (independent) variable in these examples was a hypothesized cause, while the measured outcome (dependent) variable was the hypothesized effect. Other ex-post-facto designs may focus on a presumed *effect* of some cause. For example, two groups may be formed on the basis of whether they dropped out of high school (the effect) while searching for the influence regarded as the cause (e.g., lack of a mentoring relationship). Or consider a researcher who might group students according to their difficulty learning to read (the effect), and then search for the presumed cause (little exposure to written materials prior to kindergarten, such as the amount of time a parent spent reading to a child).

Whether the researcher is forming groups out of an interest in a cause or an effect, the basic design is the same. Groups are formed on some basis (a presumed cause or a presumed effect), then compared on the basis of another variable to shed light on cause-and-effect relationships. The price of this simplicity is counteracted by the difficulty with interpretation. Despite the general name for these types of designs (*causal comparative*), such designs are weaker than true experimental designs for the purpose of establishing cause and effect.

Strong Inference. Ex-post-facto designs frequently lack strong controls for plausible rival explanations. They can, however, be greatly strengthened by testing a plausible rival hypothesis against the research hypothesis. The concept of a design that tests a research hypothesis against an alternative hypothesis (or one that pits two theories against each other) is called *strong inference* (Platt, 1964) and is one mark of a good design. Consider each one of the ex-post-facto examples listed above, and upon reflection, alternative explanations will probably come to mind. Take the very last example as an illustration, where children who had trouble learning to read were found to have parents who rarely read to them. Does failing to read to children *cause* learning-to-read difficulties? Maybe, maybe not. Quite possibly, children who have trouble learning to read have lead poisoning (assume this is the real culprit). And it turns out that the parents who spent little time reading to their children were predominantly lower social class, living in older homes which contained peeling leaded paint, which were adjacent to freeways and expressways and surrounded with soil contaminated by cars' leaded pollution over the years. This suggests that lead removal—not reading to children—would be most helpful in ameliorating the problem these children have in learning how to read. A strong inference design would illuminate this rival interpretation by collecting data on both social class and lead poisoning in addition to data on reading skills and early reading experiences. In truth, any one effect, like difficulty in learning to read, most likely has multiple, complex causes.

Consider another relationship described above: the television/achievement link. If the group of students who watch television the most have the lowest GPAs, does this mean that watching television *causes* lower achievement? Maybe lower achievement causes more television watching, in the sense that school failure lowers the motivation to pursue school-related activities (like homework, special projects, etc.) which in turn simply frees up more time to sit in front of the television. Could the real culprit be lack of exercise? Lack of exercise may deplete the brain of chemical transmitters, making school learning more difficult (hence, a lower GPA) and it may also encourage lethargic behavior, itself very compatible with television watching. The television, then, gets turned on because the student simply sits on the couch. The researcher would know this only if data on exercise were collected as part of the design.

Further, imagine (once again) a study which determined that young children who had formal training in music (e.g., piano lessons at age six) had much greater math ability ten years later than those who did not have early training in music. Was music the cause of greater math abilities? Maybe, maybe not. Possibly, those parents who encouraged their children to take music lessons also tutored them more frequently during math homework assignments years later. The cause in this case would be the achievement orientation of the parents, not the music lessons per se. Again, a solid causal comparative design using strong inference would examine data on the achievement orientation of parents as well as music experience and math ability.

Design Controls.   Causal comparative designs are often labelled by the techniques used to create the groups for comparison. For example, a *matched group* design would involve selecting two groups who are dissimilar on a hypothesized cause, say, bottle-fed and breast-fed babies, but are the same on a matching variable believed to be a rival explanation, say, the age and socioeconomic status of the mother.

An *extreme groups* design would involve the selection of groups which represented maximum differences on the hypothesized cause (or effect), for example those who watch sixty or more hours of television per week versus those who watch very little or no television. Such extreme groups could also be matched (equated) on a variable believed to be a rival explanation, for example exercise. This would be a *matched extreme groups design*.

Spurious Relationships.   The counter explanations suggested above may not seem plausible, but we hope that the point is clear: Causal comparative studies uncover links, but the *reasons* for the links may be open to many different interpretations. Variable A may cause Variable B, Variable B may cause Variable A, or Variables A and B may be caused by Variables C, D, E, F, G, H, I, J... When the relationship between Variable A and Variable B is caused (or explained) by Variable C, it is said that the relationship between A and B is *spurious,* or not real in a sense. For example, the relationship between early music lessons (A) and math ability in high school (B), is spurious if it is known that the cause of *both* early music exposure and later math ability was the parent's priority placed on achievement (C). Here is another example: The relationship between balding and heart disease in men may be spurious if it is known that both balding and heart disease were caused by a third variable, like hormone levels. Spurious relationships can be explained away by a hidden factor. One would not conclude that balding per se caused heart disease, only that the linkage between the two was the result of some other influence. Or consider the relationship I read about in a recent newspaper article: Short men are more likely than tall men to have heart attacks. It is not height per se that causes heart attacks (short men would not take growth medicine to ward off heart attacks). A third variable, like poor nutrition in childhood, probably causes both the lack of growth and weaker hearts. The important point to remember is that two variables may be strongly related without either of them causing the other. Indeed, most relationships of interest to educational researchers are probably a tangled web of many variables. Fortunately, researchers who use causal comparative research designs often have statistical procedures that allow for greater confidence in cause-and-effect interpretations. These procedures help rule out competing or rival explanations. You may have encountered the expression *controlled for statistically*. This general collection of procedures for statistical control—partial correlation—is described briefly later in this chapter.

CORRELATIONAL RESEARCH DESIGNS

Correlational research is a close cousin to causal comparative research. They both suffer from the same limitation: lack of intervention and resultant loss of control. The main difference between causal comparative and correlational research is the type of scale used in the analysis. Correlational research uses only variables that are scaled *continuously*, like the number of hours of television watched per week. The values of such a scale have no break, so to speak, in that they can be any number from 1 to, say, 60 (they may run continuously, 1, 2, 3, 4, 5, 6, 7, 8, 9, 10, 11, 12, 13, 14, 15 and so on to 60). This continuously scaled variable can then be related to (correlated with) another continuously scaled variable, like scores on a test of vocabulary knowledge, ranging continuously from zero correct to fifty correct, the maximum possible score. Contrast these continuous scales with what are called *discrete* scales, those values that are unconnected and distinct, such as type of teaching method, type of study method, school climate, learning style, or gender. Causal comparative research, as we have seen, typically employs one discrete, or grouping, variable (e.g., male versus female, presence or absence of early music lessons, or breast fed versus bottle fed) and one continuously scaled variable (e.g., score on a test of the ability to "read" faces). Correlational research, by contrast, usually employs two continuously scaled variables such as age and reaction time.

Many complex statistical methods have been developed to analyze and help interpret research findings based on two or more continuously scaled variables. For the purposes of our discussion, these techniques may be described in terms of correlational designs. Let's examine a few common designs.

Basic Bivariate Design

This is the most fundamental of all correlational designs. The concept of a correlation was first introduced in Chapter 7 (in a discussion of reliability) but will be reviewed briefly. Two variables are measured from a sample of subjects, their data points plotted, and a statistic is calculated to summarize the overall strength and direction of the relationship, or correlation. Here is an example. A group of twenty adult learners enrolled in an intensive two-week course on accounting principles and completed a one hundred-item multiple choice test as a measure of their overall learning. At the end of the test, students also indicated an estimate of how many hours of aerobic exercise they engaged in during the same two-week period of time as the course. The researcher then plotted the twenty data points showing the relationship between test scores and hours of exercise. The plot, often called a *scatterplot* (or *scatter diagram* or *scattergram;* see Chapter 7), is shown in Figure 10.1.

The trend is clearly visible in this plot, as the points tend to "swarm" in a specific direction: from the lower left to the upper right. (You may want to review Chapter 7 where we first introduced the concept of correlation.) Low scores on the test, therefore, tend to be associated with few hours of exercise, and high test scores tend to be associated with more hours of exercise. This is the defining characteristic of a *positive* relationship (low with low, high with high). If the pattern had been different, for example if the "swarm" moved from the upper left to the lower right, a *negative* relationship would be revealed. In this case, fewer hours of exercise would be associated with higher test scores, and more hours of exercise with lower test scores.

How close the plotted scores resemble an imaginary straight line defines the strength of the relationship—the closer the points are to the line, the stronger the relationship. (This is referred to as a *regression line*.) The statistic which defines the relationship's strength (and direction) is called the *correlation coefficient*. You might remember from Chapter 7 that it is symbolized *r*. Its value can range from –1.00 (a maximized negative correlation) to 1.00 (a maximized positive correlation). An *r* value of 0 (zero) reflects no correlation, or a case in which few hours of exercise are associ-

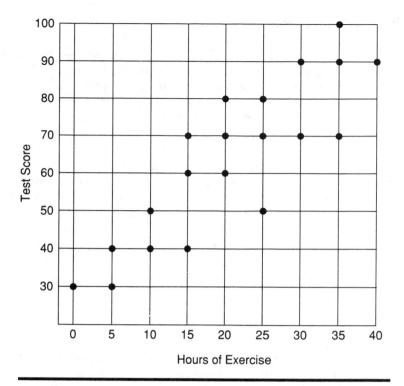

FIGURE 10.1   Scattergram showing the relationship between test scores and hours of exercise (hypothetical data).

ated with both low and high test scores (and more hours of exercise are also associated with low and high test scores). This lack of correlation would reveal itself as a circular pattern or "cloudburst" of data points. The actual correlation coefficient, r, describing the data points shown in Figure 10.1 is .87, which is positive and quite strong.

As was true with causal comparative studies, the simplicity of this correlational design comes with a price: What does this correlation mean? It is open to many interpretations. Does it mean that exercise is causally related to achievement scores, maybe through changes in brain chemistry? If those with low test scores had exercised more, would they then have had higher scores? Or is this correlation *spurious*, meaning that it is explained by reference to a third variable, such as time, not measured by the researcher? Maybe those with more time available are able to study the textbook more, and are also able to set aside time for exercise. Maybe the correlation, if spurious, is explained by yet another variable, physical health. Perhaps those who did not exercise very much have chronic health problems requiring medication, and it is the medication which interferes with attention and memory. Those who exercise more, by contrast, tend to be in better health (they exercise more because they feel better) and require no drugs which impact mental acuity.

Consider the correlation between spelling ability and shoe size: those with bigger feet spell better. (Do you remember this from Chapter 7?) How is this possible, you ask? The answer lies in the sample used to calculate the correlation: students in grades 6 through 10. Older kids have bigger feet than younger kids, and the older kids spell better too. This is another example of a spurious relationship; spelling ability and shoe size are both connected causally to a third variable, age. Correlations are sometimes very difficult to interpret because of this hidden variable problem. Remember, simply because one variable is *correlated* with another, it is not safe to assume that it *causes* the other. Correlations between variables abound, and because the world is a tangled web of complex relationships, it would be a surprise if two correlated variables were, in fact, a simple and direct causal chain.

Partial Correlation Design

Researchers who use correlational designs recognize their limitations for the purpose of establishing cause and effect. Fortunately, there exists a powerful control method very different from the type of control used by those who conduct true experiments (e.g., randomization). The correlational method of control is a type of statistical control, that is, control achieved during the analysis of data. This statistical control technique is known as *partial correlation*, and is especially useful for uncovering and explaining spurious relationships. During the analysis the variable that is believed to be a rival hypothesis—the suspected uncontrolled variable—is *partialled out*, which means that its influence is held in check. If a correlation between two variables, shoe size and spelling ability among elementary school children, for example, remains strong after the extraneous variable of age is partialled out, then it can be said that age is controlled and is not an explanation for the link between shoe size and spelling ability. In this particular case, of course, the correlation between shoe size and spelling ability would vanish when age is controlled since age is responsible for the spurious correlation. Even if the correlation did not vanish when age was controlled, there is still the possibility that some other variable, not yet partialled out, is the reason for the correlation. In other words, partial correlation can control for the influence of suspected extraneous variables, but another variable, not even measured and not part of the analysis, could always be responsible for the correlation originally obtained.

Let's see, at least conceptually, how partial correlation might work in one study. Pretend a researcher hypothesized that lead contamination caused cognitive deficits. He tested the IQs of twelve children; then he collected soil samples in their backyard (where they play) and tested it for lead content (higher numbers reflect greater amounts of lead). Table 10.1 contains his data, with the associated scatterplot shown in Figure 10.2.

The correlation between lead and IQ, as you can see from the scatterplot, is negative and very strong, $r = -.92$, meaning that higher levels of lead are linked to lower IQs (and vice versa). Knowing quite well that correlation does not mean causation,

TABLE 10.1 IQs and Backyard Lead Level Amounts for Twelve Children

Child	Lead	IQ
A	6	130
B	18	85
C	9	140
D	12	105
E	21	75
F	15	100
G	18	80
H	12	110
I	6	135
J	9	125
K	15	115
L	21	90

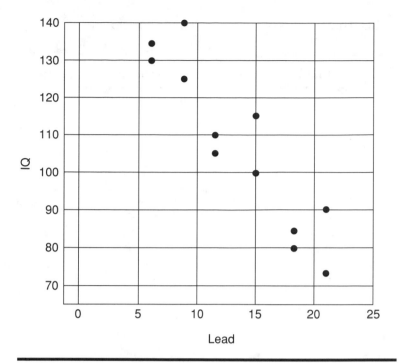

FIGURE 10.2 Scattergram of hypothetical data showing the relationship between backyard lead levels and IQ.

this researcher thinks about other variables that might help explain the finding. Maybe high levels of electric current might be an extraneous factor, resulting in a spurious lead/IQ correlation. Next, he determines how close the backyard is to the nearest high tension wire. He measures this in yards, and enters 1, 2, or 3 into his data set (1 = 100 yards or less, 2 = 100–200 yards, 3 = more than 200 yards). (A researcher would probably keep this measurement in yards, but it has been reduced to 1, 2, and 3 here for simplicity and illustration.) Table 10.2 contains his data.

When the researcher then correlated lead and IQ while partialling out (controlling for) the electric variable, the correlation dropped to zero; in other words, the lead and IQ relationship disappeared (hence, was spurious). But what does "controlled" really mean? Maybe the best explanation at this point is that the lead/IQ correlation is computed while the electric variable is held constant. That is, the lead/IQ correlation is computed only for those people coded 1 on electric; then it is computed only for those coded 2; and then only for those coded 3. Finally, a type of average is taken over the three correlations. (This is not correct technically, but I think it helps to understand the concept of control by constancy.) If you examine only the specific cases with electric equals 1—B, E, G, and L—you can see that the higher levels of lead (E and L with 21) are associated with both higher and lower IQs (90 and 75) within the simple data set of these four cases. (90 is not normally considered high, but it is high within this data set). Also, for these cases only, you can see that lower levels of lead (18 and 18) are associated with the middle values of IQ (80 and 85, neither high or low within the data set of four cases). You can see a similar lack of relationship between the variables if you examine only D, F, H, and K (electric equals 2) and cases A, C, I, and J (electric equals 3).

Researchers can extend this type of statistical control to situations where several extraneous variables can be controlled at the same time. This is possible even while examining how several other variables (presumed causes) are related to an important outcome. This widely used technique is called *multiple regression analysis,* and is the subject of more advanced courses in educational statistics.

TABLE 10.2 Levels of Electric Current as a Factor in the IQ Correlation

Child	Electric
A	3
B	1
C	3
D	2
E	1
F	2
G	1
H	2
I	3
J	3
K	2
L	1

DESCRIPTIVE DESIGNS

Frequently our understanding of educational phenomena is enhanced greatly by the process of careful description. For example, knowing how thinking changes among first-year teachers may help us design better teacher education programs. What are first-year teachers' most prominent anxieties? Their greatest disappointments? What information gained in teacher preparation courses do they feel is most valuable? What are the most frequent reasons cited among teachers who quit after their first year? What are beginning teachers' attitudes about mainstreaming? What expectations do they have regarding low socioeconomic students? What do they know about the interpretation of standardized test scores? Questions such as these are best answered with a widely used research method: the survey. Let's examine this method more closely.

Survey Designs

Surveys are typically used by researchers when they want to gather information from a group for the purpose of describing characteristics of that group. The survey may take many different forms, but the most common form is probably the written questionnaire which is familiar to most of us. The format of the questionnaire may vary, from the passive checking of rated items to more engaging open-ended essay responses. Table 10.3 presents examples of some commonly used questionnaire formats and scales.

One especially useful survey design is the *total design method,* as described by Dillman (1978). An updated discussion of the total design method is provided by Salant and Dillman (1994) and is also useful for designing and conducting your own survey. Furthermore, valuable information on conducting surveys is provided by the Phi Delta Kappa Center for Professional Development and Services in the form of PACE (Polling Attitudes of the Community on Education) materials designed for nonspecialists who want to design scientific surveys on attitudes and opinions on education. These materials provide guidance in questionnaire construction, sampling designs, and analysis of data. For more information, see Elam, Rose, and Gallup (1996, p. 59).

TABLE 10.3 Examples of Common Questionnaire Formats

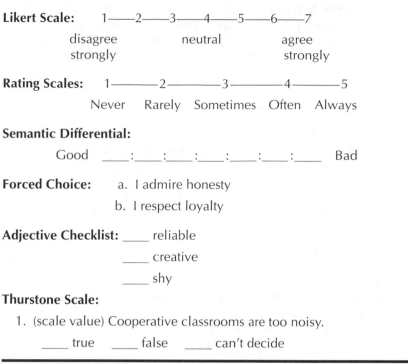

Likert Scale: 1——2——3——4——5——6——7
                          disagree   neutral   agree
                          strongly   strongly

Rating Scales: 1———2———3———4———5
                              Never   Rarely   Sometimes   Often   Always

Semantic Differential:
              Good   ____:____:____:____:____:____:____   Bad

Forced Choice: a. I admire honesty
                              b. I respect loyalty

Adjective Checklist: ____ reliable
                                    ____ creative
                                    ____ shy

Thurstone Scale:
      1. (scale value) Cooperative classrooms are too noisy.
            ____ true   ____ false   ____ can't decide

Longitudinal and Cross-Sectional Surveys. Surveys may be administered at a single point in time or they may be administered many times over a longer period. The *longitudinal survey,* for example, is well suited to describe the process of change, or trends over time. With this design, the same participants complete a questionnaire at specific intervals across time. For example, if you wanted to learn how teachers' attitudes change over a twenty-year period of time in the classroom, the same teachers may be asked for their opinions every five years. The major drawback here, of course, is the length of time required to completely describe changes (twenty years!) An alternative *cross-sectional* design, by contrast, can be completed at one point in time by surveying different teachers, say those with one year, five years, ten years, fifteen years, and 20 years experience in the classroom. For studying change, however, this cross-sectional approach has its shortcomings. The reason for this is not so obvious: cross-sectional designs confound time with subject differences. This is because as time changes (five years to ten years to fifteen years, etc.) so do naturally occurring differences in people. For example, let's presume that a cross-sectional study shows that reading teachers' beliefs about reading are more phonics-based with increasing years in the classroom. Does this mean that teachers become more phonics oriented with increasing experience in the classroom? Not necessarily. It may be that teachers attitudes don't change at all with increasing experience. It may be that teachers with fifteen and twenty years of experience simply learned how to teach reading using phonics when they were in teacher training programs fifteen or twenty years ago, and they have been using phonics ever since. And the more recently trained teachers (those with one or five years experience) learned to teach reading using whole-language methods more than phonics, and quite possibly, they will continue to use this method even after they have twenty years experience. In other words, it may be that teachers' methods and attitudes don't change at all over time; it only looks that way in a cross-sectional design because subjects at each time interval are different. In a similar way, it would be misleading for a group of people in their twenties to describe those in their nineties and reason that they, too, will be like that when they reach that age. This is because people in their nineties have had experiences that those in their twenties have not had (and probably never will have), including World Wars, the Great Depression, maybe famine, and contaminants that no longer exist. In this way, it would be hard to disentangle age effects from experience effects.

Case Study Designs

Some questions in education can be answered by intensive study of a single person (or single group). For example, one may wonder (as did Jean Piaget) what the most prominent qualitative changes in children's thinking are as they progress through the school years. Piaget answered this question, in part, by a very extensive, extraordinarily detailed study of his own children. As it turned out, Piaget's findings based on his case studies generalized remarkably well to other children. Different case studies, however, may not be so widely applicable. Let us suppose that Mrs. Rogers is immensely popular with her math students; they also outscore others by a wide margin on standardized tests of quantitative reasoning. A case study of this phenomenon may reveal charismatic personality factors coupled with very innovative and highly effective cooperative learning strategies. Yet, it is probably the case that another very popular and stellar teacher (in terms of student achievement) may share none of the charisma factors nor teaching strategies of Mrs. Rogers. The other teacher may display great humor and highly entertaining lectures.

Those who conduct case studies, however, are probably not so interested in generalizing their findings to others as they are in telling a story. The story is often full of rich narrative detail and may offer insights about complex processes not possible with, for example, simplistic rating scales that may be used in a large survey. Good case studies are usually fascinating to read; they are engaging and often speculative. Readers of case studies often find useful ideas within the rich descriptions; they may also be stimulated to look at old problems in new ways. Researchers who use case study designs often find that their research "generalizes" to the extent that others can use ideas embedded within the descriptions in some other, often personal, context.

Ethnographic Designs

Sometimes researchers investigate phenomena that do not lend themselves to straightforward quantitative approaches; they may not even know just what it is that should be measured, or if, in fact, it could be measured. A researcher in this case might use an *ethnographic* design, one of many used in qualitative approaches to educational research. Ethnographic research has been associated with the study of anthropology, in situations where the researcher observes, or even becomes part of, a group whose culture and sociology is described. For example, maybe a colony of gorillas is observed in order to understand its social network, or a recently discovered Brazilian tribe is observed to better understand its culture.

Ethnographic researchers may pose a variety of questions. For example, they may ask, "What is it like to teach in a high school that has many students with behavioral problems?" or "What is the home environment like for an at-risk preschooler?" or "What is an all-girls school like?" or "In what ways does typical Catholic education differ from typical public education?" or "Is there such a thing as a *typical* home school, and if so, what is home schooling really like for elementary school children?"

Design Features.   The design of ethnographic research usually centers on the extent to which the researcher *participates* within a group or merely *observes* a group. The participant or observer role is not a simple dichotomy. Most ethnographic designs fall somewhere on a participant–observer continuum. An ethnographer studying the lives of teachers in inner city schools may participate in teaching activities, or become involved with conflict resolution in the classroom, but might be a strict observer during faculty meetings.

Ethnographic research designs usually specify procedures and guidelines for taking *field notes*. These notes often form the backbone in the analysis of ethnographic data. The field notes may take many forms, including detailed observations and general interpretations, reflections, and summaries of recorded interviews. Ethnographic and case study designs in educational research frequently employ *triangulation*, a type of qualitative cross-validation (corroboration) or data cross-checking procedure whereby multiple data sources or data collection procedures are expected to agree. For example, a researcher might uncover a pattern in interviews, then check to see whether the same pattern holds up in written correspondence, in printed materials, in minutes of a meeting, in personal journals, or among observers. The researcher can also check to see whether the same pattern using the same data collection technique is consistent over time. If the multiple sources of data collection are in agreement, the findings are believed to be more credible. Triangulation greatly enhances the validity of qualitative findings.

Published reports of educational ethnographies reflect the rich detail of the blueprints used to carry them out. They are mostly narrative in form, and a better understanding of the phenomenon studied is often conveyed by a good metaphor or illuminating story instead of a pie chart or bar graph. Fine examples of ethnographic studies in education can be found in two journals: *American Educational Research Journal* and *Qualitative Studies in Education*.

Example: Art of Teaching. Do you remember the guided tour in Chapter 5—Flinders's study "Does the Art of Teaching Have a Future?"? It represents a blending of case study and ethnographic designs. That study was completed as a doctoral dissertation, and in 1987 it received the Association for Supervision and Curriculum Development's Outstanding Dissertation of the Year Award. The study is clearly descriptive and ethnographic, as its goal is to experience classrooms in an attempt to describe through the eyes of classroom teachers how they view professional life. Flinders's concern about an image which failed to capture the artistry suggests that teachers' views might be described best by a descriptive metaphor, in this case borrowing from fine arts. (Evidently, rating scales could not capture the essence of teachers' perceptions.) Flinders was able to describe teachers' perceptions well by extensive interviews; his questions were very effective for the purpose of understanding the art of teaching. Flinders also made careful classroom observations—his field notes—and reviewed classroom documents.

Flinders's description of teaching as an art is an insightful description; others can now understand how a lesson can be "beautiful" or a class discussion could be "well orchestrated." New ideas will undoubtedly emerge from this model of teaching and, as such, his descriptive research will have made a valuable contribution, one that would not be possible without a qualitative research design.

It is clear by now that there are literally hundreds of designs used by educational researchers. Some are simple; others are complex. They may be formal and not modifiable, or informal and dynamic. All of them, however, serve an important function in that they structure the plan for collecting data and determine how the data will be organized. Most generally, research designs help the process of research by assuring that the research question (or hypothesis) can, in fact, be answered (or tested) in a most efficient way with a minimum number of rival explanations. As is true with many qualitative research designs, most ethnographic designs have built-in flexibility that allow for adjustments as the research progresses. In fact, qualitative research designs like that are often referred to as *working* or *emergent* designs.

CHAPTER SUMMARY

Researchers often uncover relationships in the absence of any intervention or treatment. Such non-experimental research designs often yield findings that are difficult to interpret. One class of research designs is called *causal comparative,* and these designs compare groups which differ on some important dimension (e.g., heavy versus light television watchers). Researchers who use these designs are usually interested in the effects (or causes) of such differences (e.g., reading comprehension). Interpretation problems abound since the groups may differ in other important ways (e.g., heavy television watchers may also get less exercise). Researchers use *correlational designs* when subjects can be measured on a continuum (e.g., level of exercise in hours per week and speed of mental processing) as opposed to discrete groupings (as in causal comparative research). Otherwise, correlational and causal comparative designs do not differ in any fundamental way. They suffer from the same inherent interpretation problems. The difficulty with interpreting correlational findings is lessened to some extent with *partial correlation designs* which achieve control statistically. Researchers use *descriptive research designs* such as surveys to learn more about the characteristics of a particular group. Careful description often precedes the development of new theories and the search for relationships. Many descriptions are accomplished best with qualitative approaches to research.

Let's examine two non-experimental, descriptive research designs via guided tours of published research reports. The first employs a correlational research design. The second uses a blending of case study and ethnographic research designs.

GUIDED TOUR #1

Let's turn our attention now to a guided tour of published educational research. This will help solidify important terms and concepts described in this chapter.

Is Susceptibility to Distraction Related to Mental Ability?

Deborah J. Aks and Stanley Coren

University of British Columbia

Vancouver, British Columbia, Canada

In order to assess the effects of individual differences

in attentional focus on measures of mental skills, 272

This research was supported in part by grants from the Natural Sciences and Engineering Research Council of Canada and the University of British Columbia. We would like to acknowledge the assistance of Wayne Wong, Lynda Berger, Geof Donelly, and Dereck Atha, in the scoring of these data. Correspondence concerning this article should be addressed to Stanley Coren, University of British Columbia, Department of Psychology, 2136 West Mall, Vancouver, British Columbia, Canada V6T 1Y7.

university undergraduates were tested. Distractibility was determined in a speeded visual search task by comparing performance in the presence and absence of extraneous auditory and visual stimuli. Mental ability was measured using tests of crystallized intelligence and verbal ability. Although mental abilities were measured under normal (no distraction) conditions, high-distractible subjects on average were 9.4 percentile points lower than low-distractible subjects on the cognitive skills measures. This suggests that perceptual/attentional factors are an important aspect of measured intelligence.

A prevailing belief among researchers studying mental skills is that the ability to focus attention is fundamental to efficient cognitive functioning (e.g., Eysenck, 1982; Jensen, 1985). Extreme examples that support this viewpoint can be seen in attention deficit disorders and learning disabilities, where the inability to sustain attention (high distractibility) results in poor cognitive performance (Douglas, 1983). Sternberg and Berg (1986), reviewed definitions of intelligence over a 65-year period and found that the second most commonly used defining feature of intelligence contained perceptual/attentional attributes. Paradoxically, Sternberg (1982) acknowledges that a tremendous gap still exists in understanding the perceptual/attentional contribution to mental ability, because only a few recent studies have effectively focused on this issue.

One way to measure the limits of attentional focus in a normal population is to concentrate on conditions where attentional processes break down, such as when a task requires focal or selective attention and the individual is distracted by extraneous environmental stimuli. **[1]** The relationship between measured cognitive skills and attention can then be reformulated into the question: Is susceptibility to distraction

[1] *This research question investigates a non-experimental research question involving individual differences (hence correlation) since treatment groups cannot be formed via manipulation. This research tests for a relationship between two continuously scaled attribute variables, susceptibility to distraction and mental ability.*

Correlational designs play an important role in educational research. This is because in order to understand a construct (like intelligence), one must determine what other variables the construct is related to how strongly, and in which direction—positive or negative. We know a great deal about the construct of intelligence because we have uncovered many of its empirical relationships. For example, we know it is related to prenatal influences, the measured intelligence of parents, the quality of the home environment, and nutrition; maybe breast feeding, early music lessons, lead exposure, or birth order; but probably not month of birth; and definitely not astrological sign. The point is that we cannot simply make guesses about important individual differences such as intelligence; we must uncover empirical relationships with correlational (sometimes experimental) methods. Armed with scientific information about the relationships, we can then develop theories which ultimately explain the phenomenon or construct under investigation.

related to manifest mental ability? To answer this question, we conducted the following study.

Method

Distractibility Measure

Individual differences in distractibility were measured with a variant of a visual search task from the Differential Aptitude Test (Bennett, Seashore, & Wesman, 1982), in which the subject must scan a line containing letters, numbers, or both, that are in five groups of three on the left side of the page with a target group underlined. The target item must be identified in a rearranged set of five triads located on the right side of the page under speeded conditions. A control baseline was established with one test administration without distractors. To measure differences in attentional focus, each subject was tested once with visual distractors and once with auditory distractors. Visual distractors were small, meaningful pictures placed unpredictably around the search items. Because the extraneous stimuli are clearly discriminable and are not from the some cognitive category (alphanumeric stimuli) as the targets, no disembedding was required. Under auditory distraction, while subjects were performing the visual search task, 18 meaningful sounds (e.g., baby crying, car crashing) ranging from 75 to 95 dB (re $2ON^{-6}/m^2$, with A weighting) were presented. Distractibility was measured as performance decrement in the sessions with the extraneous stimuli relative to the baseline established with no distractors. Aks (1988) has demonstrated that this task produces a broad range of individual differences.

Mental Ability Measures

A set of mental abilities tests were administered under normal group testing conditions (no distractors present). The *Wonderlic Personnel Test* (Wonderlic, 1977) was administered 7 weeks after the distraction task. It is a measure of crystallized intelligence (involving analogies, logic, arithmetic, verbal problems, etc.) that has been subjected to extensive normative study and that has shown average validity coefficients of 0.97. The *Quick Test* (Ammons & Ammons, 1962), an untimed measure of verbal intelligence in which subjects select which of four pictures best fit words, was given 3 weeks after the distraction test. It is highly correlated with scores on Wechsler Adult Intelligence Scale (WAIS) verbal scales, ($r = 0.80$; Cull & Colvin, 1970). The *Spelling Component Test* (Coren, 1989) was administered 2 weeks after the distraction test. Hakstian and Cattell (1976) have shown that spelling tests are significantly correlated with school achievement (e.g., $r = 0.5$ with overall grade point average). This test requires one to fill in the missing letters needed to complete any particular word (e.g., *rest_____rant*).

Subjects and Procedures

Subjects were 272 first- and second-year university students (mean age = 18.6 years) tested in four group sessions over a period of 7 weeks. **[2]** All mental ability measures were taken under standard conditions (e.g., a quiet room, no distracting stimuli). Because of differential absenteeism, 251 individuals completed the distraction test and the Wonderlic Test, 235 completed the Quick Test, and 248 completed the Spelling Component Test.

Results and Discussion

Distractibility, defined as a performance deficit in the presence of extraneous stimuli, is computed by subtracting the score obtained under each of the distraction conditions from the score obtained under the control (no distraction) condition. To control for slight differences in the means and dispersion of the performance under visual and auditory distraction, we

[2] *Notice the relatively large sample in this study (compared with other studies we have toured). This is not uncommon in correlational designs, for in many ways they are easier to carry out than, for example, true experimental studies that require manipulation or intervention. In this study, all of the data were collected by testing college students (efficiently and without great expense). Many important correlational studies can be done without collecting new data. One can open a file cabinet in a school's central office (with permission, of course), pull together the data, and then analyze the findings in terms of correlations. For example, one could correlate scores on a standardized achievement test among fourth graders with size of family, years of preschool education, kindergarten screening test results, age in months, number of absences, or any other available measure that might help us understand achievement variation among fourth graders.*

standardized each of the individual scores to a mean of 0 and a standard deviation of 1 before combining them to create a composite distractibility score for each individual.

Perhaps the simplest procedure for looking at whether there is any relationship between distractibility and mental ability measured under conditions of no distraction is to split the sample at the mean for distractibility. Thus, individuals with a combined standardized distractibility score that is above the mean will be called high distractible, and those with a score below the mean will be called low distractible.

The performance on the Wonderlic test shows a mean advantage for individuals who are less distractible, $t(249) = 2.70$, $p < 0.01$. The corresponding percentile scores, on the basis of the North American adult norms (Wonderlic, 1977) was 72.0 for the high-distractible group and 78.3 for the low-distractible group. Thus, the low-distractible group shows a 6.3-percentile advantage over the high-distractible group.

A similar pattern appears for Ammon's Quick Test: there is a significant difference between the high- and low-distractible groups on raw performance, $t(233) = 1.98$. $p < .05$. Here the high-distractible group has a mean percentile of 42.7, and the low-distractible group has a mean percentile of 50.4; this produces a percentile difference of 7.7. These percentile scores were based on a sample of North American university students (Ammons & Ammons, 1962).

The Spelling Component Test results replicate those of the other two measures; there is a significant difference between the two distractibility groups, $t(242) = 3.30$, $p < .001$. The high-distractible group obtained a mean percentile standing of 42.0, and the low-distractible percentile mean was 56.3; this produced a percentile difference of 14.3. These percentile scores are based on a sample of North American first and second year university students (Coren, 1989).

To confirm the results of the median split analysis, we obtained Pearson product-moment correlations of the raw distractibility scores against performance for the three mental ability measures (Wonderlic, $r = -.15$, $p < .01$; Quick Test, $r = -.11$, $p < .05$; Spelling, $r = 16$, $p < .01$. **[3]** The negative correlations demonstrate the inverse relationship between measured mental ability and distractibility.

These results indicate that individuals who show high distractibility when tested under conditions where there are extraneous stimuli present show performance deficits on measures of mental ability when tested under conditions that nominally contain no distractors. The same relationship with cognitive ability holds for another performance measure of distractibility, namely, performance decrement when distractors are competing tasks, rather than extraneous stimuli (Fogarty & Stankov, 1988; Hunt, 1980). Similar results may also be inferred from Weinstein's (1978) research on individual differences in reactions to noise. Individuals who indicate that they are easily distracted by noise show poorer Scholastic Aptitude Test performance, lower percentile rank in high school, and poorer general scholastic ability.

At the theoretical level, if distractibility can be interpreted as an inability to sustain focal attention, these results may be interpreted as supporting conceptualizations of intelligence that include a perceptual/attentional component. Presumably, it is the "weak focus" in attention that accounts for both the distractibility and the reduced level of performance on the mental abilities tests. Despite the fact that we have used a fairly intelligent, normal sample of individuals in this study, and despite the fact that the individual correlation coefficients are not very large, the mean magnitude of the effect when the sample is divided into high- and low-distractible subjects is still considerable. In our data, high-distractible subjects are, on

[3] *Here are the actual correlation coefficients summarizing the strength and direction of the relationships. Recall that the correlation coefficient is written as* r. *Its value ranges from zero to one (either negative or positive), with values closer to zero indicating progressively weaker relationships (and zero revealing no association at all). Notice that the relationships between distractibility and the three mental ability measures are negative (they call this "inverse"), revealing that higher (greater) distractibility is associated with lower performance on mental ability tests. Also notice that these relationships are low; values around .1 or .2 are considered weak (if they are statistically significant). We know that these correlations, albeit weak, are statistically significant (most probably not zero in the population). We know this from the p values, as they are all less than .05. You will recall from Chapter 6 that very weak relationships can be statistically significant if large sample sizes are used in the statistical analysis. These researchers used over 200 students in their study, large by most standards. If they has used a smaller number, say fifty, these relationships would not be statistically significant.*

Notice one other interesting feature of these results. In the paragraph immediately above #3, we see that the researchers divided the scores on the distractibility measure into a low group and high group, then compared the spelling scores between the two distractibility groups. In doing so, they have used a causal comparative design. This is because they created groups based on a pre-existing attribute. Recall that correlational and causal comparative designs are very similar, the major difference being the scale, continuous or discrete, of one variable. They report what seems to be a rather large percentile difference of about fourteen points, with the high distractibility group scoring lower. This fairly hefty fourteen-point percentile difference seems to contradict the very weak correlation coefficient reported in their next paragraph. This is because there is a well-known problem with comparing percentiles near the middle of a distribution— very small raw score differences are exaggerated when expressed as percentiles. And, as such, small differences are often overinterpreted. This is because of the "bunching up" of scores near the middle of a normal distribution; they must somehow be spread out in a percentile transformation. (Percentiles are determined from equal-sized groups of scores determined after all scores have been ranked.) This exaggerated percentile difference near the middle is merely an artifact of the percentile transformation of raw scores into percentiles. (This phenomenon cannot be corrected; it is a natural consequence of such a transformation.) A true relationship is revealed by the weak but significant correlation coefficient, in this case r = -.16. *It is not uncommon for different methods of data analyses in all fields to reveal somewhat different findings. These differences can sometimes be explained by data transformations.*

average, 9.4 percentile points lower in manifest mental ability than their low-distractible counterparts. This suggests that individual differences in focal attention capacity may have a sizable effect on measures of cognitive skill in normal populations. The educational implications of these results are that poor performance on mental abilities measures may reflect deficits in focal attention, rather than intellectual capacity. They further suggest that poor classroom performance may reflect individual differences in distractibility, rather than in gross intellectual ability.

References

Aks, D. J. (1988). Predicting individual differences in distractibility. *Unpublished master's thesis*, University of British Columbia, Vancouver.

Ammons. R. B., & Ammons, C. H. (1962). The Quick Test (QT): Provisional manual, *Psychological Reports, 11*, 111–161.

Bennett, G. K., Seashore, H. G., & Wesman, A. G. (1982). Differentiation aptitude tests. New York: Psychological Corporation.

Coren, S. (1989). The Spelling Components Test: Norms and factorial structure. *Educational and Psychological Measurement, 49*, 961–971.

Cull, J. G., & Colvin, C. R. (1970). Correlation between the Quick Test (QT) and the WAIS Verbal Scale in the rehabilitation setting. *Psychological Reports, 27*, 105–106.

Douglas, V. I. (1983). Attentional and cognitive problems. In M. Rutter (Ed.), *Behavioral Syndromes of Brain Dysfunction in Childhood.* New York: Guilford Press.

Eysenck, M. W. (1982). *Attention and arousal: Cognition and performance.* New York: Springer-Verlag.

Fogarty, G., & Stankov, L. (1988). Abilities involved in performance on competing tasks. *Personality and Individual Differences, 9*, 35–49.

Hakstian, A. R., & Cattell, R. B. (1976). Manual for the Comprehensive Ability Battery (CAB). Champaign, IL: Institute for Personality & Ability Testing.

Hunt, E. (1980). Intelligence as an information processing concept. *Journal of British Psychology, 71*, 449–474.

Jensen, A. (1985). Methods and statistical techniques for the chronometric study of mental abilities. In C. R. Reynolds & V. L. Willson

(Eds.), *Methodological and statistical advances in the study of individual differences* (pp. 51–116). New York: Plenum Press.

Sternberg, R. J. (1982). *Handbook of human intelligence.* Cambridge, England: Cambridge University Press.

Sternberg, R. J., & Berg, C. A. (1986). Quantitative integration: Definitions of intelligence: A comparison of the 1921 and 1986 symposia. In F. J. Sternberg & D. K. Detter (Eds.), *What is intelligence?* Norwood, NJ: Ablex.

Weinstein, N. D. (1978). Individual differences in reactions to noise: A longitudinal study in a college dormitory, *Journal of Applied Psychology, 63,* 458–466.

Wonderlic, E. F. (1977). *Wonderlic Personnel Test Manual.* Northfield, IL: Wonderlic.

Received April 10, 1989

Revision received September 1, 1989

Accepted September 20, 1989

GUIDED TOUR #2

Let's turn our attention now to a guided tour of published educational research. This will help solidify important terms and concepts described in this chapter.

Importance of Classroom Climate for At-Risk Learners

Cecilia Pierce

The University of Alabama at Birmingham

Abstract

Although previous research has developed scales that measure the situational variables found in classroom

Address correspondence to Cecilia Pierce, School of Education, Department of Curriculum and Instruction, The University of Alabama at Birmingham, 210 Education Building, 901 South 13th Street, Birmingham, AL 35294-1250.

climates, it has failed to address the question of how such climates are created. The purpose of the following case study was to examine how one effective teacher, teaching primarily at-risk learners, created a classroom climate that enhanced learner outcomes. Data, collected through participant observation and interviews, were categorized, analyzed, and interpreted using an analytic induction approach. The major assertion generated from the data analyses was that the normative nature of this particular classroom was intimately entwined with academic learning.

For average students enrolled in secondary schools throughout the nation, the classroom is often a dull and uninteresting place (Goodlad, 1984). However for those students who have been labeled "at risk," the classroom can be profoundly alienating. In the current literature, the term *at risk* appears to be a euphemism for students who exhibit a wide range of educational problems, including the failure to respond positively to the instruction offered in basic academic skills, the manifestation of unacceptable social behavior in school, the inability to keep up with their classmates in academic subjects, and a limited repertoire of experiences that provide background for formal education (Howard & Anderson, 1978; Slavin, 1989).

Underlying these characteristics of the at-risk learner are complex factors, many of which are outside the control of the school. Social problems such as poverty, dysfunctional family life, lack of positive role models, poor medical care, and inadequate diet complicate the teaching-learning process. These students frequently come to school lacking the cognitive schemata upon which classroom instruction is ordinarily based. The prognosis for the majority of these learners is that they will drop out of school prior to graduation. Statistics from the U.S. Department of Education (1987) support this prognosis by indicating a nationwide dropout rate of 30%. In urban environments, where poverty is concentrated, the dropout rate is estimated to be as high as 50%.

Hahn, Danzberger, and Lefkowitz (1987) have argued that these statistics raise a question concerning the responsibility of the nation's schools in relation to the at-risk student. They have maintained that the obligation of the school is to serve the at-risk learner in ways that are helpful, while avoiding practices that can augment the student's problems. Unfortunately, the recent attention given to testing and academic achievement has encouraged classroom teachers to focus more on immediate learning outcomes and less on classroom structure, where many of the practices that tend to reinforce the student's problems occur. Often, decisions concerning classroom organization are made without an understanding or the role played by classroom climate toward the ultimate achievement of these outcomes. This is especially important when teaching the at-risk learner.

My purpose of this article is to discuss the findings of a qualitative case study of an effective seventh-grade social studies teacher who taught primarily at-risk students in an urban setting and to describe how she created a classroom environment that diminished the risk factors involved in learning and, as a result, increased the students' level of academic achievement. [1]

Review of Related Literature

The classroom is a critical locus for student interpersonal and educational development. The notion that classrooms have distinct atmospheres or climates that mediate this development has been in the working vocabulary of educators and researchers for years (Anderson, 1939; Fraser, 1987; Walberg, 1969; Withall, 1949, 1951). Previous research has shown that

[1] *The researcher describes her design as a "qualitative case study," but as you read it you will probably notice elements of ethnography. Qualitative research often uses blended research designs; in fact, an "ethnographic case study" is quite common in the research literature. We also see here that the study is not experimental; it is descriptive, since the purpose was to describe in a natural environment how one teacher created a climate that enhanced learning.*

student outcomes, such as subject matter achievement and attitude toward a school subject, might be improved by creating classroom environments that are more conducive to learning (Cort, 1979; Fraser, 1986; Haladyna, Shaughnessy, & Redsun, 1982; Walberg, 1969). These findings tend to agree with Goodlad's (1984) definition of classroom environment as the physical, emotional, and aesthetic characteristics of the classroom that tend to enhance attitudes toward learning.

Research on classroom climate began as early as 1936 when Lewin (1936) recognized that both the environment and its interaction with personal characteristics of the individual were potent determinants of human behavior. Building on the findings of Lewin, Murray (1938) identified a needs-press model of interaction. According to Murray, personal needs, defined as motivational personality characteristics, represent tendencies to move in the direction of certain goals, whereas environmental press provides an external situational counterpart that supports or frustrates the expression of internalized personality needs. Therefore, situational variables found in the classroom environment may account for a significant amount of behavioral variance.

To identify these situational variables, various researchers began developing rating scales designed to measure classroom climate. The research of Anderson and Walberg (1968), Walberg and Anderson (1968), and Moos and Houts (1968) formed a starting point. As part of the Harvard Project Physics (1968), Walberg developed the Learning Environment Inventory (LEI), which identified 10 dimensions relevant to classrooms: cohesiveness, diversity, formality, difficulty, apathy, democracy, cliqueness, satisfaction, disorganization, and competitiveness (Anderson & Walberg, 1968; Walberg & Anderson, 1968). Around the same time, Moos developed a social climate scale that ultimately resulted in the development of the Classroom

Environment Scale (Moos & Houts, 1968). The pioneering work of Walberg and Moos on perceptions of classroom environment has developed into major research programs and spawned an abundance of other research.

Allinsmith and Grimes (1961) identified a relationship between student compulsivity, anxiety, and performance in both structured and unstructured environments. Their findings indicated that anxiety and compulsivity interacted with one another and with teaching methods. In a structured setting, compulsive children performed better; in an unstructured environment, anxiety impeded performance. Trickett and Moos (1970) found that significant amounts of variance resided in interactions between students by classrooms. Positive student-teacher interactions resulted in course satisfaction and in higher student achievement.

Thus, data from previous research support the assertion that the interaction of a person and setting contributes significant amounts of behavioral variance. One can further assume that having a positive classroom environment is an educationally desirable end in its own right. Moreover, the comprehensive evidence presented by the research establishes that the nature of the classroom environment has a powerful influence on how well students achieve a range of desired educational outcomes. Therefore, constructive educational climates can be viewed as both means to valuable ends and as worthy ends in their own right.

When applied to the at-risk learner, these findings become even more relevant to effective teaching. At-risk learners often enter the classroom discouraged and disillusioned as the result of their repeated failures. Their self-esteem is low, and they frequently believe themselves incapable of learning. A climate that is focused primarily on production and outcomes reinforces these insecurities. They associate the classroom environment with failure; expecting to fail, they often do. By recognizing that the learning environment can either enhance or detract from the student's ability to achieve, teachers can help to change this attitude. The question then becomes one of how to create such a classroom climate. By observing and analyzing classroom interactions in effective classrooms serving at-risk students, a body of case study research can be developed that will better inform teachers of the various ways in which one may achieve such an environment. Such was the purpose of the following case study.

Research Design

The subject of this study was Mary Morgan, a middle school teacher with 24 years of teaching experience. Her effectiveness in teaching at-risk students was determined by the recommendations of teachers, administrators, parents, and former students. I verified these recommendations through preliminary observations.

Participant observation was the method of data collection. I observed the selected teacher on a daily basis for 12 weeks in the natural environment of her classroom. **[2]** I recorded observations in the form of audiotapes and field notes; I especially cited verbal and nonverbal teaching behaviors and patterns, teacher personality characteristics, and the way in which these factors facilitated student learning. Using students as key informants, I triangulated the observations and conclusions of myself, the teacher, and students to increase the accuracy of recorded data.

The collected data were categorized, analyzed, and interpreted, using an analytic induction approach, according to the context in which they occurred. From the initial classroom observations, questions were generated that tended to focus subsequent observations on specific types of classroom interactions and behaviors. **[3]** Repeating patterns of behavior began to emerge, creating specific categories and subcategories

[2] *This paragraph reveals Pierce's study to be ethnographic, as participant observation and the use of informants as a method of data collection are hallmarks of ethnographic research designs. Notice also her use of the term* triangulation, *as described earlier in this chapter. The accuracy of her data is increased to the extent that all three sources—the researcher, teacher, and students—are in agreement and converge on the same finding.*

[3] *Notice how the design of the study shapes the hypothesis (or* working hypothesis*). This is radically different from experimental designs used in quantitative research whereby hypotheses are arrived at deductively from theory, as explained in Chapter 3. Hypotheses derived from theory are fixed for the duration of the research; hypotheses derived from descriptive observations are flexible. Also notice the next section of Pierce's report describing the context of the study. Ethnographic, case study designs are holistic, in the sense that the person is total (unified) and cannot be fragmented into independent parts. Holistic description also suggests that the naturalistic setting must be preserved and interpreted in a richly complex social context.*

that were used to develop a working hypothesis tentatively explaining how this specific classroom operated. I then attempted to identify behaviors and interactions that agreed and disagreed with the working hypothesis, I used the cases of disagreement to reformat the hypothesis until an accurate description of the phenomenon was developed (Robinson, 1951).

Context of the Study [4]

Mary Morgan taught in a community located in the southeastern United States. It is an area of diverse economic activity containing a broad array of major business, industrial, educational, and health-related institutions. Figures provided by the local Chamber of Commerce at the time of the study indicated an unemployment rate of 5.4% for the community, as compared with 7.1% for the state and 5.4% for the nation. Although the socioeconomic status (SES) of the community was above average when compared with that of the total state, there were pockets of poverty located throughout the community. Recent demographic changes had resulted in a concentration of low-income, minority families in the urban center of the community. These families, who lived in government housing projects and other low-rent housing districts, constituted the population served by Morgan's school.

The inner-city school in this study was located in the central business district because of the commercialization of the surrounding community. The student population was predominantly Black; the racial composition of the entire seventh grade was 38.1% White and 61.9% Black. The majority of the students could accurately be described as at risk. Sixty-seven percent received free or reduced lunches, and 58% came from single-parent homes.

The focus of this study was Mary Morgan's fifth-period Eastern Hemisphere class. The class included 21 students; 29% were White and 71% were Black. Seventeen of the students

[4] *The context provides an important backdrop for all qualitative studies. One cannot fully understand the case (as in a case study) without analyzing how it is embedded within the environment.*

had been identified as at risk by the guidance counselors and the teacher, based on their SES, family network, and prior school performance. From information contributed by the guidance counselor, I presumed that the majority of these students did not see the benefits of education reflected through their parents. As a result, they exhibited the qualities of hesitancy, fear, and insecurity when confronted with the demands of school. To effectively teach these students, Morgan maintained that "a classroom environment which recognized and minimized these attributes had to be developed."

Results and Discussion [5]

The major assertion generated from the data analyses was that the normative nature of this particular classroom was intimately entwined with academic learning. The classroom ambiance developed through the behaviors and interactions of the teacher and students was one in which the threat of failure was diminished and in which the at-risk students had the opportunity to participate actively in the learning process. The students were provided a "safe-haven" atmosphere that enhanced learning outcomes of at-risk students. The following primary questions were developed as the study progressed: (a) What were the effective behaviors exhibited by the teacher? and (b) How did these behaviors facilitate the student/teacher interactions that led to the development of the safe-haven atmosphere?

The ambiance of Morgan's classroom was closely related to her understanding of the students she taught. She argued that at-risk students needed structure and organization, self-esteem, and a belief in their abilities to learn. In other words, they needed a safe haven that would afford them the opportunity to learn in a non-threatening environment. The climate in Morgan's classroom had three identifiable components; (a) a classroom organization based upon correct standards of be-

[5] *You won't find levels of statisitcal significance in this section, as this is a qualitative analysis. Here you'll find an "assertion." Also notice that qualitative research questions can be developed as the study progresses.*

havior and a sensitivity toward others, (b) a variety of roles assumed by the teacher to give support to the students, and (c) the teacher's enthusiasm for the students. **[6]**

Classroom organization.   The specific pattern of classroom organization selected by Morgan had a considerable impact on the manner in which the students and teacher related to each other and on the students' performance. In determining the most appropriate classroom organization, Morgan considered the nature and character of the students she taught. The majority of the students who entered her class exhibited a "loser's mentality." They had faced failure many times in their lives, as demonstrated by their school records, and as a result, they were often insecure, had poor self-concepts, and frequently believed themselves to be incapable of learning much above the basic level. Morgan defined her role as having a responsibility to change these students from "losers to winners" by instilling in them a belief in their abilities to learn and a desire to achieve. To accomplish these goals, Morgan selected a classroom organization that provided the students with a risk-free environment.

Morgan described her classroom as a place where each child knew that he/she was valued. She explained:

> I think it's important, especially at this age, to give the children a sense of self respect. I think it's important for these children to have a good self-concept, a good self-image. I can sense when they are in my room and from how they behave in other classes, sort of a settling down; sort of a comfortableness in that they know what the structure is.

This type of classroom climate did not happen by accident. Morgan entered the classroom at the beginning of the year with a plan in mind. She planned for the class to bond into a

[6] *These components were undoubtedly the result of Pierce's careful process of categorization in her analysis. Qualitative data is often categorized in some form or another.*

cooperative unit based upon the mutual respect of each student for the others. Her plan included a classroom structure that was internalized by the students and that emphasized correct standards of behavior and a sensitivity toward each other.

In establishing the classroom structure, Morgan began the first day by discussing why rules were important. She started with the world and gradually focused on the classroom. In discussing the need for rules and regulations in society, she developed a structure based upon a common understanding. In explaining her reasoning for approaching the year in this way, she said:

> I plan for them to be safe and secure, and in setting some rules it gives them structure and security because they know this is the way we do things, and they are reasonable rules.

The rules were not developed by Morgan, but by the students. By soliciting suggestions from the students concerning what the rules of the classroom should be, the rules ceased to be the teacher's rules and became the students' rules. Thus, the students entered into a participatory process for the operation of the classroom for the remainder of the year. Their input had been solicited and valued, thus establishing a relationship between the students and the teacher that was developed more fully as the year progressed.

Over a prolonged period, I observed that the students understood and had actually internalized the rules and regulations. Morgan explained:

> Occasionally we will refer to the rules. They seem to know when they get a little bit away from them but they seem to understand that the reason for them is for the safety of everybody and the well-being and har-

mony of everybody; and that it's necessary to care about each other.

At the beginning of the year, Morgan also focused the students' attention on improper behavior by identifying it as it happened and discussing why it was improper. She and the students then explored alternatives to such behavior. In analyzing this process through the eyes of the students, Julie, a gregarious 13-year-old, said:

> Mrs. Morgan didn't put on a tough guy act at the beginning of the year. She didn't say you can't do this or that. She let it work it's way out. Like, she would let something happen, and then she would explain to us why this was not appropriate in her class. She teaches us not only what not to do but why we should not do it.

Thus, Morgan developed within the students a rationale for specific behavior. She reinforced the standards of behavior through consistency, which eventually resulted in the internalization of the rules and standards of behavior by the students.

Roles assumed by the teacher. Morgan taught through example. She said:

> In my class, I try to be an example for the students as far as manners, sensitivity, and consideration for other people are concerned. I think that's important, and I think a lot of children that I teach are not getting that at home.

Morgan modeled behaviors by assuming a multitude of roles that included the teacher as a person, a safety net, an encourager, and a counselor. Each of these roles contributed to the classroom ambiance. [7]

[7] *"Ambiance" is a difficult quality to describe. Pierce uses quotations to help capture its essence.*

In assuming the role of a person, Morgan displayed her awareness of, and caring for, the students as individuals. She allowed her students to share in her life by discussing with them her feelings about life, what was important to her, her values, and personal stories concerning her relationship with her family. She openly admitted her mistakes and developed an understanding among the students that no one is perfect. Although humor was an important element in Morgan's classroom, she was careful to avoid sarcasm. She expected the students to treat each other with respect and to use proper manners in the classroom. Morgan demonstrated concern for the students outside as well as inside the classroom. The students exhibited a comfortableness in talking with her about their problems. They were not afraid to physically touch her, and Morgan never pulled away. She also felt free to touch her students. She often rubbed their backs to gain their attention and sometimes hugged them as they came into class. The students interpreted these behaviors as attitudes of caring and concern. Taurus, a 13-year-old described by his peers as "very scared and sensitive," said:

> Mrs. Morgan, she gives me the courage to pick up what I'm doing and do my homework and get up to where I can deal with other subjects. It's like everyday I see her smiling. Her smile just…a lot of teachers don't smile. Every time I see her smile it gives me the courage to just go on through the next period. No big people scare me in her class.

Julie described Mary as understanding:

> She takes things from the kid's point of view. I look forward to coming in here. When I have problems, I know I can talk with Mrs. Morgan. When I go into

other classes I am just there. When I come in here, I'm alive. I look forward to it.

Morgan also served as a safety net for her students. She reflected a desire to ensure that students would not fail or experience mental or emotional discomfort in the required class interactions and assignments. To illustrate how this was accomplished, consider the following vignette: **[8]**

[8] *Vignettes, or very brief stories or incidents, are also used commonly by qualitative researchers to support an assertion.*

Mary: What do we call the number of people in a
region or country?

Jenny: Census.

Mary: Census? It's interesting that you say that because this is the year of the census. Does everyone know what Jenny is talking about when she says census? It's when we count all of the people in the United States. April of 1990 is the census month. I'm glad you said that because we needed to think about that, but I was thinking about something else. Can anybody help me with that?

In the above dialogue we see Jenny, who was an extremely shy and sensitive student, giving an obviously wrong answer. However, instead of merely saying, "No, that is wrong," Morgan used the answer to introduce a future topic of study. This let the student know the answer was wrong but did not hurt her self-esteem. As a result, the student was more likely to answer later in the lesson. Thus, Morgan had served as her safety net and cushioned her failure. As a result of this behavior, one student said, "I feel comfortable letting Mrs. Morgan know that I don't understand something. I could not come out and say I don't understand in another teacher's class."

[9] The role of teacher as a safety net was closely related to the role of encourager. As an encourager, Morgan used positive reinforcement frequently. She used such words as "good," "excellent," "Oh, you are so smart," "I am very proud of you," and "Give yourself a pat on the back." She often accepted the student's answer and then elaborated on it to make another point. In this case, the information used was the student's information that he or she had shared with Mary and the other class members. This encouraged the students to supply more information and to respond to other questions. The result was an active dialogue between teacher and students. Julie explained the interaction in this way: Mrs. Morgan tells us we did a good job or that's really good. Those comments really help a lot. Her approval is very important.

Part of the communication network established by Morgan was based on her ability to listen when the students were talking. When a student talked to Morgan, she tried to understand exactly what the student was attempting to communicate to her. According to Morgan, "What they have to say is valuable. I think one of the most important things is to be a good listener." Randy, a very active 13-year-old who often found it difficult to sit still for a period longer than 10 min, said:

> It makes me feel real good when she listens to me because it makes me feel like I have really done something. I love to bring things in to show her, I love to impress Mrs. Morgan. It makes me feel good that I have helped her.

Because of this attitude, the students felt free to discuss a wide range of topics with Morgan. They knew she would accept their comments and would be honest and truthful with them. This built a relationship of trust between the students and the teacher.

[9] *Notice Pierce's use of the "safety net" metaphor. Such metaphors are invaluable communication devices for qualitative researchers.*

By assuming the role of counselor, Morgan helped the students with their personal problems as well as problems they were having in other classes. This talk took place both inside and outside of the class and was usually student initiated. For example, one day Taurus came to class crying. Blair, a student who exhibited compassion for everyone in the class, told Mary that Taurus had a problem and that he was crying. The teacher thanked Blair and said that she would speak to him. Mary knelt beside Taurus and talked quietly with him concerning his problem. Later, as I questioned Taurus about his feelings pertaining to Mrs. Morgan, he said:

> Mrs. Morgan, she brightens my day. It's like she cares about us. She's really nice to talk to because she deals with us. She likes to help out with our problems at home and at school. She acts like she cares more about us than she does herself.

Julie summed up the situation when she said, "I would come to her before I would go to the counselor. I feel safer with her. She doesn't threaten me. I feel secure with her." [10]

Teacher's enthusiasm for students. Morgan's enthusiasm for her students has been acquired developmentally and is conditioned by both her life experiences and her experience in the formal educational setting. Over time, certain attitudes toward others and even certain dispositions toward teaching have developed and are carried into the teaching role. Morgan has taught at every grade level from Grade 3 to 12. However, she has decided that seventh grade is where she belongs. In describing the seventh-grade student, she said:

> I think the seventh grade is so much fun because you really never know what they are going to say. I like this grade so much. You really have to like seventh

[10] *At this point, don't you feel that you really know Mary Morgan? This familiarity is one mark of a good case study; the reporting of her numerical test scores from a battery of measuring instruments would pale by comparison.*

grade to teach it. If you don't like seventh grade, you have no business teaching it.

The atmosphere in Morgan's class was relaxed. The students crowded around her before class and told her things that were happening in school and to them personally. She always paid attention to them and had a warm smile on her face. The students liked her smile. Julie observed that Mary "never seems mad." She said:

> It doesn't seem like you could get her real angry. I know you probably could, but she doesn't show it. I've had other teachers in the past where if they had a bad day at their house or had a fight or something, they would come and take it out on their students. But she doesn't. When she comes to school, it's like a whole new dimension.

Freedom of movement was another component of Morgan's relationship with her students. Mary understood that this age group was active and social. When the students participated in groups assignments, she observed their movements. Instead of scolding them for moving without permission, she often praised their show of initiative and responsibility for their own learning. During such groups activities, the students could be observed freely exchanging conversation and laughing, but all were clearly on task.

Conclusions and Implications

Morgan's classroom climate was created primarily through her exhibited behaviors, which nurtured the emotional needs of her students. Showing care, respect, and physical closeness demonstrated these qualities. The classroom organization that she developed diminished the possibility of failure in her room and developed within the students a sense of safety and security. These results helped to increase the students' level of academic achievement and their formation of more positive attitudes toward school and self. These outcomes were demonstrated both quantitatively and qualitatively.

Quantitatively, the progression of scores on 6-week examinations confirmed the increased level of academic achievement. At the end of the first 6-week grading period, the median score for the class was 58. By the third grading period, the median score had increased to 65, and by the fifth grading period, the median score was 72. SRA reading scores also increased from a mean in September of 5.9 to a mean in April of 7.1.

An equally important measure of learning outcomes was gathered from the qualitative data concerning attitudes toward school, learning, and the ability to learn. [11] These data were collected from student interviews, participant observation field notes, and an archival search of attendance records and behavior referral forms. They confirmed a reduction of inappropriate classroom behavior, an increase in attendance, and a reduction in the number of assignments not completed. When questioned concerning their attitudes toward the study of Eastern Hemispheric Studies, the class consensus was "in Mrs. Morgan's room, it's fun to learn."

What does this study offer to teachers who work with at-risk students? It suggests that many of the routine organizational decisions made by teachers have important consequences that are not evident when the teacher focuses only on immediate outcomes. It is important that teachers be aware that many decisions about classroom organization have ramifications for students' beliefs about themselves and about tasks. These beliefs, in turn, will mediate the effects of academic instruction.

When teachers can provide environments in which students have adequate information about the environment on

[11] *Here is another illustration of triangulation, or the use of multiple sources of confirming data.*

which to base decisions, and in which students do not feel that their sense of competence is personally threatened by public competition, students' motivational beliefs will more likely develop in a direction that supports self-regulation and enhances learning outcomes.

References

Allinsmith, W., & Grimes, J. W. (1961). Compulsivity, anxiety, school achievement. *Merrill-Palmer Quarterly, 7,* 247–271.

Anderson, H. H. (1939). The measurement of domination and of socially integrative behavior in teachers' contacts of children. *Child Development, 10,* 73–89.

Anderson, G. J., & Walberg, H. J. (1968). Classroom climate and group learning. *International Journal of Educational Services, 2,* 175–180.

Cort, H. R., Jr. (1979). A social studies evaluation. In H. J. Walberg (Ed.), *Educational environments and effects: Evaluation, policy, and productivity* (pp. 235–257). Berkeley, CA: McCutchan.

Fraser, B. J. (1986). *Classroom psychology.* London: Croom Helm.

Fraser, B. J. (1987). Classroom learning environments and effective schooling. *Professional School Psychology, 2*(1), 25–41.

Glaser, G. G., & Strauss, A. L. (1978). *Advances in the methodology of grounded theory.* Mill Valley, CA: The Sociology Press.

Goodlad, J. I. (1984). *A place called school: Prospects for the future.* New York: McGraw-Hill.

Hahn, A., Danzberger, J., & Lefkowitz, B. (1987). *Dropouts in America: Enough is known for action.* Washington, DC: Institute for Educational Leadership.

Haladyna, T., Shaughnessy, J., & Redsun, A. (1982). Relations of student, teacher, and learning environment variables to attitudes toward social studies. *Journal of Social Studies Research, 6,* 36–44.

Howard, M. A., & Anderson, R. J. (1978). Early identification of potential school dropouts: A literature review. *Child Welfare, 57*(4), 221–31.

Lewin, K. (1936). *Principles of topological psychology.* New York: McGraw.

Moos, R., & Houts, P. (1968). Assessment of the social atmospheres of psychiatric wards. *Journal of Abnormal Psychology, 73,* 595–604.

Murray, H. A. (1938). *Explorations in personality.* New York: Oxford University Press.

Robinson, W. S. (1951). The logical structure of analytic induction. *American Sociological Review, 16*, 812–818.

Slavin, R. E. (1989). Students at risk for school failure: The problem and its dimensions. In R. E. Slavin, N. L. Karweit, & N. A. Madden (Eds.), *Effective programs for students at risk*. Needham Heights, MA: Allyn and Bacon.

Trickett, E. J., & Moos, R. H. (1970). Generality and specificity of student reactions in high school classrooms. *Adolescence, 5*, 373–390.

U.S. Department of Education. (1987). The Department of Education wallchart. State Education Statistics. Washington, DC: Author.

Walberg, H. J. (1969). The social environment as mediator of classroom learning. *Journal of Educational Psychology, 60*, 443–448.

Walberg, H. J., & Anderson, G. J. (1968). Classroom climate and individual learning. *Journal of Educational Psychology, 59*, 414–419.

Withall, J. (1949). Development of a technique for the measurement of socioemotional climate in classrooms. *The Journal of Experimental Education, 17*, 347–361.

Withall, J. (1951). The development of a climate index. *The Journal of Educational Research, 45*, 93–99.

APPLICATION EXERCISES

1. For each of the scenarios below, determine whether the researcher is conducting a non-experimental study or an experimental study. If non-experimental, decide whether it is causal-comparative, correlational, or descriptive.

   a. A researcher studied the influence of class size on reading achievement among fourth graders. Three randomly formed class sizes were studied (twelve, eighteen, twenty-four) using a total of thirty schools.

   b. A researcher studied the influence of a new Spanish Immersion program that she designed and implemented at a large urban school. Achievement across several subject areas in the immersion school was compared with a school across town that was similar in student population but more traditional in its foreign language programs.

   c. A researcher studied how spanking as a punishment in childhood is related to criminal activity in adolescence. Three groups of adolescents were formed: those whose parents used spanking frequently, infrequently, or not at all. Arrest records were then compared across the three groups.

d. A researcher wondered how adults' reading to children was related to later reading achievement. The reading achievement of two groups of sixth graders were compared: those who were read to frequently as young children and those who were not.

e. A researcher wondered how the general trait of happiness was related to intelligence. Young adults' intelligence was measured using a traditional IQ scale; their level of happiness was also measured on a scale ranging from one to twenty. The researcher found no association (link) between these two measures.

f. A researcher wondered whether the time required to complete a multiple-choice test was related to performance on the test. One hundred college students enrolled in General Psychology took an untimed 120-item test; their tests were marked with a ranking reflecting the sequential order they were turned in. The researcher found no association between the test scores and the time spent completing the exam.

g. A researcher wondered whether principals' effectiveness, as determined by teachers' perceptions, was related to their level of educational attainment. Those principals with doctorates were perceived as more effective than those without doctorates.

h. A researcher wondered how much time parents spend per week helping their children with homework. A questionnaire was administered to a sample of parents in representative school districts across the country.

i. A researcher wanted to learn more about the moral thinking of contemporary high school students. About 1200 high school seniors were interviewed and asked to provide judgments about hypothetical moral dilemmas. The researcher found that most students' moral development had not progressed beyond what he called "conventional."

j. A researcher studied master teachers in their classrooms, and the narrative summary of his field notes revealed that most master teachers view teaching as a type of "heartfelt artistic expression."

k. A researcher studied the extraordinary accomplishments of a one hundred-year-old full-time teacher and was convinced that the "mind is a muscle."

l. A researcher wondered if children breast fed as infants had better memories than those who were bottle fed. Two groups of ten-year-olds were compared (breast versus bottle) and were found to have the same memory capacity.

2. Imagine a researcher who is planning a correlational study and will use partial correlation as a statistical method of control. Based on what you know about partial correlation and its uses, name one variable that would be a prime candidate for control via partial correlation in the following studies.

a. A researcher investigated the charge that there was sex–salary inequities at the district offices of large urban school districts. As a first step, she calculated the correlation between sex (male, female) and annual salary. What would be an appropriate variable to control via partialling?

b. A researcher investigated the relationship between vocabulary knowledge and head circumference in a population of elementary school children. What would be an appropriate variable to control via partialling?

c. A researcher investigated the suspected relationship between IQ and size of family; he found lower IQs among later borns (as the number of brothers and sisters increase, the IQ becomes lower). What would be an appropriate variable to control via partialling?

d. A research investigated the relationship between learning disabilities and the consumption of junk foods (the more junk foods consumed by a family, the greater is the learning disability). What would be an appropriate variable to control via partialling?

MULTIPLE CHOICE QUESTIONS

1. What is the defining characteristic of causal comparative designs?
    a. random assignment
    b. pre-existing group differences
    c. pretest plus posttest
    d. counterbalancing
    e. case studies

2. If a relationship is spurious, then we know that it is:
    a. explained away by a hidden factor
    b. nearly always cause and effect
    c. partially regressed
    d. ethnographic and descriptive
    e. true or quasi-experimental

3. If data are presented in a scatterplot, we know that data were collected in accordance with which of the following designs?
    a. ex-post-facto
    b. case study
    c. ethnography
    d. correlational
    e. survey

4. Correlational designs often achieve their control through which of the following procedures?
    a. counterbalancing
    b. pretesting
    c. partial correlation
    d. random assignment
    e. random selection

5. A common questionnaire format that uses a scale along a 7-point agreement continuum is referred to as a _____ scale.
    a. Thurstone
    b. forced choice
    c. semantic differential
    d. rating
    e. Likert

6. One major problem with cross-sectional survey designs is the difficulty associated with:
    a. statistically analyzing the data
    b. obtaining informed consent
    c. connecting the findings with existing theories
    d. separating age effects from experience effects
    e. generalizing from only one respondent

7. Which of the following designs is better suited to "tell a story" than generalize to large groups?
    a. case study
    b. causal comparative
    c. correlational
    d. survey
    e. longitudinal

8. The design of ethnographic studies often varies as a function of the role of the researcher as:
   a. recorder-manipulator
   b. analyst-philosopher
   c. participant-observer
   d. theorist-pragmatist
   e. statistician-storyteller

9. The use of multiple data sources or data collection procedures as a method of qualitative cross-validation is known as:
   a. quality control
   b. triangulation
   c. counter-control
   d. verification
   e. collaboration

10. What type of research design is most likely an *emergent* one?
   a. ethnographic
   b. correlational
   c. causal comparative
   d. survey
   e. partial correlation

Answers: 1) b   2) a   3) d   4) c   5) e   6) d   7) a   8) c   9) b   10) a

DATA ANALYSIS

OVERVIEW

Educational researchers are faced with an interesting problem after they collect data to answer questions or test hypotheses. The essence of the problem is this: What can I infer about the population from which my sample was drawn? They ask this question because they are usually more interested in relationships that exist within the population from which the sample was drawn, not merely within the actual sample studied. After all, if findings do not generalize beyond the sample, then researchers could never apply their findings beyond the narrow confines of the sample of subjects studied. One could reasonably ask, "Who cares about the small number of people studied? What can I say about the larger population?" The process of inferring from sample to population involves elegant statistical reasoning. Let's examine this reasoning in some detail.

COIN FLIPS AND PROBABILITY

Let us suppose that I claim to possess psychic abilities, that is, I can affect the outcome of physical events by sheer concentration. Consider a coin flip. My abilities can influence this physical event and be evidenced by the number of heads that will appear during a test of one hundred coin flips. My claim is: As I concentrate on causing the coin to land on "heads" during one hundred flips, you will find that more heads appear than you would expect by chance. Ready? Here we go…. The results are in: After one hundred flips, the coin turned up heads fifty-five times. I say, "See! I told you so! I'm psychic!"

Your best response as a critical observer is to say "Well, fifty-five heads could be a chance occurrence; maybe it would have come up heads fifty-five times if I, with no such abilities, tried to influence the number of heads." This is the crux of the problem: What are the reasonable limits of chance? Of course, the long run, theoretical expectation is that the coin will turn up heads fifty times after one hundred flips (assuming it is a fair coin). But do you actually expect such a perfect result if you were to flip a coin one hundred times? Probably not. What if the coin turned up heads fifty-one times? Would you dismiss this event as merely the working of chance? Yes, probably. What about fifty-two heads? fifty-three heads? fifty-four heads? fifty-five heads? fifty-six heads? fifty-seven heads? fifty-eight heads? fifty-nine heads? sixty heads? sixty-one heads? sixty-two heads? seventy heads? eighty heads? Clearly, you have to draw the boundary line somewhere, and if the number of heads crosses the boundary, then you would conclude that the occurrence was probably not due to chance. (Of course, even if the result were *not* due to chance, there may be explanations other than psychic ability, such as a trick coin or other extraneous influences). Fortunately, scientists have worked out a rule to follow in order to avoid being wishy-washy ("Maybe it was due to chance, maybe not, well, I don't know, looks like chance to me, sort of.") The rule is: Determine what to expect by chance ninety-five percent of the time; if the occurrence would be expected less than five percent of the time by chance, then it was probably not due to chance.

In the coin flip example, statisticians have figured that the ninety-five percent chance boundaries for the number of heads after one hundred tosses is forty-three to fifty-seven. Here is what that means. Let's say one hundred flips of a coin is one trial. After one hundred trails, you would expect ninety-five percent of the trials to yield between forty-three and fifty-seven heads, according to the laws of chance. This is very useful information, for now you can conclude that fifty-five heads is likely the workings of chance; clearly, you shouldn't be impressed with fifty-five heads. This is within the range that you would expect by chance ninety-five percent of the time. But what if the test of my psychic ability had produced fifty-nine heads instead of fifty-five heads? A very different outcome indeed, since this is more than what you could reasonably attribute to chance. Scientists have a special name for this event, *statistical significance*. One would say therefore that fifty-nine heads is a statistically significant outcome since it is expected to occur less than five percent of the time by chance. The shorthand way of stating the expression "statistically significant" is simply $p < .05$ where "p" refers to probability. This literally means that the probability is less than five out of one hundred that the results were due to chance. Always keep in mind that the results may have in fact been due to chance; statistical significance only means that the results were probably not due to chance. Remember, "p" refers to *probability*, not proof!

Sometimes, research results are presented as "$p < .01$" to convey the idea that the probability is less than one out of one hundred that the findings were due to chance. Or, findings may be presented as "$p < .001$" suggesting that the likelihood is less than one out of a thousand that chance could be responsible for the results. Statistical significance starts when the threshold of .05 is crossed, and would, of course, include any level of probability less than .05, including .01, .005, .001, or even .00000001.

Educational researchers, of course, do not spend their time challenging psychics with the coin flip test. But they do apply exactly the same logic in the analysis of educational data. Here is the logic: First, determine the boundaries to expect by chance ninety-five percent of the time. Second, compare the finding (a mean difference, a positive correlation, etc.) against the ninety-five percent chance limits. If the results fall within the boundary, then they are probably due to chance and are *not* statistically significant. If the results fall beyond the limits imposed by chance, then they are probably not due to chance and are referred to as statistically significant, or $p < .05$.

READING FACES

Let's see how this logic is used in a more realistic research setting. Let us say that I believe emotion plays a greater role in learning than was previously believed. Furthermore, I believe that learning is more difficult without an emotional component, and that our so-called "emotional IQ" may influence success in school (and life). Finally, I recognize that there is a long-held belief that women are more emotional than men. Let us suppose that being "emotionally with-it" involves correctly reading emotional expressions in faces and using this information to communicate more effectively. Given all this information, I might wonder whether girls can read faces better than boys.

To answer this question, let's suppose that a valid and reliable face-reading test had been developed. It involves making judgments about the emotions underlying facial expressions, such as fear, surprise, joy, anger, sadness, etc. (You have to assume that emotional expressions are universal, and that the test can be developed so that there exists a correct emotion for each expression). Imagine that the boys and girls were shown twenty faces and asked to choose the correct emotion as revealed by the expression (let's assume a multiple-choice format for simplicity). Furthermore, imagine that thirty boys and thirty girls from seventh and eighth grades were administered the Face-Reading Test. Here are the results, expressed as an average score on the twenty-item test:

	Mean
Boys	12.5
Girls	15.0

You can see that girls scored higher than boys, but could this be due to chance? Like fifty-five heads? Surely, even if boys and girls did not differ on this ability, you would not expect to find exactly the same mean for each; that's too perfect, akin to getting fifty heads and fifty tails. The crux of the problem is chance once again. To demonstrate chance, just imagine sixty girls being randomly divided into two groups, I and II, and then taking the Face-Reading Test. You would not expect exactly the same means for Groups I and II since chance could have easily placed a few more high scorers in one group. The means should be *about* the same, give or take a few points. This give-or-take, of course, is what most people simply refer to as "chance."

The problem of determining whether the mean difference of 2.5 points between boys and girls is larger than what you would expect by chance is solved in much the same way as the coin flip illustration. Let us suppose that the limits imposed by chance ninety-five percent of the time were 3.00 points either way (plus or minus). That is, if you repeatedly compared two groups' average scores on the Face-Reading Test (in a situation where the groups did not differ, as in the case where they were formed by random assignment), you would find that ninety-five percent of all mean differences would not be greater than 3.00 points. So, what do you make of the 2.5 difference obtained in this boy versus girl face-reading example? Clearly, the difference is not significant and could have arisen, quite reasonably, by chance. You would have to conclude that girls do not have a *significantly* greater face-reading ability. If the mean difference had been 3.5 (girls = 16.0, boys = 12.5), you would have to reach a different conclusion (one that suggests girls really do have better face-reading abilities since the difference would be statistically significant).

THE NULL HYPOTHESIS

Recall from Chapter 2 that researchers work with three different kinds of hypotheses: *research* (their hunch), *alternative* (the "something else" that caused the results), and *null*. The null hypothesis comes into play during the data analysis, and is used along with the logic we have been describing in order to reach a sound conclusion. The null hypothesis is a type of hidden hypothesis whose function waits for number crunching to begin. The null hypothesis always has the following two essential characteristics:

- it is a statement about a population (not a sample)
- the hypothesis states that there is no difference (or relationship) between the groups studied

In our case, the null hypothesis is: In the population of seventh and eighth graders (maybe one million), there is no difference between boys' and girls' ability to read the emotional expression on faces. Why would you want to presume such a thing, especially when you really believe the opposite? The answer is that its use enables a clever strategy for making an *inference* about the population, given only data from a sample. An inference is a type of specific-to-general reasoning that allows us to make a statement about something general—the population—from something specific—the sample. Let me explain.

We have seen that chance likelihood is presented (indexed) as a p value, but it is important to note now that this p value is calculated with the assumption that the *null hypothesis is true.* If we pretend, just for the moment, that the null hypothesis really *is* true, and calculate the p value with that in mind, we essentially have determined whether the null hypothesis probably is or is not true. When the p value drops below .05, as we've already seen, the results are statistically significant, but more importantly, we then know that the null hypothesis is, therefore, probably not true. Scientific researchers use the phrase "reject the null hypothesis" whenever obtained relationships are statistically significant. Researchers, in a sense, set up the null hypothesis in order to knock it down. They pretend, only while the computer is analyzing the data, that the null hypothesis is true, but hope in reality to discard it as probably not true. Because the null hypothesis is the opposite (usually) of the research hypothesis, its rejection allows the researcher to logically accept its opposite—the research hypothesis. In this case, we would say that the research hypothesis was *supported,* not proven, since there always exists the possibility that the difference did occur by chance (a fluke), even though that likelihood is small (less than .05).

Let's review the role of the null hypothesis. The researcher assumes that the null hypothesis is true: there is no difference between groups in the population. (There still exists a distribution of scores in the population; it is the difference between groups that is zero.) If one finds a difference between groups in the sample drawn from the population, the question for the researcher becomes What is the probability that I drew just those subjects whose values on the variables show up as significant in the sample? It is this probability that the results reveal: the likelihood that the obtained findings could be attributed to the workings of the random process. And when that likelihood is less than .05, the researcher concludes that the findings are statistically significant.

THE p VALUE DETERMINATION (CONCEPTUALLY)

You are probably wondering how the computer determines the p value, or as we've seen, the probability that the null hypothesis is true. This is accomplished with the famous bell curve, or normal distribution, as it is usually called. Let's see how this curve can help us determine the p value in the boy–girl face-reading study. The ideas presented for this example can be logically extended to different situations, like those involving more than two means, or to different types of data (correlations or frequency counts). We will not cover all of these applications, but you can be assured their conceptual basis is very similar.

Figure 11.1 shows an idealized (perfect) version of a normal distribution. Recall from Chapter 6 that this shows how scores "stack up" when their values are plotted against their frequency of occurrence. Recall further that in addition to the shape of the distribution (a bell), the distribution can be described in terms of its central tendency (the mean) and its variability (the standard deviation). The mean falls at the hump of the bell, and the standard deviation corresponds to a specific cutoff in the distribution such that sixty-eight percent of the cases in the distribution fall between the mean plus and minus 1 standard deviation, ninety-five percent falls within two standard deviations, and ninety-nine percent falls within three standard deviations.

Mean Differences

Think again about the null hypothesis in our example of boy versus girl face reading ability: "In the population of seventh and eighth graders, there is *no* difference between boys' and girls' ability to read faces." If this is true, you can imagine sampling thirty boys, thirty girls, testing them, computing their means, and, finally, finding a mean dif-

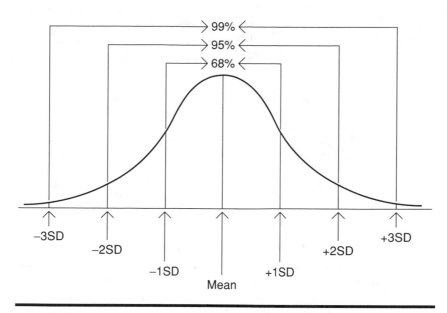

FIGURE 11.1   An idealized normal curve. Note the symmetry in the bell and the standard deviation (*SD*) points defining areas of the curve in percentages.

ference. Here's a concrete example, again emphasizing, for the moment, that the null hypothesis is true. The boys' mean = 14.9, girls' mean = 15.2, mean difference (boys' minus girls') = -.3. Imagine doing this again: Boy mean = 13.5, girl mean = 13.0, mean difference = .5. Imagine again: boy mean = 15.6, girl mean = 15.2, mean difference = .4. Imagine again: Boy mean = 14.1, girl mean = 15.2, mean difference = –1.1. Imagine again: Boy mean = 15.0, girl mean = 13.5, mean difference = 1.5. Imagine again: Boy mean = 15.0, girl mean = 16.00, mean difference = -1.00. Thus far, we could imagine these mean differences:

$$-.3$$
$$.5$$
$$.4$$
$$-1.1$$
$$1.5$$
$$-1.0$$

Let your imagination run wild and pretend that this study was replicated a thousand times (each time a new sample of boys and girls was chosen from the population) and, most importantly, each time, the null hypothesis was presumed to be true. We would have a long, long string of mean differences, and the mean of these *mean differences would be equal to zero if in fact the null hypothesis were true.* All of the chance differences, positive and negative, would wash out and balance to zero. It is important to understand that the mean of this make-believe sampling of a thousand mean differences would be zero assuming the null hypothesis is true. Do you see why?

Furthermore, there is a theorem in statistics which states that the *shape of the distribution of mean differences will be normal.* In other words, the bell curve would be duplicated in this situation, with most of the differences hovering around zero and increasingly fewer mean differences approaching the extremes. The distribution would therefore look like the one shown in Figure 11.2, a normal "bell" with mean = 0.

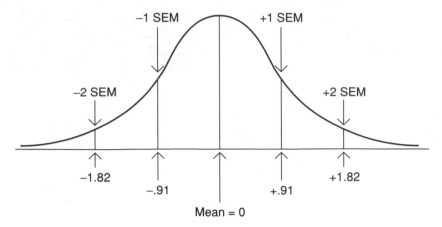

Note: SEM = standard error of the mean differences

FIGURE 11.2 A sampling distribution of mean differences retains a bell shape with a mean of zero and a standard deviation equal to a value known as the standard error of the mean differences. Mean differences that fall within two times this value (+ and -1.82) are believed to be due to chance.

Standard Error of Mean Differences

The missing piece of information thus far is the standard deviation. Not to worry, for this information can be estimated quite accurately. The standard deviation of this sampling distribution of mean differences has a special name: the *standard error of mean differences,* and its calculation is based on the standard deviation of the two sample groups. Let's see how this is done. Assume that the standard deviation of the boys' face-reading scores was 3.0 (with a mean of 12.5, recall) and the standard deviation of the girls' face-reading scores was 4.0 (with a mean of 15.0, recall). Also recall that the sample size (n) was thirty per group. The calculation of the standard error of the mean differences is as follows:

$$\sqrt{\left(\frac{3}{\sqrt{30}}\right)^2 + \left(\frac{4}{\sqrt{30}}\right)^2} = .91$$

This value of the standard error of the mean differences, .91, is a very important statistic. Because it is the standard deviation of the sampling distribution of mean differences (assuming the null hypothesis is true), it tells us the reasonable limits of chance differences. Doubling (approximately) the value of this statistic (.91 × 2 = 1.82) will form the cutoffs of a distribution such that ninety-five percent of the cases are contained within that boundary (recall that this is a basic property of the normal distribution). Figure 11.2 shows the sampling distribution of mean differences with the standard error of mean differences marked in the same manner as standard deviations.

Therefore, if the null hypothesis is true, we would expect mean differences attributable to chance between boys and girls not to exceed 1.82 (in either direction). We have essentially solved the problem related to the interpretation of the mean difference of 2.5 between boys and girls in our example. Since the obtained mean difference is larger than 1.82, we must conclude that the difference is statistically significant and, as a result, reject the null hypothesis since it is probably not true. Because the difference falls outside of the ninety-five percent chance limits, we can say that the probability of obtaining a mean difference as large as 2.5 (or larger) is less than five out of one hundred, or simply $p < .05$. The value of p itself is often referred to as the *level of statistical significance*. Its rejection logically entitles us to conclude that there is probably a difference in face-reading ability in the population of boys and girls from which the sample was drawn. This, then, is the basic logic of our statistical tests.

To review, researchers temporarily assume the null hypothesis is true, even though they usually believe otherwise. Then a calculation is made to determine how large of a difference chance could reasonably explain (e.g., due to chance alone, ninety-five percent of sample differences will fall within the boundaries marked by such-and-such to such-and-such). Then the obtained difference is cast against this backdrop of chance differences; if it is larger, then the results are significant (shown as $p < .05$), the null hypothesis is rejected, and it is concluded that there probably exists a difference in the population. By contrast, if the results are within the chance boundaries, the findings are attributed to chance, they are *not* statistically significant, the null hypothesis is accepted, and one concludes that there is no difference between groups in the population.

Correlation Coefficients

The same logic used to test a mean difference for statistical significance is applied to correlation coefficients, and many other types of statistics as well. Let's consider a related example—the relationship between the ability to read the emotional expression on faces and GPA. Assume sixty randomly selected college seniors were studied by administering the Face-Reading Test (scores range from zero to twenty, with high scores reflecting greater emotional intelligence). Their GPAs were also retrieved from the school records. The calculation of the correlation coefficient yielded $r = .30$. (Recall from Chapters 7 and 10 that this statistic ranges from -1 to $+1$ with $r = 0$ indicating no relationship.) As is customary, the null hypothesis is formed and assumed for the moment to be true. It asserts that in the population of college students, there is a zero correlation between face-reading ability and GPA. Next, a calculation is made to determine how high correlation coefficients would go in many samples drawn from the population *when the null hypothesis is true*. (These calculations have already been done by statisticians; their findings appear in tables found in most statistics books.) In this case, the calculation reveals that if one hundred samples were drawn from a population where the correlation were 0 between face-reading ability and GPA (the null hypothesis being true), then ninety-five percent of them would fall between $-.36$ and $+.36$. Only five percent of the samples would yield coefficients outside that range. Next, the obtained correlation of .30 is compared to this boundary expected by chance. Because it falls *within* the ninety-five percent chance boundaries, it is concluded that the correlation is *not* statistically significant and the null hypothesis is accepted as probably being true. Hence, in the population of college students, there is probably not a correlation between face-reading ability and GPA. The correlation of $r = .30$, it would appear, is a reasonably likely finding from a population with $r = 0$. The r of .30 may as well be interpreted as $r = 0$, since its departure from zero was probably the working of chance. Nonsignificant findings, as is true in this case, are sometimes written as $p > .05$, meaning the probability of the null hypothesis being true is greater than five out of one hundred, which, we have seen, is the scientific definition of "most likely due to chance."

COMMON STATISTICAL TESTS

Thus far we have seen how researchers go about interpreting their findings with a p, its value determining what should be done with the null hypothesis (accept it or reject it). There are literally hundreds of statistical tests, but they all have in common their bottom-line calculation: the *p* value. Each one of these statistical maneuvers yields what is called a *test statistic* (often symbolized by a letter, such as *t* or *F*); it is this test statistic that is translated into the *p* value, and interpreted as the probability that the null hypothesis is true. The variation in statistical tests arises from the variations in research designs and the types of data collected. Fortunately, educational researchers do not have to sort through hundreds of statistical tests. This is because many research applications in education have similarities which are appropriately analyzed with only a handful of techniques. These are described below.

The *t* test

The *t* test is one of the most common statistical tests. It is used to compare two means (one mean difference). Common applications include testing the difference between experimental and control groups, the differences between males and females, the difference between two teaching strategies, or the difference between a pretest and a posttest. As a mean difference increases (all other things being equal), the value of the *t* level increases, and the *p* level decreases. When the value of the *p* drops below the scientifically established threshold (.05), it is said that the mean difference is significant (and probably not due to chance).

Two types of *t* tests are used by researchers: *independent groups t* and *correlated groups t*. The independent groups *t* is undoubtedly the most common application of the *t* test and is used when the subjects in each group are different, as in male versus female, ninth graders versus fifth graders, or visual learners versus auditory learners. (The subjects are *independent* in the sense that the two groups are separate and not connected.) By contrast, a correlated groups *t* is used when there is a linkage between the two groups, as in the case where the same subjects are tested before and after a treatment (pre post) or when matched subjects in two groups are being compared (every subject in one group has its matched pair in the other group.) Another application of the correlated groups *t* test is found in twin studies that compare the talents of identical twins reared apart (in this case the linkage is genetic).

The *t* test usually appears in a published research report in the following way (using fictional data): *The treatment group (M = 93.56, SD = 5.32) scored significantly higher than the control group* (M = 81.67, SD = 6.21), t(75) = 5.93, p < .01. The descriptive statistics, means and standard deviation (*M* and *SD*, respectively), reveal that the treatment group scored higher than the control group and both have about the same scatter of scores around their mean. It is the mean difference of 11.89 (93.56 – 81.67) that has been standardized by the *t* test, that is, recast against the normal curve backdrop. The *t* value itself of 5.93 is an inferential statistic since it permits a decision about the null hypothesis (recall this is a statement about the population). The number is parentheses after the *t* statistic refers to the sample size. (Actually it is an *adjusted* sample size—the number of subjects less two—and is referred to as *degrees of freedom*. This topic is explained in most basic statistics textbooks). Finally, the bottom line information is conveyed by the *p* value itself, in this case it is less than .01. Because it is less than .05, the researcher is entitled to reject the null hypothesis and conclude it is probably not true. The mean difference in the sample, therefore, probably reflects a real difference in the population. The value of *p* itself is often referred to as the *level of significance*.

Although the *t* can be calculated in a wide variety of situations involving two groups, statisticians have found that the *p* value generated by the *t* test is most accurate when several conditions, or *assumptions*, exist. These are: (1) the populations from which the scores are drawn are normally distributed, as in a bell curve, (2) the variances of scores in the populations are equal, and (3) the samples are randomly selected from their populations. In truth, the *t* test is used frequently when some or all of these conditions do not exist. Yet it is generally believed that the *t* test is *robust*, meaning that the test yields reasonably accurate p values even when the data clearly do not meet the three assumptions. When researchers are not comfortable about the assumptions behind the t test, they frequently turn to *nonparametric* statistics, explained later in this chapter.

The *F* test

The F test, usually referred to as the analysis of variance or its acronym ANOVA, is probably the most widely used statistical test in educational research. (It derived its letter name from its developer, Sir Ronald A. Fisher, and is sometimes called *Fisher's F ratio.*) It is appropriate for testing the significance of two or more means. As such it could be used in place of the t to test two means, but it could also be used to test for differences among many means, like those that result from very complex (factorial) research designs. As is true with the t test, this technique yields an F statistic, which is then translated into a p value so that the researcher can make a sound decision about the null hypothesis (as with the t test, reject it if p drops below .05). This test, like all other inferential tests, has an underlying null hypothesis. Consider the case of a test to determine differences in teacher attitudes toward corporal punishment with five different levels of experience (teachers in training, first-year teachers, and teachers with 2–5, 6–10, and 11–20 years of experience). The null hypothesis would be that in the *population* of teachers, there are *no* differences in attitudes toward corporal punishment between teachers with varying levels of experience. The resultant p value, then, tells how likely it is that the null hypothesis is true.

The results of ANOVA usually appear in published research reports in the following way (using fictional data): *The analysis of variance revealed that there were significant differences among the 5 groups,* $F(4, 95) = 7.90$, MSE = 3.60, p < .05. (The reader is usually referred to a table which presents means, standard deviations, and sample sizes.) The two numbers in parentheses next to F refer to the number of groups and the number of subjects used in the test. (Actually, it is the number of groups less one, and the number of subjects in each group less one times the number of groups.) The next value is the F itself, which is translated into a p value. The *MSE* is a measure of average variability within the five groups (akin to a standard deviation). The p value is, once again, the bottom line. The reason for conducting the F test is to permit a sound decision regarding the null hypothesis. In this case, the null hypothesis can be rejected on the basis of its low value (less than .05) revealing that the mean differences are statistically significant.

As is true for the t test, the accuracy of the F test depends to some extent on statistical assumptions. The assumptions underlying the F test are the same as the t test: normality, equal variances, and random sampling. But like the t, the F is believed to be robust. Small departures from these assumptions are not likely to greatly affect the accuracy of the p value.

Test for *r*

It is also common for researchers to test the significance of a correlation coefficient, as was shown earlier in this chapter. The correlation coefficient, or r, can be tested with a t, the same test statistic used to test two means (but with a different calculation). This test is known as the *t test for r*. Another example might be a test of the relationship between high school students' test-wiseness and their scholastic aptitude. The null hypothesis would be: In a population of high school students there is *no* relationship between level of test-wiseness and scholastic aptitude. Is the null hypothesis probably true? Only the p value can tell (not for sure, but probably). In a published report, the significance of *r* is usually shown simply as, for example, $r = .59$, $p < .01$. The researcher would conclude that the correlation coefficient of .59 is statistically significant, therefore probably *not* zero in the population.

Chi-square test

Quite often, researchers also test for relationships involving *frequency* data in the form of tallies or percentages. This is accomplished with a statistical test called *chi square* (symbolized X^2). For example, one might test whether there is a relationship between a decision to quit teaching after one year (yes or no) and the type of teacher training program that prepared the teacher (say, traditional versus nontraditional). Or a researcher might test whether there is a difference in teachers' preference for fifty-minute versus ninety-minute classes. The corresponding null hypotheses would be: In a population of first-year teachers, there is no relationship between type of training programs and decision to leave the profession, and in a population of teachers, there is no difference in their preferences regarding fifty- or ninety-minute classes.

The chi-square test usually appears in a published report in the following way: $X^2(4, N = 90) = 9.34$, $p < .05$. The numbers in parentheses following the chi-square symbol refer to the number of groups (adjusted somewhat, but often the number of groups less one) and the number of subjects (N). The chi-square value itself is shown, followed by the all-important p value. The researcher who used chi-square would decide to reject the null hypothesis since there existed a statistically significant relationship in the sample.

PARAMETRIC VERSUS NONPARAMETRIC TESTS

Most statistical tests used by researchers are classified as *parametric* because they hold certain assumptions about population characteristics (known as *parameters*). For example, we have seen that the *t* and *F* tests assume that samples are drawn randomly from populations that are normal with equal variances. For researchers who are uneasy about these assumptions, another class of statistical tests is available. Appropriately termed *nonparametric*, these tests are used when one believes that the assumptions about the underlying parameters are probably not true ("violated").

Nonparametric tests are also appropriate when the type of data being analyzed (called the *scale of measurement*) is *nominal* or *ordinal* as opposed to *interval*. Nominal scales simply use numbers as labels with no implied order, as in 1 = male, 2 = female. Ordinal scales imply a ranking or continuum, as in 1 = fastest, 2 = next fastest, etc. Interval scales imply an equal distance between values on a continuum, as is a temperature scale where 30° to 40° represents the same difference as 90° to 100°. Parametric tests such as the *t* and *F* are most appropriately applied to interval data. Statisticians appear split on the type of data used in many educational research studies such as achievement test scores, as they appear to fall somewhere between ordinal and interval. In reality, many researchers treat most educational data as interval, hence the wide-spread use of the parametric *t* and *F*. Nevertheless, most parametric tests have nonparametric counterparts for use when parametric assumptions appear in doubt or when the type of data is clearly not interval scaled. Three widely used nonparametric tests are the *Mann-Whitney U* (counterpart to the *t* for independent groups), *Wilcoxon Matched-Pairs Signed-Ranks T* (counterpart for the *t* correlated groups), and the *Kruskal-Wallis H* (counterpart for ANOVA with one independent variable). The chi-square test for frequency data described earlier is also a nonparametric test, as frequency data is considered to be a type of nominal data. Nonparametric tests yield *p* values in the same manner as parametric tests, and they are used in the same way and with the same rules (if less than .05, reject the null hypothesis). Finally, measures of relationships—correlations—have parametric and nonparametric counterparts. The widely used *Pearson product-moment correlation coefficient (r)* is parametric, and the *Spearman rank order correlation coefficient (r_s)* is nonparametric.

STATISTICAL ERRORS

Type I

It is important to remember that the researcher's decision to accept or reject the null hypothesis may be wrong. A sampling oddity may lead to a decision to reject the null hypothesis when in fact it is true. Consider the Face-Reading Test once more, and assume for the moment that there are no differences whatsoever in the population between males and females in their face-reading ability; that is, the null hypothesis is true. A researcher's sample of women, albeit random, may simply be over-represented with skillful face-readers. The men's sample, likewise, may contain a disproportionate number of males with less skill in face-reading. This is simply a fluke, or a coincidence, like picking up the phone to call a friend only to find the friend on the phone line before you even dialed. Simply, you both had the same idea at the same time. Rare events, like being struck by lightning or winning a lottery, do in fact happen. Researchers call this problem *sampling error.*

There is a name (not a very creative one) for this type of sampling error: a Type I error, sometimes called *alpha* or *alpha error.* (Note: This term is totally unrelated to Cronbach's alpha described in Chapter 7.) It refers to mistakenly rejecting a true null hypothesis, that is, concluding there is a relationship in the population when in fact there is not. The likelihood of such an error is determined by the *p* value itself. For example, if you reject the null hypothesis, as you should, with a *p* value of .001, then you know that the likelihood of this Type I error is simply .001. This is very unlikely indeed, but it is still possible. Researchers never know for certain whether they fell victim to a Type I error. (The strongest evidence of its existence would be a series of replications of the original study which produced the significant finding, all of which by contrast, accept the null hypothesis.) It is not the type of mistake that a researcher could be faulted for; researchers have no control over random oddities.

Type II

There is another type of error in statistical reasoning called a Type II error, sometimes called *beta* or *beta error.* With this mistake, the researcher would wrongly accept the null hypothesis when in fact it was false, that is, conclude wrongly that there is no relationship in the population. The only explanation for this occurrence is, once again, chance or sampling error. In the face-reading example, it may in fact be true of the population that females really do have a better ability to read the emotional clues on faces. But the sample may have simply over-represented females with poor ability in face-reading; conversely, the sample may have been over-represented by men with good ability in face-reading. Once again, this could result from a random oddity in the random number table. The true difference in the population, therefore, would be wiped out in the sample. In this case, the researcher, based on a *p* value greater than .05, would have no choice but to accept the null hypothesis (wrongly) and be unaware that a mistake was made. In a sense, this Type II error might be more serious than the Type I error since it is a "missed chance." For example, a drug may really be a cure for a disease, but the results would be nonsignificant due to a Type II error. This overlooked cure may go unnoticed because other researchers may not replicate the study. Replicating nonsignificant findings is less exciting, usually, than replicating significant findings. Type I errors would be discovered during replications of a significant finding, whereas Type II errors would not be as frequently double-checked. The relation between Type I and Type II errors and the null hypothesis is summarized in Table 11.1.

The Accuracy of *p*

It is important to realize that the calculation of *p* in order to be accurate, assumes that "all else is fine." By this I mean that subjects were selected randomly from a population and then assigned randomly to groups, and there were no threats to the internal validity of the study, no blunders, biases, artifacts, confoundings, and so forth. In the case of serious flaws in the methodology, the *p* value may not be at all accurate, and the inference about the population may be completely wrong. This is a far more serious and culpable error than a Type I or Type II error. Consider an example of a researcher testing whether there are sex differences in aerobic exercise frequency (measured in the form of hours of exercise, on average, in one week). Assume for this example that there are in fact no differences in the population between males' and females' exercise frequency (the null hypothesis is indeed true). Let's assume further that the male researcher is a frequent exerciser (this seems reasonable since he is interested in research on exercise). For convenience, the researcher samples twenty-five of his male friends ("birds of a feather flock together"), and determines that they exercise 4.6 hours per week on average. Furthermore, he samples only a few of his female friends, and must rely on "shopping mall" tactics to complete the survey of twenty-five females (by just walking up to agreeable looking shoppers and soliciting the information). Pretend that the (mostly solicited) females, on average, exercised 2.6 hours per week. Upon analysis the researcher find a *p* value of .001, revealing a significant difference between the two samples. Remember that the null hypothesis is true in this scenario, and the usual interpretation—there is less than one out of a thousand chances that one would find a mean difference that big in the sample if the null hypothesis were true—is patently false. The major point here is that there is nothing in the statistical analysis that fixes or compensates for procedural blunders prior to the analysis. For the *p* value to be accurate, the researcher should have *randomly* sampled men and women from the population and obtained true (valid) information with little or no loss of subjects. Otherwise, the problem is akin to the old adage *Garbage in, garbage out.*

THE IMPORTANCE OF POWER

The statistical power of a test is akin to the power of a microscope or telescope. (The concept of power was first introduced in Chapter 6.) Strong power in a microscope allows biologists to see differences between cells very clearly. Strong power in a telescope allows astronomers to see clearly the differences between planets. Likewise, researchers want to be able to see differences between groups or correlations between variables very clearly. The power of a test is defined more formally as the *ability to uncover relationships in the sample if there are in fact true relationships in the population.* Pow-

TABLE 11.1   Type I and Type II errors

	Null Hypothesis Really Is:	
Your Decision:	**True**	**False**
Accept	No error	Type II(missed chance)
Reject	Type I (false alarm)	No error

erful statistical tests enable you to find relationships when they are present. Power is indexed as a probability, and as such falls between zero and one. Think of this as the probability of detecting a relationship if there is one to detect. Strong power is obviously desirable, and most researchers want to arrange for power to be about .90. This means that if there is a relationship present in the population, the probability of detecting it in the sample with the statistical test is .90, a very good bet.

Power is calculable in the planning stages of a study. Its value is determined by several factors, such as the strength of the effect (which researchers usually have little control over) and the sample size (which researchers can adjust). Statistical power always increases with increasing sample size. The answer to the question, "How many subjects do I need?" is usually determined in large part by the level of power that is desired. (See Chapter 6 for a review of sample size estimation). Sample size determination is especially important prior to carrying out a study, for it might be determined that power (as planned) is low, say .15. One could reasonably ask why carry out the study, for there is only a .15 probability that a relationship (if one existed) would be detected. You can see the futility of conducting a study with such low power, yet in fact it is probably true that many researchers are unaware of their low statistical power. Such studies with low power (e.g, less than .50) are very difficult to interpret, for a *non*significant finding could be due to *either* low power *or* a true lack of relationship in the population. The crux of the problem is that there may in fact be a relationship in the population, but a statistical test with low power will lead to nonsignificant findings. Thus, one who uses a low-power test and accepts the null hypothesis really has not learned very much. The conclusion after the analysis is the same as the proposition before the research: There may or may not be a relationship in the population.

The calculation of power prior to data collection, if low, may lead to a revision of plans and an increase in the number of subjects required for a fair test of the hypothesis. But power analysis could also yield another type of useful information. It might reveal, for example, that the power as planned is .99, and a reduction in sample size to save time, money, and other resources may still yield a very acceptable power of .90. Why use two hundred subjects when a fair test is possible with one hundred?

Power is defined statistically as *1—beta* (recall beta is the probability of a Type II error, or mistakenly accepting a false null hypothesis). Hence, power calculation involves computing beta, and easy methods (e.g., Kraemer & Thiemann, 1987) have been developed for accurately estimating beta. Beta decreases as sample size increases; hence, as previously described, one simple and direct way to increase power is to increase sample size.

QUALITATIVE DATA ANALYSIS

Its Challenge

The process of qualitative data analysis is concerned with the *qualities* exhibited by data more than their *quantities*. As such (I believe), it is a far more challenging, time consuming, and creative endeavor. It is less technical, prescribed, and "linear," but more iterative ("back and forth") than quantitative analysis. In fact, the analysis is often performed *during* data collection with emerging interpretations—a working hypothesis—guided by a theoretical framework. It is probably more accurate to say that qualitative data analysis *evolves* throughout the whole research project. It is clearly not summarized by a single number such as a *p* value, as is the case with quantitative studies. Interviews often produce hundreds of pages of transcripts, as do detailed field-notes from observations. All of this information requires critical examination, careful interpretation, and a comprehensive synthesis. A good qualitative analysis discovers patterns, coherent themes, meaningful categories, new ideas, and, in general, a better understanding of a phenomenon or process. In fact, some qualitative researchers prefer the term *understanding* of data instead of analysis of data. The analysis of rich descriptions occurring throughout the course of a project often provides new perspectives, and its analysis of interconnecting themes may provide useful insights. The depth afforded by qualitative analysis is believed by many to be the best method for understanding the complexity of education in practice. Qualitative analysis is also well suited for exploration of unanticipated results.

Good qualitative data analysis often impacts readers through powerful narrative such as stories. For example, Clark et al. (1996) begin the data analysis section of their qualitative study of teacher-researcher collaboration by stating "Our story comes from the words and voices of the people involved" (p. 203). Miles and Huberman (1994) state that "Words, especially organized into incidents or stories, have a concrete, vivid, meaningful flavor that often proves far more convincing…than pages of summarized numbers" (p. 1). Researchers with a qualitative orientation often view their work as a challenging craft or art and it shows in their writing. The Clark et al. (1996) study presents data in a form they call "Readers Theater," a written script based on the dialogues and interactions during the meetings of ten teacher-researchers. A good qualitative analysis often yields stimulating conclusions and sometimes affords a new and useful way to view old problems.

Credibility

The most important criterion for judging a qualitative study is its *credibility* or trustworthiness. To assess credibility, one would zero in on the data, its analysis, and resultant conclusions. Any weak link here would threaten the usefulness of the study. According to Miles and Huberman (1994, p. 11–12), qualitative analysis includes three streams of activity: *data reduction* (simplifying complex data by, for example, extracting recurring themes via coding), *data display* (e.g., matrices, charts, graphs, even stories), and finally *drawing conclusions* and verifying them as a means for testing the validity of findings. Qualitative researchers often rely on the principle of *triangulation* to enhance the credibility of the study. Recall from Chapter 10 that this refers to the use of multiple sources of data and collection strategies, all of which should agree in their findings.

Essentially, the daunting task for qualitative researchers is to take massive amounts of data, often in the form of interviews or detailed field notes from extensive observations, and communicate what it reveals in a credible way. The interpretation of qualitative data depends on the background and creativity of the researcher far more than does quantitative research. Also, there are no agreed-upon, ten-step procedures which all qualitative data interpreters use. Nevertheless, in some way or other most will face the task of organizing the data to enhance the study's credibility. This nearly always involves *coding*, a modifiable system for categorizing the information in the data. In the following section, we'll describe a representative qualitative analysis using coding for the purpose of making some of these abstract ideas more concrete.

Example: Parent Involvement in Early Education

Neuman, Hagedorn, Celano, and Daly (1995) described teenage mothers' beliefs about learning and literacy in an African American community through a series of peer-group discussions. After identifying the beliefs of nineteen low-income adolescent mothers, these researchers hoped to use them in ways to enhance their children's literacy opportunities. All lived in impoverished areas and had toddlers enrolled in an early intervention program. The mothers themselves had dropped out of high school and were attempting to complete adult basic education. These researchers noted that parental beliefs have been described using a variety of empirical, self-report instruments but are problematic since they tend to reflect mainstream culture and solicit "it depends" type reactions. They opted for open-ended interview discussion formats in the hope that they might lead to "far richer and more accurate understandings of beliefs" (p. 807). The ten hours of discussions were videotaped while observers took notes in an adjacent observation room.

The researcher's task of converting data into codable categories was guided by the *constant comparative method* (Glaser & Strauss, 1967), a continuous process of category identification and clarification that results in well-defined categories and clear coding instructions. The research team viewed tapes and read transcripts independently and began to identify themes (categories) by "highlighting particular words or phrases—their tone and intensity—which reflected these themes" (p. 809). Examples of categories which emerged from the data included "how children learn" ("being told" versus "experience or interaction") and the mother's role and responsibility in schooling.

The next phase of the analysis was directed toward finding linkages between categories that reflect similar views. They found, for example, close ties between all of the following: learning is telling, teachers' role is training, their method is drill and practice, and learning is demonstrated by recitation. This was a different perspective from categories linked by play, imagination, and meaningful activities. The mothers' views of themselves as teachers were also examined via comparisons and contrasts of categories which fit a common perspective (what they called "typology"). This was followed by an assessment of the credibility of the categories and representations by members of the research group who had not been involved with the data reduction (coding into categories). The researchers then presented their analytic categories and interpretation to knowledgeable outsiders for examination and revision. The researchers wanted to be certain that their reconstructions accurately reflected the reality of their subjects. Finally, they "derived a set of theoretical propositions within and across categories and perspectives that seemed to best encompass parent's beliefs about learning and literacy for their children" (p. 810). They concluded that mothers' beliefs fall on a continuum of perspectives on learning (what they labelled "transmissive," "maturational," and "transactional)" and that "through a better understanding of parental beliefs, parental involvement programs may be designed to enable culturally diverse parents to realize their aspirations for their children" (p. 822).

Studies such as Neuman et al. (1995) illustrate the challenge of qualitative data analysis. Good interpreters must tolerate ambiguity as they search for recurring regularities in complex data. Their thinking must be flexible; they must attend to counterevidence as well as evidence as they clarify categories and themes. They must also present their findings in ways that preserve its validity and full meaning and show how a better understanding afforded by the data can be useful for readers.

There has been an explosion of interest in qualitative research and analysis in recent years. As a result, there are many valuable sources available for those wanting to learn more about qualitative research and analysis in education. Sage Publications of Thousand Oaks, California publishes a wide variety of qualitative research books (their qualitative methods catalogue lists over fifty titles, including software to help analyze qualitative data). Many other publishers include qualitative research references in their holdings; one of the most widely cited is Bogdan and Biklen (1992).

CHAPTER SUMMARY

Educational researchers are usually interested in going beyond the sample studied, that is, making generalizations or inferences about the entire population represented by the sample. This process is accomplished through the use of *inferential* statistical tests. Central to this process is the idea of chance or sampling error. Researchers consider any outcome to be *statistically significant* if it can be attributed to chance with a probability less than .05 (usually symbolized "$p < .05$," where p is sometimes called the *p value* or *level of significance*). The best interpretation, therefore, of statistically significant findings is "probably not due to chance."

Researchers make one seemingly odd but very important assumption during the calculation of the p value: they assume that there is no relationship between the variables being studied in the population. This is referred to as the *null hypothesis* and is assumed to be true for the calculation of the *p* value. Because this temporary belief is contrary to the research hypothesis (usually), it is set up only to be rejected (hopefully) if the *p* value drops below .05. Its rejection, then, is synonymous with statistical significance.

In its simplest sense, the *p* value can be thought of as the likelihood that the null hypothesis is true. Many statistical tests have been developed for researchers (e.g., ANOVA) and they all have in common the bottom line summary: a *p* value which tells the researcher whether to reject the null hypothesis ($p < .05$) or to accept it ($p > .05$). This is the basis of the inference that is made regarding the population represented by the sample. For example, if one finds a statistically significant difference between boys' and girls' spatial ability in the sample, one can infer that there is a real difference in the population of boys and girls. Such inferences are warranted only when the study is not jeopardized by methodological flaws like biased sampling, threats to internal validity, or any other sources of contamination.

Qualitative data analysis, by contrast, cannot be summarized by a single *p* value. The interpretation of interviews and observations usually requires coding of categories and themes and the analysis itself evolves throughout the course of a study. This process is less mechanical and far more creative (akin to an art). The result is often powerful narrative in story form.

GUIDED TOUR

Let's turn our attention now to a guided tour of published educational research. This will help solidify important terms and concepts described in this chapter.

Brief Report

EFFECTS OF CUING ON MIDDLE-SCHOOL STUDENTS' PERFORMANCE ON ARITHMETIC WORD PROBLEMS CONTAINING EXTRANEOUS INFORMATION

K. Denise Muth

University of Georgia

The purpose of this study was to determine what effect cuing students to the possibility of extraneous information in word problems has on students' problem-solving performance. Eighth-grade students solved problems with and without extraneous infor-

Correspondence concerning this article should by addressed to K. Denise Muth, Department of Elementary Education, 427 Aderhold Hall, University of Georgia, Athens, Georgia 30602.

mation. Some students were cued to the fact that word problems sometimes contain extraneous information. The results indicated that students who were cued performed significantly better than students who were not cued and as well as students who did not have extraneous information in their problems. The results suggest that cuing may be a simple yet powerful tool for helping students cope with the presence of extraneous information in word problems.

It is well established that middle-school students have difficulty solving word problems. In particular, recent research (e.g., Kouba et al., 1988; Muth, 1984; Sowder, 1989) indicates that these students perform poorly on problems containing extraneous information. Although researchers know students have difficulty solving problems containing extraneous information, very little research has examined the question of why. The present study addresses this question.

Word problems involving extraneous information may be difficult for students to solve because of the misconception many students have that "all the numbers in a word problem must be used" (Muth, 1988, p. 237). It may be that students *can't* solve these problems correctly. Or it may be that students *don't* solve these problems correctly because of interference generated by the misconception. If the latter hypothesis is true, then students may find it easier to solve this type of problem if they are cued to the fact that they don't always have to use all the numbers in word problems. I conducted the present study to test this hypothesis.

Method

Subjects

The subjects were 60 eighth-grade students from a large suburban middle school.

Materials

A 14-item word-problem test was constructed for use in the present study. The word problems were adaptations of sample problems supplied by the *National Assessment of Educational Progress.* The problems dealt with the following concepts: distance, interest, perimeter of a rectangle, area of a rectangle, circumference, area of a circle, and volume. There were three versions of the test: (a) no extraneous information, (b) extraneous information–uncued, and (c) extraneous information–cued. The following problem versions illustrate the extraneous information manipulation.

No Extraneous Information:

"Beverly wants to buy a tarp to cover the top of her round pool. Her pool has a radius of 10 feet. How much tarp should she buy?"

Extraneous Information:

"Beverly wants to buy a tarp to cover the top of her round pool. Her pool is 8 feet deep and has a radius of 10 feet. How much tarp should she buy?"

In the versions with extraneous information, one item of numerical information was not necessary. The problems in the versions with extraneous information were otherwise identical to those with no extraneous information.

Cuing was done through a set of directions on the cover page of each test booklet. In the uncued versions, the directions on the cover page said "Remember to show all of your work and work as carefully as possible." In the cued version, the directions on the cover page said "As you work, keep in mind that word problems sometimes contain numbers that are not needed to get the correct answer. Remember to show all of your work and work as carefully as possible."

Procedure

In three eighth-grade classrooms, the three versions of the test were randomly assigned to the students with the restriction that an equal number of students receive each version. The general directions, read aloud to all students, encouraged them to work carefully and reminded them to show all of their work. They were also told that if they thought they knew how to solve a problem, but could not do the calculations, to show how they would set it up or write down the formula they would use. (All students who participated in the study demonstrated knowledge of the seven formulas to a criterion of 100% accuracy.) Students were then told to write their names on the front of their booklet and to "carefully read the directions on the front of your booklet." After all students had written their names and read the directions, they were instructed to "take a few seconds and read the directions again very carefully." After about 15 seconds, students were told they could open their booklets and begin.

Performance Measures

Three measures of performance were used to assess the solution of the word problems: (a) total correct answers, (b) total correct setups, and (c) total correct formulas.

Correct answers. Students received one point for each problem that had been carried out correctly and whose final answer was correct. Thus, subjects applied the correct operation(s) (i.e., addition, subtraction, multiplication, and/or division) to the appropriate numbers and computed the correct answer.

Correct setups. Subjects received one point for each problem that had been set up correctly, even if the final answer was incorrect. That is, if a subject indicated the correct operation(s) that were to be applied to the correct numbers, but did not carry out the operations or carried them out incorrectly, he or she still received one point for the problem. Thus, a correct setup was a more liberal measure of problem solving performance than a correct answer.

Correct formulas. Subjects received one point for each problem that had a correct formula associated with it, even if no other work was done on the problem or if work that was done was incorrect. Thus, a correct formula was the most liberal or the three performance measures.

Results

Means and Standard Deviations

The students correctly answered 40% of the 14 problems ($M = 5.65$, $SD = 3.23$) and correctly set up 44% of the 14 problems ($M = 6.10$, $SD = 3.35$). [1] Students listed correct formulas for 51% of the 14 problems ($M = 7.12$, $SD = 3.2$).

Relations Among Performance Measures

Correct answers were positively correlated with correct setups ($r = .98$) and with correct formulas ($r = .88$, both $ps < .001$). [2] In addition, correct formulas were positively correlated with correct setups ($r = .89$, $p < .001$).

Analyses of Variance

One way analyses of variance were performed to assess the effects of test version on correct answers, correct setups, and correct formulas. [3] Because the three performance measures proved to be highly correlated, in order to avoid redundancy, only the results of the correct answer measure will be reported here. The results indicated a significant difference among the versions, $F(2, 57) = 4.09$, $p < .05.$, $MS^e = 9.45$. Tukey's honestly significant difference test (alpha = .05) was used to follow up the analysis of variance results. Significantly more problems were solved correctly in the no extraneous information version

[1] *These means (M), standard deviations (SD), and percentages are descriptive statistics; they merely describe characteristics of the sample without making any inferences about the population via statistical significance. We know this because there are no p values in this section, and as we have seen in this chapter, p values are needed to make a sound decision about the null hypothesis.*

[2] *This section does not present the main findings related to the research hypothesis; this is an extra analysis in order to see how the performance measures were interrelated. This section, though, illustrates the basic principles of statistical inference and is worth the trek, maybe as a warmup for interpreting the major findings in #3 below. You will recognize the r value as a correlation coefficient. In the case of r = .98, it tells us the extent to which the correct answers were associated with correct setups. There is evidently a near perfect relationship between correct answers and correct setups; if the problem is not set up correctly, then the answer will invariably be wrong. The p value associated with this r of .98 tells us that a statistical test has been conducted. Every p value signals a statistical test. The test in this case assesses whether the correlation coefficient is different from zero. Of course, you might say, since .98 is not zero! There is still, and always will be, the possibility that the .98 could have arisen by chance in the sample, even when the true value is zero in the population. The p value of < .001 tells us that there is less than one out of a thousand chances that this is true. Remember that it is the null hypothesis that is assessed directly by this test. The null hypothesis in this case is that there is zero correlation in the population. The probability of that being true is less than .001, so we reject the null hypothesis and conclude that there is probably a strong relationship between these two measures in the population of students like these. Remember: Any p value less than .05 provides grounds for rejecting the null hypothesis, therefore concluding that there exists a significant relationship among the variables tested.*

[3] *This section tests the main research hypothesis, differences in performance across three conditions: no extraneous information, extraneous information cued, and extraneous information uncued. You'll see further in the paragraph that the means (descriptive statistics) for these groups, respectively, are: 6.35, 6.55, and 4.05. The questions needing answers in the analysis are all conceptually related: Are these means significantly different? Could their differences reasonably be attributed to the workings of chance factors? Do they represent true differences expected in a population of students like these? Are these differences large enough to warrant rejecting the null hypothesis? These interrelated questions are answered by an inferential statistical test known as the analysis of*

($M = 6.35$, $SD = 2.96$) and in the extraneous information–cued version ($M = 6.55$, $SD = 3.22$) than in the extraneous information–uncued version ($M = 4.05$, $SD = 3.03$). The difference between the no extraneous information version and the extraneous information–cued version was not significant.

Discussion

This study replicates and extends previous findings. It replicates previous findings by demonstrating that the presence of extraneous information in word problems reduces the accuracy of students' answers and by showing that students have a misconception that all the numbers in a word problem must be used.

This study extends previous research by showing that cuing students to the fact that word problems sometimes contain extraneous information increases the accuracy of their answers. In fact, students who were cued to extraneous information did as well as students who did not have extraneous information in their problems. This finding suggests that cuing may be a simple yet powerful tool for helping students cope with the presence of extraneous information in word problems.

In conclusion, middle-school teachers and text authors are encouraged to include some extraneous information in the word problems they ask students to solve. Teachers and authors are also encouraged to make students aware that they do not always have to use all the numbers in a word problem. Helping students recognize and respond to extraneous information in classroom situations may better prepare them to deal with it in applied problems later in life.

References

Kouba, V. L., Brown, C. A., Carpenter, T. P., Lindquist, M. M., Silver, E. A., & Swafford, J. O. (1988). Results of the fourth NAEP assess-

variance (or ANOVA). This is appropriate since more than two means are being compared. The ANOVA test statistic appears as an F, but the bottom-line summary is the informative p value. We see that the p, or level of statistical significance, is reported as "p < .05." Because the p has crossed the .05 threshold, we know that the mean differences are probably not due to chance, the null hypothesis can be rejected, the mean differences are statistically significant, and there probably exists a real difference in a population of students like those tested in this experiment.

One last point must be mentioned. The ANOVA test is a general test, in the sense that it tests for the differences among means overall. It does not pinpoint the mean differences for us, although inspection of the means suggests that the uncued condition (4.05) is different from the other two conditions (6.35 and 6.55). This pinpointing test is accomplished by another test, called the Tukey test, with the level of significance (what they call "alpha") set at the customary level of .05. This Tukey test revealed that, as suspected by the inspection of means, significantly more problems were solved in the no extraneous version (6.35) and in the cued extraneous information version (6.55) than in the uncued version (4.05). Although they did not report the specific level of p for this test, we know it had to be less than .05 since they reported that "significantly" more problems were solved ("significantly" implies statistical significance). Finally, notice the last sentence in this section. They are reporting that the Tukey test revealed that the means of the two highest scoring groups (6.35 and 6.55) were not themselves significantly different. The p value in this case must have been greater than .05, consequently accepting the null hypothesis concerning these two means and concluding that the mean difference of .20 was most likely due to chance. This, of course, suggests that there are not true differences in a population of students tested with the no extraneous information version and the cued extraneous information version.

ment of mathematics: Measurement, geometry, data interpretation, attitudes, and other topics. *Arithmetic Teacher, 35,* 10–16.

Muth, K. D. (1984). Solving arithmetic word problems: Role of reading and computational skills. *Journal of Educational Psychology, 76,* 205–210.

Muth, K. D. (1988). Effects of extraneous information and multiple steps on the problem solving performance of middle school students. *Proceedings of the Tenth Annual Meeting of the North American Chapter of the International Group for the Psychology of Mathematics Education,* 236–242.

Sowder, L. (1989). Story problems and students' strategies. *Arithmetic Teacher, 9,* 25–26.

Received October 10, 1989

Revision received June 11, 1990

Accepted June 16, 1990

APPLICATION EXERCISES

1. For each research question below, determine whether you think the question could be answered best with quantitative analysis or qualitative analysis. Explain your decision.

   a. How do teachers' implicit theories about students' learning change as they progress from novice to expert?

   b. How do Japanese methods of instruction compare to American methods?

   c. What stages in the development of vocational interests typify high school students?

   d. How does the gap in standardized achievement between students of differing socioeconomic status change during their progression through grade levels?

   e. How would you characterize the ideas of educators with forty or more years of classroom teaching experience?

   f. Is there a relationship between speed of learning and long-term retention of the learned material?

2. How would you answer the following questions posed by a teacher with no background in scientific research methods?

   a. The null hypothesis seems rather paradoxical to me. Why do researchers hypothesize that *no* relationships exist when they really don't believe that?

   b. The term *statistically significant* when applied to research findings suggests to me that the research findings are important. Isn't this true?

   c. What is meant by the term *statistical test*? Is this like a test that is administered to students?

   d. What do all those *p* letters mean that are littered all over the results section of a published research report?

    e. Why would an experienced researcher make those mistakes called I and II?

    f. Is the term *statistical power* at all related to the power that might be applied to a telescope or microscope?

    g. What do all those letters like *t*, *F*, and *r* refer to in a published report?

3. Locate a recent published report of qualitative research in education in a premiere journal such as the *American Educational Research Journal*. Focus on the data analysis section and summarize how the researchers established the *credibility*, or trustworthiness of their findings.

MULTIPLE CHOICE QUESTIONS

1. Which of the following is a shorthand method for expressing "statistically significant"?
   a. $p > .05$
   b. $p = .05$
   c. $p < .05$
   d. $p < .50$
   e. $p = .99$

2. What does "*p*" refer to in the analysis of data?
   a. prove
   b. significant
   c. power
   d. probability
   e. important

3. Which of the following captures the meaning of the null hypothesis?
   a. there are no alternative explanations
   b. there are no relationships in the sample
   c. there are no controls in the sample
   d. there are no statistical tests
   e. there are no relationships in the population

4. What is the mean of a sampling distribution of mean differences if the null hypothesis is true?
   a. 0
   b. 1
   c. 2
   d. −1
   e. −2

5. What is meaning of the term *nonsignificant* in data analysis?
   a. probably due to chance
   b. not important
   c. probably of little practical value
   d. not replicable
   e. definitely not due to chance

6. If a researcher wanted to test for differences across three means, which of the following test statistics would be most appropriate?
   a. t
   b. p
   c. F
   d. X^2

e. *d*

7. If a *t* were calculated to be 1.30, what would be its associated *p*?

    a. > .05
    b. < .05
    c. < .01
    d. < .001
    e. none of the above

8. Falsely accepting the null hypothesis reflects _____; falsely rejecting the null hypothesis reflects _____; rejecting the null hypothesis when it is false reflects _____

    a. power; Type I error; Type II error
    b. Type I error; power; Type II error
    c. Type II error; Type I error; power
    d. Type II error; power; Type I error
    e. Type I error; Type II error; power

9. Which of the following best describes the nature of qualitative data analysis?

    a. simple
    b. evolving
    c. uncreative
    d. cozy
    e. chancy

10. Qualitative data analysis often involves _____, and the most important criteria for evaluating the analysis of a qualitative study is its _____.

    a. decisions; simplicity
    b. teamwork; creativity
    c. coding; believability
    d. manipulation; "seamlessness"
    e. "playing"; readability

Answers: 1) c   2) d   3) e   4) a   5) a   6) c   7) a   8) c   9) b   10) c

Chapter 12

RESEARCH CRITIQUES

OVERVIEW

At this point in your study of educational research, you are quite familiar with reading a published research article. You are aware of the general format of a report, the methodological procedures used by researchers, and their scientific way of thinking. This background allows you to read published research with comprehension sufficient enough for a critical review. This chapter will guide you through that process.

WHAT IS A CRITICAL REVIEW?

It should be noted that there is no one standard format for a critical review of published research (unlike the format required for presenting the research findings in a journal article). Nevertheless, there is general agreement about the components of a review. What follows is a recommendation based on other reviewers' suggestions for the content and format of a review and observations of reviews as they are currently practiced.

A *critical review* (or *critique*) of published research is not a closed-minded attack of its worth based on its shortcomings, limitations, or flaws. It is more like a movie review, where the critical reviewer tells us what the movie is about (the plot), general reactions (e.g., one of the year's best), how it achieved its most prominent characteristics (fear, humor, intrigue, etc.), strengths (e.g., superb acting, special effects), weaknesses (e.g., too-familiar story line, slow pace), and an overall recommendation ("thumbs up or down").

The critical reviewer of published educational research engages in much the same task. The review may begin with a description of what the research is all about, or its general purpose (the research question or hypothesis and its placement within a broader context, namely the theoretical framework and literature review), overall reactions (e.g., a much needed and well executed study), how it handled methodological issues (e.g., its research design, control procedures, instrumentation, sampling, etc.), strengths (e.g., large sample size, proper control techniques such as blinding, engaging discussion), weaknesses (e.g., doubtful validity of some measures, high loss of subjects, poorly written, outdated literature review, etc.), and an overall judgment (e.g., a professor's grade, a journal editor's recommendation to accept it for publication, an administrator's decision to change policy, or a teacher's decision to apply findings to classroom instruction).

GUIDELINES FOR CRITIQUES

Purpose

A critical evaluation of research often begins with an introductory statement regarding its purpose. Why was the research done? What question or questions did it answer? What hypothesis was tested? The reviewer is probably not neutral with regard to the purpose of the research; hence, it is appropriate to evaluate the overall purpose. On the positive side, the research might attempt to answer a question that might lead to solutions to very practical problems, shed new light on old problems, provide support for a theory which guides sound decision making, advance our understanding of a complex phenomenon, or test the limits of general applicability through the replication of others' findings. In a general sense, research is potentially useful to the extent that it has theoretical value through its impact on ideas, or research which has practical value through its influence on practice.

The purpose of the research, of course, does not exist in a vacuum. The larger context, or prior research, is relevant to the evaluation of purpose. Issues here might include how well embedded the research is, using prior research findings and ideas as a context. This is not an easy task, for it involves a type of synthesis, or the creation of a framework for understanding how new research might "fit in." The framework for understanding may be as straightforward as a summary of previous research findings with a statement about a void (gap) in knowledge or understanding that the research is attempting to fill. Or it may be as ambitious as a literature review that culminates in a new theory or model (or a major revision of an existing theory) that is tested by the research. One hallmark of a good research question or hypothesis is that the findings are informative no matter what the outcome. This is especially true if the research compares two competing theories, with one outcome supporting one theory and a different outcome supporting the other. This is an application of strong inference (Platt, 1964) described in Chapter 10. Needless to say, the research purpose and its context should discourage any reader from saying, "So what?"

Overall Reaction

It is almost natural after reading a research report to have an overall evaluation. It seems reasonable that this reaction results from a complex combination of preconceived biases (e.g., an orientation which favors qualitative methodologies, or a preference for field studies in a natural environment), an evaluation of purpose and context, methodology, and a weighing of unique strengths and weaknesses. Perhaps the overarching question at the heart of an overall reaction is, "Does the research make any contribution?" The potential contribution could come in many forms including, for example, support (or lack of it) for a new or established theory, the application of old models in new situations, the extension (generalization) of others' findings, the generation of empirically-based novel ideas, or the reinterpretation of earlier findings based on new data. This list is not exhaustive; it merely describes a few ways that research results may add to our existing knowledge, understanding, and way of thinking about education and the teaching and learning process.

It is important to note that empirical research may make a significant contribution without being especially strong in its methodology, sampling, instruction, and so forth. This may sound paradoxical, but once again, consider the classic case in point: the famous "Pygmalion in the Classroom," a study of the role of teachers' expectations in the determination of students' intellectual development (Rosenthal & Jacobson, 1968). This was a blockbuster idea, to be sure, and it remains one of the most cited educational studies ever conducted. You will recall, as it turned out, the validity of the study was seriously challenged by Elashoff and Snow (1971), among others, and today it is largely discredited. This is not to distract, however, from the study's monumental contribution. There is a widely held belief today that teachers in fact do have many expectations of students' abilities based on a large variety of preconceived ideas, and that these stereotyped expectations do affect students in many complex ways, but probably not in the simplistic and dramatic way described by Rosenthal and Jacobson (1968).

By contrast, an exceptionally strong study from a methodological point of view (adequate controls, representative sampling, valid instrumentation, etc.) may leave a reviewer wondering, "Who cares?" Other studies may "beat a dead horse" by replicating an empirical "given," such as the relationship between socioeconomic status and school achievement without providing any new insight into an old relationship.

Methodological Issues

Every research study must grapple with methodological problems. Some problems are relatively easy to overcome; others are more difficult. How a study comes to terms with its methodological challenges often sets it far above (or far below) other studies in a particular area. Consider research design, for instance, and the concept of control. This is a good focal area because nearly all researchers are interested in the bases of relationships which my be discovered. We know that true experimental designs, executed with proper control over extraneous influences, are especially strong for the purpose of detecting cause-and-effect relationships. In a research area dominated by correlational findings, such as the link between violence on television and aggressive behavior, any research study using an experimental design should be evaluated with particular attention to its handling of this ever-present methodological concern.

Another ubiquitous methodological issue is bias. Lack of attention to this issue may be significant enough to completely discredit a research finding. Just as you would probably doubt a research study conducted by a tobacco company showing that smoking does not cause lung disease, you would also probably doubt a drug maker's research-based claim that a particular prescription has no side-effects, or a book publisher's research-based claim that children learn to read better from books than from computer screens. As we have seen, bias can be very subtle, even "subconscious" (as well as blatant and deliberately distorting), and could affect even the best-intentioned researcher.

Yet another methodological issue that many evaluators focus on is measurement and central concerns of reliability and validity. Studies that employ the strongest designs, the tightest controls, and the best checks against bias may still be rendered questionable if measures are full of error (unreliable) or if they are off target in terms of their purpose (invalid). The process of measurement (instrumentation) is one of the most frequently occurring sources of limitation in educational research.

On the positive side, many studies are noteworthy for their creative methods for solving methodological dilemmas, or at least overcoming inherent weaknesses in research designs. One example here might include *triangulation,* or the use of multiple methods to answer a research question. When the answers to one question all agree (or *converge*), despite the variation in methods used to gather information, the answer is judged to be more believable. The counterpart in a court of law might be evidence from a variety of sources including, for example, eyewitness testimony, fingerprints, and physical evidence such as DNA found at the scene of the crime.

Other methods for overcoming methodological obstacles may involve novel methods of collecting data. For example, if a researcher wants to learn how often high school students worry about family related problems, one possible method would involve asking students at the end of the day to estimate how many times (and for how

long) they have had episodes of "family worry." We know that memory, being recon-
structive, is a very unreliable indicator of "what was" and that people can grossly un-
der- or over-estimate the frequency of specific behaviors. A more suitable method
might involve the students' wearing of beepers, and when they were beeped at random times for each student throughout the day, they would immediately write down
their current thoughts and, if they were worrying, a description of their concern. Of
course, merely telling students what the study is all about before they were outfitted
with beepers might unintentionally increase the frequency of such worries, since the
wearing of beepers would be a constant reminder of the study's purpose. But not in-
forming students of the true purpose of the study will raise ethical issues. They might
also be hesitant to report the true content of their thoughts, thinking that they might
be labelled as abnormal and referred to therapy. This is precisely what is meant by an
ethical dilemma—one choice of method may introduce a bias, and a different choice
of method will introduce another problem or a different bias.

Weaknesses and Strengths

One could argue, quite logically, that all studies in education are, at least to some extent, seriously flawed at worst and seriously limited at best. The process of sampling
always limits the applicability of generalizations, the instruments are never perfectly
reliable and valid, the inferential statistics are never evidence of proof (recall the probability statements arising from the *p* value), randomization never guarantees group
equivalency, some respondents do not tell the truth or lack the motivation to perform
their best, and so on. Because these criticisms are universal and can be applied to all
educational research, they add nothing to our evaluation of specific studies. The following section is concerned with addressing weaknesses that are relatively common
and can be applied to specific studies as appropriate.

Educational research cannot easily be faulted for lack of good ideas, useful theories, creative thinking, statistical sophistication, or strong designs. It appears that
three of the most common weaknesses in educational research are poor instrumentation, limited generalization, and alternative explanations or counter interpretations.
These might be good candidates to focus on if asked to discuss a study's weaknesses.
Let's take each one of these facets in turn.

Instrumentation.   At the heart of sound measurement, you will recall from Chapter 7,
are the notions of reliability and validity. We have seen how difficult it is to measure
well such important constructs as, for example, self-esteem, creativity, motivation, or
emotionality. The construct of intelligence stands in sharp contrast to other complex
constructs, for there is general agreement that intelligence can, under the right circumstances, be measured reliably and validly, in the sense that intelligence tests seem to
yield consistent (stable) scores that can be used to predict school success. It should be
emphasized, however, that this apparent success with instrumentation is narrowly
confined to *verbal/analytical* intelligence (reasoning with language and symbols) and
cannot be claimed for other important facets of intelligence, such as interpersonal,
emotional, or practical intelligence. With this in mind, it is probably wise to scrutinize
very carefully those educational research findings investigating constructs which are
difficult to measure, such as creativity or character.

The measurement of school achievement poses another challenge for researchers.
So-called "bubble tests," such as the *Stanford Achievement Tests*, are without question
reliable and content-valid to the extent that their content matches the school curriculum (which it does quite well for most schools in most subject areas). But it is a brief
snapshot at best, and clearly does not assess how students' thinking becomes organized over time and how their knowledge and skills translate into real-world prod-

ucts and activities. Even when they are taken by sufficiently motivated students, the standardized achievement tests, such as the *Stanford Achievement Tests,* tend to measure end-state knowledge of the convergent variety (where there is agreement about a single correct answer). Portfolio assessment, by contrast, tells a story about a student's effort and progress as well as achievement progress over time. And its focus on products and accomplishments is something that is meaningfully valued by students. The problem with portfolio assessment (besides practicality) from a research perspective is, you guessed it, reliability (in particular, inter-rater agreement).

Generalization. Limited applicability of generalizations, or the failure of research findings to extend beyond the borders of a study (subjects, setting, measures, etc.) also appears to be a common weakness of educational research (and research in other fields, such as medicine, as well). Because of this caution, it would not be surprising if one were to adopt a reading program which was shown to be effective in a study for one group of first-graders into his own classroom only to find very different results. The fact is that teaching and learning are complex processes, most probably characterized by innumerable interactions and very few main effects (see Chapter 9). One can speculate about reasons for this lack of generalization, but it seems plausible that many educational treatments are complex bundles, not as simple as a name or summary may suggest. Because treatments do not occur in a vacuum, you might think of an educational intervention as a "treatment with trappings." The trappings (extraneous variables) might include the personalities of teachers, the environmental conditions of the classroom, the climate within the school building, the variation in parental involvement, the presence of teaching aides, class size, and so on. To the extent that any of the trappings interact with the treatment, a different finding may result. For example, the success of a program may depend on the context of its implementation. If its implementation is "top down" or mandated by high-level administrators, its success might be unlikely. But if teachers' "grass roots" movements leads to the adoption of the same treatment, then its success might be more likely.

In addition to this "treatment-as-a-bundle" phenomenon, there exists the inescapable fact that individual differences among students are enormous, and they can react to different treatments in many different ways. This can be explained, in part, by differences in learning style, motivation, interest, or aptitude, just to name a few of the thousands of potential interacting variables.

Alternative Explanations. Undoubtedly one of the most difficult weaknesses to identify in educational research is the alternative explanations or counter interpretations of data. Because most alternative explanations do not pop out in an obvious way, they often remain hidden, to be revealed only by persistent researchers who dig deeper for the best interpretation. For example, Gerald Bracey (1992), who writes a research column for the *Phi Delta Kappan,* argues that studies of international achievement comparisons which reveal low United States rankings are "fatally flawed" because so many variables were not under the control of the researchers and had not been "factored out" (p. 568). After some digging, Bracey turned up evidence to challenge the assertion that America's public schools are failing. It constitutes what he calls "The Big Lie" (Bracey, 1991). Suffice it to say that nearly all educational research findings have counter interpretations.

Not considering alternative, yet plausible, interpretations would be regarded as a weakness in any study. Also, a weakness would also be evident if a written report of the research did not state the limitations or problems with the study as perceived by the researcher. After all, who is in a better position to critique the study, having actually planned and carried it out? In other words, a stronger study is one which makes a true confession. This is because all studies in education are, to some extent, limited and prone to methodological problems.

Research studies can circumvent some of these common weaknesses of educational research and, to that extent, would be regarded as strengths. "Trappings" could be built into the design of the study, individual differences could be identified and analyzed as part of the findings, and alternate explanations could be anticipated and evaluated for their plausibility with additional data. Apart from this, readers of educational research, at least in the premiere journals such as the *American Educational Research Journal,* can usually expect characteristic strengths such as a comprehensive review of the literature, a meaningful research question, reasonable controls for obvious biases, proper analysis, and a thought-provoking discussion that is logically related to the actual findings.

Overall Recommendation

After reviewing a research study, reviewers are often faced with the difficult task of recommending whether or not the study should be published, presented, awarded, funded (as in the case of a research proposal), replicated (because of its potential for changes in practice), included (as in a review of the literature, or in a meta-analysis), disseminated (in the case of influencing public policy), discarded, and so forth. This decision undoubtedly involves a complex weighing of all relevant criteria, inevitable personal bias, a counterbalancing of weaknesses and strengths, maybe even "gut" reactions, and countless other factors. The final decision, though, is often a simple *yes* or *no.* It is no wonder, then, why reviewers of educational research often do *not* agree on seemingly simple decisions such as "accept" or "reject." (This is just another instance of poor reliability in educational research.) Of course, all of the research studies you have read in the previous chapters have been regarded by at least some reviewers in the field as worthy, since they have all been published in reputable journals.

GOOD CRITIQUES TAKE PRACTICE

We conclude this chapter by examining a study that was not only published, but also was given an award. On occasion, the editors of the *Journal of Educational Research* announce competition for the Meritorious Contribution to Educational Practice Through Research Award which recognizes and honors research published in their journal. One award winner was Carolyn M. Evertson's "Training Teachers in Classroom Management: An Experimental Study in Secondary School Classrooms" published in the *Journal of Educational Research* [September/October 1985, Vol. 79 (No. 1), pp. 51–58]. We are reprinting this article at the close of this chapter (and at the end of the book). We will provide a brief critique of this research, to give you an example from which to work. We hope your insight will add to this critique. Your instructor may choose another activity related to this award-winning research. In either case, we trust you will be able to read this article with far better comprehension and be able to discuss it more meaningfully than you would have prior to this guided tour through educational research. Further, we hope you will take this opportunity to see how educational research is truly an *integrative process,* where one step leads to another.

Finally, studying educational research in discrete chapters (such as this text) does not foster a connective, process-oriented view of research. This is unfortunate. That is why it is important in this final chapter to think about all the research concepts and principles you have learned and try to see how they all fit together into a meaningful whole.

GUIDED TOUR

Let's turn our attention now to a guided tour of published educational research. This will help solidify important terms and concepts described in this chapter.

Training Teachers in Classroom Management: An Experimental Study in Secondary School Classrooms

Carolyn M. Evertson

Peabody College, Vanderbilt University

Abstract

The purpose of this study was threefold: (a) to validate principles of classroom organization and management shown in correlational research to be related to management effectiveness in secondary classrooms; (b) to determine if school district personnel could deliver teacher workshops and collect data on implementation of the principles; and (c) to assess whether training in classroom management techniques would provide additional skills to teachers who had already been trained in a statewide instructional skills program. Results indicated that training and observations could be done by district personnel, and the trained group exceeded the control group on both management skills and student task engagement.

[Students:] *Use this space for making notes*

The work reported here was sponsored in part by the Arkansas Department of Education, Little Rock, Arkansas, and by National Institute of Education Grant 83-0063. The opinions expressed are those of the author and no official endorsement by these agencies is implied.

Address correspondence to Carolyn M. Evertson, Department of Teaching and Learning, Box 330, Peabody College, Vanderbilt University, Nashville, TN 37203.

Creating and maintaining an orderly, productive class-room environment has long been viewed as one of the essential elements in teaching competence. Not only is there little argument as to the importance of these elements from the common sense point of view, but research has also shown that a number of management variables are also correlated with pupil achievement (Good, 1979; Medley, 1977).

Studies in the primary grades (Anderson, Evertson, & Brophy, 1979; Brophy & Evertson, 1976) and more recently in the secondary grades (Evertson, Anderson, Anderson & Brophy, 1980; Evertson & Emmer, 1982a) show that the more academically effective teachers in those studies generally had better-organized classrooms and fewer behavior problems. Additionally, research indicates that the key to managing classrooms effectively begins from the first day of school with a systematic approach, advance preparation, and planning (Brophy, 1992; Evertson & Emmer, 1982b).

While research has supported the importance of classroom management as a necessary condition for effective teaching, studies which have sought to train teachers in principles of effective classroom management derived from research are rare (Borg & Ascione, 1982; Emmer, Sanford, Clements, & Martin, 1981; Evertson, Emmer, Sanford, & Clements, 1983). Those that have been conducted indicate that recommendations and suggestions for teachers aimed at planning rules and procedures ahead of time, presenting these to students along with expectations for appropriate behavior, maintaining a systematic approach through monitoring student academic work and behavior, and providing feedback to students among other things, can result in improved student task engagement, less inappropriate student behavior, and smoother instructional activities when compared with a control group without such

[Students:] *Use this space for making notes*

training. Experimental field studies showing the efficacy of such training have been completed.

While research on classroom management and effective teaching has progressed (Brophy, 1979; Good, 1983), there has been at the same time interest from practitioners in using these results in inservice and preservice teacher training. In several instances, this interest has been both statewide and nation-wide through various divisions of state education agencies, district and regional agencies, and teachers' unions.

[Students:] *Use this space for making notes*

The following is a report of an experimental study under-taken in one of six Arkansas school districts involved in devel-oping and testing statewide a model for improvement of classroom management and instruction using the findings from classroom research. The research that was the focus for the classroom management model was conducted in a large metropolitan school district in Texas (Emmer, Evertson, San-ford, Clements, & Worsham, 1982; Evertson et al., 1983).

Several reasons existed for conducting additional studies in Arkansas schools rather than simply adopting the results of the Texas studies.

1. The experimental studies conducted in Texas suggested that brief (½-day) workshops and teacher manuals were enough to produce changes in teacher behavior in the desired direction; however, more specific information about the nature of the training was needed to support the development of an exportable statewide model with recommendations and guidelines for use.

2. The role that classroom observation could play in en-couraging teachers to practice and perform the desired behav-iors needed to be explored further.

3. Questions remained about whether findings from field studies conducted in one state, where the participating school

district was familiar with the research and used it in its own inservice programs, could be replicated in another state where the material was new but where there had already been extensive statewide training on instructional skills. That is, could classroom management training add anything new to previous training in instructional skills?

4. In the Texas studies, the training workshops and the classroom observations were handled by members of the research team. Developing an exportable model would require that school personnel be trained to provide the workshops for their teachers and to provide follow-up observations and conferences. Hence, guidelines for training and observing would have to be developed. This required a study in which the training phase included careful outlining and specification of the content and activities used in training the teachers to determine the most effective means.

To gain answers to some of these questions the following studies were conducted in six school districts in Arkansas.

Method

Participating in the studies were 102 teachers from six Arkansas school districts: 70 in grades 1–6, with 35 serving in the experimental group and 35 in the control group; and 32 teachers in junior high and high school, 16 experimental and 16 control.

Experimental-group teachers were each given a one-day workshop in their respective school districts using the manuals that had been produced in the Texas studies of effective management. The workshop content is described in the section below on training. A one-day follow-up workshop was conducted in mid-October to reemphasize management principles and discuss problems.

Teachers were randomly assigned to the experimental and control groups. Prior to randomization a step was taken to prevent an imbalance across groups on teaching experience and grade level. Teachers were blocked into matched pairs on these characteristics, and then members of each pair were assigned randomly to either the control or experimental group. One requirement for participation in the studies was that all teachers, both experimental and control, were to have had previous training in instructional skills through the state's Program for Effective Teaching (PET). This was necessary in order to gain a clear assessment of the relative contribution of classroom management training to the teachers' overall performance.

Because the intent of the studies was to explore both the content and the processes involved in developing a model for classroom management training which school districts could use, personnel from within each school district had to be trained to carry out the research.

In the summer prior to the 1982 school year, administrative staff members from each of the six school districts met in Little Rock with the principal investigator for a one-day training session. One requirement for being designated as a trainer was that the staff member also be certified as an instructor in the state's PET program in instructional skills as well. The reason for this was to capitalize on talent already available in each of the districts, thereby saving time and resources, and, more importantly, to supply a common orientation and background for the training procedures.

The objective of this session was to provide personnel in each district with specified content and procedures for the before school workshop. (One day later in the fall was set aside for planning the follow-up workshop scheduled for mid-October.) Material used to train teachers was taken partially from a booklet (Sanford, Clements, & Emmer, 1981) that contained case studies, procedures, and activities to accompany material in the teachers' manuals (Emmer et al., 1982; Evertson, Emmer, Clements, Sanford, & Worsham, 1981). Additional activities

[Students:] *Use this space for making notes*

were developed by trainers and incorporated in the training procedures systematically to insure that all teachers received similar content in the workshops.

Content presented to the teachers was outlined in terms of tasks to be accomplished in the order needed to prepare for the start of school and to maintain this start throughout the year. The following outline was developed and used as a guide to specify the content and activities in the workshops and emphasized three key activities: planning before school begins; presenting information about rules, procedures, and expectations; and maintaining the learning environment (see Figure 1).

[Students:] *Use this space for making notes*

I. Planning (before school starts)
    A. Use of space (readying the classroom)
    B. Rules for general behavior
    C. Rules and procedures for specific areas
        1. Student use of classroom space and facilities
        2. Student use of out-of-class areas
        3. Student participation during whole class activities/ seatwork
        4. Student participation in daily routines
        5. Student participation during small-group activities
    D. Consequences/incentives for appropriate/inappropriate behavior
    E. Activities for the first day of school
II. Presenting the rules, procedures, and expectations (beginning of school)
    A. Teaching rules and procedures
        1. Explanation
        2. Rehearsal
        3. Feedback
        4. Reteaching
    B. Teaching academic content
    C. Communicating concepts and directions clearly
III. Maintaining the system (throughout the year)
    A. Monitoring for behavioral and academic compliance
    B. Acknowledging
    C. Stopping inappropriate behavior
    D. Consistent use of consequences/incentives
    E. Adjusting instruction for individual students/groups
    F. Keeping students accountable for work
    G. Coping with special problems

FIGURE 1 Outline of Workshop Content for Experimental Group

Since the design of the study included observing all teachers (trained and untrained) to determine the degree to which teacher behavior and student task engagement was or was not affected by training, it was necessary to train observers in each of the school districts to carry out this function. Eleven school district administrative staff members met with the principal investigator for a one-day training session in the use of the classroom observation instruments designed for the study. Like the trainers, the observers were required to be certified observers trained in observation procedures in the state's PET program instructional skills component.

Observers were given manuals containing descriptions of rating scales. They participated in one full day of intensified training using both written scripts of classroom situations and videotapes. Reliability checks during training indicated that by the end of the training all observers had reached 80–90% agreement in use of the items.

Observers were trained to collect data pertaining to the variables of interest in classroom management. To do this a variety of measures was used.

Narrative records. These records were used to gather qualitative data about classroom activities and behaviors of both teachers and students. During each observation observers recorded notes on narrative record forms. After the observation, the observer used the notes to dictate onto audiotape a complete description of the context, activities, etc., in each classroom. Observers were asked to preserve the correct sequence of activities, noting teacher and student behaviors and recording as much classroom dialogue as possible. Training procedures emphasized the dimensions relevant to classroom management skills while also noting the overall organization of the observation period. Observers also collected time information, which allowed an estimate of the length of activities and transitions.

[Students:] *Use this space for making notes*

Student engagement rates. Beginning at a randomly determined time during the first 10 minutes of the observation period, observers stopped notetaking and categorized each student in the room in one of the following three categories of engagement: (a) definitely on task: student is obviously engaged in the task at hand as defined by the teacher at the time; (b) probably on task: student appears to be engaged, but there is some question as to whether attention is wandering or not; (c) off-task: student is not engaged in what he or she is suppose to be doing.

A score for each category was obtained by dividing the number of students in each category by the total number of students present yielding a percentage of students classified in one of the above categories. Student engagement rates were recorded on the narrative forms enabling one to see also what activities were taking place at those times.

Classroom rating scales. After each observation, a set of classroom rating scales was used by the observer to assess teacher and student behavior on several variables relating to aspects of management of student conduct and management of instruction. These five-point rating scales were defined in manuals given to the observers during training. The ratings required observers to rate all teachers on various aspects of lesson management, monitoring student behavior, class climate, handling of student misbehavior, etc. They also included ratings on the degree and frequency of student disruptive or inappropriate behavior.

Summary ratings. When all observations were completed in November, a set of 31 summary ratings of each teacher was filled out by the observer who saw a given teacher at least twice. In many instances, two sets of ratings were filled out because there were two observers who each saw a given teacher. In these cases, observers were asked not to discuss their rat-

[Students:] *Use this space for making notes*

ings and to do them independently. Observer agreement tended to be high on most items. Summary ratings were designed to assess several variables that could be rated only after several visits to a class, such as the overall amount of time students spent waiting for the next assignment, decreases in student attention from the first of the year to later in the school year, smoothness of transitions between activities, or teachers' characteristic methods of giving feedback to students.

Data collection. All observations and data collection began on the first day of school after teachers had received the first workshop. Observers visited classrooms for 30–45 minutes and tried in elementary classrooms to plan their observations for the beginnings of lessons. In secondary classrooms, observations were conducted for the full class period. Observers were not told the identity of the trained teachers, and each observer saw both trained and untrained teachers. Teachers likewise were told the design of the study and were asked not to share information or materials from the workshops or to discuss this with observers. Control-group teachers were told the general nature of the study and its importance. Their role was explained, and they were promised that they would be the next group to receive training.

Observations were planned so that observers saw all teachers four times after the first (before school) workshop beginning with the first day of school and twice after the second workshop given in mid-October. The purpose of observing after the second workshop was to assess the possible effects of the second workshop in helping teachers maintain their management skills.

Results

The remainder of this paper will focus on the quantitative findings from the study in secondary classrooms in particular.

[Students:] *Use this space for making notes*

A framework for qualitative analyses of lesson content in these classrooms is reported in Green and Weade (1984).

The component ratings and student engagement ratings were analyzed using two-way analysis of variance, one between-groups factor to assess overall treatment and control group differences and one within-groups factor to determine the difference in mean scores before and after the second workshop (see Table 1).

Of the 35 five-point ratings used to assess teachers' management practices after each observation period, 22 (61%) were significant in favor of the treatment group. Additionally, treatment group means exceeded control group means in the predicted direction on all but one of the variables. The $p \leq .10$ level of significance was chosen because the small sample size reduced the likelihood of detecting a significant finding at a more stringent probability level. Nevertheless, the acceptance of this significance level did not change the interpretations or patterns of the findings. First we will examine the group differences.

Instructional management. Eight of the eleven ratings were significant in favor of the treatment group, and the remaining three means indicated trends in favor of that group. It may be more illuminating to discuss those three variables. Each of these had to do with materials and their use. The means indicate that in neither group did the variety of materials used exceed the minimum, nor were there many assignments for different students. This might be explained by the fact that these were secondary classrooms that were departmentalized and ability grouped with relatively focused curricula. Few teachers departed from the basic text in their classes, and most of the instruction was tied directly to the assigned text.

Room arrangement. Neither variable was significant for the arrangement of the room. Again this is most likely due to

[Students:] *Use this space for making notes*

TABLE 1 Means for Component Ratings for Secondary Classrooms: Experimental and Control Groups × Time of Workshop[a]

	Treatment		Time	
	Experimental $n = 8$	Control $n = 8$	Post treatment Time 1 $n = 16$	Post Treatment Time 2 $n = 16$
Instructional management				
Describes objectives clearly	4.95	4.27**	4.56	4.65
Variety of materials	1.23	1.08	1.31	1.00*
Materials are ready	4.92	4.65	4.76	4.81
Clear directions for assignments	4.66	4.15**	4.35	4.46*
Waits for attention	4.42	3.87**	4.30	4.00
Encourages analysis	4.34	3.46*	3.65	4.15***
Assignment for different students	1.38	1.17	1.15	1.40
Appropriate pacing of the lesson	4.15	3.41*	3.73	3.84
Clear explanations	4.45	3.85*	4.06	4.25
Monitors student understanding	4.46	3.92*	4.10	4.28
Consistently enforces work standards	4.27	3.41**	3.68	4.00
Room Arrangement				
Suitable traffic patterns	4.75	4.73	4.98	4.50***
Good visibility	4.76	4.73	4.98	4.50***
Rules and Procedures				
Efficient routines	4.58	4.42	4.47	4.53
Appropriate general procedures	4.57	4.15*	4.35	4.37
Suitable routines for assigning and checking work	4.53	4.20*	4.23	4.50*
Meeting student concerns				
High degree of student success	4.36	3.85***	4.12	4.09
Level of student aggressive	1.03	1.40**	1.19	1.25
Attention spans considered	3.87	3.28	3.46	3.68
Activities related to students' interests	3.82	3.11	3.03	.90***
Managing student behavior				
Restrictions on student movement	4.07	2.96***	3.48	3.56
Rewards appropriate performance	3.93	3.08	3.67	3.34
Signals correct behavior	3.27	2.08***	2.98	2.37**
Consistency in managing student behavior	4.06	2.97**	3.60	3.43
Effective monitoring	4.05	3.33*	3.70	3.68

Continued

TABLE 1 *Continued*

	Treatment		Time	
	Experimental $n = 8$	**Control** $n = 8$	**Post treatment Time 1** $n = 16$	**Post Treatment Time 2** $n = 16$
Student misbehavior				
Amount of disruptive behavior	1.16	1.41	1.33	1.25
Amount of inappropriate behavior	1.95	2.76**	2.40	2.31
Stops inappropriate quickly	3.10	3.23	3.61	2.71**
Ignores inappropriate behavior	2.51	4.10**	3.37	3.25
Classroom climate				
Conveys value of the curriculum	4.48	3.60**	4.03	4.06
Task-oriented focus	4.53	3.85***	4.26	4.12
Relaxed, pleasant atmosphere	4.52	3.82**	4.16	4.18
Miscellaneous				
Listening skills	4.08	3.30	3.72	3.65
Avoidance behavior during seatwork	1.28	1.87***	1.69	1.46
Participation in class discussions	3.61	3.14	3.38	3.37
Percentage of students engaged				
% of students off-task	7.09	14.79**	9.32	12.56
% of students probably on-task	4.96	9.68	5.21	9.44
% of students on-task	87.95	75.53**	85.47	78.00**

Note. Means for the component ratings are based on 5-point scales: 1 = low occurrence or least characteristic; 5 = high occurrence or most characteristic.
[a]There was one significant interaction for Treatment × Time for level of student aggressive behavior at $p = .06$.
*$p \leq .10$.   **$p \leq .05$.   ***$p \leq .01$.

the fact that most secondary classrooms leave little flexibility in the ways one can arrange the classroom.

Rules and procedures. Appropriate procedures and suitable routines for assigning and checking work were the two significant variables of the three listed under this heading. These procedures were also emphasized heavily in the workshops.

Meeting student concerns. Although level of student aggressive behavior was minimal in either group (1.03 and 1.40

on a 5-point scale), it appeared significantly greater in the control group classes. This type of misbehavior more often took the form of "sassing" or defying the teacher or being generally uncooperative or belligerent. The treatment group appeared to be able to maximize the match between materials and students' skill levels such that there appeared to be more student success in their classrooms.

Managing student behavior. By far the greatest mean differences for treatment and control groups appeared for this group of variables. The treatment group exceeded the control group on all the ratings and significantly so for four of the five. One strong effect of the training appeared to be the direct management of student behavior even to restricting students' freedom of movement in and around the classroom. Still, these restrictions did not appear to have an effect on classroom climate as will be seen later.

Student misbehavior. Misbehaviors were divided into two types depending upon the severity. Disruptive behavior was problematic student behavior that actually disrupted the class activities. This type of misbehavior seldom occurred in any of the classrooms. However, inappropriate student behavior, behavior which involved inattention, uncooperativeness, chatting with friends, etc., occurred slightly more frequently, and significant differences were found between treatment and control groups. Treatment teachers had less inappropriate behavior in their classes, and they were less likely to ignore it when it did happen. Interestingly, the quickness with which such inappropriate behavior was stopped did not differ between the two groups, and both groups tended to be less diligent about putting a stop to inappropriate behavior as time went on.

Classroom climate. Treatment teachers received significantly higher ratings for all the classroom climate variables. These findings suggest that in spite of the fact that they were

[Students:] *Use this space for making notes*

rated significantly higher on managing and controlling variables, the classroom atmosphere did not appear to suffer. Students also seemed to adopt a more task-oriented attitude including greater cooperation in doing seatwork assignments.

Student engagement. Treatment classrooms had significantly fewer students off task (7.09% as opposed to 14.8% in the control-group classes). Since the average class size was 23, this would amount to an average of 1 to 2 students off task in the trained teachers' classrooms but 3 to 4 students off task in the untrained teachers' classrooms. Findings were parallel for on-task behavior. In treatment classrooms, 88% of the students were on task (over 20 of the students), whereas only 76% of the students in the control classes were on task (only 17 of the average 23 students). While these differences appear small, when calculated over the period of several months they represent a significant problem for control and attention. Not surprisingly, on-task behavior in both treatment and control groups dropped across time, probably an indication that there is a natural letdown as the year progresses. Some support for this phenomenon comes from Evertson and Veldman (1981) who found an increase in mild misbehaviors and evidence that life in classrooms tended to deteriorate toward the end of the year, though not dramatically. What is more, these trends tended to obtain in both the classrooms of effective and ineffective teachers.

Differences across time. Nine of the 35 ratings (26%) showed differences for time of year across the two groups. The purpose of examining these differences was to see if the trained behaviors maintained and/or if the second workshop was effective in helping to sustain the desired behaviors. The data indicate that for five of the variables behaviors did drop off as time progressed. The variety of materials used in classes changed from a small variety to the minimum, usually only the textbook. Traffic patterns and the degree of visibility the

[Students:] *Use this space for making notes*

students had to the instructional areas were judged to be less effective as time went on. Also, teachers tended to do less signalling of correct behavior and to stop inappropriate behavior less quickly. However, four of the significant differences showed an improvement between the first and second workshops. Teachers improved the clarity of their directions for assignments, encouraged student reasoning and supplied rationales, and provided activities more closely related to students' backgrounds and interests. Teachers were also judged to have more suitable routines for assigning and checking work as time went on.

[Students:] *Use this space for making notes*

Only one interaction appeared significant between treatment group and time of workshop and that was the incidence of student aggressive behavior. Aggressive behavior was almost nonexistent in the treatment-group classrooms, but tended to increase with time in the control-group classes.

Summary observer ratings. These ratings were filled out by observers at the end of the data collection period. One set was completed for each teacher and served as a summary of observer impressions from the first of the year (see Table 2).

Nine of the 31 ratings (29%) were significant, and the patterns tended to support the component ratings just discussed. Treatment teachers were perceived to exceed the control group in two general areas: (a) the physical management of space and student behavior and (b) the management of academic work and student accountability for work. Treatment teachers were seen as having their classrooms ready for school, using their space more efficiently, having more efficient transitions between activities, stopping student disruptive behavior quickly, not allowing the class to get out of hand, and not dealing with students who continually come up for help. Assignments in the treatment classrooms were judged to be more appropriate (i.e., not too hard or too easy), students cooper-

TABLE 2 Treatment and Control Group Comparisons for Summary Observer Ratings of Secondary Classrooms

	Treatment		Control		
	$\bar{X}$	SD	$\bar{X}$	SD	$p \leq$
Classroom is ready for school	4.69	.53	3.94	1.12	.10
Class gets out of hand	1.31	.70	2.37	1.38	.07
Students wander around the room	1.38	.69	2.25	1.31	
High noise level	1.56	1.05	2.50	1.31	
Students talk during seatwork	3.56	.90	3.13	.69	
Efficient transitions between activities	4.81	.53	3.81	1.13	.04
Students come up for help frequently	1.63	1.38	2.31	1.13	
Teacher ignores "come-ups"	1.38	.58	1.63	1.06	
Teacher sends "come-ups" back to seats	1.38	.52	1.81	.53	
Teacher answers "come-ups" questions	2.56	1.91	4.13	.92	.05
Students leave their seats to get help	1.86	1.19	2.38	.95	
Students hold up hands to get help	3.63	1.36	3.50	.87	
Students call out to get help	1.69	.88	2.50	1.16	
Teacher leaves room often	1.31	.37	1.19	.26	
Teacher stops disruptive behavior quickly	4.63	.88	3.31	1.41	.04
Good use of space	4.56	.42	3.88	.88	.06
Teacher plans enough work	4.94	.18	4.13	1.36	
Teacher allows activities to go on too long	1.75	.85	2.44	1.12	
Assignments are too hard	2.06	1.12	2.50	.71	
Assignments are too short and easy	1.13	.23	1.81	.96	.07
Teacher checks for understanding	4.13	.79	4.25	.71	
Teacher keeps students responsible for their work	4.56	.62	3.75	.80	.04
Teacher is confident	4.44	1.05	4.69	.37	
Teacher is warm and pleasant	4.50	1.04	4.06	.78	
Teacher is enthusiastic	4.31	.84	4.00	.71	
High average attention	4.44	.50	3.81	.92	
Students begin work quickly without dawdling	4.63	.52	3.69	1.03	.04
Short amount of time waiting for next assignment	3.75	.85	2.88	1.51	
Student attention stays high from the beginning of school	1.69	.46	1.50	.46	
Attention improved from the first of school	1.44	.42	1.38	.52	
Attention level remains the same from the first of school	1.38	.35	1.19	.37	

Note: The first 28 items were based on 5-point scales: 1 = low occurrence or least characteristic; 5 = high occurrence or most characteristic; the last 3 items are based on 2-point scales: 1 = no; 2 = yes

ated in getting seatwork done without dawdling, and students were kept accountable for their work and assignments.

Discussion

The question of whether training in classroom management techniques could provide additional skills to teachers over and above their training in instructional skills seems to have been answered, at least indirectly by the results of this study. Since both treatment and control groups had received extensive training in instructional skills, the treatment group differences at the end of the management training study indicate that classroom management training enhanced these teachers' skills.

We also wanted to learn whether management training would enhance differences in the skills of secondary teachers and if this would coincide with increases in student on-task behavior. Apparently, it did. The question of whether management training sustains over a significant part of the year can be answered with less assurance. There does appear to be a decrease in some areas (i.e., stopping inappropriate behavior quickly), while others maintain. However, there are increases in other areas. Routines become more efficient, clarity of directions improves, and teachers apparently use more questions that elicit rationales and higher order thinking skills.

There are some limitations to the study, namely that we have no pre-measures of teachers' performance before training; nevertheless it is assumed that a control for initial differences would be effected by the matching procedures used and the fact that the most powerful prior training (instructional skills) was held constant. This assumption may be unwarranted; however, preliminary data from the elementary classrooms show similar differences between treatment and control groups.

[Students:] *Use this space for making notes*

The findings nevertheless suggest that management training similar to that described here is both a successful staff development activity and a relatively cost-efficient one. School districts with trained personnel can accomplish the required teacher training and follow-up. What is more, these studies provide evidence that we can export findings from tightly controlled research to the field with some success. Part of this success no doubt lies with the idea that none of the trained behaviors are startling or new to teachers. It is likely that the ordering of them and the rationales for their use provide a conceptual framework from which teachers can make the critical decisions about their teaching on an everyday basis.

[Students:] *Use this space for making notes*

References

Anderson, L., Evertson, C., & Brophy, J. (1979). An experimental study of effective teaching in first-grade reading groups. *Elementary School Journal, 79*, 193–223.

Borg, W., & Ascione, F. (1982). Classroom management in elementary mainstreaming classrooms, *Journal of Educational Psychology, 74*, 85–95.

Brophy, J. (1979). Teacher behavior and its effects. *Journal of Educational Psychology, 71*, 733–750.

Brophy, J. (1982). Supplemental group management techniques. In D. Duke (Ed.) *Helping Teachers Manage Classrooms.* Alexandria, VA: ASCD.

Brophy, J., & Evertson, C. (1976). *Learning from teaching.* Boston: Allyn & Bacon.

Emmer, E., Evertson, C., Sanford, J., Clements, B., & Worsham, M. (1982). *Organizing and managing the junior high classroom.* Austin, TX: Research and Development Center for Teacher Education.

Emmer, E., Sanford, J., Clements, B., & Martin, J. (1981). *The design of the Junior High Management Improvement Study* (Rep. No. 6150). Austin, TX: Research and Development Center for Teacher Education.

Evertson, C., Anderson, C., Anderson, L., & Brophy, J. (1980). Relationships between classroom behaviors and student outcomes in junior high mathematics and English classes. *American Educational Research Journal, 17*, 43–60.

Evertson, C., & Emmer, E. (1982a). Effective management at the beginning of the school year in junior high classrooms. *Journal of Educational Psychology, 74,* 485–498.

Evertson, C., & Emmer, E. (1982b). Preventive classroom management. In D. Duke (Ed.) *Helping teachers manage classrooms.* Alexandria, VA: ASCD.

Evertson, C., Emmer, E., Clements, B., Sanford, J., & Worsham, M. (1981). *Organizing and managing the elementary school classroom.* Austin, TX: Research and Development Center for Teacher Education.

Evertson, C., Emmer, E., Sanford, I., & Clements, B. (1983). Improving classroom management: An experiment in elementary classrooms. *Elementary School Journal, 84,* 173–188.

Evertson, C., & Veldman, D. (1981). Changes over time in process measures of classroom behavior. *Journal of Educational Psychology, 73,* 156–163.

Good, T. (1979). Teacher effectiveness in the elementary school. *Journal of Teacher Education, 30,* 52–64.

Good, T. (1983). Research on classroom teaching. In L. Shulman & G. Sykes, (Eds.) *Handbook of leaching and policy.* New York: Longman.

Green, J., & Weade, R. (1984). *Taking a closer look: Qualitative explorations of task management.* Paper presented at the annual meeting of the American Educational Research Association, New Orleans.

Medley, D. (1977). *Teacher competence and teacher effectiveness: A review of process-product research.* Washington, DC: American Association of Colleges for Teacher Education.

Sanford, J., Clements, B., & Emmer, E. (1981). *Communicating results of classroom management research to practitioners.* (Rep. No. 6051A)/ Austin, TX: Research and Development Center for Teacher Education.

Evertson, C. M. (1985). Training teachers in classroom management: An experimental study in secondary school classrooms. *Journal of Educational Research, 79*(1), 51–58. Reprinted with permission of the Helen Dwight Reid Educational Foundation. Published by Heldref Publications, 1319 Eighteenth St., N.W., Washington, D.C. 20036-1802. Copyright © 1985.

This article illustrates many hallmarks of quality research. It has a very clear purpose (three, in fact, as revealed in the abstract). In her introduction and review of the literature, Evertson recognizes that correlational research has yielded potentially useful findings, but by its very nature, is weak with regard to discerning causal relationships. A meaningful research question thus becomes, "Can we take correlational findings and demonstrate causal relationships?" It is this type of research that Evertson reports as "rare." Her research attempts to fill this void in the literature. As such her research is very applied; it has immediate and obvious consequences for improving the practice of teaching. It is less theoretical in scope; in fact, as revealed in her literature review, no theory is being tested explicitly. She is answering several applied research questions, not testing research hypotheses born from a theory. Her reasons for conducting this study are clearly stated immediately above her Method section.

Several methodological issues are worthy of mention in this article. Her research design is truly experimental, involving a manipulation and random assignment to experimental (workshop) groups and control groups. In fact, she used a technique prior to random assignment which guaranteed equivalence between experimental and control groups on the extraneous variables of experience and grade level. "Blocked into matched pairs" means that teachers were first sorted into grade levels and ranked in terms of years of experience; a similar pair was then randomly assigned to the experimental or control group. For example, two teachers, both third-grade teachers each with five to ten years of experience, were considered a matched pair; one was assigned to the treatment group, the other to the control group. This type of paired randomization over 102 teachers was certain to produce comparable experimental and control groups, a powerful control procedure. Furthermore, the sample size appears adequate, fifty-one teachers in each group, and generalizable across all levels.

Another important methodological issue is instrumentation, and you can see that careful attention was paid to maximizing both the quality and array of measures used. Notice that both qualitative and quantitative data were collected (although the qualitative findings are described in another report). A variety of observational measures were collected over multiple observation periods, and Evertson made certain that their recordings were reliable. Furthermore, observers were also blinded ("not told the identity of trained teachers," p. 54), another important control procedure. Overall, this study seems well executed, with appropriate measures in place to counteract biasing influences and alternative explanations.

Notice another measure of quality research near the end of the Discussion Section: a recognition of the study's weaknesses. Recall that all research is limited to some extent; most readers need a reminder of this fact. Some limitations may only be recognized from the vantage point of the researcher; it was she, after all, who lived and breathed with this study for so long and undoubtedly has deeper insight into some of the problems. This reference to limitations could undoubtedly be expanded into an entire section, not only in this report, but in all published research reports. Yet any recognition of a study's limitations, subtle or obvious, is clearly a positive feature of the research.

What do you think about this study?

CHAPTER SUMMARY

A critical review of published research involves careful analytic judgment. Guidelines for critiquing have been offered, including the focus on purpose, overall reaction, methodological issues, weaknesses and strengths, and overall recommendations. Educational research could be improved by greater attention to instrumentation, measures of generalization, alternative interpretations or explanations, and explicit descriptions of a study's weaknesses and limitations. Critiquing skills can be enhanced with practice, and the practice itself helps foster a view of research as an integrative process.

APPLICATION EXERCISE

Form a small study group of four to six classmates based on your common interests in education. As a group, locate one published research report in your field, but *independently* review the study using guidelines offered in this chapter. Then meet as a group to share your reviews. Discuss areas in which there is disagreement and try to understand others' rationale for their evaluations. Be prepared for different reactions, which can sometimes be radical. Disagreements are common even among expert reviewers of manuscripts submitted to journals for publication in education.

MULTIPLE CHOICE QUESTIONS

1. Which of the following best describes the meaning of a research critique?
   a. attack
   b. review
   c. censure
   d. belittle
   e. scrutinize

2. When evaluating the purpose of a study, reviewers should look for the:
   a. cost-benefit ratio
   b. reference length
   c. larger context
   d. citation index
   e. multicultural orientation

3. The "Pygmalion in the Classroom" study was described as being seriously flawed in its methodology; it could also be described as which of the following?
   a. monumental in its contribution
   b. "beating a dead horse"
   c. exemplary in mix of quantitative and qualitative research
   d. useful in "pitting" of two theories
   e. descriptive and experimental

4. All of the following would be considered methodological issues *except:*
   a. design
   b. sampling
   c. control
   d. theory
   e. measurement

5. Which of the following is regarded as true?
   a. All educational research is ethically controversial.
   b. All educational research is generalizable.
   c. All educational research is flawed or limited to some extent.
   d. All educational research is nontheoretical.
   e. All educational research is applied.

6. Which of the following is regarded as a common problem in educational research?
   a. lack of good ideas
   b. useless theories
   c. statistical flaws
   d. weak instrumentation
   e. poor designs

7. One common weakness of educational research is the failure of findings to extend beyond the borders of a study, a problem known as:
   a. limited applicability of generalizations
   b. internal invalidity

  c. measurement unreliability
  d. test insensitivity
  e. statistical restriction

8. It is suggested in this chapter that reports of educational research would be improved if the authors:
  a. used *non*parametric statistics
  b. wrote in "plain" English
  c. made true "confessions"
  d. excluded all statistical "mumbo-jumbo"
  e. were not theoretically "vacuous"

9. The evaluation of published research allows one to see how educational research is a(n):
  a. illogical puzzle
  b. problem-free activity
  c. all-or-nothing task
  d. uncreative endeavor
  e. integrative process

10. The chapter points out that one of the most difficult weaknesses to identify in educational research is the:
  a. extent to which the data satisfy assumptions
  b. connection to a larger body of literature
  c. extent to which ethical guidelines are followed
  d. alternative explanations or counter interpretations
  e. plausibility of the theoretical background

Answers: 1) b 2) c 3) a 4) d 5) c 6) d 7) a 8) c 9) e 10) d

REFERENCES

Adair, J. B., Sharpe, D., & Huynh, C. (1989). Hawthorne control procedures in educational experiments: A reconsideration of their use and effectiveness. *Review of Educational Research, 59,* 215–228.

American Psychological Association. (1994). *Publication manual of the American Psychological Association* (4th ed.). Washington, DC: Author.

Berger, K. S. (1991). *The developing person through childhood and adolescence.* New York: Worth.

Bloom, B. S. (1976). *Human characteristics and school learning.* New York: McGraw-Hill.

Bogdan, R. C., & Biklen, S. K. (1992). *Qualitative research in education.* Boston: Allyn and Bacon.

Bowers, C. A., & Flinders, D. (1990). *Responsive teaching.* New York: Teachers College Press.

Bracey, G. W. (1991, October). Why can't they be like we were? *Phi Delta Kappan, 71*(2), 104–117.

Bracey, G. W. (1992, March). Culture and achievement. *Phi Delta Kappan, 73*(7), 568–571.

Byrd, P. D., & Byrd, E. K. (1986). Drugs, academic achievement, and hyperactive children (meta-analysis of research). *The School Counselor, 33,* 323–331.

Calhoun, E. F. (1993). Action research: Three approaches. *Educational Leadership, 51*(2), 62–65.

Campbell, D. T., & Stanley, J. C. (1963). *Experimental and quasi-experimental designs for research.* Chicago: Rand McNally.

Campbell, F. A., & Ramey, C. T. (1995). Cognitive and school outcomes for high-risk African-American students at middle adolescence: Positive effects of early intervention. *American Educational Research Journal, 32,* 743–772.

Casto, G., & Mastropieri, M. A. (1986). The efficacy of early intervention programs: A meta-analysis. *Exceptional Children, 52,* 417–424.

Chadwick, B. A., Bahr, H. M., & Albrecht, S. (1984). *Social science research methods.* Englewood Cliffs, NJ: Prentice-Hall.

Childs, T. S., & Shakeshaft, C. (1986). A meta-analysis of research on the relationship between educational expenditures and student achievement. *Journal of Education Finance, 12,* 249–263.

Chinn, C. A., Waggoner, M. A., Anderson, R. C., Schommer, M., & Wilkinson, I. A. G. (1993). Situated actions during reading lessons: A microanalysis of oral reading error episodes. *American Educational Research Journal, 30,* 361–392.

Clark, C., Moss, P. A., Goering, S., Herter, R. J., Lamar, B., (1996). Colloboration as dialogue: Teachers and researchers engaged in conversation and professional development. *American Educational Research Journal, 33*(1), 193–231.

Coopersmith, S. (1967). *The antecedents of self-esteem.* San Francisco: Freeman.

Cunningham, A. E., & Stanovich, K. E. (1990). Early spelling acquisition: Writing beats the computer. *Journal of Educational Psychology, 82,* 159–162.

Davenas, E., Beauvais, F., Amara, J., Oberbaum, M., Robinzon, B., (1988). Human basophil degranulation triggered by very dilute antiserum against IgE. *Nature, 333,* 816–818.

Dillman, D. A. (1978). *Mail and telephone surveys: The total design method.* New York: John Wiley & Sons.

DuBois, P. H. (1966). A test-minded society: China 1115 B.C.–1905 A.D. In A. Anastasi (Ed.), *Testing problems in perspective* (pp. 29–36). Washington, DC: American Council on Education.

Edelman, G. (1992). *Bright air, brilliant fire: On the matter of the mind.* New York: Basic Books.

Eisenhart, M., & Borko, H. (1993). *Designing classroom research: Themes, issues, and struggles.* Boston: Allyn and Bacon.

Elam, S. M., Rose, L. C., & Gallup, A. M. (1996, September). The 28th annual Phi Delta Kappa/ Gallup poll of the public's attitude toward the public schools. *Phi Delta Kappan, 78*(1), 41–59.

Elashoff, J. D., & Snow, R. E. (1971). *Pygmalion reconsidered.* Worthington, OH: Jones.

Fletcher-Flinn, C. M., & Gravatt, B. (1995). The efficacy of computer assisted instruction (CAI): A meta-analysis. *Journal of Educational Computing Research, 12,* 219–241.

Flinders, D. (1993). Researcher's comments. In W. Borg, J. Gall, & M. Gall, *Applying educational Research: A practical guide* (3rd ed.), 209. New York: Longman.

Franke, R., & Kaul, J. (1978). The Hawthorne experiments: First statistical interpretation. *American Sociological Review, 43,* 623.

Gagne, R. M. (1985). *The conditions and learning and the theory of instruction* (4th ed.). New York: Holt, Rinehart and Winston.

Gardner, H. (1983). *Frames of mind: The theory of multiple intelligences.* New York: Basic Books.

Glaser, B. G., & Strauss, A. L. (1967). *The discovery of grounded theory: Strategies for qualitative research.* New York: Aldine.

Guskey, T. R., & Pigott, T. D. (1988). Research on group-based mastery learning programs: A meta-analysis. *The Journal of Educational Research, 81,* 197–216.

Hembree, R. (1990). The nature, effects, and relief of mathematics anxiety (meta-analysis of research). *Journal for Research in Mathematics Education, 21,* 33–46.

Hembree, R., & Dessart, D. J. (1986). Effects of hand-held calculators in precollege mathematics education: A meta-analysis. *Journal for Research in Mathematics Education, 17,* 83–99.

Holmes, C. T., & Matthews, K. M. (1984). The effects of nonpromotion on elementary and junior high school pupils: A meta-analysis. *Review of Educational Research, 54,* 225–236.

Horton, P. B., McConney, A. A., & Gallo, M. A. (1993). An investigation of the effectiveness of concept mapping as an instructional took (meta-analysis of research). *Science Education, 77,* 95–111.

Howell, D. C. (1982). *Statistical methods in psychology.* Boston: Duxbury Press.

Kagan, D., Dennis, M. B., Igou, M., Moore, P., & Sparks, K. (1993). The experience of being a teacher in residence. *American Educational Research Journal, 30,* 426–443.

Khalili, A., & Shashaani, L. (1994). The effectiveness of computer applications: A meta-analysis. *Journal of Research on Computing in Education, 27,* 48–61.

Kiewra, K. A., DuBois, N. F., Christian, D., & McShane, A. (1988). Providing study notes: Comparison of three types of notes for review. *Journal of Educational Psychology, 80,* 595–597.

Kourilsky, M., & Wittrock, M. C. (1992). Generative teaching: An enhancement strategy for the learning of economics in cooperative groups. *American Educational Research Journal, 29,* 861–876.

Kraemer, H. C., & Thiemann, S. (1987). *How many subjects? Statistical power analysis in research.* Newbury Park, CA: Sage.

Kulik, C. C., & Kulik, J. A. (1982). Effects of ability grouping on secondary school students: A meta-analysis of evaluation findings. *American Educational Research Journal, 19,* 415–428.

Kulik, C. C., Kulik, J. A., & Bangert-Drowns, R. L. (1990). Effectiveness of mastery learning programs: A meta-analysis (with discussion). *Review of Educational Research, 60,* 265–307.

Landon, 1,293,669: Roosevelt, 972,897. (1936, October 31). *Literary Digest,* p. 5–6.

Madden, N. A., Slavin, R. E., Karweit, N. L., Dolan, L. J., & Wasik, B. A. (1993). Success for all: Longitudinal effects of a restructuring program for inner-city elementary schools. *American Educational Research Journal, 30,* 123–148.

McGinnies, E. (1949). Emotionality and perceptual defense. *Psychological Review, 56,* 244–249.

McGiverin, J., Gilman, D. A., & Tillitski, C. (1989). A meta-analysis of the relation between class size and achievement. *The Elementary School Journal, 90,* 47–56.

Mills, M. B., & Huberman, A. M. (1994). *Qualitative data analysis* (2nd ed.). Thousands Oaks, CA: Sage.

Naftulin, D. H., Ware, J. E., & Donnelly, F. A. (1973). The Dr. Fox lecture: A paradigm of educational seduction. *Journal of Medical Education, 48,* 630–635.

Neuman, S. B., Hagedorn, T., Celano, D., & Daly, P. (1995). Toward a collaborative approach to parent involvement in early education: A study of teenage mothers in an African-American community. *American Educational Research Journal, 32,* 801–827.

Neuman, S. B., & Roskos, K. (1993). Access to print for children of poverty: Differential effects of adult mediation and literacy-enriched play settings on environmental and functional print tasks. *American Educational Research Journal, 30,* 95–122.

Newkirk, T. (Ed.). (1992). *Workshop by and for teachers: The teacher as researcher.* Portsmouth, NH: Heinemann.

Oberg, A., & McCutcheon, G. (1987). Teachers' experience doing action research. *Peabody Journal of Education, 64,* 116–127

Otto, W. (1985). Homework: A meta-analysis. *Journal of Reading, 28,* 764–766.

Perry, R. P., Abrami, P. C., & Leventhal, L. (1979). Educational seduction: The effect of instructor expressiveness and lecture content on student ratings and achievement. *Journal of Educational Psychology, 71,* 107–116.

Pfungst, O. (1911). *Clever Hans.* New York: Holt, Rinehart and Winston.

Platt, J. R. (1964). Strong inference. *Science, 146,* 347–353.

Popham, W. James (1993). *Educational evaluation* (3rd ed.). Boston: Allyn and Bacon.

Powell, B. (1993, December). Sloppy reasoning, misused data. *Phi Delta Kappan, 75,* 283, 352.

Rice, B. (1982, February). The Hawthorne Defect: Persistence of a flawed theory. *Psychology Today,* 70–74.

Roethlisberger, F. J., & Dickson, W. J. (1939). *Management and the worker.* Cambridge, MA: Harvard University Press.

Roopnarine, J. L., Ahmeduzzaman, M., Donnely, S., Gill, P., Mennis, A., (1992). Social-cooperative play behaviors and playmate preferences in same-age and mixed-age classrooms over a 6-month period. *American Educational Research Journal, 29,* 757–776.

Rosenthal, R., & Jacobson, L. (1968). *Pygmalion in the classroom: Teacher expectations and pupils' intellectual development.* New York: Holt, Rinehart and Winston.

Sagor, R. (1992). *How to conduct collaborative action research.* Alexandria, VA: Association for Supervision and Curriculum Development.

Salant, P., & Dillman, D. A. (1994). *How to conduct your own survey.* New York: John Wiley & Sons.

Santa, C. M. (1993). Researcher's comments. In W. Borg, J. Gall, & M. Gall, *Applying educational Research: A practical guide* (3rd ed.), pp. 401–402. New York: Longman.

Santa, C. M., Isaacson, L., & Manning, G. (1987). Changing content instruction through action research. *The Reading Teacher, 40*(4), 434–438.

Schlaefli, A., Rest, J. R., & Thoma, S. J. (1985). Does moral education improve moral judgment? A meta-analysis of intervention studies using the Defining issues test. *Review of Educational Research, 55,* 319–352.

Scriven, M. (1967). The methodology of evaluation. In R. E. Stake (Ed.), *Perspectives of curriculum evaluation.* American Education Research Association Monograph Series on Evaluation, No. 1. Chicago: Rand McNally.

Scruggs, T. E., & Mastropieri, M. A. (1994). Successful mainstreaming in elementary science classes: A qualitative study of three reputational cases. *American Educational Research Journal, 31,* 785–811.

Scruggs, T. E., White, K., & Bennion, K. (1986). Teaching test-taking skills to elementary-grade students: A meta-analysis. *The Elementary School Journal, 87,* 68–82.

Snow, R. E. (1969). Unfinished pygmalion [Review of the book *Pygmalion in the classroom*]. *Contemporary Psychology, 14,* 197–200.

Smart, J. C., & Elton, C. F. (1981). Structural characteristics and citation rates of education journals. *American Educational Research Journal, 18,* 399–413.

Stampfer, M. J., Willett, W. C., Colditz, G. A., Rosner, B., & Speizer, F. E., (1985). A prospective study of postmenopausal estrogen therapy and coronary heart disease. *The New England Journal of Medicine, 313,* 1044–1049.

Stanford Achievement Test Series, Eighth Edition (1989). *National norms booklet.* San Antonio, TX: The Psychological Corporation.

Stufflebeam, D. L., Foley, W. J., Gephart, W. J., Guba, E. G., Hammand, R. L., Merriman, H. O., & Provus, M. M. (1971). *Educational evaluation and decision making.* Itaska, IL: Peacock.

Sylwester, R. (1993/1994). What the biology of the brain tells us about learning. *Educational Leadership, 51*(4), 46–51.

Tabachnick, B. G., & Fidell, L. S. (1983). *Using multivariate statistics.* New York: Harper & Row.

Tomchin, E. M., & Impara, J. C., (1992). Unraveling teachers' beliefs about grade retention. *American Educational Research Journal, 29,* 199–223.

VanSledright, B., & Brophy, J. (1992). Storytelling, imagination, and fanciful elaboration in children's historical reconstructions. *American Educational Research Journal, 29,* 837–859.

Wallen, N. E., & Fraenkel, J. R. (1991). *Educational research: A guide to the process.* New York: McGraw-Hill.

Watson, James D. (1968). *The double helix: A personal account of the discovery of the structure of DNA.* New York: Atheneum.

Weinburgh, M. H. (1995). Gender differences in student attitudes toward science: A meta-analysis of the literature from 1970 to 1991. *Journal of Research in Science Teaching, 32,* 387–398.

White, W. A. T. (1988). A meta-analysis of the effects of direct instruction in special education. *Education and Treatment of Children, 11,* 364–374.

Willig, A. C. (1985). A meta-analysis of selected studies on the effectiveness of bilingual education. *Review of Educational Research, 55,* 269–317.

Wilson, P. W. F., Garrison, R. J., & Castelli, W. P. (1985). Postmenopausal estrogen use, cigarette smoking, and cardiovascular morbidity in women over 50. *The New England Journal of Medicine, 313,* 1038–1043.

Wineburg, S. S. (1987). The self-fulfillment of the self-fulfilling prophecy: A critical appraisal. *Educational Researcher, 16,* 28–37.

Worthen, B. R., & Sanders, J. R. (1987). *Educational evaluation: Alternative approaches and practical guidelines.* New York: Longman.

INDEX